Prisoners of Britain

Prisoners of Britain

German civilian and combatant internees during the First World War

Panikos Panayi

Manchester University Press
Manchester and New York
distributed in the United States exclusively by Palgrave Macmillan

Published by Manchester University Press
Oxford Road, Manchester M13 9NR, UK
and Room 400, 175 Fifth Avenue, New York, NY 10010, USA
www.manchesteruniversitypress.co.uk

Distributed in the United States exclusively by
Palgrave Macmillan, 175 Fifth Avenue,
New York, NY 10010, USA

Distributed in Canada exclusively by
UBC Press, University of British Columbia, 2029 West Mall,
Vancouver, BC, Canada V6T 1Z2

British Library Cataloguing-in-Publication Data is available

Library of Congress Cataloging-in-Publication Data is available

ISBN 978 0 7190 9563 4 *paperback*

First published by Manchester University Press in hardback 2012

This paperback edition first published 2014

Printed by Lightning Source

Contents

Tables

Illustrations

Preface

The origins of this book lie in my Ph.D. thesis, which I completed over twenty years ago and which appeared in 1991 as *The Enemy in Our Midst: Germans in Britain during the First World War*. This work focused upon all aspects of the experiences of German civilians in Britain during these years, who effectively faced a process of ethnic cleansing as a result of property confiscation, mass rioting and deportation. Before deportation, however, males of military age experienced incarceration, which could last for over four years. In one sense, this volume returns to the two chapters from *The Enemy in Our Midst* which dealt with internment and expands them.

However, rather than focusing simply upon civilian incarceration, I have also examined the experiences of soldiers who were captured on the western front and increasingly brought to Britain in the latter stages of the war, mostly for the purpose of utilizing their labour power. Furthermore, I discovered during the current research that, while most of the civilian internees were men who found themselves in Britain in 1914, either as part of the established German community or as visitors during that summer, the British government also transported Germans from the British and German Empires to Britain, as well as seizing Germans upon ships, who suffered the same fate. The book therefore recognizes three types of internees in First World War Britain: civilians already present in the country in August 1914; civilians brought to Britain from all over the world; and combatants, primarily soldiers from the western front, but also naval personnel and a few members of zeppelin crews whose vessels fell to earth. These three groups faced different internment experiences, particularly in terms of the length of time they spent behind barbed wire and their ability to work.

Many combatants viewed internment almost as a relief from the fighting they had experienced on the western front, while, for civilians, the spell behind barbed wire represented their key wartime experience. Throughout the narrative, from the first days behind barbed wire until the last, the book recognizes the varying experiences faced by the differing groups of prisoners. Nevertheless, we need to consider all internees together because they became victims of one of the first mass incarcerations in history. While the prisoner of war has a long history, imprisonment on the scale practised in the First World War, by both Britain and the other belligerent states, of both soldiers and civilians, represents a new phenomenon.

Following on from my previous work, I have chosen to focus upon German prisoners held within Britain, rather than all of those captured by the British Empire during the course of the First World War, which would have placed this project, as one based upon primary sources, on a much larger and potentially unmanageable scale, certainly from a publishing point of view. Britain and its empire also incarcerated German civilians and soldiers, together with those from Austria-Hungary and the Ottoman Empire, although Germans always formed the vast majority of those who found themselves behind barbed wire. Although much of the British archival material tackles internment on an imperial scale, I chose to also use all of the available German material, which allows a much more focused project. At the same time, individual projects have been published upon experiences in other parts of the empire. My central concern is German internees upon the British mainland.

The history that follows, by using a wide range of sources, both personal and official, tries to outline the evolution of internment policy and its consequences for the individuals concerned. Chapter 1, 'Forgetting, remembering and the beginnings of a history', investigates the reason for the absence of any previous volume on internment in First World War Britain a century after the conflict. From a British point of view, I suggest that this links with the Germanophobia of the Great War, which lasted into the 1920s and beyond. In the German case the memory of imprisonment in Britain and elsewhere remained strong until the Second World War, when the attention received by internees of the 1939–45 conflict, especially those who took years to return from the Soviet Union, drowned out that of the First World War internees. I recognize that the forgetting was not total. Chapter 2, 'Arrest, transportation and capture', looks at the varying experiences of civilians resident in Britain, those brought to Britain from colonies and the high seas and combatants. I try to explain the reasons for the adoption of mass incarceration before moving on to outline the scale of interment. I then examine the development of policy towards our three groups and outline the way in which they initially experienced it through arrest, transportation and capture. Chapter 3, 'The camp system', takes a necessarily top-down approach, using official sources, in order to demonstrate the scale of internment in Britain. It initially outlines the ministries involved before moving on to examine the nature and extent of the camp system. Most of the chapter focuses upon the camps themselves, which are divided into six different types: first, the smaller establishments which held non-combatants, consisting of the initial short-lived camps and those which would emerge in 1915 and survive the duration of the war; second, special camps, which held distinct groups of prisoners; third, the Isle of Man camps; fourth, military camps; fifth, military hospitals; and finally, working camps, which proliferated at the end of the war.

Chapters 4–6 in many ways form the core of the book, as they deal with life behind barbed wire as lived by individuals, using a wide range sources which allow us to understand the experience of internment. Chapter 4, 'Barbed wire disease and the grim realities of internment', examines the evolution of the concept of barbed wire disease, popularized by A. L. Vischer of the Swiss Embassy in London, who visited the Isle of Man camps in particular on behalf of the German government. The chapter engages with Vischer's ideas before examining the everyday realities of life behind barbed wire. Vischer took a basically negative view of internment. The alternative perspective came from John Davidson Ketchum, who spent the war in Ruhleben, the civilian internment camp for Britons in Berlin, and who, decades after his life there, wrote a narrative of his experiences from the point of view of his training as a social psychologist, in which he recognized 'Prison Camp Societies'. Unlike Vischer, who concentrated upon the problems thrown up by internment, Ketchum focused upon the ways in which internees came to terms with their incarceration by constructing a variety of pastimes. Chapter 5 deals with these by examining them under the headings of: religion; reading, writing and learning; high culture; and sport. Vischer recognized that the main solution for barbed wire disease was employment, which is the focus of Chapter 6. However, under the Hague Convention only combatants could work. This chapter outlines the evolution of employment policy in Britain and then moves on to consider the tasks actually undertaken by both civilians and combatants. It concludes by discussing the importance of employment, which proved more significant for the prisoners themselves than it did for the British economy because of the relatively small numbers of people employed in comparison with those employed by other twentieth-century European war economies.

Chapter 7 tackles 'Public opinion'. The plight of prisoners became an important issue in the Anglo-German propaganda war. Essentially, both sides, especially through the press and parliament, claimed that the enemy mistreated their own internees while they treated their foreign prisoners well. The chapter will examine this perception and will also tackle the rise of humanitarianism towards internees. However, it points out that, rather than acting as a foil to Anglo-German hatred, this humanitarianism simply formed part of it because the main driving force for helping German prisoners in Britain consisted of the German Red Cross and other similar German charities, largely driven by the desires of relatives to maintain contact.

Chapter 8, 'Escape, release and return', tackles the end of internment from the point of view of both policy and its meaning for the individuals involved. While the German side wanted wholesale exchange from the early stages of the war, the British rejected this because of the inequality in numbers. Although various schemes meant that some people returned during the course of the conflict, most went back home at its conclusion. However, hundreds, and possibly thousands, tried to escape, although only three people succeeded in getting back to Germany. Return to a Germany in economic and political upheaval during 1918 and 1919 often proved a traumatic experience, especially for those deported immigrants who had not seen the country for decades and for their English wives, who had never previously visited the country.

Chapter 9 tries to understand 'The meaning of internment in Britain during the First World War' by placing it into three contexts. First is its importance to the lives of those affected, and second is its significance as state policy. Thirdly, we need to place the control of Germans in Britain within the broader European picture of persecution during the First World War in particular and try to understand its meaning within the age of total war in the first half of the twentieth century, but also to view it as a turning point in the history of mass incarceration.

The book has used a wide range of sources in an attempt to give a complete picture of the experiences of the internees against the background of the policies pursued by the British government. It has therefore utilized both official and unofficial information. This falls into several categories. Archival material has proved of central importance. It includes the official documents produced by German and British government departments. Much of the German material consists of correspondence of the Auswärtiges Amt with the British Foreign Office, via the United States and Swiss Embassies, in an attempt to establish the treatment of individual prisoners. At the same time, the Reichsmarineamt interviewed numerous returnees throughout the conflict. Each individual gave an account of their experiences. Official British archival material also includes a variety of correspondence with the United States and Swiss Embassies, often dealing with individual prisoners. Both British and German official archives also contain hundreds of United States and Swiss consular reports on individual camps, allowing a reconstruction of virtually every place of internment, from the smallest farm holding a few dozen working military prisoners to Knockaloe, the symbol of First World War British internment, which held tens of thousands of civilians. Unofficial archival material also proves important, including papers of humanitarian organizations such as the Frankfurt Red Cross, held in the Bundesarchiv in Berlin, and of several groups in the Evangelisches Zentralarchiv, Berlin.

The voice of the prisoners themselves proves central for this project. This comes through in a variety of sources including letters. I have made use of personal accounts written during and after the conflict. Those in the Manx National Heritage in Douglas and the Elsa Brändström Gedächtnis collection in the Militärarchiv in Freiburg proved especially helpful. Both of these collections also contain camp material, including not only diaries but also concert programmes, details of educational activity and newspapers. I also utilized the books published by prisoners during and after the First World War. While some of these remain brief and often focus upon events outside camps, especially when capture took place beyond Europe or when an escape occurred, some of the narratives provide profound insights into the everyday realities of internment. Where the original sources are in German, I have provided translations in all cases.

This book has also made use of newspapers. These include not only those published within the internment camps themselves, but also those from the localities in which the camps existed. I initially wished to look at the latter in order to gauge public opinion in the areas which held camps, but, in the case of the Isle of Man newspapers in particular, I found that they actually provided much information on events behind the barbed wire, including deaths and criminality. The camp publications prove particularly important for reconstructing leisure activities, while British and German national publications act as a good indicator of public opinion, as do the records of British and German parliamentary debates.

What follows is therefore the first attempt, a century after the end of the conflict, to reconstruct the history of First World War German internment in Britain. While the everyday lives and activities of the prisoners form the central focus, they receive contextualization in the actions and decisions of the British state during this conflict, which, mirroring the actions of other belligerents, took the decision to intern vast numbers of males for years in many cases.

In methodological terms the book can be viewed as an example of *Alltagsgeschichte* in the German historiographical tradition of the history of everyday life or as a British example of history from below, which now increasingly uses life stories to drive forward its narrative. Certainly, the central chapters on the experience of internment as well as Chapter 8 have personal experiences at their heart. Nevertheless, this is also partly a history of administrative solutions and policy decisions in a conflict which represented a turning point in the growth of state intervention in the lives of Britons in particular. While the personal accounts provide us with much of the information for the life of prisoners, the official record allows us to reconstruct the state policies, although the range of such records and the wealth of information they contain also help us in the reconstruction of everyday life.

Acknowledgements

Of those I would like to thank in connection with the project, I must first mention the British Academy. This body initially financed my Ph.D. thesis in the second half of the 1980s. More importantly, I received a small grant lasting from early 2009 until the end of 2010, which allowed me to make visits to Bedford, Berlin, Douglas, Freiburg, Hull, Leipzig, London and Stuttgart, where I completed all of the archival and other primary source research. Thankfully, the government has saved the Small Grants scheme, which is priceless for historians, despite the apparently 'small' sums it provides. I am also grateful to a series of bodies for allowing me to use the following illustrations: the Bildagentur für Kunst und Geschichte Berlin for Figure 5.5; the Bundesarchiv, Militärarchiv for Figures 1.2, 4.2, 4.3 and 5.1; and Graham Mark for Figure 3.3 and an adaptation of his original map for Figure 3.1. Every effort was made to trace the copyright holders of the other images.

I would also like to thank a variety of individuals who have helped in various ways as this project has evolved. First of all, I owe a long-term gratitude to Colin Holmes, who set me on my academic career when he supervised my original Ph.D. thesis on 'Germans in Britain during the First World War'. Similarly, I would also like to reiterate my thanks to Roland Quinault, who suggested that I should look at the German community in Britain at the outbreak of the First World War for my undergraduate dissertation. An important turning point for this project came, however, when I was asked by Jochen Oltmer in 2000 to write an essay for a collection he was editing on prisoners in Europe during the Great War. Rather than asking me to regurgitate my original work, he also wanted me to look at combatants. While researching for this essay I realized the enormous amount of information available, especially in the Foreign Office files in London, which really made up my mind to pursue this as a significant project. Other academic colleagues whom I would like to thank and who have helped in various ways in bringing this project to fruition include Stefan Berger, Yvonne Creswell, Tony Kushner, Stefan Manz, John Martin, Tammy Proctor, Dieter Steinert and Mathew Stibbe. I am also grateful to Alison Welsby, who originally commissioned this volume while at Manchester University Press, and Emma Brennan, who saw it to fruition.

I would also like to thank my wife Mundeep, who accepted that writing an Anglo-German history project meant that I had to spend seven weeks in Germany and another on the Isle of Man. In fact, she came to see me in Berlin and Freiburg, where the places we visited included Lake Titisee on a wet afternoon in August 2010 and Kreuzberg on a hot afternoon in July 2009, after half a day in the Evangelisches Zentralarchiv. Mundeep also cultivated the garden vegetables in my absence so that we enjoyed a rich harvest during both of these years.

I would also like to mention my (first) cousin (once removed), Anna Kourdoullou (junior), who came to visit me on one of my other archival trips to Berlin on a very hot weekend, just after Germany lost to Spain in the World Cup semi-final of 2010, which meant that neither of us found ourselves in a country which had reached the World Cup final. Anna came just before embarking on her history degree at Queen Mary, and during the weekend she managed to see some of the main sites of the Nazi terror. I think I inspired her to undertake her history degree from quite an early age and I hope that, in the era when degrees have become tied to the labour market, she can go on to pursue a career in which her history degree proves useful.

Unfortunately, just after I submitted the original typescript her grandfather, and my uncle, Panayiotis Kourdoullou, died. He had spent most of his life in England, arriving in the late 1950s, having left the village of Rizokarpazo in the Karpasia Peninsula in Cyprus, where the fish was always fresh and always will be. In 1974 his village experienced the type of ethnic cleansing which would start to become commonplace during the First World War and would continue for much of the twentieth century, which meant that he never went back to his village after 1974. I would like to devote this book to his memory.

Abbreviations

Admiralty	ADM
AIR	Ministry of Air
BA	Bundesarchiv
BL	British Library
BLARC	Bedford and Luton Archives and Record Centre
CAB	Cabinet
DRK	Deutsches Rotes Kreuz
EZA	Evangelisches Zentralarchiv
FO	Foreign Office
HHC	Hull History Centre
HO	Home Office
IWM	Imperial War Museum
LBWHS	Landesarchiv, Baden-Württemberg, Haupstaatsarchiv Stuttgart
LMA	London Metropolitan Archives
MA	Militärarchiv
MEPO	Metropolitan Police
MNH	Manx National Heritage
NA	National Archives
NATS	Ministry of National Service
RH	Chef der Heeresarchive
SBB	Staatsbibliothek zu Berlin
WL	Wellcome Library
WO	War Office
WW1/AC	War Agricultural Executive Committee

1

Forgetting, remembering and the beginnings of a history

> She loves this German – she who had loathed all his race as no one else had ever hated them! Everybody knows it, too, and everybody loathes her.[1]

Forgetting

It seems astonishing that almost a century after the outbreak of the First World War, no academic study has yet appeared upon the experiences of German prisoners of war in Britain, either in English or in German, despite the fact that hundreds of thousands of Germans found themselves behind barbed wire during the conflict, reaching a peak of 115,950 in November 1918.[2] This seems even more surprising when we consider the fact that the study of the Great War has become a key theme in understanding the twentieth century. The lacuna in this field finds no replication in the study of German internees in Britain between 1939 and 1945, who have received much attention, both in popular memory and in academic circles. This assertion applies especially to the study of civilian prisoners. While the experience of German internment in First World War Britain has not yet resulted in the publication of an academic monograph, this group did not disappear completely from either academic or popular consciousness during the course of the last century, even though long periods existed when this theme remained forgotten, within both Britain and Germany.

Before demonstrating the ways in which the amnesia about our subject did not become total, it seems important to ask why we have had to wait for a century before the appearance of the first volume on German prisoners in Britain during the Great War. The reasons in Britain and Germany differ. In the former, the main explanation would be the Germanophobia which gripped the country both during and after the First World War. As my original study on German civilians has demonstrated,[3] and as stressed by a small number of writers at the time, British state and society during the First World War became saturated with hatred of Germans. After the sinking of the *Lusitania* by a German submarine off the coast of Ireland on 7 May 1915 with the loss of over 1,000 lives, D. H. Lawrence could write, 'I am mad with rage myself. I would like to kill a million Germans – two millions.'[4] After the war, Lawrence could, however, write that from 1916 to 1919 'a wave of criminal lust rose and possessed England', resulting in a 'reign of terror' led by a 'criminal mob' which meant that a man lost 'his sense of truth, of justice and of human honour'.[5]

This intolerance and hatred of all things German manifested itself most obviously in propaganda campaigns, particularly as conscription became operational only at the beginning of 1916.[6] For those who wanted to fight the war at home, the most obvious target for their Germanophobic hatred, in both Britain and other parts of the empire,[7] consisted of victimizing the German minority in their midst, although other persecuted groups included pacifists.[8] The hostility towards Germans, driven by the popular press and sections of the radical right of the Unionist Party, resulted in the ethnic cleansing from Britain of the thriving group which had emerged during the course of the nineteenth century. In the first place, rioters destroyed virtually every German-owned shop in Britain. Meanwhile, the Trading with the Enemy Acts eliminated any remaining German business in Britain, from butchers and bakers to the London branches of the Deutsche Bank and Dresdner Bank, whose assets went towards the reparations payments under the Treaty of Versailles. Britain also implemented a policy of wholesale internment of males of military age, who, along with women and children, would face deportation to Germany, meaning that the size of the community declined from 57,500 in 1914 to 22,254 in 1919.[9] Studies of Britain during the Great War published since *The Enemy in Our Midst* have incorporated its findings.[10] At the same time, subsequent work on the German community in Glasgow has confirmed them.[11] The hatred of all things German included all German internees in Britain, not simply those who had resided in the country before 1914 but also those brought to Britain from French battlefields, from ships on the high seas and from the colonies. All of these groups became caught up in a propaganda campaign which contrasted the humane treatment received by German prisoners in Britain with the alleged brutality faced by Britons in Germany.[12]

The Germanophobia of the Great War clearly played a role in the lack of attention devoted to German prisoners of war in Britain during the conflict. Anti-German hostility remained a factor of British life.[13] During the inter-war years, when social history remained in its infancy and focused upon the British working classes,[14] the small numbers of professional historians writing in Britain completely ignored the experiences of German prisoners of war, although they did make some impact upon popular memory. John Bourne in his study of the country during the conflict wrote, in contrast to D. H. Lawrence, who lived through the war, that 'The British people were not "militarized". Wartime excesses of chauvinism, anger and hate became regarded with incredulous embarrassment and were then *forgotten*. Patience, tolerance and generosity returned.'[15] I have italicized the key word here. The forgetting of 'wartime excesses' also meant sweeping the victims of these excesses under the carpet, especially the German community in Britain. The prisoners remembered by British society were those held by the Germans, especially in Ruhleben. One of the reasons for the contrast lies in the individual memories of British victims who survived.[16] This was not true in the case of Germans in Britain, even though some of the civilian internees remained in the country. The residual Gemanophobia of the inter-war years meant that such individuals wished to become assimilated, rather than set up groups to remember their collective experiences,[17] as happened in the case of those who had been interned in Ruhleben and other German camps. At the same time, a focus among historians upon civilian internees in Britain and the more general treatment of the German community in the country during the Great War would undermine the myths of British tolerance towards ethnic outsiders. Unlike German historiographers, who have questioned everything about the nature of German national identity and the actions of the German nation state in the aftermath of actions of the Third Reich, British historians have never had such a conversation with themselves.[18] Part of the reason for this contrast may lie in the fact that Britain never descended into the all-pervading inhumanity practised by the Nazis during the Second World War. Yet the country did oversee the two largest acts of ethnic cleansing in history, in the form of the deportation of Germans from the East in the aftermath of the Second World War and the mass expulsions which happened in India and Pakistan following partition,[19] as well as fully participating in and leading the destruction of German cities and the murder of civilians as a result of the air war between 1943 and 1945.[20] For Britons the war in the air focuses upon either the heroism of those who killed German civilians,[21] the bravery of the spitfire pilots in the summer of 1940[22] or the consequences of 'the blitz'.[23] These remained the unquestioned myths of Second World War Britain, in which Nazis symbolized evil, with Britons playing the roles of victims and heroes. Such a viewpoint also extends to prisoners of war. In British popular consciousness, the key experience in the history of prisoners of war is that of those Britons held by the Japanese during the Second World War,[24] who again play the role of victims and fit into mainstream British views regarding participation in war.

While, as we shall see, traces of the experience of German prisoners during the Great War in Britain did not completely disappear, they were drowned out in the popular and academic memory set by the paradigms in which Britons play the role of either heroes or victims. Little space has existed in the context of the world wars for Germans as anything other than perpetrators. While the First World War resulted in mass memorialization by state and individuals of those who died during the conflict, the memorialization became highly selective and operated along national and ethnic lines. Little space existed for outsiders. This remembering encompassed monuments, poems, novels and films as trauma and loss became a core aspect of life, in the 1920s in particular.[25]

The above discussion has also touched upon a second reason for the absence of a substantial study of German prisoners in Britain during the Great War: the increasing dominance of the Second World War over the First in popular and academic consciousness. This may partly result from the sheer scale of the Second World War in comparison with the First. The more important explanations probably consist of the number of survivors of the Second in comparison with the First, who, in terms of British combatants, have now disappeared, following the death of Harry Patch in July 2009[26] as well as the visual memory through films in particular.[27] While scholars such as Paul Fussell and Jay Winter have stressed the importance of First World War memory, the memory of the Second World War appears to have become more ubiquitous.[28]

The Second World War internment experience helps to illustrate this. To begin on a personal note, during the course of the research for this book several friends and academic colleagues asked me: 'What are you working on at the moment?' I then proceeded to tell them that I was looking at German prisoners in Britain during the First World War, at which stage, either because they did not hear me or because they had no awareness of or no interest in this subject, they simply started speaking to me about German captives in Second World War Britain. Part of the explanation for this probably lies in the existence of a larger body of literature on German Second World War internees. Focusing upon civilian internees, two edited volumes have appeared in recent decades. The first emerged from a conference to commemorate the fiftieth anniversary of the decision to implement the internment of both Italian and German (mostly Jewish refugee) civilians in June 1940. While my own essay in this volume focused upon the First World War, the book contained five contributions simply dealing with the Second. It also contained one personal testimony from a First World War internee and four from individuals incarcerated during the Second World War. Just as interesting from the point of view of this discussion is the fact that the original conference also included former Second World War internees, who described some of their experiences.[29] Twelve years after the publication of *The Internment of Aliens in Twentieth Century Britain*, there appeared a volume edited by Richard Dove focusing upon both world wars. While, on this occasion, contributions on the First World War by Yvonne Creswell, Jutta Raab Hansen and Stefan Manz accompanied my own essay (making four in all), the volume contained seven essays on the Second World War.[30] Similarly, any study of monographs on civilian internment reveals the existence of at least seven focusing simply upon the Second World War.[31] In addition, several other volumes, concerned primarily with Jewish refugees from Nazism, also examine the Second World War internment experience.[32] This contrasts starkly with the treatment of the Great War, where my own volume and those by Stefan Manz and J. C. Bird deal with internment as part of a broader narrative.[33] In addition to the amount of work on civilian internment from 1940 to 1942, an English-language volume also exists on German military prisoners in Britain during the Second World War and its immediate aftermath,[34] while the book by Johannes-Dieter Steinert and Inge Weber-Newth on Germans in early post-war Britain includes coverage of those German prisoners who decided to remain.[35] We should also mention here Lucio Sponza's volume, which, although focusing upon Italians, examines both civilian and military prisoners.[36]

In the British case the study of the First World War German prisoner experience either does not fit into British national myths about tolerance, heroism and victimhood or, more recently, has become overshadowed by the focus upon the Second World War. As we shall see, however, Britons did not suffer from total amnesia in this field. When we turn to German historiography and memory, the absence of a monograph on our theme may seem even more surprising. The idea of Germans not playing the role of victims would appear irrelevant here, except for the fact that much writing and memory work after 1945 involved forgetting the experiences of the Second World War and focusing upon the victims of the Nazis. Liberal German nationalism since 1945 has essentially revolved around the idea of recreating a new form of identification in which remembering the crimes of the Nazis, and those who suffered as a result, became central.[37] However, the feeling of victimhood certainly existed after the First World War being linked with the Versailles Treaty and encompassing a variety of groups, including those who now found themselves under foreign rule as a result of boundary changes and German prisoners, particularly those held by the French, Russians and Soviets. In the inter-war years those Germans who faced internment certainly impinged on the public consciousness. No full-scale academic study emerged on the British experience, but some academic coverage did occur.[38]

In the German case, to an even greater extent than in Britain, where concern with German prisoners barely surfaced during the 1920s and 1930s, the Second World War experience almost completely drowned out that of the Great War. While the Federal Republic officially accepted the post-1945 boundaries and the millions of ethnic Germans who had moved westward in consequence, those who had undergone expulsion clung on to the idea of returning home. At the same time a large academic literature in German has emerged on those who faced expulsion, with its origins in the immediate post-war years.[39] Robert Moeller has demonstrated that the expellees became a central theme in early West German popular culture.[40]

Prisoners of war also became a major concern for post-war Germans. This seems unsurprising given the fact many did not return until the second half of the 1940s, while the last of those who found themselves in the Soviet Union did not leave that country until Konrad Adenauer visited it in 1955. In the popular culture and academic literature of the Federal Republic, the term 'prisoner of war' has therefore tended to refer to those individuals who faced incarceration during the Second World War, even though their experiences resembled those of their forefathers during the Great War, whose internment had remained largely forgotten. An important academic literature has grown up on those incarcerated from 1939 to 1955, which has included both general and specific accounts focusing particularly upon the Soviet Union but has also resulted in a recent study on those Germans held captive in Britain.[41]

However, the term 'prisoners' in the post-1945 period in Germany also has a second meaning, referring to those individuals who found themselves working for the Nazi economy between 1939 and 1945, whose numbers may have reached 15 million in total. In the immediate post-war period the main popular memory of these individuals focused upon their alleged criminality upon their liberation following the Allied invasion. By the 1960s an academic literature began to develop upon this theme, and it has burgeoned from the 1990s.[42] The issue of foreign workers came to the forefront of the historical memory of Nazism at the start of the twenty-first century, being connected with the attempt to gain compensation for those affected. After the German government agreed to payments in 2000, all manner of organizations, including both major churches, admitted to having employed foreign workers during the war.[43] By this time, studies had also begun to appear on the experiences of foreign workers on a local scale during the Second World War[44] as part of the obsessive focus of post-war German historiography upon the Nazis and the Second World War within this theme, which applies not simply to Germans but also to British, American and Israeli scholars. Only recently have historians turned their attention to the experience of prisoners in Germany during the Great War.[45]

Remembering

Consequently, the Great War prisoner experience has become something of a distant memory, particularly in popular discourse, although academics and others, in both Britain and Germany, have not completely ignored the story of what happened between 1914 and 1919. The amnesia about this subject was partial rather than total, as an examination of surviving academic and other literature in Britain and Germany demonstrates.

A focus upon Britain reveals two clear patterns in the memory of German prisoners. Although the Germanophobia of the First World War and inter-war years remained potent, it did not prevent the publication of a handful of volumes on the experiences of individual internees. These included translations of German works. After 1945, while academic historians began to turn their attention to Great War internment, local historians focused upon some of the camps which emerged, above all those on the Isle of Man, particularly Knockaloe, which held tens of thousands of people between 1915 and 1919.

The war years themselves proved too poisonous for Britons to devote much attention to the sufferings of Germans. A small number of exceptions exist to this rule, especially as a result of the efforts of a few charities and individuals including the Society of Friends and Karl Emil Markel.[46] In addition, a volume of photographs appeared, probably in early 1917, taken at six camps on the mainland by 'the photographic section of the Royal Flying Corps' in response to 'a request made by the American Ambassador in Berlin' (as the United States acted as the mediator for relations between Britain and Germany until 1917) for an exhibition at Württemberg. But even the single page of text making up the foreword of this publication could not escape the Germanophobic atmosphere of the time, concluding that the photographs 'show that the excellence of the conditions in which the prisoners live are in striking contrast with the regime which obtains in many of the prisoners' camps in Germany'.[47]

In the early 1920s there followed the only English literary work to have appeared on the experience of internment, focusing upon Knockaloe and written by Hall Caine, who, while not born on the Isle of Man, had become one of the most famous writers associated with it. *The Woman of Knockaloe*, which first appeared in 1923,

Figure 1.1 Donington Hall. During the course of the First World War this camp would become synonymous, in the eyes of the British press, with the luxurious treatment of German officers, despite the fact that the reality remained different.

centred upon the relationship between Mona Craine, the daughter of the local farmer, and one of the internees brought here from the mainland, Oskar Heine, an engineer previously employed by an English firm on the Mersey. Although Mona initially has strong prejudices against Germans, the first meeting with Oskar, who has come to collect milk from the farm, results in instant attraction, and also means that she now sees the internees as humans rather than as outsiders and barbarians. Caine stresses the strong prejudice which exists towards to any relationship from both their families, who each suffer losses during the conflict. Mona's father dies after a fit of anger while condemning her feelings for Oskar, and Oskar's mother refuses to allow him to bring Mona back to Germany at the end of the war, as Mona faces eviction from her farm for her actions. Caine emphasizes the potency of the hatred in a desperate final scene in which the two lovers throw themselves, arm in arm, off a cliff and into the sea below. *The Woman of Knockaloe* provides a good indication of the level of Germanophobia which existed in Britain both during and after immediately after the Great War. The novel also has a strong Christian message, with Caine emphasizing Christianity over the intolerance of nationalism, especially in the final chapter as the lovers hurl themselves into the sea. A reading of the book also reveals that Caine had a detailed knowledge about the everyday realities of internment and the geography of Knockaloe, so that it had to come with a statement that 'nothing in this book is intended to refer to real-life persons in the Isle of Man'.[48]

The novel also became an American film, *Barbed Wire*, in 1927. While the characters of Mona and Oskar remain the same, the setting changes from the Isle of Man to Normandy, and, in the need to have a Hollywood 'happy ending', 'Mona's blinded brother returns from the war and shames the people with an impassioned plea for love and forgiveness'.[49] The Germanophobic reaction to the film in Britain incensed Caine, and, in a letter to the *Sunday Times*, he outlined that the story came to him while he was living on the Isle of Man during the war and, in particular, during one night at the end of the conflict, when he had a vivid dream about the relationship between a local farmer's daughter and an internee, who had become outcasts but disappeared in unity off the edge of a cliff. In a further indication of the potency of Germanophobia in inter-war Britain, Caine's letter objected to the 'monstrous' and 'malicious' misrepresentation of the film by 'certain sections of the press', which described it as 'pro-German', even though it was 'only and always pro-human . . . with the sole desire of preserving peace'.[50]

Against this background it therefore proved difficult to publish anything positive about the experiences of Great War German internees during the 1920s and 1930. One other exception, *Time Stood Still* by Paul Cohen-Portheim, is perhaps the most accurate account of the realities of internment and the boredom it produced for those civilians unable to work under the Hague Convention. Cohen-Portheim, actually an Austrian, found himself painting in England in the summer when the war broke out, but could not return home. He therefore spent much of the conflict in the middle-class camp in Wakefield, where he remained until release in February 1918. His account is a scathing and penetrating attack on the futility of internment and the orderliness of the society created, with much detail about the feelings of boredom that he experienced.[51]

The only other types of narrative which appeared in inter-war Britain were escape stories by military internees, aimed at a male audience and including translations of German works. Some of these came together in a collection of accounts originally published in 1932 under the title of *Escapers All*,[52] based upon a series of sixteen talks organized by the BBC in the summer of 1931: 'thirteen were given by Englishmen who escaped in Germany and Turkey, two by Germans who escaped in England, and one by a German who escaped from a British island in the Indian Ocean'.[53] The Germans trying to flee from England consisted of Heinz E. Justus, who unsuccessfully attempted to escape on several occasions, and Gunther Plüschow, who escaped from the officers' camp at Donington Hall and managed to return home to Germany, where he received an Iron Cross for his efforts. In fact, as the volume on escape points out, the Plüschow story is an extract from his book originally published in German in 1916 as *Die Abenteuer des Fliegers von Tsingtau: Meine Erlebnisse in drei Erdteilen* (referring to the fact that he initially faced capture in China on the outbreak of war) and appearing in an English edition as early as 1922.[54] Similar narratives on internment experiences had appeared in German during both the war and its immediate aftermath, although few would make it into English editions. The exceptions include Carl Spindler's *Das geheimnisvolle Schiff*, published in 1921 and appearing in English ten years later, about Spindler's capture off the Irish coast, his experiences in several camps and his eventual return to Germany.[55] Similarly, one of the few other successful escapees during the war, Pál Stoffa, actually an Austro-Hungarian, captured in Russia and finding himself in the camps at Alexandra Palace and Knockaloe, also had his originally German narrative issued in English.[56]

These few accounts inevitably had a small readership, with the exception of the *Woman of Knockaloe*, which went through several editions. However, at the height of the Second World War one of the most important fictional German prisoners appeared in the Michael Powell and Emeric Pressburger film *The Life and Death of Colonel Blimp*. We can read this film in many ways, but from our own point of view, it offers a sympathetic perception of Anglo-German relations from the eve of the Great War to the Second World War through the relationship between the leading characters, the British officer Clive Wynne-Candy, the German officer Theodor Kretschmar-Schuldorff and Edith Hunter, an Englishwoman with whom both fall in love. Wynne-Candy and Kretschmar-Schuldorff meet when they fight an inconclusive duel in pre-war Berlin, after which they become friends. Theo (rather than Clive) actually marries Edith, but this does not affect their relationship. They next meet at the end of the First World War when Theo finds himself interned in a British camp, which Clive visits to find him listening to a concert. Theo does not speak to him, but he telephones Clive while making his way back to Germany and visits him at his house, where he talks to him and other British officers, expressing his doubt about the way in which Germany would be treated. We next see Theo during the Second World War as an enemy alien, who has fled the Nazis and has been saved from internment by Clive. In the context of its appearance in 1943 we might see this aspect of the film as catching an anti-internment mood of this year and looking forward to a positive post-war post-Nazi Anglo-German future: the Ministry of Information partly financed it. The film partly came from the personal experiences of Pressburger, a Hungarian Jew educated in Germany who had worked in Berlin and fled the Nazis to face an aliens' tribunal, which had to decide whether to intern him in 1940.[57]

Colonel Blimp, along with *The Woman of Knockaloe*, remains one of the few fictional accounts to deal with German prisoners in First World War Britain. In the aftermath of the Second World War, as popular memory focused upon this conflict, the experiences of individual German internees during the Great War became irrelevant. As in the German case, 'prisoner of war' now had a specific meaning, denoting the defiant victims of the Nazis, epitomized both in film and in the Colditz television series of the 1970s,[58] or those who had suffered at the hands of the Japanese.[59]

This focus of popular culture on prisoners of the Nazis and the Japanese essentially drowned out German internment experiences, certainly from the Great War, until the very end of the century. The only exceptions appear to consist of a local history account of a camp in Jersey[60] and a few chapters in an autobiographical study published in 1956 by the German anarchist Rudolf Rocker, who found himself interned in a number of London camps, including Alexandra Palace.[61] Some attention also refocused upon the long-standing camp in Stobs, near Hawick, in 1988.[62] By the 1990s local historians began to pay attention to places which hosted internment camps, including those at Lofthouse Park in Wakefield,[63] Pattishall[64] and Skipton.[65] In addition, since the middle of the 1980s, several pamphlets on individual camps, published by local enthusiasts, have also appeared.[66] Most interesting of all perhaps, two 'amateur' historians have actually published books covering internment. The first, eighty-nine pages in length, is a patchy account of the treatment of civilians and appears to have its origins in the experiences of the author's German grandfather, who found himself in Knockaloe.[67] The other volume, while it may lack academic rigour, is a different type of work. At 258 pages in length and published by the Postal History Society, with a focus upon prisoners, mail, it has a basis in a thorough knowledge of the local history of internment.[68]

This recent growth in the interest in internment among historical enthusiasts may have several explanations. In the first place, it almost certainly links with the expansion of popular interest in history, perhaps best epitomized by the arrival of *BBC History Magazine*, but also with the growth in genealogy, witnessed by the explosion in the number of magazines which focus upon this subject and, once again, driven forward by the BBC, this time as a result of the celebrity ancestor-tracing *Who Do You Think You Are*, which has now gone through several series.[69] But decades before this programme emerged on television screens, the Anglo-German Family History Society came into existence in 1987. The group has held annual meetings, has produced publications about the history of Germans in Britain and has offered genealogical guidance and information to Britons wishing to trace their German ancestry. It also has a deep interest in the history of internment in Britain.[70] This growth in popular interest in internment has also received stimulation from serious academic study, including my book on the First World War German community.

Local enthusiasts on internment, as well as professional scholars, have particularly focused upon the Isle of Man, which seems inevitable in view of the tens of thousands of Germans and other nationalities held there during the Great War. Nevertheless, this interest has only really surfaced in recent decades, assisted by a collection policy at Manx National Heritage which is aimed at gathering internment material.

Before moving further, however, we need to stress the absence of any sort of serious memorial to the tens of thousands of Germans and other enemy aliens who lived in the barracks established at Knockaloe Farm during the Great War. While some artefacts have survived at Manx National Heritage, anyone passing Knockaloe Farm today would remain completely unaware of the presence of an enormous concentration camp here at the start of the twentieth century. Only three clues survive. First, the Manx Department of Agriculture, Fisheries and Forestry has put up a small sign (under a larger one pointing out the present use of the site as an experimental farm). The plaque reads:

> KNOCKALOE CAMP
> Knockaloe Farm served as an internment camp for over 20,000 German Civilians interned during the period of the Great War, 1914–1918.

In fact, internees remained here well into 1919. Second is a similar plaque put up by the Anglo-German Family History Society.[71] The only other trace consists of graves at Patrick Church, next to the camp. Those still maintained consist of two Jewish headstones and seven Turkish ones, with a marble commemoration in front of them declaring: 'Here are buried seven Turkish internees who died in the 1914–1918 war.' Both of these headstones were replaced during the course of the 1970s.[72] Archival sources, however, confirm that numerous Christian Germans found their resting places here. An index of graves held in the Bundesarchiv in Freiburg lists almost eighty plots, including the Turkish one noted above, holding a total of 221 graves.[73] Several line drawings in a Freiburg file confirm this.[74] However, none of these graves appear visible because in July 1962, after a public meeting, the 245 prisoners buried here were moved to the German Military Cemetery in Cannock Chase by the Imperial War Graves Commission. 'The operation was kept as quiet as possible. Screens were erected at the Manx Churchyard to hide the work going on and sightseers were discouraged.' Within one month '69 graves, each with up to five prisoners in them, were opened up. The coffins were burned and the gravestones were broken up and thrown into the open ground before they were refitted.'[75] But the almost complete amnesia on the Isle of Man in terms of any form of surviving sites seems remarkable when compared with the situation in Germany, which has preserved countless former concentration camps, admittedly from the Second World War.[76] This lack of a memorial provides the best indication of the amnesia about internment in First World War Britain. While the Federal Republic maintains memorials in numerous Nazi concentration camps, Britain can spare only a small commemorative plaque which, unless an individual seeks it out, remains invisible. This absence of any sort of memorial needs further contextualization in the countless monuments to British troops killed during the Great War.[77] German internees simply did not fit into any of the memorialization of the inter-war years. The deportation of the Germans at the end of the First World War and the level of Germanophobia meant that there existed no enthusiasm for the erection of such a memorial. The situation has not changed since 1945.

Writers, meanwhile, began to devote attention to Isle of Man internment in the last two decades of the twentieth century. Until that time few books seriously considered First World War internment. They included B. E. Sargeaunt's 1922 volume *The Isle of Man and the Great War*, which had an important focus upon internment.[78] Similarly, a study of Cunningham's holiday camp, which was turned into the place of internment in Douglas, also focused upon this subject,[79] as did the biography of the Quaker James T. Baily, who did much to help Manx internees.[80] More recently, a series of academic and amateur historians have turned their attention to First World War internment. Perhaps most importantly and symbolically, volume 5 of the official history of the Isle of Man covering the years 1830–1999 contains a section on internment under a subheading of 'The 1914–18 War and the Internment Camps'.[81] This contrasts with Margery West's account of the Manx experience during the Great War, which devotes three chapters and almost thirty pages to internment, although we would expect this.[82] Academic studies include the work of Jennifer Kewley Draskau[83] and the Manx archivist Yvonne Creswell,[84] as well as Gerald Newton.[85] We should also mention the efforts of

Figure 1.2 Patrick churchyard with German graves. Most of those who died in Knockaloe would have been buried here, as this illustration from the early 1920s demonstrates, although all but a small number of Jews and Turks would subsequently face transfer to the German Military Cemetery in Cannock Chase.

Robert Fyson[86] and the account of Pat Kelly, whose narrative on Knockaloe evolved from her mother-in-law's experiences.[87]

German accounts of First World War internment differ from British ones in several ways. In the first place, the most important period for remembering prisoners was the Great War and the inter-war years, when numerous personal accounts appeared and when prisoner-of-war associations came into existence. At the same time, while English-language publications have mostly concerned themselves with civilian internment, those published in German have covered all types of prisoners. Although personal accounts predominated between 1915 and 1939, these did not have the same concern with the locality, other than the camp itself, which many of the later British narratives did.

A whole series of personal accounts began to appear during the course of the conflict itself, written by internees who, for a variety of reasons, spent only part of the war in British camps. The demand for these testimonies finds partial explanation in the propaganda war between Britain and Germany, in which the treatment of prisoners formed a key element.[88] Nevertheless, few of the accounts published during the conflict, or indeed after it, have mistreatment by the British as a central theme. Those published between 1915 and 1918 prove easier to understand if analysed in two groups. On the one hand, we can identify those in which adventure provides a key element, with a story which involves capture in the colonies and then a long journey to a camp in England. On the other hand, there appeared several books which essentially concentrate upon life behind barbed wire, often with a focus upon one individual camp where the author spent most of his period of incarceration.

At least five accounts of capture in the colonies and subsequent transportation to Britain appeared during the course of the Great War. Two of these, by Heinrich Norden and Gotthilf Vöhringer, focus upon the same episode in the form of the seizure and subsequent transportation of German civilians living in Cameroon in September 1914, following the invasion of this German colony by French and British troops. Much of the narrative of both authors concentrates upon events in Africa, the description of various places of internment, the journey to England and subsequent incarceration there. Both of these individuals found themselves lucky enough to return home at the start of 1915. Both display much indignation at the collapse of the German Empire in Africa and the incarceration of thousands of Germans at British hands.[89] Philipp Hecklinger, another missionary in Cameroon, appears to have endured a similar experience to Norden and Vöhringer, although his account appeared in the form of a diary. Like them, he faced capture and internment in West Africa at the outbreak of war, followed by a journey to England and a short period of incarceration in Queenferry, before sailing to Germany at the start of 1915.[90] Georg Wagener, meanwhile, the first German pastor of the Protestant community in Cape Town, found himself interned in South Africa before transportation to England, where he spent time in the Alexandra Palace and Stratford internment camps.[91] The short account by the missionary J. Maue, who lived in India at the outbreak of war, includes a chapter on 'Hatred of the Germans'. Maue describes the journey which took him to the major internment camp used by the British in India, located in Ahmednagar, and his experiences there. A long journey from there, described in some detail, eventually brought him to Alexandra Palace, which he described as having better conditions than Ahmednagar. After eighteen months behind barbed wire in both camps he eventually found himself back in Germany. Maue, like Wagener, ultimately accepted his fate as a result of his religious conviction, and his conclusion reasserts his faith in God.[92]

Most of the other personal accounts published during the First World War did not have the same level of excitement as those which featured scenes from the colonies and the journey to England, although those on Knockaloe, written by pastors who had worked there, did have some circumspection. Hans Erich Benedix published one of the longest wartime accounts of internment in England. In fact, rather like some of the missionaries brought to the country from beyond Europe and reflecting the experiences of other people who found themselves interned in Britain in the autumn of 1914, he began his path to incarceration while travelling on a ship in the high seas, in this case on the *Potsdam* on a passage from New York to Germany. The pages which follow the details of his capture prove a useful account of internment in Britain. Benedix provides details of his own personal experiences, from his capture to a description of all of the individual camps in which he found himself, Stratford, Alexandra Palace and the German Hospital in Dalston, when he fell ill, and his release and return home. Benedix further offers an overview of internment in Britain, outlining the major camps. In addition, his own experience allows him to provide an interesting and useful analysis of specific aspects of internment including culture and the celebration of German national days and Christmas. While the book may have had some propaganda value, Benedix wrote in a generally objective manner.[93] Bruno Schmidt-Reder also found himself captured by the British while travelling on the *Potsdam* from New York. He spent time in Dorchester but had returned to Germany by the end of December 1914.[94] D. W. Pult wrote one of the few accounts by a military prisoner published during the war. He actually arrived as early as 1915, following capture in France, which probably explains the appearance of his book before the end of the war, as the increase in military internees did not occur until 1917 and 1918. Pult provides a fairly matter-of-fact account of his experiences, focusing upon his capture and release and also on the description of camp life in Portsmouth, Holyport and Leigh, where he found himself interned.[95]

The two accounts of Knockaloe published during the war came from pastors who had worked in the camp. Adolf Vielhauer wrote a brief but detailed factual account, which provides information on the location of the camp, the space available to internees and their activities. Vielhauer also focuses upon religious life. He concludes that the prisoners in Knockaloe suffered physically and spiritually and asked his readers to pray for their release.[96] The account produced by R. Hartmann, formerly camp parson in Knockaloe, also provides insights into the realities of life in the camp, focusing upon the activities of the internees.[97]

A small number of books and pamphlets on the experience of internment in Britain therefore appeared during the course of the war. Most of these remained fairly brief, ranging from ten pages to slightly over 100. Despite the potential propaganda value of these accounts in the Anglo-German battle over the treatment of prisoners, the books considered here generally took an objective approach to their subject, outlining the realities of life behind barbed wire. If a message did come through it was in several cases one of maintaining faith in God.

The experience of prisoners remained an important theme in German war memory throughout the inter-war years. Those interned in Britain formed one part of a wider narrative also including those held in France and Russia, who usually fared worse than those captured by the British.[98] Part of the remembering occurred through the issue of further memoirs by those who found themselves interned during the war. In addition, prisoner-of-war groups constituted part of a paramilitary scene which had emerged in the early Weimar Republic and was made up of young men formed by combat.[99]

In the immediate aftermath of the conflict, the state played a role in the creation of a prisoner-of-war consciousness through the establishment of bodies concerned with re-integrating internees into German society, above all the Reichszentralstelle für Kriegs- und Zivilgefangene, which published a regular newsletter.[100] The Reichsbund zum Schutze der Deutschen Kriegs- und Ziviligefangenen emerged in the immediate aftermath of the war, largely out of concern for those prisoners who had not yet returned home.[101] It appears to have subsequently become the Volksbund zum Schutze der Deutschen Kriegs- und Ziviligefangenen, again with its own newsletter.[102] The largest veterans' group was the Reichsvereinigung Ehemalige Kriegsgefangene, founded in December 1918.[103] A report from 1926 claimed that this organization counted 510 branches with at least 9,000 members, although the total may have reached about 400,000 in the early 1920s, which would mean a third of all former prisoners.[104] It also tried to establish an archive and museum for prisoners of war (Archiv und Museum der Kriegsgefangenschaft).[105] During the course of the 1920s its fundamental task consisted of improving the image of prisoners of war and ensuring that they had the same status as other soldiers.[106]

One of its concerns was the situation of German prisoner graves abroad, including those in Britain. Its publication listed graves in Manchester and Stobs in 1922.[107] In 1936 representatives of this group travelled to England to take part in a wreath-laying ceremony in what had emerged as the main graveyard for those prisoners who had died in England, Cannock Chase Military Cemetery, which is still maintained by the German War Graves Commission and is one of the few visible and tangible signs of the German prisoner-of-war experience in Britain between 1914 and 1918. The May 1936 visit actually formed part of a meeting of ex-servicemen from fifteen different states.[108] The Reichsvereinigung Ehemalige Kriegsgefangene and the Volksbund zum Schutze der Deutschen Kriegs- und Ziviligefangenen ensured that the German prisoner of war received space in the memorialization of the conflict during the inter-war years.[109]

The efforts of these groups went hand in hand with a whole series of personal accounts published after 1918. Although the immediate post-war years witnessed a spate of these, publishers continued to issue them even during the Second World War. It may seem tempting to view these publications as part of an Anglophobic discourse, but the diversity does not lend itself to such a generalization. We can divide them into four general categories. Firstly, we can identify a group of official and semi-official accounts. Second, a couple of escape stories appeared, which did not undergo translation. We can also identify a third group of fictional publications produced by those who spent some time behind barbed wire. Finally, the largest sub-genre consists of factual narratives produced by former prisoners themselves. While the range of the books in this last group varies in quality, some are literary in nature and offer important insights into the realities of internment. Once again, the publications of those interned in England need contextualization in a wider remembering of former prisoners who had faced incarceration in a variety of European locations.

This becomes clear in the official and semi-official volumes, each of which deal with Britain as one case study. Two of these from 1919 appear to have the same text. The Vereinigung Wissenschaftlicher Verleger issued *Deutsche Kriegsgefangene in Feindesland*.[110] The year 1919 also saw the publication of two volumes of overtly official material under the title *Kriegsgefangene in Feindesland*, with one focusing on France and the other on England. The main concern of the latter (with the same text as *Deutsche Kriegsgefangene in Feindesland*) was the treatment of German internees during the conflict. While taking a fairly objective approach to these issues, it concentrated upon the poor conditions of the early camps, the mistreatment of those Germans working under British control in France and the experiences of submarine prisoners, as well as the attitude of the British press.[111] Another official-style account on English camps appeared in 1922, consisting primarily of reports by internees. The central focus, however, was accounts of the British controlled camps in France.[112] This appears to be the last official-style volume. The main aim of these publications was to inform Germans of the realities of internment in the immediate aftermath of the war.

The demand for personal accounts survived throughout the inter-war years. Two of these sold themselves as escape narratives, probably aimed at a younger male audience and at those who had experienced internment during the war, and focused upon the thrill and risks of escaping. Albrecht Brugger, for instance, faced capture as late as October 1918 and found himself imprisoned in Lofthouse Park. While spending some time on his seizure and his journey to England and Lofthouse Park, the overwhelming majority of this short book focuses upon his plan for escape and his journey back to Germany, which did not occur until the autumn of 1919, just before the camp closed. Published in 1937, this volume, which begins with a statement asserting its accuracy, is very much a product of Nazi Germany, as after escaping and arriving in London, Brugger and his companion tried to find a Mr Saloman. 'The Jew had no Fatherland and no national feeling', despite his German nationality, and did not therefore offer them any financial help. Brugger and his friend were recaptured but stayed only a few more days in Lofthouse Park camp because of its closure in mid-December, consequently returning home by the end of 1919.[113] The other escape narrative, by Wilhelm Kröpke, appeared in 1938 and almost presents a thrill a minute. Like several accounts which had appeared during the conflict, his journey begins in East Africa, from where he subsequently faced transportation to Britain. He spent time in Queensferry, from where he tried to escape (and therefore faced transfer to carry out hard labour in Knutsford), Stobs and Alexandra Palace, from which he successfully fled. The journey back to Germany, which actually occurred via Scotland, is described in some detail.[114] The books by Brügger and Kröpke offer themselves to a series of interpretations. On the one hand, they represent simple escape narratives in which the constant threat of capture plays a significant role. However, both have much information on Britain and the British in their accounts of journeys to escape ports, involving description of British people, landscape and cities. With war again approaching such stereotypes may have proved interesting for those who wanted a simple insight into potential foes.

We can also mention two fictional works which appeared in Germany during the inter-war years and which form part of wider genre which emerged during the 1920s in particular, with a particular focus upon experiences in Russia, leading to titles such as *Die magischen Wälder*.[115] Christoph Wohlenberg's pamphlet is a play, or sketch, of seventeen pages set in an English internment camp. It consists of a discussion between German internees and a Danish pastor, involving religion and German and north European identities and concluding with a rendition of the German patriotic hymn 'Ein feste Burg ist unser Gott'.[116] The other literary account on First World War internment in Britain which appeared in the inter-war years also came from the pen of a former internee, on this occasion Heinrich Eckmann. Set in a working camp in Wales, the book, according to the foreword, appears to represent a fictional account of his wartime experiences. Although none of the locations which Eckmann describes existed, he clearly had knowledge of the realities of internment, as revealed in his descriptions of camp life, his relations with other internees and camp staff and his experiences of work as a farmer and gardener.[117]

The remaining six volumes on prisoner-of-war experiences in Britain sell themselves as factual narratives. Four are bulky volumes which focus upon experiences in one camp and provide important insights into the realities of internment, having been written by individuals who thought about and analysed their wartime situation. The other two, fairly thin volumes, do not carry the same weight. Despite its grand title, which apparently tells the story of all Germans interned in Britain, the account published by Karl von Scheidt and Fritz Meyer focuses upon their own personal experiences following capture on a journey from New York to Europe. This short book does, however, provide useful insights, as well as interesting illustrative material.[118] The volumes of Wohlenberg and von Scheidt and Meyer both appeared in 1919, when hundreds of thousands of Germans still found themselves behind barbed wire. So did an account by Otto Schimming, another missionary transported from West Africa to Britain, which provides a similar narrative to the accounts of religious men published during the conflict.[119]

The other four autobiographical accounts published in German during the inter-war years provide us with the sort of detail on the realities of everyday life offered only by Paul Cohen-Portheim in English. They would have appealed to a more educated audience than did some of the escape narratives. Read collectively, together with Cohen-Portheim, they would reveal the monotony, boredom, hopelessness and camaraderie experienced by many educated internees. The military prisoners Fritz Sachse and Paul Cossmann spent time in a camp in Skipton and while there wrote an account which they claimed to have subsequently revised on their way back to Germany. The strengths of this volume include its description of the routine of everyday life, while it also provides a vivid account of the layout of the camp.[120] J. Machner wrote a similarly detailed and considered account of his year spent in Ripon following capture in France in September 1918. This volume of 392 pages provides both details of the environment in which he found himself and his perceptions of it.[121] Meanwhile L. Bogenstätter and H. Zimmermann wrote a rich description of the camp established in Handforth, near Manchester. This actually takes a partly chronological perspective. Although the authors almost certainly spent time here to judge from the vividness of their observations, they actually wrote in the third person.[122] While these three volumes appeared in the immediate aftermath of the First World War, the other similar account was published at the beginning of the Second, which suggests that the new conflict may have provoked interest in the personal experience of Frederick Lewis Dunbar-Kalckreuth. The author, with Scottish origins but holding a German passport, was studying English in St Leonard's on Sea on the outbreak of war but found himself classified as an alien enemy. Unable to return home, he spent most of the war in the internment camp in Douglas on the Isle of Man. This publication consists of a series of diary entries covering each part of Dunbar-Kalckreuth's experiences, from his idyllic summer in England in 1914, through the tension caused by the outbreak of war, to his arrest and his return home. With the title *Die Männerinsel*, the majority of the volume focuses upon his experiences in Douglas.[123]

Despite the richness of the experiences revealed in many of the accounts published by and about First World War internees, Dunbar-Kalckreuth's volume appears to have been the last German-language book in probably the last possible year when such a publication would attract public interest. The following years would result in an even greater conflict than the First World War, with Germans becoming far more interested in the battle they were currently fighting, which resulted in the capture of millions of German prisoners of war, some of whom would not return home until the 1950s. The events of the Second World War and its aftermath overshadowed the memory of the experience of the First, certainly in the area of prisoners of war.

Beginnings of a history

Only at the end of the twentieth century did professional historians, both German and otherwise, seriously begin to turn their attention to the experiences of German internees during the First World War, partly in the context of the emergence of a discipline of 'First World War studies', which now includes at least one journal.[124] However, most general accounts of the First World War have ignored prisoners. Those which have devoted attention to them include Tammy Proctor's examination of civilian experiences during the Great War, which takes an individual approach, using personal testimonies, while also recognizing the global nature of civilian internment. She sees the First World War as a turning point in the history of mass incarceration.[125] Niall Ferguson's volume devotes an entire chapter to military prisoners.[126] As he demonstrates, between 6.9 and 8.7 million people faced incarceration during the conflict, making up around 25 per cent of all 'casualties'.[127] Ferguson's chapter, entitled 'The Captor's Dilemma', appears to have partly emerged from an article he published on prisoner taking and killing[128] and offers a general introduction to the subject of captivity. Stéphane Audoin-Rouzeau and Annette Becker's history of the First World War also carries a chapter on prisoners under the title 'The Camp Phenomenon: The Internment of Civilians and Military Prisoners', recognizing the Great War as a turning point in the mass incarceration of males but also devoting attention to mistreatment and humanitarianism.[129] Focusing upon French and German experiences, the authors recognize the commonality of experiences between military and civilian internees and assert that 'soldiers in the Great War were really civilians in uniform'.[130]

Like Ferguson, those who have written volumes about internment during the Great War usually focus upon this issue in a European-wide context. Furthermore, they often concentrate upon one particular theme. This approach dates back to the inter-war years. One of the most interesting studies in this context is Hermann Pörzgen's *Theater ohne Frau*, an analysis of the role of plays within camps for German internees throughout Europe, a theme which would receive attention once again at the start of the twenty-first century with a focus upon issues of sex and sexuality.[131] In this context we can also mention the work of Rainer Pöppinghege, who has examined the role of the newspapers which emerged in German, British and French prisoner-of-war camps during the First World War.[132]

Attention has also focused upon the rights and treatment of prisoners of war, which are usually contextualized historically, sometimes in a narrative dating back to antiquity. One of the most important volumes to take this approach appeared in Berlin at the height of the Nazi war effort.[133] More recently, Stefan Oeter has dealt with the subject,[134] while Matthew Stibbe has seen it as one of the key themes in the study of civilian internment during the Great War. Most recently Heather Jones's study of prisoners in Britain, Germany and France has focused upon the memory and reality of mistreatment.[135] As the present volume will demonstrate, those prisoners who found themselves in camps within Britain rarely experienced deliberate mistreatment. The British generally played by the rules established by the Hague Convention in 1907. The various government departments responsible for internment also placed no obstacles in the way of the United States Embassy and subsequently Swiss Embassy officials who acted as intermediaries between the British and German governments during the war. One of their key tasks consisted of visiting the internment camps for both civilian and military prisoners during the conflict.[136] Humanitarian organizations, which also have recently received attention, also proved important in the fair treatment of prisoners held on British soil.[137]

The United States and Swiss Embassy reports provide much information on the employment of internees, another theme which has received attention from historians. In fact, while it remains brief and covers both world wars, Gerald Davis's article on this subject, published in 1977, signalled a re-emergence of academic interest in First World War captivity.[138] Ten years later a German book appeared on this subject. While covering a long time period and not truly academic, it provides some useful insights.[139] Most recently, Matthew Stibbe has contextualized prisoner-of-war labour between 1914 and 1920 in an edited volume also dealing with captivity and forced migration during these years.[140]

Some general volumes have also appeared in recent decades on the history of prisoners of war over a long time period, aimed at both an academic and a general market, probably those with an interest in all things military. Those in the latter category, which predate the serious academic interest in the subject, include A. J. Barker's *Behind Barbed Wire*.[141] Among the academic studies, Arnold Krammer's handbook provides an outline of the history of prisoner-of-war captivity dating back to antiquity and stressing the cruelty the prisoners faced. Krammer also devotes attention to 'The Search for Legal Protection', stressing the role of the Enlightenment and also focusing upon the foundation of the Red Cross and the Hague and Geneva Conventions.[142] More recently, Sibylle Scheipers, introducing her edited volume on prisoners of war through the ages, has also examined cruelty and humanitarianism. She suggests that internees offer an insight into other aspects of war. Their treatment 'seems to be a litmus test for compliance with cultural, legal and moral norms aimed at mitigating the effects of war', while the 'issue of prisoners in war tells us something about the success and progress of the humanitarian project as such'.[143] Scheipers examines the uses of prisoners for strategic, economic and political purposes, as well as the issue of reciprocity.[144] From the point of view of the present volume, Scheipers's perspective has some value, especially as both the British Foreign Office and the German Auswärtiges Amt became obsessed with reciprocity, exchanging thousands of letters over the relative treatment of their captives during the conflict and egged on by their own public opinion. Rüdiger Overmans too covers the issue of the significance of prisoners for other aspects of war and also outlines historical continuities and discontinuities. He further stresses the First World War as a turning point, especially in view of the numbers of males who found themselves behind barbed wire after 1914. In addition, like Audoin-Rouzeau and Becker in particular, he also devotes attention to civilian internees, on this occasion focusing upon Germans abroad.[145]

This brings us to general studies of captivity in the First World War, most importantly Jochen Oltmer's edited volume on this subject, with contributions on the experiences of military prisoners in particular throughout the European continent. The essays are divided into three sections focusing upon 'Prisoners of War as a Problem of European States', humanitarianism and repatriation.[146] In his introduction, Oltmer stresses that the prisoner-of-war problem was a mass phenomenon never previously experienced. He also points to the varying attitudes of individual states, as well as to the fact that captivity represented an individual experience for each prisoner. He views the prisoner-of-war phenomenon as a military problem, a foreign policy issue and an internal and security question.[147] We should also mention Alan R. Kramer's article on prisoners of war between 1914 and 1918.[148]

The above outline of recent historiography points to a concern of historians with several key issues when studying the First World War. These include the scale of the problem, mistreatment, humanitarianism and the role of internees in relations between combatant states. None of these form a key element in the current volume, although I do address them within the narrative. The book that follows, focusing upon one individual case study, takes a similar approach to two of the other recent books on First World War internment, Alon Rachamimov's study of Austro-Hungarian military prisoners in Russia, who totalled 2.8 million people,[149] and Matthew Stibbe's book on the approximately 5,500 British civilians held at the Ruhleben internment camp in Berlin,[150] which harks back to the classic account on this subject written by John Davidson Ketchum, who spent much of the war there.[151] Like these two volumes, the narrative which follows essentially focuses upon the everyday lives of the internees. We can see it in the German tradition of *Alltagsgeschichte*[152] or the well-established British historical tradition of history from below, which now increasingly uses 'life stories'.[153] The research is contextualized in writing on wartime captivity from both the time and subsequently. This volume begins with the journey to an internment camp and continues through the experiences of the prisoners, in a series of chapters, to their ultimate release. The lives of the prisoners find contextualization in the attitudes and actions of British and German government and public opinion, and in the work of humanitarian groups.

Notes

1 Hall Caine, *The Woman of Knockaloe: A Parable* (London, 1923), p. 99.
2 NA/WO394/10, Statistical Abstract, 1 November 1918.
3 Panikos Panayi, *The Enemy in Our Midst: Germans in Britain during the First World War* (Oxford, 1991).
4 D. H. Lawrence, *Selected Letters* (Harmondsworth, 1978), p. 83.
5 D. H. Lawrence, *Kangaroo* (1923; reprint Harmondsworth, 1985), pp. 235–6.
6 Cate Haste, *Keep the Home Fires Burning* (London, 1977); Gary S. Messinger, *British Propaganda and the State in the First World War* (Manchester, 1992); R. J. Q. Adams, *The Conscription Controversy in Great Britain, 1900–18* (Basingstoke, 1987).

7 Gerhard Fischer, 'Fighting the War at Home: The Campaign against Enemy Aliens in Australia during the First World War', in Panikos Panayi, ed., *Minorities in Wartime: National and Racial Groupings in Europe, North America and Australia during the Two World Wars* (Oxford, 1993), pp. 263–86; Andrew Francis, '"To Be Truly British We Must be Anti-German": Patriotism, Citizenship and Anti-Alienism in New Zealand during the Great War' (Ph.D. thesis, Victoria University of Wellington, 2009).

8 Gerard J. DeGroot, *Blighty: British Society in the Era of the First World War* (London, 1996), pp. 140–60.

9 Panayi, *Enemy*.

10 DeGroot, *Blighty*, pp. 157–60; Adrian Gregory, *The Last Great War: British Society and the First World War* (Cambridge, 2009), pp. 234–48.

11 Stefan Manz, *Migranten und Internierte: Deutsche in Glasgow, 1864–1918* (Stuttgart, 2003), pp. 231–95; Ben Braber, 'Within our Gates: A New Perspective on Germans in Glasgow during the First World War', *Journal of Scottish Historical Studies*, vol. 29 (2009), 87–105.

12 See Chapter 7 below and Matthew Stibbe, *British Civilian Internees in Germany: The Ruhleben Camp, 1914–18* (Manchester, 2008).

13 John Ramsden, *Don't Mention the War: The British and the Germans since 1890* (London, 2006); Ruth Wittlinger, 'Perceptions of Germany and the Germans in Post-War Britain', *Journal of Multilingual and Multicultural Development*, vol. 25 (2004), 453–65.

14 The Pioneering works include: G. D. H. Cole and Raymond Postgate, *The Common People* (London, 1938); and J. L. and L. B. Hammond, *The Skilled Labourer, 1760–1832* (London, 1919).

15 John Bourne, *Britain and the Great War, 1914–18* (London, 1989), p. 236.

16 Stibbe, *British Civilian Internees*, pp. 162–76.

17 See Chapter 7 below.

18 Colin Holmes, 'The Myth of Fairness: Racial Violence in Britain, 1911–19', *History Today*, vol. 35 (October 1985), 41–5; Tony Kushner and Kenneth Lunn, 'Introduction', in Tony Kushner and Kenneth Lunn, eds, *The Politics of Marginality: Race, the Radical Right and Minorities in Twentieth Century Britain* (London, 1990); Panikos Panayi, 'Anti-Immigrant Violence in Nineteenth and Twentieth Century Britain', in Panikos Panayi, ed., *Racial Violence in Britain in the Nineteenth and Twentieth Centuries* (London, 1996), pp. 1–2. For an introduction to German debates see Richard J. Evans, *In Hitler's Shadow: West German Historians and the Attempt to Escape from the Nazi Past* (London, 1989).

19 Panikos Panayi and Pippa Virdee, eds, *Refugees and the End of Empire: Imperial Collapse and Forced Migration during the Twentieth Century* (Basingstoke, 2011).
20 See, for instance: Jörg Friedrich, *The Fire: The Bombing of Germany, 1940–1945* (New York, 2006); and A. C. Grayling, *Among the Dead Cities: Was the Allied Bombing of Civilians in WWII a Necessity or a Crime?* (London, 2006).
21 John Sweetman, *Bomber Crew: Taking on the Reich* (London, 2005).
22 See, for example, Malcolm Brown, *Spitfire Summer: When Britain Stood Alone* (London, 2000).
23 Angus Calder, *The Myth of the Blitz* (London, 1991).
24 For the academic literature see: R. P. W. Havers, *Reassessing the Japanese Prisoner of War Experience* (London, 2003); Brian MacArthur, *Surviving the Sword: Prisoners of the Japanese 1942–45* (London, 2005); and Philip Towle, *Japanese Prisoners of War* (London, 2003).
25 Jay Winter, *Sites of Memory, Sites of Mourning: The Great War in European Cultural History* (Cambridge, 1995); Paul Fussell, *The Great War and Modern Memory* (Oxford, 1975).
26 *Guardian*, 25 July 2009.
27 Robert Murphy, *British Cinema and the Second World War* (London, 2000).
28 Winter, *Sites of Memory*; Fussell, *The Great War and Modern Memory*.
29 David Cesarani and Tony Kushner, eds, *The Internment of Aliens in Twentieth Century Britain* (London, 1993).
30 Richard Dove, ed.,*'Totally un-English'? Britain's Internment of 'Enemy Aliens' in Two World Wars* (Amsterdam, 2005).
31 François Lafitte, *The Internment of Aliens* (1940; London, 1988); Peter and Leni Gillman, *'Collar the Lot': How Britain Interned and Expelled its Wartime Refugees* (London, 1980); Ronald Stent, *A Bespattered Page? The Internment of His Majesty's 'Most Loyal Enemy Aliens'* (London, 1980); Miriam Kochan, *Britain's Internees in the Second World War* (London, 1983); Erich Koch, *Deemed Suspect: A Wartime Blunder* (Toronto, 1980); Connery Chappell, *Island of Barbed Wire: Internment on the Isle of Man in World War Two* (London, 1984); and Maxine Schwartz, *We Built Up Our Lives: Education and Community among Jewish Refugees Interned by Britain in World War II* (London, 2001).
32 Werner E. Mosse et al., eds, *Second Chance: Two Centuries of German-Speaking Jews in the United Kingdom* (Tübingen, 1991); Gerhard Hirschfeld, *Exile in Great Britain: Refugees from Hitler's Germany* (Leamington Spa, 1984).

33 See Panikos Panayi, 'A Marginalized Subject? The Historiography of Enemy Alien Internment in Britain', in Dove, ed., *Totally Un-English*, pp. 17–26.

34 Matthew Barry Sullivan, *Thresholds of Peace: Four Hundred Thousand German Prisoners and the People of Britain, 1944–1948* (London, 1979).

35 Johannes-Dieter Steinert and Inge Weber-Newth, *German Migrants in Post-War Britain: An Enemy Embrace* (London, 2006).

36 Lucio Sponza, *Divided Loyalties: Italians in Britain during the Second World War* (Frankfurt, 2000).

37 See Mary Fulbrook, *German National Identity after the Holocaust* (Cambridge, 1999).

38 See the discussion below.

39 As an introduction to these issues, see, for example, David Rock and Stefan Wolff, eds, *Going Home to Germany? The Integration of Ethnic Germans from Central and Eastern Europe in the Federal Republic* (Oxford, 2002).

40 Robert G. Moeller, *War Stories: The Search for a Usable Past in the Federal Republic of Germany* (London, 2001).

41 Ibid., pp. 88–170; Albrecht Lehmann, *Gefangenschaft und Heimkehr: Deutsche Kriegsgefangene in der Sowjetunion* (Munich, 1986); Annette Kaminsky, ed., *Heimkehr, 1948* (Munich, 1998); Andrea Hilger, *Deutsche Kriegsgefangene in der Sowjetunion, 1941–1956: Kriegsgefangenenpolitik, Lageralltag und Errinerung* (Essen, 2000); Renate Held, *Kriegsgefangenschaft in Grohßbritannien: Deutsche Soldaten des Zweiten Weltkrieges in britischem Gewarhsam* (Munich, 2008).

42 Eva Seeber, *Zwangsarbeiter in der faschistischen Kriegswirtschaft* (Berlin, 1964); Hans Pfahlmann, *Fremdarbeiter und Kriegsgefangene in der deutschen Kriegswirtschaft, 1939–1945* (Darmstadt, 1968); Ulrich Herbert, *Hitler's Foreign Workers: Enforced Labour in Germany under the Third Reich* (Cambridge, 1997); Mark Spoerer, *Zwangsarbeit unter dem Hankenkreuz: Ausländische Zivilarbeiter, Kriegsgefangene und Häftlinge im Deutschen Reich und im besetzten Europa* (Stuttgart, 2000).

43 For an introduction to these issues see Spoerer, *Zwangsarbeit*, pp. 233–51.

44 See, for example, Gabriele Freitag, *Zwangsarbeiter im Lipper Land: Der Einsatz von Arbeitskräften in der Landwirtschaft Lippes, 1939–1945* (Bochum, 1996); Heinrich Burgdorf et al., eds, *Zwangsarbeiterinnen und Kriegsgefangene in Blomberg (1939–1945)* (Bielefeld, 1996); Volker Issmer, *Niederländer in verdammten Land: Zeugnisse der Zwangsarbeit von Niederländern im Raum Osnabrück*

während des Zweiten Weltkrieges (Osnabrück, 1998); Jens-Christian Wagner, *Ellrich 1944/45: Konzentrationslager und Zwangsarbeit in einer deutschen Kleinstadt* (Göttingen, 2009).

45 See, especially, Uta Hinz, *Gefangen im Grossen Krieg: Kriegsgefangenschaft in Deutschland, 1914–1921* (Essen, 2006).

46 'Karl Emil Markel', *Der Auslandsdeutsche*, vol. 15 (November–December 1932), 317–19; Anna Braithwaite Thomas, *St Stephen's House: Friends Emergency Work in England, 1914 to 1920* (London, 1920), pp. 63–4; Leslie Baily, *Craftsman and Quaker: The Story of James T Baily, 1876–1957* (London, 1959), pp. 86–107. See also Panayi, *Enemy*, chapter 9.

47 *German Prisoners in Great Britain* (London, n.d.).

48 Caine, *Woman of Knockaloe.*

49 Roland V. Lee, director, *Barbed Wire* (1927).

50 The letter was reprinted in *Isle of Man Examiner*, 27 May 1927. For more on Hall Caine, *The Woman of Knockaloe* and the reaction to it see: Peter Skirne, 'Hall Caine's *The Woman of Knockaloe*: An Anglo-German War Novel from the Isle of Man', in Susanne Stark, ed., *The Novel in Anglo-German Context: Cultural Cross-Currents and Affinities* (Amsterdam, 2000), pp. 263–76; and Vivian Allen, 'Caine, Sir (Thomas Henry) Hall (1853–1931)', *Oxford Dictionary of National Biography*, online edn, www.oxforddnb.com/view/article/32237 (accessed 5 October 2010).

51 Paul Cohen-Portheim, *Time Stood Still: My Internment in England* (London, 1931).

52 The volume was subsequently reissued as Hugh Durnford et al., *Tunnelling to Freedom and Other Escape Narratives from World War One* (Mineola, NY, 2004).

53 Ibid., p. 5.

54 Gunther Plüschow, *My Escape from Donington Hall* (London, 1922). This story has an enduring appeal; it led to an article in the *Observer* by James Leasor on 27 October 1974, while a further English-language edition appeared in 2004.

55 Carl Spindler, *The Phantom Ship* (London, 1931).

56 Pál Stoffa, *Round the World to Freedom* (London, 1933).

57 Michael Powell and Emeric Pressburger, directors, *The Life and Death of Colonel Blimp* (1943). Interpretations of this film include: James Chapman, 'The Life and Death of Colonel Blimp (1943) Reconsidered', *Historical Journal of Film, Radio and Television*, vol. 15 (1995), 19–36; A. L. Kennedy, *The Life and Death of Colonel Blimp* (London, 1997); and Kevin Macdonald, *Emeric Pressburger: The Life and Death of a Screenwriter* (London, 1994). Unlike the First World War those interned in 1940 only spent a short time behind barbed wire.

58 S. P. Mackenzie, *The Colditz Myth: British and Commonwealth Prisoners of War in Nazi Germany* (Oxford, 2004).
59 See, for example, MacArthur, *Surviving the Sword.*
60 T. E. Naisk, 'The German Prisoners of War Camp at Jersey during the Great War, 1914–1918', *Bulletin of the Société Jersiaise*, vol. 15 (1955), 269–80.
61 Rudolf Rocker, *The London Years* (1956; Nottingham, 2005). See also the typescript written by Rocker entitled 'Alexandra Park Internment Camp in the First World War', held in the BL, Printed Books Section.
62 Judith Murray, 'Stobs Camp, 1903–1959', *Transactions of the Hawick Archaeological Society* (1988), 12–25; Julie M. Horne, 'The German Connection: The Stobs Camp Newspaper, 1916–1919', *Transactions of the Hawick Archaeological Society* (1988), 26–32. See also, more recently, Stefan Manz, 'New Evidence on Stobs Internment Camp', *Transactions of the Hawick Archaeological Society* (2002), 59–69.
63 Peter Wood, 'The Zivilinternierungslager at Lofthouse Park', in Kate Taylor, ed., *Aspects of Wakefield 3: Discovering Local History* (Barnsley, 2001), pp. 97–107.
64 Richard Moss and Iris Illingworth, *Pattishall: A Parish Patchwork* (Astcote, 2000), pp. 80–5.
65 Geoffrey Rowley, *The Book of Skipton* (Buckingham, 1983).
66 Leslie Smith, *The German Prisoner of War Camp at Leigh, 1914–1919* (Manchester, 1986); Laurence and Pamela Draper, *The Raasay Iron Mine: Where Enemies Became Friends* (1990; fifth printing Dingwall, 2007); Janet Harris, *Alexandra Palace: A Hidden History* (Stroud, 2005).
67 John Walling, *The Internment and Treatment of German Nationals during the 1st World War* (Grimsby, 2005).
68 Graham Mark, *Prisoners of War in British Hands during WW1: A Study of their History, the Camps and their Mails* (Exeter, 2007).
69 These magazines include: *Genealogy Magazine*; *Ancestors*; *Family History Monthly*; *Who Do You Think You Are?*; *Your Family Tree*; *Family History*; and *Family Tree Magazine.*
70 www.agfhs.org.uk (accessed 15 September 2010). The group has published pamphlets on internment including Roy Bernard, *My German Family in England* (Maidenhead, 1993); and Anglo-German Family History Society, *An Insight into Civilian Internment in Britain during WWI* (Maidenhead, 1998).
71 See the photograph on the society's website: www.agfhs.org.uk/about/history.html (accessed 15 September 2010).

72 Margery West, *Island at War: The Remarkable Role Played by the Small Manx Nation in the Great War 1914–1918* (Laxey, 1986), pp. 106–7.

73 BA/MA/MSG200/2074.

74 BA/MA/MSG200/2706.

75 West, *Island at War*, p. 107. See also *Isle of Man Weekly Times*, 24 August 1962, which points out that some of the 245 graves were located in the Douglas Borough Cemetery and at Rushen and Braddan. This date appears to coincide with the beginning of Cannock Chase Cemetery, and the article mentions that prisoners graves from all over Britain were being sent there.

76 See contributions to Bill Niven and Chloe Paver, eds, *Memorialization in Germany since 1945* (Basingstoke, 2010).

77 Alex King, *Memorials of the Great War in Britain: The Symbolism and Politics of Remembrance* (Oxford, 1998).

78 B. E. Sargeaunt, *The Isle of Man and the Great War* (Douglas, 1922).

79 Jill Drower, *Good Clean Fun: The Story of Britain's First Holiday Camp* (London, 1982).

80 Baily, *Craftsman and Quaker*, pp. 86–107.

81 Derek Winterbottom, 'Economic History', in John Belchem, ed., *The New History of the Isle of Man*, vol. 5, *The Modern Period, 1830–1999* (Liverpool, 2000), pp. 235–44.

82 West, *Island at War.*

83 Jennifer Kewley Draskau, 'Prisoners in Petticoats: Drag Performance and its Effects in Great War Internment Camps on the Isle of Man', *Proceedings of the Isle of Man Natural History and Antiquarian Society*, vol. 12 (April 2007–March 2009), 187–204; Jennifer Kewley Draskau, 'Written Between the Lines on Devil's Island: The "Stobsiade" Anthology 1917: Great War Internment Literature from the Isle of Man', in Richard Pine and Eve Patten, eds, *Literatures of War* (Newcastle-upon-Tyne, 2008), pp. 104–17; Jennifer Kewley Draskau, 'Relocating the Heimat: Great War Internment Literature from the Isle of Man', *German Studies Review*, vol. 32 (2009), 83–106.

84 Yvonne Creswell, ed., *Living with the Wire: Civilian Internment in the Isle of Man during the Two World Wars* (Douglas, 1984); Yvonne Creswell, 'Behind the Wire: The Material Culture of Civilian Internment on the Isle of Man in the First World War', in Dove, ed., *'Totally un-English'?*, pp. 45–61.

85 Gerald Newton, 'Wie lange noch? Germans at Knockaloe, 1914–18', in Gerald Newton, ed., *Mutual Exchanges: Sheffield Münster Colloquium II* (Frankfurt, 1999), pp. 103–16.

86 Robert Fyson, 'The Douglas Camp Shootings of 1914', *Proceedings*

of the Isle of Man Natural History and Antiquarian Society, vol. 11 (April 1997–March 1999), 115–26.

87 Pat Kelly, *Hedge of Thorns: Knockaloe Camp, 1915–19* (Douglas, 1993).

88 See Chapter 8 below.

89 Heinrich Norden, *In englischer Gefangenschaft* (Kassel, 1915); Gotthilf Vöhringer, *Meine Erlebnisse während des Krieges in Kamerun und in englischer Kriegsgefangenschaft* (Hamburg, 1915).

90 Philipp Hecklinger, *Tagebuchblätter über Krieg und Kriegsgefangenschaft in Kamerun und England* (Stuttgart, 1916).

91 Georg Wilhelm Wagener, *Meine Gefangenschaft in Südafrika und England vom 15. Sept. 1914 bis 18. Juni 1916* (Brunswick, 1917).

92 J. Maue, *In Feindes Land: Achtzehn Monate in englischer Kriegsgefangenschaft in Indien und England* (Stuttgart, 1918).

93 Hans Erich Benedix, *In England interniert* (Gotha, 1916).

94 Bruno Schmidt-Reder, *In England kriegsgefangen! Meine Erlebninsse in dem Gefangenenlager Dorchester* (Berlin, 1915).

95 D. W. Pult, *Siebzehn Monate in englischer Kriegsgefangenschaft* (Siegen, 1917).

96 Adolf Vielhauer, *Das englische Konzentrationslager bei Peel (Insel Man)* (Bad Nassau, 1917).

97 R. Hartmann, *Bilder aus dem Gefangenenlager Knockaloe in England* (Bad Nassau, 1918).

98 Alon Rachamimov, *POWs and the Great War: Captivity on the Eastern Front* (Oxford, 2002); *Bretagne 14–18*, vol. 3 (2002); Georg Wurzer, *Die Kriegsgefangenen der Mittelmächte in Russland im Ersten Weltkrieg* (Göttingen, 2005).

99 See, for instance: George L. Mosse, *Fallen Soldiers: Reshaping the Memory of the World War* (Oxford, 1990), pp. 159–200; Rainer Pöppinghege, '"Kriegsteilnehmer zweiter Klasse": Die Reichsvereinigung ehemalige Kriegsgefangener 1919–1933', *Militärgeschichtliche Zeitschrift*, vol. 64 (2005), pp. 391–423.

100 *Nachtrichtenblatt der Reichszentralstelle für Kriegs- und Zivilgefangene*. See also Chapter 8 below.

101 See copies of *Mitteilungen des Reichsbund zum Schutze der deutschen Kriegs- und Ziviligefangenen*.

102 *Mitteilungen des Volksbundes zum Schutze der deutschen Kriegs- und Ziviligefangenen*.

103 See: Pöppinghege, 'Kriegsteilnehmer'; BA/MA/MSG3/2733, Reichsvereinigung ehemalige Kriegsgefangene, 'Fest-Schrift zum bayerischen Gautag in München, Pfingsten, 1929', p. 9: Heather Jones, *Violence against Prisoners of War in the First World War: Britain, France and Germany, 1914–1920* (Cambridge, 2011), p. 345.

104 BA/MA/RH18/1300; Pöppinghege, 'Kriegsteilnehmer', pp. 401–6.
105 BA/MA/MSG3/2728, *Mitteilungen der Bundesleitung der Reichsvereinigung ehemaligen Kriegsgefangen*, January 1929, March 1934. This group eventually became absorbed into the Nazi state, for which see ibid., June 1936, July 1937.
106 Pöppinghege, 'Kriegsteilnehmer', pp. 408–10.
107 BA/MA/MSG3/2728, *Mitteilungen der Bundesleitung der Reichsvereinigung ehemaligen Kriegsgefangen*, September 1922.
108 *Cannock Chase Courier*, 22 May 1936; BA/MA/MSG200/2423; Volksbund Deutsche Kriegsgräberfürsorge, Cannock Chase, www.volksbund.de.kgs/stadt.asp?druckvorschau-true+stadt-1068&st-1 (accessed 15 September 2010). The cemetery holds graves of both First and Second World War German prisoners.
109 Pöppinghege, 'Kriegsteilnehmer'.
110 Vereinigung Wissenschaftlicher Veleger, *Deutsche Kriegsgefangene in Feindesland* (Leipzig, 1919), pp. 5–39.
111 *Deutsche Kriegsgefangene im Feindesland: Amtliches Material*, vol. 1, *England* (Berlin, 1919).
112 Albin Eckhardt and Kurt Maul, *Was wir in englischer Kriegsgefangenschaft erlebten und erlitten* (Frankfurt, 1922).
113 Albrecht Hermann Brugger, *Meine Flucht aus dem Kriegsgefangenen-Lager Lofthouse-Park* (Berlin, 1937).
114 Wilhelm Kröpke, *Meine Flucht aus englishcher Kriegsgefangenschaft 1916: Von Afrika über England nach Deutschland zur Flandern-Front* (Flensburg, 1937).
115 Heinz Gumprecht, *Die magischen Wälder* (Gütersloh, 1933).
116 Christoph Wohlenberg, *Kriegesgefangenen in England! Dramatische Beschreibung des 22. Juni 1919* (Bordessholm, 1919).
117 Heinrich Eckmann, *Gefangene in England* (Leipzig, 1936).
118 Karl von Scheidt and Fritz Meyer, *Vier Jahre Leben und Leiden der Auslandsdeutschen in den Gefangenenlagern Englands* (Hagen, 1919).
119 Otto Schimming, *13 Monate hinter dem Stacheldraht: Alexandra Palace, Knockaloe, Isle of Man, Stratford* (Stuttgart, 1919).
120 Fritz Sachse and Paul Nikolaus Cossmann, *Kriegsgefangen in Skipton: Leben und Geschichte deutscher Kriegsgefangenen in einem englischen Lager* (Munich, 1920).
121 J. Machner, *Gefangen in England: Erlebnisse and Beobachtungen* (Hildesheim, 1920).
122 L. Bogenstätter and H. Zimmermann, *Die Welt hinter Stacheldraht: Eine Chronik des englischen Kriegsgefangenlagers Handforth bei Manchester* (Munich, 1921).
123 Frederick Lewis Dunbar-Kalckreuth, *Die Männerinsel* (Leipzig, 1940).

124 The International Society for First World War Studies publishes *First World War Studies*.
125 Tammy Proctor, *Civilians in a World at War, 1914–1918* (London, 2010), pp. 203–38.
126 Niall Ferguson, *The Pity of War* (London, 1998), pp. 367–94.
127 Ibid., p. 369.
128 Niall Ferguson, 'Prisoner Taking and Prisoner Killing in the Age of Total War: Towards a Political Economy of Military Defeat', *War in History*, vol. 11 (2004), 148–92.
129 Stéphane Audoin-Rouzeau and Annette Becker, *14–18: Understanding the Great War* (New York, 2002), pp. 70–90.
130 Ibid., p. 71.
131 Hermann Pörzgen, *Theater ohne Frau: Das Bühnenleben der kriegsgefangenen Deutschen, 1914–1920* (Königsberg, 1920); Alon Rachamimov, 'The Disruptive Comforts of Drag: (Trans)Gender Performances among Prisoners of War in Russia, 1914–1920', *American Historical Review*, vol. 111 (2006), 362–82; Draskau, 'Prisoners in Petticoats'.
132 Rainer Pöppinghege, *Im Lager unbesiegt: Deutsche, englische und französische Kriegsgefangenen-Zeitungen im Ersten Weltkrieg* (Essen, 2006).
133 Franz Scheidl, *Die Kriegsgefangenschaft von den ältesten Zeiten bis zur Gegenwart: Eine völkerrechtliche Monographie* (Berlin, 1943).
134 Stefan Oeter, 'Die Enwicklung des Kriegsgefangenenrechtes: Die Sichtweise eines Völkerrechtes', in Rüdiger Overmans, ed., *In der Hand des Feindes: Kregesgefangenschaft von der Antike bis zum Zweiten Weltkrieg* (Cologne, 1999), pp. 41–59.
135 Stibbe, *British Civilian Internees*, pp. 10–12; Jones, *Violence*.
136 See Richard B. Speed III, *Prisoners, Diplomats, and the Great War: A Study in the Diplomacy of Captivity* (London, 1990).
137 Matthew Stibbe, 'The Internment of Civilians by Belligerent States during the First World War and the Response of the International Committee of the Red Cross', *Journal of Contemporary History*, vol. 41 (2006), 5–19; Heather Jones, 'International or Transnational? Humanitarian Action during the First World War', *European Review of History*, vol. 16 (2009), 697–713.
138 Gerald H. Davis, 'Prisoners of War in Twentieth Century Economies', *Journal of Contemporary History*, vol. 12 (1977), 623–34.
139 Heinz-Peter Mielke, *Kriegsgefangenen Arbeiten aus zwei Jahrhunderten* (Viersen, 1987).
140 Matthew Stibbe, ed., *Captivity, Forced Labour and Forced Migration in Europe during the First World War* (London, 2009).
141 A. J. Barker, *Behind Barbed Wire* (London, 1974).

142 Arnold Krammer, *Prisoners of War: A Reference Handbook* (London, 2008), pp. 2–14, 17–23.

143 Sibylle Scheipers, 'Introduction: Prisoners in War', in Sibylle Scheipers, ed., *Prisoners in War* (Oxford, 2000), pp. 1–2.

144 Ibid., pp. 3–9, 14–16.

145 Rüdiger Overmans, '"In der Hand des Feindes": Geschichtsschreibung zur Kriegsgefangenschaft von der Antike bis sum Zweiten Weltkrieg', in Overmans, ed., *In der Hand des Feindes*, pp. 9–14, 20–34.

146 Jochen Oltmer, ed., *Kriegsgefangene im Europa des Ersten Weltkrieges* (Paderborn, 2005).

147 Jochen Oltmer, 'Einführung: Funktionen und Erfahrungen von Kriegsgefangenschaft in Europa des Ersten Weltkrieges', in Oltmer, ed., *Kriegsgefangene*, pp. 11–23.

148 Alan R. Kramer, 'Prisoners in the First World War', in Scheipers, ed., *Prisoners in War*, pp. 75–90.

149 Rachamimov, *POWs and the Great War.*

150 Stibbe, *British Civilian Internees*, p. 2.

151 John Davidson Ketchum, *Ruhleben: A Prison Camp Society* (Toronto, 1965). Ketchum was actually Canadian but the camp held people from throughout the British Empire.

152 As an introduction see Alf Lüdtke, ed., *The History of Everyday Life: Reconstructing Historical Experiences and Ways of Life* (Princeton, NJ, 1995).

153 A good example of such an approach is Kathy Burrell, *Moving Lives: Narratives of Nation and Migration among Europeans in Post-War Britain* (Aldershot, 2006).

2

Arrest, transportation and capture

In the small hours of Tuesday morning the HMS *Tynwald* arrived in Douglas Bay, having on board just over 200 German and Austrian males who, as a consequence of the outbreak of war between Great Britain and Germany, had been arrested in various parts of the United Kingdom.[1]

Introduction

Eric Hobsbawn began his history of the twentieth century in 1914, believing that it marked the beginning of the 'Age of Catastrophe', which lasted until the end of the Second World War. The First World War 'marked the breakdown of the (western civilization) of the nineteenth century', whose characteristics had included the fact that it was 'liberal in its legal and constitutional structure' with a belief in 'the advance of science, knowledge and education, material and moral progress'.[2] One of the nation states which encapsulated these features was Great Britain, where, in A. J. P. Taylor's famous phrase, 'Until August 1914 a sensible, law-abiding Englishman could pass through life and hardly notice the existence of the state, beyond the post office and the policeman'.[3]

The First World War had a profound impact upon the liberalism and relative peace and tolerance which had characterized the nineteenth century. Hobsbawn pointed out that from 1914 human beings learnt to live 'under the most brutalized and theoretically intolerable conditions', returning 'to what our nineteenth century ancestors would have called the standards of barbarism'.[4] Stéphane Audoin-Rouzeau and Annette Becker have entitled one of three sections of their volume on understanding the Great War 'Violence'.[5] This choice of word may seem obvious in view of the central meaning of First World War combat. But it differs from the approach of, for instance, Niall Ferguson, who deals with such issues in a much broader approach to the conflict.[6] Audoin-Rouzeau and Becker encapsulate a key meaning of the war. Their section on 'Violence' includes a chapter on 'Battle, Combat, Violence',[7] which focuses upon the events on the battlefields and its consequences, a topic which Ferguson also tackles in a chapter entitled 'The Death Instinct: Why Men Fought'. In addition, Ferguson's book includes a chapter on 'Strategy, Tactics and the Net Body Count', which is primarily about the first two of these issues, rather than the third. Nevertheless, he provides figures for casualties, which total almost 33 million, including deaths (9.45 million), wounded (15,404,905) and prisoners of war (7,924,921).[8] In the third chapter in their section on 'Violence', Audoin-Rouzeau and Becker cover the theme of 'The Camp Phenomenon', including both military and civilian internment.[9] Uta Hinz has correctly described the First World War as the period which witnessed 'the first great camp system of the twentieth century', paving the path for what would follow between 1939 and 1945.[10] All three of these authorities view the plight of prisoners of war in the context of the overall violent consequences of the Great War. Between their first and third chapters, Audoin-Rouzeau and Becker cover the theme of 'Civilians: Atrocities and Occupation', and their focus includes the bombardment of civilians and the Armenian genocide,[11] the worst atrocity of these years, but one which fits into a context of brutalization in which ethnic cleansing and genocide began to emerge as part of the state-building process of the early twentieth century.[12] At the same time, to give another example of the way in which killing left the battlefield and impacted upon civilians, we also need to remember the actions of the German armies, especially in Belgium.[13]

Internment and the capture of prisoners of war therefore needs contextualization in the brutal and murderous consequences of the First World War, which, unlike many nineteenth-century conflicts, moved away from battles between armies to incorporate all civilians. To return to the work of Arthur Marwick in particular, the Great War constituted a total war, in which all sections of society participated, whether they fought on the battlefield or not.[14] While this total participation partly accounts for the brutalization and all-encompassing nature of warfare and the emergence of mass killing, it also helps to explain the extension of state power over all sections of the war effort including the economy. This control of industrial production, however, needs contextualization in the increasing growth of the role of the state over its population in the First World War. This is most obvious in the use of conscription, which existed in many continental countries by 1914 and also came into use in Britain by the beginning of 1916.[15] Tens of millions of people found themselves fighting unknown and unseen enemies. The increasing state control affected not only members of dominant populations but also those conceived as outsiders. This could result in forced migration, as encapsulated by the fate of millions of Armenians who were taken to the Syrian desert from their historic homelands in 1915. Part of the reason for this event lay in the Ottoman perception of Armenians as traitors, some of whom fought on the side of Russian army and against Turkey.[16] This illustrates the concern with what we would now call 'security', but which in the era of the First World War attracted descriptions including 'spying' and 'treachery'. In the total mobilization of the years 1914-18, all individuals came under the control of the state, including those perceived as having any connection with the enemy, who would face a whole series of measures, culminating in internment.[17] For Britain as a global power, this policy towards outsiders affected not simply those who lived in its northern European heartland but also those who resided in the whole empire and even those caught on ships in the high seas, for the concept of Britannia ruling the waves still survived.

The context of the First World War, above all the growth of state power and increasing brutalization, therefore provides a background for the mass incarceration which took place, especially that of civilians. However, we also need to bear in mind historical precedents: the British navy, in seizing enemy nationals on the high seas, was simply continuing traditions established at the height of British sea power.[18] More importantly, as recent historiography has demonstrated, prisoner-taking has formed an aspect of war throughout history. In fact, in opposition to the perspective outlined above, several scholars have focused upon the increasing humanity shown towards those prisoners who found themselves taken into captivity from the Enlightenment onwards,[19] as reflected in the situation of internees on British soil, who did not face deliberate systematic mistreatment, even though it did occur. One of the most important, but now dated, studies of prisoners of war in

Britain before 1914, which actually appeared in that year, argued for the humanity which Britain had shown towards both American and French prisoners in the vast period between 1756 and 1815.[20] In contrast, general overviews of the treatment of prisoners before the eighteenth century have pointed to massacres, ransoming and economic exploitation.[21]

A full understanding of incarceration during the First World War needs to accept the circumstances and immediate background of the Great War, including the mass mobilization of populations and the increasing control exercised by the state. While we also need to bear brutalization in mind, something of a paradox emerges when we consider historical patterns of prisoner capture and mistreatment. It seems tempting to view the incarceration of prisoners of war through a Foucaultian lens which places the growth of the prison as part of the evolution of modern society, a process involving the marginalization and imprisonment of those regarded as different. While they may, during the First World War, have received better treatment than their historical predecessors, they faced marginalization in the same way as criminals or the mentally ill. We might simply see mass incarceration as part of the modernization process which displays elements of relative humanity but, on the other hand, reflects the way in which industrial liberal societies punish those regarded as different.[22]

On the other hand humanitarianism may have reached something of a peak during the First World War, although it was usually carried out on behalf of the states whose citizens faced capture.[23] But we need to reiterate its juxtaposition with violence and brutality. Apart from the fate of the Armenians, some of whom perished in concentration camps,[24] other examples of deliberate mistreatment certainly exist, especially involving reprisals between Britain and Germany.[25] While Britain may have a basically positive record in its treatment of internees on British soil, those who found themselves working for the British behind the frontline in France did face mistreatment, reflecting the actions of the French and German armies.[26]

Numbers

Mass incarceration became a characteristic of the First World War, with all of the major combatants having millions of internees under their control, especially in the latter stages of the conflict. The figures for those held in Britain remained fairly constant until about 1917, when increasing numbers of German soldiers became prisoners in France. War Office records classify those held in Britain in various ways, especially into categories of civilians and military captives,[27] although they also identify naval internees and officers. However, it seems best to separate captives held in Britain into three categories. These three groups partly follow the narratives which have survived, but also find reflection in both British and German official documentation.

In the first place we can indentify civilian internees who were resident in Britain in 1914 either as settled immigrants or as visitors and who would, during the course of the war, find themselves behind barbed wire. Significantly, all of them, with a tiny handful of exceptions, were males of military age because, in contrast with the practice during the Second World War[28] and in other parts of the empire,[29] the British state did not order female internment. The history of captivity in First World War Britain is therefore one of an almost entirely male experience, with wives and children left to fend for themselves with some help from the Local Government Board and charities. While statistics exist for civilian internees, numbers for the second category remain largely absent from the official record. This category essentially consisted of males of military age who were seized either on the high seas or in colonies and were then transported to Britain. Official statistics place them into the categories of civilian or military prisoners, although they recognize naval internees, essentially those who formed part of the German imperial navy. Civilians of this type were incarcerated in the early stages of the war, and many would return to Germany years before it ended. The final group of prisoners consisted of military captives made up of small numbers of naval internees and an even smaller group of members of zeppelin crews, but with an overwhelmingly majority of soldiers, both privates and officers, captured on French battlefields especially in the latter stages of the war.

Only 3,100 of the 13,600 internees held in Britain on 22 September 1914 had come from the battlefields. Most of the remaining 10,500 came from the German civilian community in Britain.[30] Numbers of captured naval and military personnel remained low throughout the early stages of the war. By 1 February 1915 'there were 400 officers (including a few Austrians),

Table 2.1 Number of internees in Britain, 1914–19

Date	Civilian	Military (including naval)	Total
22 September 1914	10,500	3,100	13,600
1 May 1915	20,000	6,900	26,900
20 November 1917	29,511	49,815	79,326
1 November 1918	24,522	91,428	115,930
5 July 1919	3,373	86,903	90,276

Sources: NA/WO394/20, Statistical Information Regarding the Armies at Home and Abroad, 1914–1920; NA/WO394/1, Statistical Abstract, December 1916; NA/WO394/5, Statistical Abstract, November 1917; NA/WO394/10, Statistical Abstract, 1 November 1918; NA/WO394/15, Statistical Abstract, 1 September 1919.

6,500 soldiers and naval sailors, and between 19,000 and 20,000 merchant sailors and civilians (German and Austrian) interned'.[31] By November 1915, following the decision in May of that year to intern all enemy aliens of military age, the number of civilian internees had reached 32,440.[32]

The number of military prisoners did not begin to increase until 1917, when the numbers of German soldiers captured in France grew. Thus in that year, 73,131 combatants fell into British hands on French soil, followed by another 201,633 during 1918, the vast majority of them, 186,684, captured between 12 August and 9 December as the German armies faced defeat.[33] These figures translated into an increase in the numbers of military personnel held in Britain. Thus in December 1916 the figure stood at 876 officers and 24,251 men. Naval personnel totalled 120 officers and 1,286 men, all but one of them Germans.[34] By 20 November 1917 79,326 people found themselves interned in British camps, including 29,511 civilians.[35] In November 1918 the British held a total of 207,357 prisoners of war throughout the world. The figure within Britain had reached 115,950, of whom 89,937 consisted of military staff (including 5,005 officers) together with 1,491 naval personnel.[36] By January 1919 the British held a global total of 507,215 prisoners of war, including 343,512 Germans and 119,159 Turks, and the peak figure in the UK had reached 128,043, made up of 122,121 Germans, 5,644 Turks, 23 Bulgarians and 158 others. The British also held a total of 199,840 Germans in France.[37] By 5 July 1919 the British held responsibility for 458,392 internees globally, and on home soil the figures had declined to 90,276, including 3,373 civilians, 2,899 naval personnel and 84,004 soldiers.[38] While the number continued to fall during the summer, 'general repatriation' began on 24 September and lasted until 20 November. During this time 4,161 officers and 73,118 German men went home. A further 3,624 prisoners, including 704 Austrians and Hungarians, returned between 26 November and 29 January. Finally, on 9 April 1920 '3 officers' and '9 other ranks (specially retained)' completed the repatriation of Germans interned on British soil during the Great War.[39]

As these statistics suggest, the overwhelming majority of internees were Germans, although they included some Austro-Hungarians, Turks and Bulgarians. A further dissection of the figures would also show that the earlier figures referred predominantly to civilian internees, but that the growth from 1917 onwards mainly resulted from the increasing numbers of men taken by the British army in France.

Behind these statistics lie countless personal experiences preserved in a variety of sources. The main purpose of this chapter is to outline the development of internment policy and its immediate impact for individuals. Civilians faced arrest, or simply gave themselves up, while those conveyed to Britain upon ships essentially experienced transportation. Germans taken to Britain from France may have been captured but they also surrendered. In fact, all of the various categories of prisoners involved there essentially capitulated, because of the futility of doing otherwise. Niall Ferguson has partly explained this through the guarantees of the Hague Convention, which protected the rights of prisoners, and the fact that many of the military prisoners were reluctant conscripts and soldiers.[40]

Arrest

In the first three years of the war the majority of Germans who found themselves behind barbed wire in Britain were therefore civilians. Most of these came from the German community which had evolved during the course of the nineteenth century and which, by the outbreak of the First World War, numbered 53,324 people, of whom 63.1 per cent were males and only 2.9 per cent under fifteen years of age,[41] although children born to German parents in

Britain automatically assumed British nationality and would often find themselves in the British army fighting against the land of their fathers. The established community was concentrated particularly in London, where about half of the Germans lived, especially in the area between Goodge Street and Tottenham Court Road, although settlements existed throughout the capital, while German communities had also evolved in northern cities, including Manchester, Bradford, Glasgow, Liverpool and Sheffield.[42] By the outbreak of the First World War the Germans in Britain had become a diverse social group, ranging from the destitute through artisans, shopkeepers, teachers and governesses to merchant bankers.[43] Some of them, especially the wealthier ones, acquired British nationality through naturalization. The number of Germans as defined through birth or German parentage therefore exceeded the official census figure given above.[44] Nevertheless, during the course of the war only non-naturalized males of military age would automatically find themselves behind barbed wire. The majority of the civilian internees arrested in Britain, therefore, had already settled in the country, often many years previously. These included, for instance, Richard Noschke, a resident of the East End of London, who had worked for the same firm for twenty years.[45] But the civilian internees also included individuals spending time in Britain in the summer of 1914, some of whom would experience long periods behind barbed wire. Two of the most important accounts of First World War internment in Britain come from such individuals.[46]

The round-up of civilians in Britain did not proceed smoothly, as the policy went through fits and starts in the early stages of the war. In fact, immediately before the outbreak of the conflict no plans existed for the internment of Germans and other alien enemies. Instead, the Committee of Imperial Defence[47] had decided in August 1913 to allow all enemy subjects to leave, except for those suspected of spying.[48] The first few months of the war, however, witnessed a schizophrenic policy influenced by uncertainty, a hostile, intolerant and demanding Parliament and press-led public opinion transformed by the success of German armies on the continent and the fear of imminent invasion which this instilled, and no living memory of internment since the Napoleonic Wars. Until the decision to introduce wholesale internment for enemy aliens of military age in May 1915, policy went through various twists and turns. Internment also represented just one method by which the government controlled the activities of Germans: even when they remained at liberty, they had restrictions upon their residence, movement and other aspects of their lives, especially as a result of the Aliens Restriction Act, passed immediately after the outbreak of war.[49]

On 7 August 1914 the General Staff decided to intern all Germans and Austrians aged between seventeen and forty-two, yet, on the following day a conference involving the War Office, Foreign Office, Home Office and Colonial Office reversed this decision, with chief constables informed that they should intern only those regarded as dangerous to the safety of the realm. The number of internees totalled 1,980 on 13 August but had increased to 4,300 by 28 August.[50] The early prisoners included reservists in the German army attempting to return home, such as the hundreds 'who were made prisoners of war when about to leave this country' sent from Falmouth to Dorchester, one of the earliest camps, while a 'detachment of Sherwood Rangers' went to the 'colliery village of Haworth and arrested sixteen reservists'.[51] Meanwhile, in one of the other early internment camps, Queensferry near Chester, internees arrived 'in batches of forty or more at a time by train under military escorts'.[52] The *Londoner General-Anzeiger*, one of the leading German newspapers in London, shortly before it faced closure under the terms of the Aliens Restriction Act,[53] reported the arrest of Germans in several locations. They included Max Kulmer in Nottingham, 'arrested as a spy. In his home the Police found a loaded revolver, maps of Nottingham, Brussels and German cities, and several German letters.'[54] Those sojourners who happened to find themselves in Britain at the outbreak of war included Willi Kortmann from Duisburg, who worked in the German seamen's mission in South Shields. Twenty of its residents faced immediate arrest, including the pastor.[55]

By the end of August 1914 the Home Office and the War Office had become increasingly concerned about the potential threat posed by those German reservists still at large. Consequently, an intensification of arrests occurred from late August until 20 September. By 9 September the Manchester police had seized 107 enemy aliens, most of whom would make their way to Queensferry. On 8 September the local constabulary acted in a heavy-handed manner when they arrested fifty-five Germans and Austrians, who 'were manacled and chained together, and were under an escort of policemen armed with rifles'. A Manchester chief superintendent claimed that the reason for the round-up lay in the fact that the German advance on Paris had led some of those facing arrest to 'freely express their satisfaction at the German successes and to boast of what they would do as soon as German soldiers landed in England'.[56] Similar events occurred in Scotland, although without the manacles.[57]

The arrests of late August and September increased the number of internees from 4,300 on 28 August to 13,600 by 23 September. The latter figure included 2,100 military captives, although the remaining 11,500 would also have included some people arrested on ships. However, space had run out by this time, and the War Office suggested that only those regarded as an immediate threat should be incarcerated. Some arrests therefore continued during late September and early October 1914. One letter to a German newspaper claimed that 'At 7 am on 12 October we were brought in a covered wagon with two lieutenants and sixty men to Newbury.' The writer stated that the men had to carry their own bags, despite the size and weight of many of them, while those who were too weak received no help. He claimed that 'during the whole journey' they 'had no opportunity to purchase anything. Food, drink, nothing. We arrived at 5. During the journey no attention was paid in any way towards catering. The wagons were closed for the whole journey. We only received a cup of tea and some dry bread when we reached Newbury.'[58]

The rapid advance of German armies through Belgium during October 1914 led to the first peak of Germanophobia in wartime Britain, which resulted in riots in Deptford and Crewe in the second half of the month. The Home Office now resumed internment partly in the interests of public safety, although, once again, a lack of space meant that this policy lasted for only a few days.[59] Newspaper reports in the week following 21 October again give details of arrests taking place. *The Times* of 22 October reported wholesale incarceration throughout the country in cities including Manchester, Bradford, Coventry and Reading, and on the following day it listed more towns where Germans faced arrest and carried a feature on the community in the East End of London. The *Daily Express* of 22 October focused upon Reading, where 'a jeweller was taken into custody as he was putting up his shutters at one o'clock and conveyed to the police station in a taxicab'. Meanwhile, 'a detective arrived as the family were at dinner, laughing and chatting' and arrested 'Max Seeburg, a publican, formerly a member of Reading football team'.

The contrasting reports quoted above from German and English sources partly point to the role of internment in the propaganda war. Throughout the conflict, while the German sources nearly always emphasized the depressing aspects of the experiences of Germans behind barbed wire, the English ones ignored any negative impact (despite the reporting of journals such as the *Manchester Guardian*, which remained an exception). The extract from the *Daily Express* ignores any trauma of separation and dislocation caused by the actions of the local police, although we need to place the experiences of these civilian internees in the context of millions of males who left their families during these years on their way to fight upon European battlefields.[60] The arrest of Rudolf Rocker, the London German anarchist, which occurred in December 1914, gives an insight in the grim and poignant reality of arrest and separation:

> They took me away on 2 December at 7pm. I had been expecting it, so it didn't come as a surprise. Milly was very brave about it. My son Rudolf, Milly's sister Polly, and a few friends who were there pressed my hand silently. I said goodbye to my young son Fermin. He was only seven. The child burst into tears. The two plain clothes policemen were as much moved by his crying as we all were. We couldn't pacify him. He was still crying when I left under escort the home to which I never returned.[61]

After late October 1914 civilian internment policy reached something of a stasis. Although some growth in the numbers of those incarcerated occurred as a result of people being transported to camps from the colonies and from ships on the high seas, the overall number of internees declined, with about 3,000 released between November and early February.[62] But during the winter and spring of 1914-15 the Douglas and, more especially, Knockaloe camps on the Isle of Man (where the overwhelming majority of civilian internees would eventually find themselves) came into their own, with regular sailings from the mainland to the ports of Peel and Douglas bringing internees from smaller and temporary accommodation in England.[63] By 27 March 1915 Knockaloe housed 4,000 prisoners, while 2,400 lived in Douglas.[64] The policy of general release of enemy aliens had ceased by the end of January 1915. The suspension arose partly from nervousness in the Home

Office but partly from a reaction to public opinion, especially in the House of Commons and in certain sections of the press. Reginald McKenna, the Home Secretary at this time, felt vilified because some enemy aliens remained at liberty.[65] The radical right-wing Conservative MP William Joynson-Hicks led the criticism[66] and received support from Lord Charles Beresford, who summed up the desire of many when he declared in the House of Commons, 'I want them all locked up.'[67]

Beresford's wish came true following the sinking of the *Lusitania*, which represented the crossing of the Rubicon in British First World War civilian internment policy. The sinking of the passenger liner in the Irish Sea on 7 May by a German submarine, with the loss of over 1,000 lives, led to the most widespread riots in twentieth-century Britain, fuelled by a press reaction whose viciousness was summed up by Horatio Bottomley's magazine *John Bull* declaring on 15 May that he wanted 'to exterminate every German-born man (God forgive the term!) in Britain'. In this atmosphere virtually every German shop in Britain had its windows broken during a week of pogroms.[68]

Demands from both newspapers and radical right-wing MPs accompanied the rioting and the victimization of the German community in Britain, linking them with the actions of the German armed forces. The *Daily Sketch* declared, 'Lock Them All Up!' and 'Clear Out the Germans'.[69] A slightly more circumspect, but no less demanding, editorial in *The Times* declared: 'After the numerous inhuman outrages committed by the enemy, there will be no restoration of calmness while very many thousands of Germans, including large numbers of military age, are enjoying almost complete liberty in this country.' The Germans had 'become a danger to the public welfare' because their liberty actually caused rioting. The piece also suggested that 'segregation will become desirable for the safety and the protection of the Germans themselves, just as much as for the preservation of public order'.[70] On 12 May Joynson-Hicks and Beresford presented a petition to the House of Commons 'signed by a quarter of a million of the women of our Islands, asking this honourable House immediately to take the necessary steps to ensure the safety of their homes, by interning all alien enemies of military age'.[71]

On the same day the Prime Minister, Herbert Asquith, declared that the government was 'carefully considering the practicability of the segregation and internment of alien enemies on a more comprehensive scale', firstly because of the military dangers and secondly because, referring to the actions of the German military and the reaction of the British population towards enemy aliens, 'innocent and unoffending persons are in danger of being made to pay the penalty of the crimes of others'.[72] Alien enemies were therefore interned partly to protect them from rioters and partly from a security point of view. Asquith outlined the new internment policy on 13 May; 'it would be a 13th of course', wrote Paul Cohen-Portheim.[73] Asquith stated that enemy aliens in Britain were divided into those with enemy nationality and those who had become naturalized. The former included 19,000 already interned men together with 40,000 people who remained at large (24,000 men and 16,000 women). All 'adult males' of military age (seventeen to fifty-five) should 'for their own safety, and that of the community, be segregated and interned'. Women, children and males above fifty-five would be repatriated. A judicial body would look at those seeking exemption from internment. The round-up would begin when suitable accommodation became available. The 8,000 naturalized enemy aliens would be interned only if evidence existed to prove them a threat.[74]

Arrests began immediately, with 3,339 males interned by 5 June and 1,000 people per week making their way to camps by the end of July. One Advisory Committee made up of MPs and judges considered cases of exemption for England and Wales, while a second dealt with Scotland. They considered 16,000 applications for exemption from internment and granted 7,150. By 22 November the number of civilian internees had reached 32,440, an increase of 12,871 from 13 May.[75]

The decision taken on 13 May had a significant impact upon both the development of internment camps and individual Germans. Those from London faced incarceration in Frimley and Stratford, on the Isle of Man and on ships anchored off the south-east coast, while those from Liverpool also went to the Isle of Man as well as to Stobs near Hawick.[76] The increase in the numbers held at Douglas and Knockaloe illustrates the experience of civilian internment, as well as pointing to the increasing concentration upon the Isle of Man. Thus the total of 4,931 in Knockaloe on 1 May 1915 had increased to 21,305 by January of the following year, with a peak figure of 22,693 on 1 August 1916.[77] During the summer and autumn of 1915 boats landed regularly in Peel and Douglas with hundreds of prisoners on board.[78]

Germans and other enemy aliens reacted in a variety of ways to the decision of 13 May and its aftermath. Despite the increase which occurred in the following months, many people clearly made efforts to maintain their liberty, as indicated by the 16,000 who appealed to the Advisory Committees. These actually outnumbered the increase which would take place after May, even though 8,850 failed in their attempts. Nevertheless, if we accept an increase of 12,871 until 22 November, only 4,000 of these actually went to camps without challenging the decision. Unfortunately, the documentation of the Advisory Committees has not survived and the impression left by other sources suggests a largely obedient process of either surrender or arrest.

In the immediate aftermath of the 13 May decision the press wrote of the surrender of Germans, especially in London. Those who lived in the West End, particularly around Soho, included many single waiters, who were working in the capital to improve their English in the hope of subsequently securing a good post in a continental hotel or restaurant.[79] Most had few family attachments in Britain, and their decision to surrender appears to have been partly motivated by this factor, as well as by 'the terror created by the riots'.[80] Others had lost their employment, partly as a result of anti-German boycotts, which had resulted in the sacking of German employees.[81] Aliens therefore 'simply went to the police-station, and announced that they were ready for internment'.[82] Voluntary surrenders appear to have been less usual in the East End of London, where a more settled community including families had developed from the middle of the nineteenth century, although some appear to have taken place. In fact, because of a lack of space in the short run, the police had difficulties in dealing with the number of surrenders.[83]

Those arrested included Dunbar-Kalckreuth, who had moved to Putney after the outbreak of war and received a visit on Ascension Day from 'two gentlemen from the police' who told his landlady that he should be ready at 11.00 the following morning. In fact, he saw the prospect of internment, in which he would spend time with fellow Germans, as preferable to his current solitary life away from his friends and family.[84] A police visit formed part of the process for those who had not surrendered. Cohen-Portheim wrote that on 24 May 'a detective called on me: I was to appear at the police station at 10 o'clock next morning. "Why?" I asked. "To be interned", he replied.' Cohen-Portheim requested to see the necessary papers authorizing his internment. 'I had not the slightest idea of what internment meant.' He asked the policeman what he should pack, to which the officer replied: '"I would pack as if you were going for a holiday". It was to be a protracted holiday.'[85] Meanwhile, an account written by an internee describing himself simply as a 'leather specialist' recounts his experiences as follows:

> On 22 June 1915 I received a communication to report to the Police Station on Harrow Road, Paddington, at 10 in the morning in order to be interned. Led by my wife who could hardly believe what was happening, and following a tearful farewell, the drama began. With hundreds of fellow sufferers, for whom, like me everything seemed unreal, in consequence of the short amount of time available to sort out any private or business matters, we spent the time until 2 in the afternoon in the cellar of the police station where we had been penned together.

The internees were then taken to the camp at Stratford, although many of them would eventually find themselves in Knoackloe.[86] Most of the arrests continued in this well-ordered manner until the autumn. Another German wrote a letter to his local church magazine declaring that 'At seven o'clock in the morning I dressed and after a sad farewell I went about 8.50 to Hornsey Police Station'; he subsequently made his way to an unnamed camp via Kentish Town police station and Waterloo Station. He asserted that 'the authorities want to do everything to make us as comfortable as circumstances permit'.[87]

Most of the above narratives point to an acceptance of the inevitability of internment, whether through voluntarily walking to the local police station without instruction or through obeying the orders to go there. The main form of resistance consisted of appealing to the Advisory Committees. Nevertheless, some individuals took the most extreme of actions:

> Dread of internment was stated to be the reason for the suicide of Heinrich Hertnam Hauck, a German tailor, on whom an inquest was held at Westminster yesterday.
>
> It was stated that he endeavoured to commit suicide last December, but promised his wife, an Englishwoman, that he would not again make an attempt on his life.

> When the recent internment order was issued he became depressed and said he dreaded leaving his wife and daughter. He left home last Thursday and was found dead in the Serpentine on Friday morning.
> The jury returned a verdict of 'Suicide during temporary insanity'.[88]

Such an action points to the terror which the prospect of internment could instil.

The peak of the process of interning German males occurred between May and September 1915, even though many had already found themselves in camps before the *Lusitania* pogrom. From 1916, we can identify a series of strands in internment policy. In the first place, about 12,000 enemy aliens males remained free, including 4,000 'technical' Germans such as Czechs, Poles and Alsatians, about 1,500 males over seventy, some males who carried out valuable work for the war effort, and up to 6,000 who had resided in Britain for over thirty years and had sons fighting for the British army.[89] The number of internees would gradually decrease, as the result of a series of repatriation initiatives, until the general release, which occurred in 1919.[90] However, sections of the press and several MPs continued to badger the government about the apparent laxity of its internment policy, which reached a series of peaks, above all in the summer of 1918.[91] For individual civilians, the period which followed their initial internment could mean either years in the same camp or movement from one location to another. Cohen-Portheim, for instance, spent time in Stratford, Knockaloe and Wakefield, while the unnamed leather specialist who surrendered at the police station in Paddington initially went to Stratford before moving to Knockaloe.[92] Those wives left behind largely depended upon handouts from the British and German governments and charity, while others faced deportation.[93] Separation put much strain on marriages, especially those between Germans and English wives, and some did not survive the long separation. In at least one case a German internee obtained a divorce while in Alexandra Palace.[94]

Transportation

Those German civilians who had lived in Britain before 1914 faced some of the longest periods behind barbed wire. After their arrest, military escorts would take them to one or more places of internment. While some of these internees had settled in Britain, others had the misfortune to find themselves in the country when the war broke out. Those counted as civilians in official statistics also included people transported to Britain, mostly in the early stages of the conflict. Some of these simply found themselves on sailing vessels of varying types in British waters or in areas which the British navy felt it controlled. Others who lived in British colonies or in German possessions overrun by the British at the start of the war faced ethnic cleansing from India or Africa. It is important to view the camps in Britain as part of a global internment system which counted both military and civilian internees and which lasted for the entire duration of the conflict. Those in Britain made up a minority of the prisoners held throughout the empire.[95]

Little official evidence exists to indicate whether the British government pursued a deliberate policy of either taking Germans off ships or transporting them from colonies from the British Empire or the collapsing German Empire. A memorandum from early 1915 suggests that all males between seventeen and fifty-five taken from enemy ships in particular should be interned, while the advice upon those on neutral ships remained ambiguous.[96] Personal narratives, together with a few newspaper articles, allow a reconstruction of this policy.

Some of those who faced internment were North Sea fishermen. Probably because of their non-literate backgrounds and their greater readiness to accept their fate in contrast to some of the more educated people captured on passenger liners, relatively little survives about this group. A report in the *Scotsman* in late August 1914 claimed that of 600 men held in a tented camp in Redford, near Edinburgh, 'fully eighty per cent are sailormen that work the fishing grounds of the North Sea and most are in the garb which they were in when British cruisers or torpedo boats hovered in sight and swiftly shepherded their hardy little vessels into the nearest Scottish port'. The article claimed that because many of them 'know well the coastline and harbours of the North' they 'would be of great value to the German fleet'.[97]

Perhaps for this reason, the British navy continued to capture and intern German fishermen who entered British territorial waters into 1915. Their narratives emerge in official statements that they gave upon returning to German ports after release from internment. Among them was Mathias Jörgensen, a cook upon the trawler

Risle, which sailed from Geestenmünde on 5 October 1915 and found itself two days later near Hornsriff, where a flotilla of British cruisers captured the ship and escorted it to Hull, while the *Aurora* took the fishermen to Harwich. Jörgensen claimed: 'We stayed in Harwich for two days. On the morning of 11 October we were taken to Stratforth [sic]. On the journey to Stratforth we were constantly harassed and insulted by the civilian population and on the way from the station to the camp stones were thrown at us. The soldiers who accompanied us did not intervene.' Meanwhile, another cook, Paul Sappelt, who worked upon the trawler *Roland*, claimed that on 17 August 1915, two days after he sailed out to sea, a party of eleven English destroyers intercepted his ship and subsequently sank it. The *Maridiane* took the crew to 'Sherness' and they then went by tug to a military prison with primitive conditions in 'Champton' before eventually going to Handforth in Cheshire and subsequently to Knockaloe. Max Scharff sailed on another trawler, the *Elma*, on 2 October 1915 and was 'surprised by a great number of English destroyers' two days later. A party came on board and took most of the crew to Harwich, where Scharff also claimed they faced insults and missiles without any protection from their guard. Upon arrival in Stratford they experienced abuse from women and children. Meanwhile, Heinrich Klockgether sailed on the *Herbert* on 29 September 1915 and on 7 October fifteen English ships took the crew unawares:

> An English party came on board and we had to take our own ship under this guard to Grimsby, where we arrived on 9 October; we were kept there out of necessity for three days on a passenger liner. The English only gave us bread, while the cook from the trawler *Paul*, which was also interned there, provided us with leftover food. On 12 October we were transported on foot to a military camp in *Reiwyk* [sic]. The march lasted for 5½ hours. We remained here in makeshift accommodation until 18 October on slender rations. We were then further transported with 82 men to Grimsby and from there to Alexandra Palace.

Klockgether also claimed that his party faced a hostile reception in Grimsby.

These four narratives share a series of characteristics and, in fact, if read as a group,[98] tell similar stories of sudden interception, transportation to an east coast port, poor initial conditions in a temporary camp and abuse from English onlookers. We can see this as evidence of a collective experience which befell those fishermen unfortunate enough to find themselves captured by the British navy. However, similarities in the narratives might suggest some intervention in their construction. They certainly point to the regularity of the capture and internment of North Sea German fishermen, most of whom appear to have returned home before the end of the war, but it proves difficult to find any statistics. While the above stories refer to events in the autumn of 1915, trawlers faced capture and even sinking later in the war.[99]

Together with fishermen, numerous other German males who found themselves on ships virtually anywhere in the world, whether registered as German or not, might face transportation to a British internment camp at any stage of the First World War, especially in the immediate aftermath of the outbreak of the conflict. Again, the numbers of German sailors who found themselves behind barbed wire in Britain proves difficult to establish, but on 30 January 1916 over eighty 'captains and nautical and technical ships' officers of the German and Austro-Hungarian mercantile marines', overwhelmingly Germans, wrote to the United States Embassy in London with a series of complaints about their internment in Knockaloe, including the fact that 'those who were formerly in positions of authority are forced to live promiscuously among and in the closest association with their subordinates', which suggests that a far larger number of members of the mercantile marine were held here.[100]

The British authorities seized German ships that were in British ports when the war broke out, including the *Levensau*, *George Harper*, *Lucinda*, *Altje*, *Ursus*, *Hyland* and *Friedesware*, and interned the men on board.[101] Germans on neutral vessels also found themselves taken to internment camps, including thirty passengers on board the Dutch steamer *Gelria* in Falmouth.[102]

The British navy also took Germans from ships all over the world, but especially from the North Atlantic and North Sea, as a few examples will illustrate. For instance, Captain Johannes Schmidt-Klafleth, sailing on business to New York on 25 August 1914, actually reached his destination, despite the fact that his ship was intercepted and the fact that he underwent interrogation in Dover. However, he had less luck on the return journey, when he found himself taken to the camp at Newbury after landing at Plymouth.[103] Meanwhile, P. Ernst Goretzki, a resident of Perth

Amboy, New Jersey, returning home from a visit to Germany to see his mother on board the SS *Bergensfjord*, described how English officers from the cruiser *Ebro* took him off his ship 'near the North Islands of Scotland'.

Teenagers also faced capture. For instance, Willi Haas wrote to the United States Embassy in London in February 1916 from Knockaloe complaining that he had been 'taken from the Norwegian sailing vessel' *Zambeese* when only fourteen years old.[104] Similarly, sixteen-year-old Johannes Buschmann ended up in Knockaloe following a journey to the United States on board the Dutch steamer *Rotterdam*, which left Rotterdam on 20 June 1915. He travelled 'with the intention to emigrate' but 'on the following day the steamer had to stop and I was captured and eventually interned in this camp'.[105] In fact, these two cases seem to represent the tip of a small iceberg. In August 1915 the camp at Lancaster held a total of 216 Germans under seventeen, of whom 183 consisted 'of persons whose occupation is on the sea'.[106]

As an indication of the global nature of the British internment system during the First World War, some prisoners actually made their way to camps in Britain from places of internment elsewhere in the empire. These included Gibraltar. Edwin Mieg sailed on an Italian ship, the *America*, back to Europe from New York, where he was working upon the outbreak of war. After initial internment in Gibraltar, he subsequently found himself in Alexandra Palace and then Knockaloe.[107] Similarly, Lieutenant Klapproth, travelling back to Europe from a training exercise in New York aboard the *President Grant* on the outbreak of war, spent time in the internment camp in Gibraltar from 24 August until 24 December 1914. He was then transported to England and spent time in Holyport, Plymouth, Southampton, Donington Hall and Wakefield.[108]

One of the most celebrated cases of Germans taken from a ship and transported to England was that of those travelling upon the Dutch steamer *Potsdam*, which left New York for Germany with about 450 German passengers on 15 August. On 24 August the English cruiser *Diana* approached the *Potsdam* near Falmouth and forced it to dock there. As many as 394 passengers were interned, including an overwhelming majority of Germans and a few Austro-Hungarians. Initially taken to the early camp at Dorchester, many of the prisoners would remain interned into the following year, by which time they had been moved to other locations including, eventually, the Isle of Man.[109]

In the early stages of the war in particular, Britannia still ruled the waves and would flex its muscles when it found Germans sailing on the high seas, whether they offered any realistic threat to the British war effort or not.[110] The fishermen taken off trawlers well into the First World War provide the best example of this fact. As well as demonstrating their global power at sea by taking people from ships, the British army and navy displayed their international status by transporting Germans from colonies taken over by France and Britain once the war broke out. Such actions again point to the global nature of British internment.

Most transportation of Germans from the colonies occurred immediately after the outbreak of war in the autumn of 1914. However, we again need to remember that some parts of the British Empire established their own camps, among them India, Australia and New Zealand,[111] although some individuals were certainly deported from the first of these.[112] Much transportation from the colonies was actually from West Africa. Some of the victims were Germans already resident there and finding themselves unprotected following the collapse of the German Empire, while others were taken there upon ships crossing the South Atlantic.

The most famous case of the latter was that of the Dutch steamer *Hollandia*, on its way from Buenos Aires to Amsterdam in August 1914 but intercepted by the British cruiser *Cornwall*, which took fifty-eight German prisoners, many of whom resided in South America. The *Cornwall* escorted the *Hollandia* to the Cape Verde Islands to join eight other ships held there. The Germans from the *Hollandia* were then taken to Freetown in Sierra Leone and then to a camp on shore on 22 September, and did not leave for England until 18 January.[113] A similar sequence of events was experienced by the passengers on the *Professor Woermann* sailing from Tenerife to Las Palmas, which ended up in Freetown and then sailed to Britain.[114]

In addition to those Germans sailing from West Africa to Britain after removal from ships in the South Atlantic were long-term German residents both in British colonies and from the overrun German possessions.[115] Those in the former category included Wilhelm Kröpke, who had lived in Nigeria from 1913 but was arrested on 9 August 1914. He initially spent time in a cell in Lagos before transportation to a camp in Ibaddan and subsequently to Britain.[116] Most of those Germans initially interned in Africa and subsequently taken to Britain lived in the German possessions of Togo and, more especially, Cameroon. Among those captured in the former were German missionaries, who were initially taken to Accra and subsequently sailed to Plymouth.[117] Two narratives appeared in 1915 on the conquest of Cameroon and its consequences for the local German population. The turning point was the fall of Duala on 27 September, after which the Germans were arrested. Heinrich Norden wrote of a journey with between 150 and 200 people taken to a camp for two days and then upon the *Bathurst* to Nigeria and subsequently Accra; he remained there until the end of December, when he sailed to Liverpool for a short spell of detention in Britain. Other ships carried German internees to Britain in November.[118] Later in the war some Germans also found themselves transported to Britain from German South-West Africa as well as South Africa.[119]

Capture

While the British internment system operated globally during the First World War, only a minority of those who spent a spell in a camp in Britain came either from a ship or from a British or German colony. Most originated either among the Germans resident in Britain when the war broke out or, increasingly as the conflict progressed, among German soldiers captured in the battle zone which separated Germany from France.

The term usually used to describe the initial encounter of combatants with the prospect of internment is 'capture', but we need to accept Ferguson's assertion that, in many cases, probably the vast majority, the correct phrase is actually 'surrender', partly because most men who became prisoners were conscripts who had little desire to fight for the German army.[120] By 1918, as a result of disillusionment, exhaustion and the realization of the overwhelming forces against them, surrender occurred *en masse* in an ordered fashion.[121] A. J. Barker has addressed the issue of capture versus surrender:

> In the simple case, a man becomes a prisoner because he cannot continue to fight, and cannot get away. He may have been overpowered,

> or run out of ammunition; alternatively he or his commander has voluntary opted to give in. Whatever the cause he is helpless and hors de combat, and when his opponents realise it they take control.

Barker also considers the possibility of reaching a 'point where the choice is capitulation or death', when 'most westerners choose to surrender'.[122]

While capture may offer one perspective on the initial moment of captivity, the concept of surrender proves equally useful. In addition, some Germans who fell into British hands did so when wounded, sometimes seriously, and found themselves in wings of hospitals in Britain specially given over to caring for them. Thousands of Germans wounded and helpless on French battlefields during 1917 and 1918 therefore spent their final days in a British hospital, officially categorized as prisoners.

The vast majority of military internees who found themselves in Britain therefore originated in the deciding battles of the First World War, those from 1917 onwards. In addition, some of those in British camps were individuals involved in other forms of combat. These actually included a few members of zeppelin crews. For instance, on 24 September 1916 an airship fell to earth in Little Wigborough in Essex; this led to a search for the crew involving '120 men' and resulting in the capture of two officers and nineteen men. Eighteen of the men and two officers went to the 'detention barracks' in Colchester (although they were kept separately), while one wounded member of the crew found himself in Colchester Hospital. All of them faced transfer to London two days later.[123] By 1918 over 150 Germans from zeppelins found themselves interned in camps throughout the country and on the continent where they faced transfer. The thirty-eight-member crew of the L33 was distributed in a variety of locations including Donington Hall, Frongoch, Kegworth, Brocton and Pattishall, as well as the Netherlands and Switzerland, awaiting repatriation.[124]

Although several thousand sailors from the German navy were interned in Britain during the First World War, relatively little information upon them has survived. They included those crew and officers on the dregs of the German navy interned at Scapa Flow at the end of the war, whose numbers totalled close to 5,000. Arriving in December 1918, the officers scuttled the captured ships on 21 June 1919 by opening the sea cocks, which resulted in them being taken to Royal Navy battleships and subsequently to internment camps including Lofthouse Park and Donington Hall. They complained about their treatment and the fact that they remained the last German prisoners left in England.[125]

Some information survives on the crews of German submarines captured during the First World War, and emerged against the background of the outrage which their actions in sinking merchant ships and passenger liners caused, which reached a peak in the *Lusitania* riots.[126] Crews faced either arrest or capture following the torpedoing of their vessels by the Royal Navy. In the spring of 1915 they began to arrive in Britain. The U8 'was sunk in the channel off Dover by destroyers' on 4 March, and the crew of twenty-five men and four officers landed in Dover on the following day.[127] 'Large numbers of people had assembled in the vicinity of the Dockyard and at various points on the road . . . including a number of women, many being the wives of boatmen and seamen', in order to watch the landing and escort of the captives.[128] A letter from (what appears to be) the captain of the U8 describes his thoughts on the moment following the sinking, where he reflected on the choice between 'eternal imprisonment by death' and 'imprisonment by the enemy'. He chose the latter. Like other submarine crews, that of the U8 found itself in the 'Royal Detention Quarters in Chatham'.[129] Those taken prisoner from the U8 joined others from the U12 and, despite complaints from the German government about their mistreatment as retaliation for the plight of British prisoners in Germany, United States Embassy officials claimed that the twenty-nine internees received fair treatment. Statistics even emerged to demonstrate that the crews had not lost weight. By June they had been transferred to other military camps.[130] These allegations did not disappear, however, leading to further British denials.[131] The Admiralty printed a document on 'Prisoners Taken from Submarines' outlining their treatment, which began, 'Prisoners captured from enemy submarines will be subjected to a searching interrogation by Naval Officers from the Admiralty', meaning that they would remain in naval custody for up to a week. This 'differentiation in the treatment of these prisoners is in no way meant to be punitive' but, instead, was to allow the naval authorities 'the opportunity of obtaining useful information and to render it more difficult for news of their capture immediately to reach the enemy'.[132] The interrogators certainly carried out their work effectively by asking questions about a whole series of issues including strategy, journeys and mine-laying.[133]

Two surviving letters in a British Admiralty file reveal the prisoner-taking process following the sinking of three submarines in 1917, although the main focus is the moment of explosion and the immediate aftermath. Reinhard Schirm, writing to his mother, described the sinking of the UC32 while laying mines off Sunderland, from which he escaped and 'swallowed a good deal of oil which was floating about on the surface of the water'. He continued:

> At last I saw a light, and soon after a second one. The first one was the Sunderland Lighthouse, the second the light of an English patrol boat. I swam towards the latter, as it was the nearest. But I was getting weaker every moment. When I was about 20 metres from the steamer, somebody threw me a lifebelt, and I clung to it. Then I saw a lifeboat coming towards me on the right. A sailor handed me an oar, and I was dragged into the boat by it. 'Hullo, Schirm, you here too?' said a voice from the boat, and I recognised the Captain. I then fainted. When I came to, I found myself on board the steamer, and heard that only 3 men had been saved out of 25.

Meanwhile, a letter from Kurt Tebbenjohannes, the sole survivor of the sinking of the UC44, to his parents stated that 'With God's help I found my way to the surface out of the sunken boat.' He mentioned 'the kind people from Dunmore, who sent out boats directly after the explosion, picked me up and treated me with greatest kindness'.[134] If anything, the experiences of these two sailors merit description as rescue rather than capture or surrender. If they surrendered, they did so to those who saved their lives.

The vast majority of prisoners of war by 1917 consisted of those who had fought on French battlefields, although such captives had arrived in Britain from the early stages of the conflict, as newspaper accounts colourfully described. Thus, on 11 September 1914, the *Daily Express* reported 'Uhlans in England' and continued: 'Four German officers and about seventy-five men, who were captured in action, were landed at Southampton yesterday by a naval vessel.' In the following month: 'On an afternoon in October a great company of German officers marched between English guards through the lanes of Hampshire. At Farnborough they had to pass through the gateway-lodge of an avenue leading up through a wide park to a mansion and a wooded path.'[135] Further stories about the arrival of German prisoners also subsequently appeared in the *Daily Express*, including one on 1,000 'Germans from Neuve Chapelle at Southampton'. They came 'not as conquerors, but as prisoners of war, guarded by British bayonets'.[136] In July 1916 the same paper wrote: 'Two Thousand Germans Land at Southampton' in 'two batches'. They temporarily remained there 'pending their removal to a concentration camp', and a crowd gathered out of 'curiosity to see what manner of men the captives were'.[137]

The arrival at Southampton represented part of a journey to captivity which began for soldiers on a French battlefield and ultimately ended in a camp. As the narratives by some of the civilian internees above indicate, many moved around during their time in Britain. Combatants, unlike civilians and officers, could work under the Hague Convention, which meant that the British government transported them to places which needed their labour.[138] We can divide the process of becoming a prisoner of the British into two stages: the moment of capture in France, and the journey to and within Britain, which involved marching, rail travel and a sea crossing.

Personal narratives, consisting of letters and subsequently published memoirs, provide an insight into the way in which German soldiers fell into British hands, which involved a combination of capture and surrender. Dr Funk from Magdeburg, of the 4th rifle battalion, described the moment when he became a captive following his return to Germany in early 1915. On 10 September 1914 his 'battalion found itself bringing up the rear of a retreating cavalry division following the battles in Jonavre and La Ferté on the Marne on the 8th and 9th, as behind Gandeln enemy artillery suddenly started firing in the morning – and infantry fire attacked the marching column'. He escaped into the wood with three officers and eighty-five men as the British approached. 'It was impossible to go any further as all the streets were occupied by the quickly approaching English army. In the still grey of the morning we attempted to escape but we were noticed by a patrol and surrendered, as more troops with machine guns arrived.' Funk ultimately surrendered; he implied that fighting would have resulted in almost certain death.[139] Richard Schmitt described the moment when he fell into captivity in a statement upon his return to Germany. He found himself as a sergeant of the '3. Komp. E. R. 245' on patrol with Lieutenant Mauthe and Private Biersack in Richebourg, where they were captured during the night of 12-13 April 1916 by an English patrol of about twenty men.[140] At the end of the war, in September 1918, J. Machner found himself in British captivity. He and his companions received leaflets from the air telling them to surrender because they would be treated well in captivity. On 27 September Scottish guards surrounded them and then took them to a holding camp in Le Havre.[141] Another account simply states, without any further details, 'On 14 October I fell, with the majority of my Regiment, in Flanders, north west from Cheluwe, into English imprisonment', although this may have something to do with the fact that Alfred Brugger's 1937 story focused upon his escape.[142] Some German prisoners held by the British appear to have fallen initially into French hands, as suggested by the case of Dr Otto Coester, captured near Reims on 15 September 1914. He seems to have made a train journey to St Nazaire and then got onto a ship bound for Portsmouth.

Coester mentioned the good treatment he experienced at the hands of the British when handed over by French troops.[143] But in early 1916 allegations emerged about the shooting of a German tied to a tree in the previous March. The British authorities carried out an investigation in an attempt to disprove this.[144] However, numerous accounts focus upon the fact that German troops had their possessions confiscated when they were first taken prisoner. For instance, officers captured in the early 1917 offensive in Arras and Flanders complained that they were 'cleaned out by English troops. Gold, watches, wedding rings and equipment were taken under the threat of violence.'[145] Similar reports emerged during the course of 1918.

Some of the assertions concerned the robbing of wounded soldiers,[146] and it is clear from a variety of sources that many of those German soldiers taken prisoner by the British had suffered injuries as a result of combat. A series of files in the Bundesarchiv in Berlin, held by the Frankfurt Committee of the Red Cross,[147] contain thousands of death certificates compiled by the Prisoners of War Information Bureau, which had as one of its central tasks the transmission of information on individual captives to their families.[148] The details contained in the certificates include place and date of death and place of burial. Among the deaths were those of civilians (who remained in the minority) and increasing numbers of soldiers who died of influenza and its symptoms during 1918. But the majority of these death certificates point to mortality in military hospitals which had wings for prisoners, as a result of wounds sustained in France. Thus we learn of Private Peter Pohla, brought to Nell Lane Military Hospital in Manchester, who died a fairly gruesome death as a result of 'Gunshot wound: face, jaw, shoulder' and 'septic broncho-pneumonia' on 24 October 1918. The death certificate, under the heading 'Other features of interest to his relatives', asserted that 'The prisoner of war, died quite resigned. He was buried in the presence of his companions.'[149] Similarly, Julius Otto Rossberg died at the prisoner-of-war hospital in the Brocton camp on 12 December 1918 of 'Gunshot wound: left leg (amputated) and septic pneumonia', although the assertion that 'The prisoner of war did not suffer much' seems hard to believe in such circumstances.[150]

Arriving in Britain with injuries, sometimes of a life-threatening nature, represented a normal form of capture on French battlefields. Some of those who survived their wounds kept a record of their ordeal. Clemens Prinz, for instance, fell into the hands of the British after injury on 16 June 1916. In a statement he made to a military court in Eslingen on 18 July 1918 upon his return he also pointed to the fact that British soldiers took his papers together with his jewellery and 'immediately put them in their bag and kept them'. Between 16 and 22 June he spent time in a field hospital in Calais before going to Netley Hospital (until 20 July) and then on to the camp at Dorchester.[151] Meanwhile, a first lieutenant was seriously wounded at the Battle of Orly on the Marne on 8 September 1914, when a bullet lodged itself just below his right eye. He described the taking of his weapons by British soldiers, but also the confiscation of his personal possessions and money. He travelled for four days on a train until he reached St Nazaire. An Australian doctor operated upon him there and removed the bullet from his face. He sailed for Portsmouth on 17 September, and when he arrived there he encountered a German doctor, who asserted that the English surgeon had not dealt properly with his wound, which had now reopened, and therefore operated upon it with two other German surgeons.[152] On the other hand, Dr Funk commented on positive treatment at the hands of the English. After capture on the Marne in September 1914 he found himself caring for injured Germans. 'Our seriously wounded remained in Rouen, those with less serious wounds travelled with a hospital ship to Southampton and from there with a good hospital train to Devonport and were cared for and treated well.'[153]

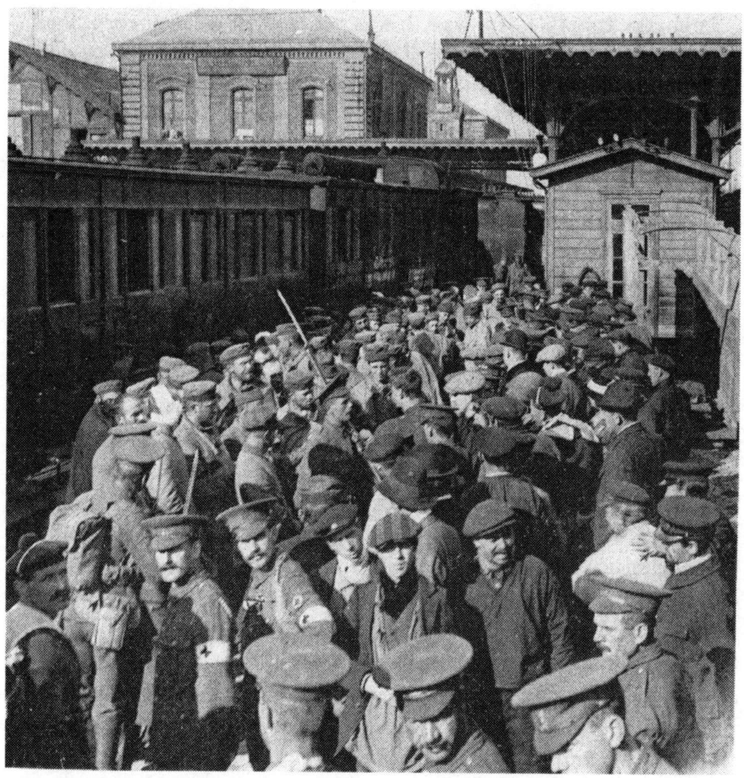

Figure 2.1 German prisoners of war in Boulogne awaiting transportation to England. Those combatants who faced capture in France would experience a journey which involved a rail trip to a French Channel port, a sea crossing and then a short spell of time in a reception camp on the south coast before transfer by rail to a more permanent place of incarceration.

These experiences illustrate the journeys that prisoners made after their capture. The lieutenant quoted above had an especially bad voyage to Britain, as did other wounded soldiers suffering from the pain of their injuries. In fact, on at least one occasion, on 17 April 1917, a German torpedo sank a hospital ship crossing the English Channel, as is indicated by letters written by three survivors from this crossing. Lieutenant Richard Schmidt provided the following details to his mother:

> I am now happily in England. It was not easy for we were torpedoed on the way over. After a good dinner there was a heavy bang and everything shot upwards. We were put into lifeboats and later taken on board the accompanying British torpedo boat. It was coming up to 7 p.m. and, thank God, was still light. The ship's crew, and also the English sailors, behaved towards us in an exemplary manner.[154]

Crossing the English Channel and arriving on the south coast of England formed part of the German prisoner's journey. As some of the narratives quoted above indicate, the first stage consisted of reaching a ship in northern France. In most cases this happened shortly after capture. Albrecht Brugger recalled a three-day march from Cheluwe to Poperinghe, where 'we were crammed into cattle trucks, which took us on a slow journey via Calais to Abbeville. The men were separated from us there and freighted to the French interior. On the following morning we arrived starving and frozen in Le Havre.' Brugger spent several days there before sailing for Portsmouth.[155] Another soldier complained about his journey across France, which involved the internees standing together in crammed railway carriages, while one of his companions found himself in chains for complaining.[156] Some German prisoners initially remained in France providing labour for the British army,[157] and faced transfer to Britain subsequently. Among them was E. Wolff, captured at the Somme in the summer of 1916 then taken to a camp in Le Havre in September and subsequently to a working camp in Calais, where he remained until his transfer to Southampton in February 1918.[158]

Few accounts spend much time on the Channel crossing,[159] focusing instead upon the internees arrival and the English journey to the place which would hold them. Most prisoners initially spent time in a holding camp on the south coast. Two of the most important of these were Shirley Rink and Bevois Mount, both of which appear to have existed from 1915. When soldiers arrived here they remained for about five days before transfer to a camp in another part of Britain.[160] Wolff 'entered the gates of an old skating rink at Shirley in Southampton' before being transferred to Brocton, where 'All pockets, bags, boxes, valses and packets were exhaustively searched and many a thing was flung on the piles of prisoners' property.'[161] Walter Scheller wrote of 'the Paradise of Southampton', where he initially spent time before his transfer to a camp with worse conditions.[162] D. W. Pult, meanwhile, initially found himself in a girls' school in Portsmouth after arriving from France on 10 March 1915 and was subsequently transferred to Holyport.[163] Similarly, Brugger arrived in Portsmouth and then went to Wakefield via London.[164]

Conclusions

During the course of the First World War the number of Germans interned in Britain gradually increased until it eventually reached its peak in early 1919. While the initial captives largely consisted of those civilians living in Britain at the outbreak of war, together with smaller numbers of people brought from the colonies and taken from ships, the grim and large-scale battles from 1917 onwards resulted in an increase in the numbers of combatants held in the country.

Internment policy evolved as the war progressed, largely because Britain had not fought a conflict on the scale it now experienced for a century. While security concerns played some role in deciding the fate of civilians, so did public opinion and, after the *Lusitania* riots, concern for their personal safety. The transportation of people from the colonies and from ships to Britain appears to have happened on a fairly ad hoc basis. While many of those from the British and German Empires remained for a short period in Britain, those taken off boats could spend years in a British camp, simply because they had been intercepted by a British ship. The internment of military captives essentially followed procedures which had evolved over centuries and which were formalized under the Hague Convention. But countless Germans complained of their initial treatment, pointing to a picture in which abuse represented normality.

From the point of view of the captives themselves, the main reaction to initial incarceration was essentially resignation. Most civilians obeyed orders to report to police stations and, in some cases, voluntarily surrendered, following the trauma of the *Lusitania* riots. Those taken from ships, in particular, as well as from colonies, had little choice other than capitulation. The experience of soldiers involved surrender as much as capture. The narratives quoted above all point to the fact that individuals made little effort to continue fighting when outnumbered. In many cases, the decision to succumb to captivity was a collective one reached by superiors.

All of the internees experienced an initial journey. For those already living in Britain, this remained relatively short, although moving from London to Knockaloe meant a wrench from family. Those taken from ships found themselves making journeys thrust upon them which they had not envisaged, whether they were fishermen or passengers upon ocean-going liners. Individuals transported from the colonies underwent some of the most dramatic journeys. Finally, soldiers seized in France faced a relatively short journey to Britain. Unlike those civilians in Britain who experienced a separation from family, these combatants would enter a safer experience in a British camp away from the constant possibility of death from a British or French shell or bullet.

Notes

1 *Isle of Man Examiner*, 26 September 1914.
2 Eric Hobsbawm, *Age of Extremes: A Short History of the Twentieth Century* (London, 1994), p. 6.
3 A. J. P. Taylor, *English History 1914–45* (1965; reprint Harmondsworth, 1985), p. 25.
4 Hobsbawm, *Age of Extremes*, p. 13.
5 Stéphane Audoin-Rouzeau and Annette Becker, *14–18: Understanding the Great War* (New York, 2002), pp. 15–93.
6 Niall Ferguson, *The Pity of War* (London, 1998).
7 Audoin-Rouzeau and Becker, *14–18*, pp. 15–44.
8 Ferguson, *Pity of War*, pp. 282–317, 339–66.
9 Audoin-Rouzeau and Becker, *14–18*, pp. 70–93.
10 Uta Hinz, *Gefangen im Grossen Krieg: Kriegsgefangenschaft in Deutschland, 1914–1921* (Essen, 2006), p. 9.
11 Audoin-Rouzeau and Becker, *14–18*, pp. 45–69.
12 See the work of Mark Levene in particular, which he summarizes in 'The Tragedy of the Rimlands, Nation-State Formation and the Destruction of Imperial Peoples, 1912–1948', in Panikos Panayi and Pippa Virdee, eds, *Refugees and the End of Empire: Imperial Collapse and Forced Migration during the Twentieth Century* (Basingstoke, 2011), pp. 51–78.
13 John Horne and Alan Kramer, *German Atrocities, 1914: A History of Denial* (London, 2001). See also Alan R. Kramer, *Dynamic of Destruction: Culture and Mass Killing in the First World War* (Oxford, 2007).
14 See, for instance, Arthur Marwick, *War and Social Change in the Twentieth Century* (1965; reprint London, 1986).
15 John Stevenson, *British Society, 1914–45* (London, 1984), pp. 46–76.

16 A standard account of these events is: Vahakn Dadrian, *The History of the Armenian Genocide* (Oxford, 1995).
17 See, especially, Panikos Panayi, *The Enemy in Our Midst: Germans in Britain during the First World War* (Oxford, 1991), pp. 43–159; J. C. Bird, *Control of Enemy Alien Civilians in Great Britain, 1914–1918* (London, 1986); and Thomas Boghardt, *Spies of the Kaiser: German Covert Operations in Great Britain during the First World War* (Basingstoke, 2004).
18 Paul Kennedy, *The Rise and Fall of British Naval Mastery* (London, 1976), pp. 149–265.
19 See Chapter 1 above.
20 Francis Abell, *Prisoners of War in Britain, 1756 to 1815: A Record of their Lives, their Romance and their Sufferings* (Oxford, 1914).
21 Sibylle Scheipers, 'Introduction: Prisoners in War', in Sibylle Scheipers, ed., *Prisoners in War* (Oxford, 2000), pp. 3–4; Arnold Krammer, *Prisoners of War: A Reference Handbook* (London, 2008), pp. 3–5.
22 Michel Foucault, *Discipline and Punish: The Birth of the Prison* (London, 1977).
23 Richard B. Speed III, *Prisoners, Diplomats, and the Great War: A Study in the Diplomacy of Captivity* (London, 1990). See also Chapter 7 below.
24 See, for instance, Donald Bloxham, *The Great Game of Genocide: Imperialism, Nationalism and the Destruction of the Ottoman Armenians* (Oxford, 2005), pp. 69–96.
25 Matthew Stibbe, *British Civilian Internees in Germany: The Ruhleben Camp, 1914–18* (Manchester, 2008), pp. 111–36.
26 Peter Scott, 'Captive Labour: The German Companies of the BEF, 1916–1920', *Army Quarterly Defence Journal*, vol. 110 (1980), 319–38; Heather Jones, *Violence against Prisoners of War in the First World War: Britain, France and Germany, 1914–1920* (Cambridge, 2011).
27 Alan R. Kramer, 'Prisoners in the First World War', in Scheipers, ed., *Prisoners in War*, pp. 75–6, takes the same approach.
28 See, for example, Charmian Brinson, '"Loyal to the Reich": National Socialists and Others in the Rushen Women's Internment Camp', in Richard Dove, ed.,*'Totally un-English'? Britain's Internment of 'Enemy Aliens' in Two World Wars* (Amsterdam, 2005), pp. 101–19.
29 Tammy Proctor, *Civilians in a World at War, 1914–1918* (London, 2010), pp. 206–7.
30 NA/WO32/5368, Internment of Alien Enemies, 1914.
31 *The Times History of the War*, vol. 6 (London, 1916), p. 272.
32 Panayi, *Enemy*, pp. 75–81.

33 NA/WO394/20, Statistical Information Regarding the Armies at Home and Abroad, 1914–1920.
34 NA/WO394/1, Statistical Abstract, December 1916.
35 NA/WO394/5, Statistical Abstract, November 1917.
36 NA/WO394/10, Statistical Abstract, 1 November 1918.
37 NA/WO394/20, Statistical Information Regarding the Armies at Home and Abroad, 1914–1920.
38 NA/WO394/15, Statistical Abstract, 1 September 1919.
39 NA/WO394/20, Statistical Information Regarding the Armies at Home and Abroad, 1914–1920.
40 Niall Ferguson, 'Prisoner Taking and Prisoner Killing in the Age of Total War: Towards a Political Economy of Military Defeat', *War in History*, vol. 11 (2004), 149–52.
41 Panikos Panayi, *German Immigrants in Britain during the Nineteenth Century, 1815–1914* (Oxford, 1995), p. 108.
42 Ibid., pp. 89–107; Stefan Manz, *Migranten und Internierte: Deutsche in Glasgow, 1864–1918* (Stuttgart, 2003); Gerald Newton,'Germans in Sheffield, 1817–1918', *German Life and Letters*, vol. 46 (1993), 82–101.
43 Panayi, *Enemy*, pp. 110–44.
44 See the discussion in Manz, *Migranten*, pp. 30–41.
45 IWM, The First World War Diaries of Richard Noschke, pp. 2–4.
46 Paul Cohen-Portheim, *Time Stood Still: My Internment in England* (London, 1931); Frederick Lewis Dunbar-Kalckreuth, *Die Männerinsel* (Leipzig, 1940).
47 Franklyn Arthur Johnson, *Defence by Committee: The British Committee of Imperial Defence, 1885–1959* (London, 1960), pp. 11–162.
48 NA/WO32/5368, A. H. Dennis to the Deputy Assistant Adjutant General, 12 November 1914.
49 Panayi, *Enemy*, pp. 45–69; Bird, *Control*, pp. 14–45.
50 Panayi, *Enemy*, pp. 70–1.
51 *Daily Express*, 8 August 1914.
52 *Manchester Guardian*, 21 August 1914.
53 Panayi, *Enemy*, p. 53.
54 *Londoner General-Anzeiger*, 15 August 1914.
55 BA/MA/RM3/5371, Statement by Willi Kortmann, 20 January 1915. For more on German sailors and their homes in Britain before 1914 see Panayi, *German Immigrants*, pp. 125–6, 160–3, 178–9.
56 *Manchester Guardian*, 9 September 1914.
57 *Scotsman*, 12 September 1914.
58 The letter first appeared in the *Tägliche Rundschau* of 12 October and was reprinted in *Die Eiche* in July 1915.

59 Panayi, *Enemy*, pp. 72–4, 225–9; Bird, *Control*, pp. 63–7.
60 Michael Roper, *The Secret Battle: Emotional Survival and the Great War* (Manchester, 2009).
61 Rudolf Rocker, *The London Years* (1956; Nottingham, 2005), p. 149.
62 Panayi, *Enemy*, p. 74.
63 MNH/MS06465/1, Douglas Camp Journal, gives the number and dates of arriving prisoners.
64 *Isle of Man Weekly Times*, 27 March 1915.
65 Panayi, *Enemy*, pp. 75–6.
66 *Hansard* (Commons), fifth series, vol. 70, cols 833–47, 3 March 1915. See further David Cesarani, 'The Anti-Jewish Career of Sir William Joynson-Hicks, Cabinet Minister', *Journal of Contemporary History*, vol. 24 (1989), 461–82.
67 *Hansard* (Commons), fifth series, vol. 70, cols 889, 3 March 1915.
68 Panayi, *Enemy*, pp. 229–53.
69 *Daily Sketch*, 13 May 1915.
70 *The Times*, 13 May 1915.
71 *Hansard* (Commons), fifth series, vol. 121, col. 1618, 12 May 1915.
72 *Hansard* (Commons), fifth series, vol. 71, col. 1649, 12 May 1915.
73 Cohen-Portheim, *Time Stood Still*, p. 20.
74 *Hansard* (Commons), fifth series, vol. 71, col. 1842, 13 May 1915.
75 Panayi, *Enemy*, pp. 80–1; Bird, *Control*, pp. 92–114.
76 Panayi, *Enemy*, p. 80.
77 MNH/MS06465/5, Daily Record of Prisoners Interned, does not make it clear whether the figure represents just Knockaloe or Knockaloe and Douglas combined, but B. E. Sargeaunt, *The Isle of Man and the Great War* (Douglas, 1922), p. 67, mentions a peak of 23,000 for Knockaloe.
78 *Mona's Herald*, 26 May, 15 September 1915.
79 Panikos Panayi, 'Sausages, Waiters and Bakers: German Migrants and Culinary Transfer to Britain, c 1850–1914', in Stefan Manz, Margrit Schulte Beerbühl and John R. Davis, eds, *Migration and Transfer from Germany to Britain, 1660–1914* (Munich, 2007), p. 155–6.
80 *Manchester Guardian*, 15 May 1915.
81 Panayi, *Enemy*, pp. 197–200.
82 *The Times*, 15 May 1915.
83 Ibid., 17, 18 May 1915; *Daily Mirror*, 15 May 1915; Panikos Panayi, 'The German Poor and Working Classes in Victorian and Edwardian London', in Geoffrey Alderman and Colin Holmes, eds, *Outsiders and Outcasts* (London, 1993), pp. 53–79.
84 Dunbar-Kalckreuth, *Die Männerinsel*, p. 99.
85 Cohen-Portheim, *Time Stood Still*, pp. 20–1.
86 BA/MA/MSG200/2277, Schilderungen eines Lederfachmannes.

87 The letter is reprinted in *Hornsey Journal*, 10 September 1915.
88 *Daily Express*, 26 May 1915.
89 Panayi, *Enemy*, pp. 81–2.
90 See Chapter 8 below.
91 See Chapter 7 below.
92 Cohen-Portheim, *Time Stood Still*, pp. 25–67; BA/MA/MSG200/2277, Schilderungen eines Lederfachmannes.
93 Panayi, *Enemy*, pp. 80, 82, 259–63
94 *Hornsey Journal*, 19 May 1916; *Daily Mirror*, 12 July 1916.
95 Proctor, *Civilians*, pp. 203–38.
96 NA/FO383/107, Treatment to be Accorded to Alien Enemies and Other Persons Removed from Prizes etc. or Found on Board Vessels Entering the United Kingdom, 2 February 1915. See also NA/ADM1/8389/241, War Orders, 262, Enemy Subjects and Persons removed from Prizes or Ships Detained – Disposal.
97 *Scotsman*, 26 August 1914.
98 They can all be found in BA/MA/RM3/5388.
99 See the two accounts given by Obersteurmannsmaat Haack of the sinking of a trawler and his internment in BA/MA/RM3/5398.
100 NA/FO383/241, Joh. Schute to the US Ambassador in London, 20 January 1916.
101 BA/MA/RM3/5367, Hecksher and Sons to Gertruder Petersen, 16 September 1914; BA/MA/RM3/5368, American Consular Service, Hull, to Messrs Heckscher and Sons, 22 September 1914.
102 BA/MA/RM3/5368, 'Verzeichnis derjenigen Deutschen, die als Passagiere auf dem holländishen Dampfer "Gelria" von den englischen Behörden in Falmouth angehalten worden sind'.
103 BA/MA/RM3/5378, 'Meine Flucht aus England. Von Kapitän Schmidt-Klafleth'.
104 NA/F0383/143, letter from P. Ernst Goretzki, 11 January 1916; Willi Haas to the United States Embassy in London, 12 February 1916.
105 NA/FO383/72, Johannes Buschmann to the United States Embassy in London, 9 July 1915.
106 NA/FO383/31, M. L. Waller to Under Secretary of State, Foreign Office, 20 August 1915.
107 MNH/MS11034, Transcripted Correspondence of Edwin Mieg.
108 BA/MA/RM3/5382, pp. 324–6.
109 Hans Erich Benedix, *In England interniert* (Gotha, 1916), pp. 1–2; *Berliner Tageblatt*, 11 September 1914; NA/FO383/22, Letter from Dr Werner Kieschke, 9 February [1915].
110 The classic work on British sea power in this period is Arthur J. Marder, *From Dreadnought to Scapa Flow: The Royal Navy in the Fisher Era, 1904–1919*, 5 vols (Oxford, 1961–70).

111 Andrew Francis, '"To Be Truly British We Must Be Anti-German": Patriotism, Citizenship and Anti-Alienism in New Zealand during the Great War' (Ph.D. thesis, Victoria University of Wellington, 2009), pp. 127–72; Gerhard Fischer, *Enemy Aliens: Internment and the Homefront Experience in Australia, 1914–1920* (St Lucia, 1989), pp. 58–175; J. Maue, *In Feindes Land: Achtzehn Monate in englischer Kriegsgefangenschaft in Indien und England* (Stuttgart, 1918).

112 Maue, *In Feindes Land*, pp. 23–30.

113 BA/MA/RM3/5369, Liste der vom 'Hollandia' auf der Fahrt von Buenos Aires nach Amsterdam durch den Englischen Kreuzer 'Cornwall', kriegsgefangenen gemachten deutschen Fahrgäste; NA/FO383/81, Intercepted Letter from E. G. Müller, Prisoner of War at Wakefield.

114 BA/MA/RM3/5372, Letter from P. W. Brünger, 7 February 1915.

115 For a good introduction to the war in Africa see Hew Strachan, *The First World War*, vol. 1, *To Arms* (Oxford, 2001), pp. 495–643. For Germans in Africa, see, for instance, Daniel Rouven Steinbach, 'Defending the *Heimat*: The Germans in South-West Africa and East Africa during the First World War', in Heather Jones, Jennifer O'Brien and Christoph Schmidt-Supprian, eds, *Untold War: New Perspectives in First World War Studies* (Leiden, 2008), pp. 179–208.

116 Wilhelm Kröpke, *Mein Flucht aus englischer Kriegsgefangenschaft 1916: Von Afrika über England nach Deutschland zur Flandern-Front* (Flensburg, 1937), pp. 7–20.

117 Otto Schimming, *13 Monate hinter dem Stacheldraht: Alexandra Palace, Knockaloe, Isle of Man, Stratford* (Stuttgart, 1919), pp. 1–7.

118 Heinrich Norden, *In englischer Gefangenschaft* (Kassel, 1915). See also Gotthilf Vöhringer, *Meine Erlebnisse während des Krieges in Kamerun und in englischer Kriegsgefangenschaft* (Hamburg, 1915); BA/R901/84678, Bericht des Kapitänleutenants d. Res. Bötefur über die Erlebnisse während seiner Gefangenschaft, 31 March 1916; BA/MA/RM3/5371, Testimony of Dr Beyer.

119 FO383/276, Secretary, Prisoners of War Department, to War Office, 12 August 1917; Georg Wilhelm Wagener, *Meine Gefangenschaft in Südafrika und England vom 15. Sept. 1914 bis 18. Juni 1916* (Brunswick, 1917).

120 Ferguson, 'Prisoner Taking'.

121 Alexander Watson, *Enduring the Great War: Combat, Morale and Collapse in the German and British Armies, 1914–1918* (Cambridge, 2008), pp. 184–231.

122 A. J. Barker, *Behind Barbed Wire* (London, 1974), pp. 27–9.

123 See the correspondence in NA/AIR1/16/15/307.

124 NA/AIR1/16/15/272.

125 *Hansard* (Commons), fifth series, vol. 223, cols 431–2, 17 December 1919; NA/FO383/508, Captain Lieutenant in Command of Torpedo Flotilla, Lofthouse Park, Wakefield, to Swiss Minister in London, 2 July 1919; *Stenographische Berichte über die Verhandlungen des deutschen Reichstages*, session 138, 16 January 1920, p. 4344; Dan van der Vat, *The Grand Scuttle: The Sinking of the German Fleet at Scapa Flow in 1919* (London, 1982), pp. 117–95; Friedrich Ruge, *Scapa Flow 1919: The End of the German Fleet* (London, 1973).
126 For a study of the actions of German U-boats see, for example, Joachim Schröder, *Die U-Boote des Kaisers: Die Geschichte des deutschen U-Boot-Krieges gegen Großbritannien im Ersten Weltkrieg* (Bonn, 2003).
127 *Manchester Guardian*, 6 March 1915.
128 *Scotsman*, 6 March 1915.
129 BA/MA/RM2/5372, Letter from Chatham Naval Detention Quarters, 17 March 1915.
130 See the relevant correspondence in NA/FO383/60 and NA/FO383/61.
131 *The Times*, 15 November 1916.
132 NA/ADM1/8446/15, War Orders. Prisoners of War (NL48398-1916).
133 NA/ADM137/3897, Report of Interrogation of Prisoners from 'UC32', sunk off Sunderland on 23 February 1917.
134 The letters are in NA/ADM137/3897.
135 Tighe Hopkins, *Prisoners of War* (London, 1914), p. 107.
136 *Daily Express*, 17 March 1915.
137 Ibid., 5 July 1916.
138 See Chapter 6 below.
139 BA/R901/84674, Bericht des Stabsarztes Dr Funk.
140 LBWHS/M77/1/930, Fragebogen für die Vernehmung des aus der englischen kriegsgefangenschaft zurückgekehrten Vizefeldwebels (Offiziersaspiranten) Richard Schmitt.
141 J. Machner, *Gefangenen in England: Erlebnisse and Beobachtungen* (Hildesheim, 1920), pp. 10–27.
142 Albrecht Hermann Brugger, *Meine Flucht aus dem Kriegsgefangenen-Lager Lofthouse-Park* (Berlin, 1937), p. 9.
143 BA/R901/84676, Beglaubigte Abschrift zu Nr. 3406 15. Z. V. I.
144 See the relevant correspondence in NA/FO383/175.
145 BA/R67/1283, DRK, Interner Bericht 102, 4 March 1918.
146 See reports in BA/R901/84680. See also Brian K. Feltman, 'Tolerance as a Crime? The British Treatment of German Prisoners of War on the Western Front, 1914–1918', *War in History*, vol. 17 (2010), 435–58.
147 BA/R67/852; BA/R67/909; BA/R67/1038; BA/R67/1039; BA/R67/1040; BA/R67/1041.

148 Ronald F. Roxburgh, *The Prisoners of War Information Bureau* (London, 1915), p. 1.
149 BA/R67/1039.
150 BA/R67/1040.
151 See the statement and questionnaire completed by Prinz on pp. 138m and 138n of LBWHS/M77/1/930.
152 *Norddeutsche allgemeine Zeitung*, 28 August 1915.
153 BA/R901/84674, 'Bericht des Stabsarztes Dr Funk'.
154 WL/RAM/488, three letters written by German prisoners of war to their families about their treatment and the torpedoing of the hospital ships taking them to England.
155 Brugger, *Meine Flucht*, p. 9.
156 *Die Eiche*, July 1915.
157 Scott, 'Captive Labour', pp. 319–31.
158 IWM 82/35/1, Transcript of E. Wolff, 'My Adventures in the Great War 1914/18'.
159 But see the paragraph in Brugger, *Meine Flucht*, p. 9.
160 *Reports of Visits of Inspection Made by Officials of the United States Embassy to Various Internment Camps in the United Kingdom* (London, 1916), pp. 335; NA/FO383/277, Swiss Embassy Reports on Shirley Rink and Bevois Mount, 9 November 1917.
161 IWM 82/35/1, Transcript of E. Wolff, 'My Adventures in the Great War 1914/18'.
162 Walter Scheller, *Als die Seele starb: 1914–1918: Das Kriegserlebnis eines Unkriegerischen* (Berlin, 1931), p. 89.
163 D. W. Pult, *Siebzehn Monate in englischer Kriegsgefangenschaft* (Siegen, 1917), pp. 46–62.
164 Brugger, *Meine Flucht*, p. 9.

3

The camp system

> Wakefield was an extremely orderly place, as orderly, monotonous and drab as a lower middle-class suburb, but it was a suburb without a city, and its inhabitants suburbanites out of work. Everything was organized, everything ordered. The huts had captains, the captains a chief-captain and he an adjutant with so little sense of humour that he actually signed himself Adjutant L. and wished to be addressed by his ridiculous title. There were committees for everything, and nearly everyone was a member of one or the other or had some sort of post in the P.O. or the kitchen department or God knows what, and they all took themselves and their activities most seriously.[1]

Bureaucracy

The hundreds of thousands of German prisoners in Britain during the First World War needed a bureaucracy to control them. Although the internment system had an element of chaos within it, especially in the early stages of the conflict, by the middle of 1915 it operated effectively. The different agencies involved in the camp system stretched from the international level, in the form of United States and Swiss Embassy officials, through a series of government departments, to local councils and the bureaucracies of the camps themselves, which, in the case of Knockaloe, involved hundreds of people.

Just as the bureaucracy remained rather haphazard in the early stages of the war, so, in the same way, did the camps themselves. The government initially simply set up temporary places of internment, some of which would become permanent. But the camp system did not take long to develop. Knockaloe started taking civilians in November 1914 and gradually expanded during the course of the following year. It joined a series of other long-term civilian camps which emerged in 1914 and 1915. Soldiers captured in France increasingly found themselves interned in their own camps during the course of 1915 and beyond. By 1919 the number of places of incarceration had reached almost 600, many of which simply consisted of working camps attached to more long-standing parent institutions.

It seems tempting to compare the British camp structure established during the First World War with that set up in Germany during the Second. Although the latter may have had more sinister aims, it operated as an effective system, being required to transport, house, work and murder the people it controlled, as demonstrated by scholars such as Zygmunt Bauman and Götz Aly and Susanne Heim.[2] While the bureaucracy of British internment did not have the last aim, it did have the others.

But it might prove more useful for us to place the British internment system of the First World War within the context of other bureaucracies which developed during the course of the conflict, in particular, those required to move millions of soldiers from all parts of Britain to battlefields throughout Europe. The experience of German military captives mirrored that of British soldiers in the sense that they faced mass transportation and would live in similar standard huts (although many found themselves in trenches for years).[3] We also need to remember the expansion and even creation of ministries required to fight the war, including the Ministry of National Service and the Ministry of Munitions.[4] The former body had the employment of German prisoners as one of its aims. At the same time, as Britain generally played by the rules when it came to prisoner welfare, we also need to remember the international bodies concerned with the welfare of internees, which were allowed into the camps by the British government.

Any attempt to reconstruct the overall administration of the camp system reveals a series of layers of bureaucracy and concern, ranging from international to national and local. The international level included the German branches of charities concerned with the fate of prisoners in Britain, above all the Red Cross, together with a series of specifically German bodies, many of whom worked either with the Red Cross or with religious and other groups in Britain.[5]

The Prisoners of War Information Bureau came into existence on 17 August 1914 and lasted until 6 March 1920, employing 376 people,[6] with its headquarters at 49 Wellington Street in central London. Its establishment followed article 14 of the Hague Convention, which declared that such an organization should exist in all combatant states with the aim of replying 'to all enquiries about the prisoners' and receiving information from a range of agencies allowing it 'to make and keep up to date an individual return for each prisoner of war'. The initial return for each internee, whether civilian or military, occurred once he arrived in a camp. The bureau maintained a card index.[7]

While few papers from this body have survived, the other international organizations which looked after the welfare of prisoners, in the form of the United States and Swiss Embassies, have left thousands of pages of documentation held in both British and German official archives, upon which this chapter is largely based. As a neutral state at the beginning of the war, the USA received requests from several powers including both Britain and Germany, to protect their interests in enemy territory. These interests included the plight of both civilian and military internees. The United States operated through its embassies in the various belligerent states whose interests it protected. Thus it established a German division in Britain, which answered questions from the German Foreign Office about specific aspects of the situation of Germans in Britain. One of the key tasks consisted of the inspection of places of internment, which, in the case of Britain, occurred on a regular basis until the USA entered the war.[8] The reports which ensued are key sources for understanding the operation of individual camps, as well as the conditions within them. While a small number of these reports saw the light of day through publication, the vast majority did not. Once the United States entered the war in 1917, the Swiss Embassy took over its tasks.[9] These diplomatic overseers tried to ensure that fair play operated within the individual internment camps. Each of the reports which they produced reached the United States or Swiss Embassy in Berlin and, in turn, the German Foreign Office. It is clear that they had some influence on the running of these camps, because the Swiss and United States consular officials who constituted the inspectors spoke to individual internees within them. The complaints reached the German Foreign Office, which in turn pressurized the British government through the embassies in London, and this could often lead to an improvement in conditions.

Despite the role of charities and the United States and Swiss

Embassies, the British government, through several ministries, together with various quangos established during the course of the conflict, as well as local government bodies, controlled the bureaucracy of internment. Actually dissecting this bureaucracy proves difficult because of the range of bodies involved. Once again, one of the main problems lies in the novelty of interning hundreds of thousands of prisoners and 'the entire lack of experience or precedent': 'nothing was to be gained from a study of the conditions which obtained . . . during the second half of the 18th century and the early years of the 19th century' when Britain 'last held prisoners in considerable numbers'.[10] This situation meant that policy and responsibility evolved as the war progressed and threw up increasing numbers and new problems.

No ministry or body had overarching responsibility for internment and the camp system as a whole, and the establishment of quangos complicated the picture further. At least ten separate ministries became involved. The War Office proved one of the most important from the start of the conflict. It carried out a range of tasks. In the first place, it had at least some responsibility for virtually all of the camps in Britain, and the discipline of prisoners within them. The Army Council helped with the last task through the issue of regulations about the treatment of prisoners of war, which could change during the conflict as a result of retaliation for German actions against British internees. The War Office appears to have carried out its functions through the Directorate of Prisoners of War, established in September 1914, which initially held responsibility for deciding on individual cases for exemption before the advisory committees took over in May 1915. According to one account, the directorate employed just twenty-three people, although this number would simply consist of those at a head office and exclude the thousands involved in local camp administration. The Home Office focused upon enemy aliens in Britain, including their internment and repatriation. It held major responsibility for the Isle of Man camps, although the Scottish Office appears to have looked after those in Scotland. The Foreign Office particularly concerned itself with communication with Germany and other belligerent states through the embassies which looked after German interests. In order to help co-ordinate its activities, it established a Prisoners and Aliens Department just after war broke out for the purpose of dealing with prisoner questions as well as working with the other government departments concerned with such issues. The Colonial Office and the India Office held responsibility for prisoner-of-war issues in their respective spheres of influence, working with the War Office and Foreign Office in London. The Admiralty dealt with the sea transport of repatriated prisoners and mercantile marine internees. The Board of Trade shared the Admiralty's latter concern. The Ministry of National Service had the task of employing mostly military prisoners, especially in the latter stages of the war. The Post Office and the Treasury needed consultation for facilities, budgets and monetary exchange. Police forces arrested civilians. These responsibilities remained for most of the war, but concern had arisen by 1916 about confusion and overlap, leading to the establishment of another quango in February of that year, the Prisoners of War Department, which eventually employed forty-nine people, initially under the control of the Foreign Office and the stewardship of Lord Newton, although it quickly became independent. It communicated with foreign governments over issues regarding prisoners, and it appears to have carried out the tasks previously administered by the Foreign Office under the Prisoners and Aliens Department. More complicated still, an interdepartmental committee came into existence at the same time to co-ordinate the work of the different ministries concerned with prisoners. In September 1918 Lord Cave, the Home Secretary, took over responsibility for this committee.[11]

Despite the apparent chaos, which was emphasized by some radical right-wing MPs (including Joynson-Hicks) and the bureaucrats who worked in the different government ministries concerned with prisoners, the internment system operated effectively, especially after the initial outbreak of war.[12] The main responsibility for running the camps lay with the War Office and Home Office, as the example of those located on the Isle of Man indicates. In this case both of these ministries played a role, together with the recently established Destitute Aliens Committee and the Local Government Board, as well as the Isle of Man government. In addition, the prisoners helped with the internal administration of the camps. The complexity of Knockaloe in particular remains unique, and can be explained partly by the number of people interned here, as well as its longevity, as it lasted from 1914 until 1919.

The Destitute Aliens Committee, which was established at the start of the war and would subsequently become the Civilian

Internment Camps Committee, initiated the plan to send civilians to the Isle of Man after members of this organization went there in September 1914. This first trip led to the establishment of the Douglas camp, while another visit on 24 October led to the emergence of Knockaloe. The War Office played an overarching role in the running of the camps on the Isle of Man, with responsibility for guarding, discipline, sanitation and censorship. The Home Office, meanwhile, delegated its duties to the Isle of Man government; these consisted of the upkeep of the buildings and their equipment, the installation of lighting and water and the provision of food and clothing. While the War Office supplied the military staff, including the commandant, sub-commandants (in the case of Knockaloe) and guards, the Home Office held responsibility for civilian employees, who included censors, pursers, clerks, storekeepers, hospital dispensers and engineers. The number of staff employed in the two camps appears to have fluctuated. On 28 July 1917 the staff at Douglas numbered forty-five, while the figure for Knockaloe stood at 236 including both military and civilian employees. The latter figure seems rather low for a camp which held over 20,000 people, but finds partial explanation in the fact that internees carried out everyday tasks such as cooking.[13]

The extent and nature of the camp system

The Isle of Man, particularly the camp at Knockaloe, provides a symbol of British internment policy during the Great War, but the two camps which emerged here were simply the best-known examples of the hundreds which emerged from 1914. It would appear that the total number approached 600 in 1918 and 1919, although, as some had come and gone since 1914, especially those established in the initial stages of the war, the total number of places of incarceration for civilian and military prisoners during the entire conflict certainly exceeded 600.

We can paint an overall picture of the camps in a variety of ways. Actually establishing their total throughout the war proves problematic. Two separate sources give figures of 584[14] and 'over 500',[15] but this peak was not reached until the end of the conflict. My own research in the British and German national archives revealed United States and Swiss Embassy reports on 452 different camps during the course of the entire conflict.[16] A British publication from the end of 1914 claimed: 'In mid-October we held German prisoners of war at Blackdown, Camberley, Dyffryn Aled (North Wales), Douglas (Isle of Man), Frimley, Handforth, Lofthouse Park (between Leeds and Wakefield), Newbury, Queensferry, Templemore (Ireland), York and Olympia in London.'[17] Most of these catered mainly for civilians. A German list from May 1916 provides the names of only sixteen camps in Britain, which may reflect the true picture before the increase in military prisoners of the final two years of the war. The list certainly includes the most important camps which existed at this time.[18] The next (German) source indicating the total number of camps appeared in 1917 and consisted of a map of the world which detailed the places where Germans found themselves interned. These included ninety-five in Britain.[19] By the beginning of 1918 the figure had reached 118,[20] and it increased further to 566 a year later, reflecting the growth in the number of military internees.[21]

Britain therefore established a system of mass incarceration dependent upon a complex bureaucracy. The hundreds of camps which came into existence had as many differences as they did similarities. In the first place, the most obvious differentiation was between civilian and military places of internment. Although a few camps initially held a mixture of soldiers and immigrants in the chaos which followed the immediate outbreak of the war, separation had become the norm by 1915, which made sense because of the different regulations governing the two groups under the Hague Convention, especially regarding work.[22] Secondly, class played a major role. Knockaloe had a 'privilege' camp, for example, while the civilian internment camps at Wakefield and Douglas also catered for wealthier middle-class refugees. Some of the longest-lasting military establishments including Donington Hall, Frongoch and Dyffryn Aled held only officers, and the existence of such camps maintained military distinction and class barriers, especially as many people held here had German privates acting as servants. In terms of geography, camps existed throughout the country by the end of the war, especially with the growth in the numbers of military prisoners from 1917, which resulted in the establishment of numerous working camps. Thus virtually every corner of Britain held internees from the Isle of Raasay and the Isle of Man to Chatham, Portsmouth and Devonport. Although the use of prisoner labour in agriculture and the 20,000 people held at Knockaloe

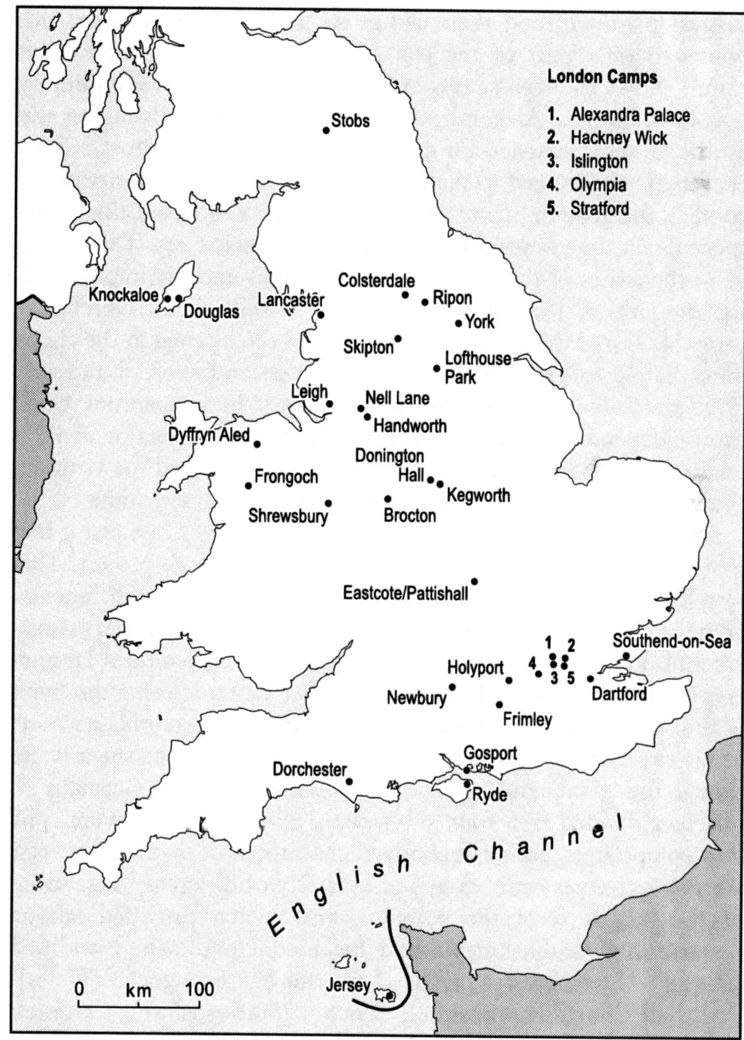

Figure 3.1 Major internment camps in Britain during the First World War. This map simply gives the locations of the most important and long-lasting of the hundreds of camps which came into existence during the course of the Great War.

suggest prisoners and their camps as a rural phenomenon, this points to only part of the truth. The 1917 map of internment camps shows eighteen camps in London, including several military hospitals, but also Alexandra Palace, Hackney Wick, Islington and Stratford, which existed for most of the war.[23] While most prisoners remained confined to their quarters for the vast majority of the conflict, the growth in working camps after 1916 meant that many spent much time beyond their barbed wire enclosures. This brings us to the issues of the longevity of the camps and, by implication, the amount of time individuals spent within them. Dorchester probably lasted the longest of all, having been opened in the chaos immediately following the outbreak of war and evolved and survived until its conclusion, by which time it had numerous work camps dependent upon it. Similarly, some of the major civilian institutions, above all Douglas and Knockaloe, lasted for virtually the whole of the conflict and into 1919. In contrast, some of the camps which emerged at the end of the war might last just a few months, especially if connected with a specific work project. This also leads us to the issue of the sizes of individual establishments. Some of these smaller working camps held only a few dozen prisoners and, in some cases, such as those holding agricultural labourers, just consisted of a farm. At the other extreme came the 'men island', the title of Frederick Lewis Dunbar-Kalckreuth's account of his experiences mostly on the Isle of Man, where he spent some time in the 'giant camp' at Knockaloe with its '25,000 Germans';[24] this was divided into four sub-camps, which, in turn, were split into compounds, each essentially a small town of men. In between the two extremes came camps of a variety of different sizes. Some of the largest were the parent camps which provided labour for working establishments and included Handforth, Blandford (Dorset), Dorchester, Leigh (Lancashire), Frongoch (Wales), Pattishall (Northamptonshire), Brocton (Staffordshire), Catterick (Yorkshire) and Shrewsbury.[25] Finally, in this introductory outline we can mention the different types of accommodation in which the prisoners found themselves, which varied greatly. Some consisted of ready-made buildings which would survive the duration of the war, including Cunningham's holiday camp in Douglas[26] and the stately homes at Donington Hall and Holyport. On the other hand, some of the early camps took over establishments which proved completely unsuitable, such as Newbury race course, the hall at Olympia and several factories, while some of the most heavily criticized places were ships anchored off Ryde, Southend and Gosport in early 1915. Standard accommodation consisted of bell tents, which were usually replaced, if the camp became long-standing, with the type of huts used for housing British troops.

While prisoners of war in Britain may have had the common characteristic of spending time behind barbed wire deprived of their liberty, the types of camp in which they found themselves varied greatly, as the outline above suggests. In order to provide more detail, it proves easiest to divide the camps into six categories, essentially maintaining the distinction between civilian and military incarceration: first, the smaller establishments which held non-combatants, consisting of the initial short-lived camps and those which would emerge in 1915 and survive the duration of the war; second, special camps, which held distinct groups of prisoners; third, the Isle of Man camps; fourth, military camps; fifth, military hospitals; and finally, working camps, which proliferated at the end of the war.

Smaller civilian camps

In the chaos which followed the immediate outbreak of the war a series of places of internment emerged, many of which would remain short-lived. These included Olympia, which started taking prisoners who lived in London from the time of the first decision to intern enemy aliens. They initially had to sleep on the floor upon arrival, although some improvement occurred subsequently. Those held here included Rudolf Rocker, who wrote that it 'was arranged in twelve camps, separated from each other by heavy ropes', each of which contained between 100 and 150 men. In total Olympia held between 300 and 1,500 men and housed prisoners only until December 1914.[27]

The camps at Frimley (near Aldershot) and Newbury had a similarly fleeting existence, although Frimley appears to have undergone several reincarnations. It used bell tents and quarters made out of galvanized iron to house internees. According to one German source, it housed as many as 6,000 captives by the middle of November 1914. Although prisoners had left here in early 1915, it came into use again later in that year and again emptied in October 1915, but reopened in 1916, and by 1918 held combatant

Table 3.1 Major internment camps in Britain, 1914–19

Name	Location	Type of camp	Duration	Approximate numbers held at any one time
Alexandra Palace	London	Civilian	1915–19	3,000
Brocton	Staffordshire	Military	1917–19	5,000
Colsterdale	Yorkshire	Officer	1917–18	400
Dartford	Kent	Hospital	1915–18	Up to 3,726
Donington Hall	Leicestershire	Officer	1915–19	500
Dorchester	Dorset	Military	1914–19	3,000
Douglas	Isle of Man	Civilian	1914–19	2,500
Dyffryn Aled	Wales	Officer	1915–18	100
Frimley	Hampshire	Civilian then military	1914–15, 1916–18	Up to 6,000
Gosport (ships)	Hampshire	Civilian	1914–15	3,600
Hackney Wick	London	Civilian	1916–17	100
Handforth	Cheshire	Civilian then military	1914–18	2,000–2,500
Holyport	Berkshire	Officer	1915–19	150–600
Islington	London	Civilian	1915–19	600–700
Jersey	Channel Islands	Military	1915–19	1,100
Kegworth	Derbyshire	Officer	1916–19	600
Knockaloe	Isle of Man	Civilian	1914–19	20,000

Leigh	Lancashire	Military	1914–19	1,500
Lofthouse Park (Wakefield)	Yorkshire	Civilian	1914–19	1,500
Nell Lane	Manchester	Hospital	1916–19	Up to 1,665
Newbury	Berkshire	Early civilian	1914–15	c.3,000
Olympia	London	Early civilian	August–September 1914	300–1,500
Pattishall (Eastcote)	Northamptonshire	Civilian then military	1914–19	Up to 4,500
Ripon	Yorkshire	Officer	1919	900
Ryde (ships)	Isle of Wight	Civilian	1914–15	2,500
Southend (ships)	Essex	Civilian	1914–15	5,000
Stobs	Roxburghshire, Scotland	Civilian then military	1914–18	4,500
Stratford	London	Civilian	1914–17	Up to 740

internees.[28] Those Germans held in Newbury found themselves living on the race course, some of them using the horse boxes as accommodation with neither heat nor light. Prisoners appear to have left here by the beginning of 1915.[29]

Wales and Scotland had similarly fleeting establishments at the start of the war. A story in the *Daily Mirror* painted a positive picture of 217 German seamen held in 'comfortable quarters at the Engineers' Drill Hall, at the back of the Post Office' in Cardiff.[30] Meanwhile, 600 Germans, again mostly sailors, found themselves housed in the ground of the Redford barracks near Edinburgh, living in close proximity to, but separately from, British soldiers. This acted as a transit camp where prisoners remained for between one and four weeks.[31]

Some of the most notorious short-lived places of internment emerged in December 1914 and January 1915 in the form of the ships moored off Gosport, Southend and Ryde and requisitioned by the War Office. Each of these locations acted as home to three vessels. Those at Ryde were the *Canada*, *Tunisian* and *Andania*, with the last of these holding combatants. The War Office had dispensed with them by March 1915. The *Scotian*, *Ascania* and *Lake Manitoba* lay off Gosport while the ships next to Southend were the *Invernia*, *Saxonia* and *Royal Edward*. The individual ships held between 795 and 2,300 internees each, overwhelmingly civilians, and they may have held close to 9,000 in all at their peak in early 1915. By the end of April 1915 only the *Saxonia*, the *Royal Edward* and the *Uranium*, which had replaced the *Lake Manitoba*, still remained in operation, and these seem to have emptied at the end of May. Personal accounts of life on these ships paint varying pictures, but none of them prove particularly positive, with many complaining about the accommodation and food, although wealthier prisoners could pay for better provisions and first-class cabins.[32]

Alexandra Palace became the home of many of the internees from these ships and counts as the largest and longest-lasting of the four major London camps, which also included Stratford, Hackney Wick and Islington. Other places of internment in London included Brixton Prison and military hospitals. Alexandra Palace, which held internees under War Office control from the beginning of May 1915, simply made use of the facilities of this pre-war entertainment and cultural centre, which had actually acted as home to Belgian refugees from September 1914. It held a peak of 3,000 prisoners at any one time, although as many as 17,000 men may have passed through it, often on their way to Knockaloe. The last prisoners did not leave until March 1919. The long-term residents consisted especially of the German community of London, although Austro-Hungarians and Turks also spent time here, as did people brought to Britain from the colonies. Little privacy existed, as the internees slept in three large halls, a common enough situation in other places, but one which irked middle-class prisoners used to their own space. As elsewhere, the prisoners were divided into groups in the form of three battalions which were in turn split into companies.[33]

Another large internment camp opened in Stratford in the east of London at the end of 1914. Those held here included Richard Noschke and Paul Cohen-Portheim, both of whom commented on the arrogant attitude of the guards, the former also criticizing two of the commandants. This camp, like several others, utilized an old factory, which meant that conditions within it remained poor, as many internees indicated, focusing upon issues such as heating and damp. One prisoner described it as 'a horrible hole in the manufacturing quarter of London. It consists of the machinery hall of an old jute spinning works. It is dirty, cold and draughty.' Few people spent any length of time here, as it acted either as a starting point for prisoners on their way to larger camps or an end point for those awaiting repatriation. It closed during 1917. It appears to have reached a peak population of 740 in May 1915.[34]

The other significant London establishment, a former workhouse in Cornwallis Road in Islington, like Alexandra Palace, held London Germans, many of whom had British-born wives. They included traders, hotel managers, waiters, commercial agents, shopkeepers, tailors, barbers and craftsmen, reflecting the major occupations of the pre-war London German community. The camp opened at the end of June 1915 and an elected committee controlled it. The number of prisoners stood at between 600 and 700, and the internees produced a variety of goods, which they managed to sell. It closed in 1919.[35]

The camp in Hackney Wick lay on the site of a former 'casual ward', where people had spent the night in return for carrying out some work. The small number of people held here, which fluctuated at around 100, again came mainly from the London German community. Hackney Wick was essentially a civilian working camp, as the prisoners consisted of skilled mechanics working for Vickers.[36]

Outside London, several civilian camps emerged in north-west England during the early stages of the war, reflecting the pre-war settlement of Germans in Manchester and Liverpool. An early camp in Lancaster used an old wagon works, but it does not seem to have survived beyond 1915. Its population of 2,000 in early 1915 included 200 boys taken from ships, who remained there well into 1915.[37] Nearby Queensferry emerged on the site of an 'industrial village' in Flintshire in the 'buildings of an old foundry, which have been unoccupied for several years'.[38] A German report from 1915 commented on the poor conditions here.[39] It did not survive beyond 1915. The camp at Handforth, which lasted until 1918, came into existence in November 1914 on the site of a former print works. Although it had developed into a military camp by 1916,[40] it initially held a combination of local Germans largely from Manchester, the crews of German trawlers, and people brought from the colonies, whose numbers totalled between 2,000 and 2,500. External visitors to the camp wrote quite favourably about it because by early 1915 it had become fairly well organized and the factory buildings held acceptable accommodation.[41]

Rather like Alexandra Palace, the camp at Lofthouse Park utilized the site of a former entertainment complex for the West Riding Tramway Company near Wakefield, which had opened in 1908 but was no longer in operation in 1913 and was taken over by the War Office when the war broke out. The first prisoners arrived here in October 1914, mainly from northern towns, although the camp held people from a variety of locations, among them Hermann J. Held, a law student at Cambridge, and Paul Cohen-Portheim, transferred there from the camp in Stratford. It appears to have reached a peak of around 2,400 prisoners, but the total averaged around 1,500 for most of the conflict, overwhelmingly Germans, but also including some Austrians and a handful of Turks. The camp was divided into three compounds. Cohen-Portheim's account stated that the south camp contained 'a good many men from the German colonies' and 'was inclined to be cranky'. The north camp 'was frigid and correct' and 'doubtlessly socially superior' and included a small number of people who had lived in England, as well as others captured in the colonies. Cohen-Portheim lived in the west camp, which 'had the least character' and essentially housed members of the Victorian and Edwardian German middle-class community in England. In fact, Wakefield was a privilege camp and internees had

Figure 3.2 Lofthouse Park. This served as 'privilege camp' where middle-class prisoners could pay to receive superior accommodation. Paul Cohen-Portheim, however, provided a vicious critique of the time he spent here in one of the most incisive personal accounts of internment in Britain during the Great War.

to pay ten shillings a week to live there in better conditions than were available in many of the other civilian camps. But its inhabitants were transferred to the Isle of Man in October 1918, when it became a camp for combatants.[42]

The most important Scottish camp by the end of 1914 was Stobs, near Hawick, on the side of a sloping hill, initially opened in 1903 for the training of Scottish regiments and still in use for that purpose when the war broke out. Taking prisoners from November 1914, it held both military and civilian internees until July 1916, when the latter were transferred to Knockaloe. Although the captives initially found themselves housed in bell tents, they subsequently lived in standard huts of 120 by 20 feet holding thirty-three men each. Stobs was divided into four compounds. In April 1916 A and B held 1,102 and 1,098 civilians respectively, while C and D housed 1,081 and 1,209 military and naval prisoners.[43] By November 1918 it held 1,867 German military prisoners, including 922 non-commissioned officers and fifty-one sailors, and had twenty-three working camps attached to it as far away as Kinlochleven and Raasay, which held 2,610 prisoners between them.[44]

A variety of establishments therefore emerged during the course of 1914 and 1915 for the purpose of housing civilians. Some of the most hurriedly assembled, such as Redford and the ships moored off south coast ports, and the most unsuitable, including Stratford, did not last for long, while others simply became transformed into camps for combatants. A few, notably Alexandra Palace and Wakefield, survived for most of the conflict. If any patterns emerge they are the use of old factories, amusement parks and standardized tents and huts.

Special camps

Each establishment holding civilians may have had its own characteristics, but the camps followed fairly standard patterns of holding internees either from Britain or from ships and the colonies. In addition, we can also identify several camps which came into operation to house distinct groups of prisoners: criminals and those regarded as a high security threat; women; and the residents of Libury Hall industrial and farm colony.

Some internees spent time in prisons, notably Brixton and Reading. At the start of the war about 100 alien men, consisting of those awaiting deportation and those regarded as a security threat, found themselves in the former. Although mostly German, they also included other nationalities, including non-enemy aliens. Inmates from Brixton, together with others from Birmingham, Leeds, Liverpool, Wakefield, Stafford and Manchester prisons, were transferred to Reading between December 1915 and January 1916, replacing the ordinary prisoners held here. After complaining about their conditions in 1917, about fifty German spies and criminals were transferred to Knockaloe, where they remained separate from the rest of the internees. A handful of Germans awaiting deportation actually remained in Brixton after the end of 1915.[45]

Although German women in Britain did not face incarceration *en masse* during the Great War, a small number regarded as hostile or as having carried out espionage found themselves held in one of the blocks of the Aylesbury Inebriate Reformatory.[46] They included Milly Rocker, arrested because of her anarchist political beliefs.[47] Hildegard Burnyeat, the German-born widow of the former MP for

Whitehaven, also spent time here, because in August 1915 'Strange bright lights were seen on the coast near Whitehaven, Parton and Harrington, in the course of which the Germans claimed to have destroyed the benzol factory.' Much 'indignation' and 'resentment' arose in the vicinity, and Mrs Burnyeat essentially got the blame, especially as the daughter of German colonel and regarded as pro-German. She faced imprisonment on what seems to have been circumstantial evidence, but the Home Secretary released her the following year for the sake of her sanity.[48]

One of the most unusual camps was the German Industrial and Farm Colony at Libury Hall near Ware in Hertfordshire, originally established in September 1900 as a home for those German males who found themselves facing economic hardship in England. By 1914 it had assisted 5,073 Germans, with 150 living here at the outbreak of war.[49] In many ways Libury Hall constituted a ready-made place of concentration which did not have the early teething problems faced by other localities, such as unsuitable accommodation. It seems to have become an internment camp in early 1915. It housed a significant percentage of residents beyond military age who did not wish to return to Germany and people who had lived here before the war, some of whom still resided here with their families after 1914. The internees seem to have totalled between 150 and 200, although this figure excludes about ten pensioners and ten colonists, as well as a staff of around twelve.[50]

The Isle of Man

The true symbol of First World War internment in Britain is Knockaloe, with the same significance for this experience that Auschwitz has for the Nazi murder of European Jewry[51] or, perhaps more aptly, that Ruhleben has for the German incarceration of Britons during the Great War.[52] Although the camp at Douglas slightly predated the one at Knockaloe, the latter grew much larger and tens of thousands of prisoners passed through it during the course of the war.

Douglas emerged from ready-made accommodation in the form of Cunningham's holiday camp, which had come into existence during the 1890s and, in the years leading up to the outbreak of war, housed male campers in bell tents. When the war broke out, 2,800 men were holidaying here, 2,000 of whom joined the army almost immediately, together with 153 from the 200 employees.[53] Following the visit of the Destitute Aliens Committee, the camp 'was transformed almost overnight. A double row of barbed wire fencing was put up around the grounds and lamps were installed to light the compounds at night'.[54] The first batch of 203 prisoners arrived on 22 September 1914, followed by a second group two days later. The initial consignment 'comprised men of all classes of society, from apparently prosperous merchants to sailors and waiters . . . A large amount of luggage belonging to the prisoners was brought over.'[55] Further boatloads of internees followed over the following weeks from a variety of locations, above all Liverpool, although they originated from temporary camps such as those at Frimley and Edinburgh, so that by the beginning of 1915 around 3,000 men lived here.[56] On 19 November 1914 a serious riot had occurred in the camp, leading the authorities to open fire and kill five of the prisoners.[57]

Despite these events, the camp survived until the end of the war, and the number of internees averaged between about 2,200 and 2,800. As late as 16 February 1919 a total of 1,354 still lived here, awaiting repatriation. Some men may have spent almost five years in Douglas, but the population appears to have changed quite regularly because prisoners moved into and out of places of internment, especially between Douglas and Knockaloe, mirroring the picture in many of the mainland camps. The Douglas camp journal reveals the extent to which movement between camps occurred. In January 1915, for instance, indicating the rate at which Knockaloe expanded, over 550 moved there from Douglas, while the Home Secretary released almost 70. During the summer of 1916 we can see the following movements: 10 went to Hackney Wick on 1 July, 19 to Feltham on 5 July, 21 to Knockaloe on 18 July and 62 to Stratford on 1 August. Reflecting the make-up of the enemy alien population in Britain at the outbreak of war, the majority of the internees in Douglas were Germans, with some Austrians and a handful of Turks. Thus, in May 1917 the 2,604 prisoners consisted of 1,914 Germans, 709 Austrians, 10 Turks and 7 people of 'other nationalities'.[58]

The internees initially lived in the bell tents used to house the holidaymakers before the outbreak of war, but standardized huts replaced these fairly quickly, although some of the prisoners appeared to have preferred living in tents into 1917. Douglas was divided into two separate compounds by early 1915, the 'ordinary' camp and the privilege camp. Most prisoners lived in the first of these, in huts holding between 110 and 120 men each.[59] Despite the fact that fewer people lived in the privilege camp, it attracted much attention after some journalists visited Douglas in 1916. The following account indicates the reality, despite the rather elaborate language used:

> Of the 2,700 prisoners, 400 or 500 are privilege prisoners. By paying 10s a week two or three may secure a small, separate hut between them, and by paying £1 a week one may have his own tent or hut. Other privileges follow. They are allowed to have their own servants, and about a hundred other prisoners, who, of course, make their own bargain, are employed in this capacity. They may have two bottles of beer or one bottle of light wine each day.

The article suggested that the camp resembled Bond Street because 'you may be shampooed by barbers who learnt their business in Paris and Berlin', buy a tweed suit made by somebody actually trained in Bond Street or even sit for a portrait. The writer contrasted this with the picture in Ruhleben.[60]

The availability of such services reflects the pre-war professions of some of the internees, as well as the fact that they had developed sophisticated artistic and cultural activities. Despite the apparent idleness and luxury suggested by this portrait, up to 85 per cent of those held at Douglas may have carried out paid employment by 1916. At the same time, the prisoners played a significant role in camp administration, even establishing a police force at one stage.[61]

In addition to the ordinary and privilege camps at Douglas, there was special provision for Jewish internees. They do not appear to have had a separate camp as such, despite an assertion in one Swiss Embassy report about one. This mentioned that the Jewish prisoners appreciated 'the facilities accorded to them by the camp authorities for the observance of their religion', referring especially to cooking,[62] which was assisted by a Committee for the Supply of Kosher Food to Interned Jews, which also serviced Alexandra Palace.[63] By 1916 the kosher kitchen, originally established in 1914, had 'been greatly extended, is very well managed and is under the supervision of a Rabbi and a special Shomer (supervisor): 4 cooks are employed and supply daily meals to over 500 people.'[64]

While Douglas may have begun to take prisoners earlier than its sister camp on the Isle of Man, Knockaloe quickly overshadowed it and developed into a small town populated entirely by men. It covered the grounds of a farm, Knockaloe Moar, which had previously served as 'a camping ground for up to sixteen thousand territorial reserves'.[65] The first prisoners arrived on 17 November 1914. Although it was initially intended for 5,000 internees, a figure it had reached by the end of May 1915, the total shot up as a result of the wholesale internment of males of military age following the *Lusitania* riots, reaching a peak of perhaps 24,000, including staff, and remaining at over 20,000 for much of 1915 and 1916. This figure would decline from 1917, but only gradually, as the last prisoners did not leave until 10 October 1919.[66] By this time, advertisements had appeared in the press, announcing that the camp was up for sale as 'surplus government property'.[67]

Many prisoners simply passed through Knockaloe. Between 17 November 1914 and 31 December 1917 30,835 men entered the camp and 12,374 left it.[68] Those passing through included Carl Hermann, a musician captured upon the *Potsdam*, whose internment history included not simply a spell in Knockaloe but also two periods in Handforth and periods in the German Hospital in London, an unnamed workhouse, Stratford and Dorchester.[69] Cohen-Portheim transferred here from Stratford. 'My first impressions of Stratford had been sickening; my first impression on seeing Knockaloe Camp in daylight was one of delighted surprise.' Nevertheless, he applied for transfer to Wakefield and had his request fulfilled. Cohen-Portheim described the prisoners at Knockaloe as 'a motley crowd' and 'quite cosmopolitan'. Those in his circle included Schulz, born in Mexico, who could speak only Spanish, and 'an extremely black negro', an Ottoman citizen. Both had been arrested on board ship. Cohen-Portheim also befriended a Bolshevik and a young man who could speak only English.[70] A similar character protested to journalists visiting Knockaloe in July 1916: 'I ain't no bloomin 'Un; I come from the smoke.'[71] The more obvious Germans included Karl von Scheidt and Fritz Meyer, originating on the *Potsdam* and brought to Knockaloe in June 1916, after spending a year in Alexandra Palace, and finally departing in April 1918.[72] Similarly, Karl Schonwalder came here from Handforth.[73] Despite Cohen-Portheim's assertions of cosmopolitanism, which certainly contain truth, the vast majority of the prisoners consisted of citizens of the states with which Britain found

Figure 3.3 Knockaloe. This is one of the many illustrations produced by some of the tens of thousands of civilians who spent time in this camp, which would last for almost five years.

itself at war. Thus, a Swiss Embassy report of 29 November 1917 listed 15,773 Germans, 2,450 Austrians, 64 Turks, 22 Bulgarians and 134 others.[74]

The scale of Knockaloe struck both contemporary observers and subsequent commentators. Scheidt and Meyer described it accurately as a 'prisoner town' in a 'valley basin' surrounded by hills and close to the Irish Sea and the small town of Peel. They also pointed out that the Isle of Man itself stretched to only thirty-three miles in length and twelve miles in breadth. Just as interestingly, the island had a resident population of only 52,000, and that the city of Douglas was 21,000, which meant that the camp exceeded the size of the capital during much of 1916 and 1917.[75] Margery West has more recently calculated that the camp covered 22 acres, within which over 23,000 people lived, and had a perimeter fence of 695 miles of barbed wire and three miles of internal roads.[76]

Such a large camp could function only if broken down into smaller units, and it actually operated as four separate camps, each one simply designated by its number and subdivided into compounds. At its height in 1916 it had a total of twenty-three compounds, divided in the following way: Camp I had seven; Camp

II had five; Camp III had six; Camp IV had five. Each compound could take up to 1,000 men.[77] The camps and the compounds within them operated as autonomous units with their own sub-commandants and deputies. Visitors from the United States and Swiss Embassies counted the populations of the individual camps separately. Thus in May 1917 the following figures emerged: Camp I numbered 5,913 internees; Camp II, 4,279; Camp III, 4,741; and Camp IV, 5,481. The same report also pointed out: 'The four camps are entirely divided from one another and their inmates are not allowed to communicate with each other. Camps III and IV are on the higher ground.' Even the compounds within each of the sub-camps remained 'separated one from the other by barbed wire fences. The inmates of these compounds cannot communicate without special permits, which are usually given.' Each compound had its own kitchen and also developed its own recreational activities.[78] Each camp also had a hospital, which employed eight doctors together with forty German attendants in May 1916. In addition there was 'an Isolation Hospital for contagious diseases, situated at a distance from the camps'.[79]

The prisoners lived in wooden huts 'of the regular War Office pattern of 30 feet by 15 feet, each section holding thirty men. Six huts are placed together, and each hut is capable of accommodating 180 men. They are provided with trestle-tables and chairs for each group of men, and each man has a bed board, mattress and three blankets.'[80] In these spaces the internees would 'sleep, eat, work, play, chat and smoke'.[81] Nevertheless, because of the dampness of the climate, but also the fairly basic nature of the huts, waterproofing proved problematic.[82] One internee in Camp II commented that the huts and the 'streets' between them 'were wittily christened' with patriotic-sounding names such as Kaiser Wilhelm Strasse, Postdamer Platz (where the post office lay), Hotel Emden and Zeppelin Villa.[83]

'The great problem of the camps is the provision of suitable employment',[84] although during the course of the conflict some internees obtained paid work, while others participated in the sophisticated entertainment and educational activities which emerged. In addition, a complex series of committees developed whereby the prisoners helped to run both the camp as a whole and each of the sub-camps. In the first place there appear to have existed both camp and compound leaders. At the same time a whole range of overarching committees, responsible for activities throughout Knockaloe, also emerged to cover relief, kitchens, prisoners' aid, sports, industry, education, a library, medical issues, dramatic activities and a sick and burial board. One prisoner produced a 'Final Report and Statistical Record on the Internal Administration of the Prisoners of War Camp No. IV, 1915–1919'. An annual report from 1916 listed all of the committees and the various social and leisure clubs which existed, drawing up a complex diagram outlining the relationships between the different bodies, together with a hierarchy of the camp administration and a list of the individuals who ran the sections.[85]

Military camps

None of the military camps grew to quite the size of Knockaloe, although a few had an equally long history, beginning, in some cases, as holding points for both combatants and civilians at the outbreak of war, but then evolving into purely military camps. Some of these would simply house officers. The prisons for combatants numbered hundreds, especially if the work camps are counted among them.[86] Rather than outlining all of them, we can simply glance at some of the longest-lasting, together with those for which the most information survives.

While this study focuses upon those German military prisoners brought to Britain, we need to acknowledge the fact that the British held some captives in northern France, where several camps evolved including Rouen, Le Havre and Dieppe. Close to the front line and essentially forming part of labour battalions, the few thousand men who found themselves in these camps endured difficult conditions, partly because the British retaliated against the treatment of their own by the German army.

The German prisoners held in camps on British soil endured more humane conditions than their counterparts in France.[87] One of the first of these utilized the building of the Royal Horse Artillery barracks in Dorchester. By November 1914, it held 950 men, a total made up of soldiers and people taken from ships, including Bruno Schmidt-Reder, brought here from the *Potsdam*, although he had returned home by the end of the year. By this time the inmates had developed their own educational and sporting activities, which would become quite sophisticated during the course of

Figure 3.4 Dorchester. This was one of the longest-lasting camps, initially accommodating a mixture of civilian and military prisoners but subsequently developing into a military establishment.

the conflict.[88] The camp would survive until 1919, during which time it essentially held military captives. It appears to have reached a peak figure of 4,407 in April 1919, when it included 49 Austrians, 152 from the German navy and 2 airmen. The number fluctuated around 3,000 for much of the war. Few officers ever seem to have spent time here. The expansion in the numbers of captives had meant the erection of huts, as the old military quarters proved insufficient. Many of the internees worked by the end of the war, when Dorchester became a hub for several working camps, mostly in southern England, whose number had reached 130 by April 1919.[89] Most of the visitors to Dorchester essentially agreed with Robert Cecil's assessment of it as 'a very satisfactory camp'.[90]

Handforth had a similar history to Dorchester in that it also began by holding a mixture of civilian and military internees, the former of which had disappeared by 1916. Numbers hovered between 2,000 and 3,000, although in their account two prisoners drew up a table to demonstrate that between October 1915 and November 1919 a total of 20,240 men had entered Handforth, while 16,312 had left, the latter figure also including transfers to a variety of other camps, especially 'branch camps', eighteen deaths and other internees who went out to work for a variety of employers, especially farmers. L. Bögenstätter and H. Zimmermann, who compiled these figures, appear to have spent over four years here. They described this location as a 'mass camp' because of its use of a factory, which, in fact, had never operated. It appears to have been divided into forty-five rooms varying from 450 to 2,300 square metres. The inhabitants consisted of both privates and officers. Its duration meant that it developed a sophisticated cultural life. Although some post-war German reports criticized the conditions in Handforth, the Swiss Embassy accounts do not support this view.[91]

The camp at Leigh in Lancashire also used the site of a factory constructed just before the outbreak of war. The first prisoners arrived before the end of 1914, and further batches would follow regularly during the course of the conflict until it closed in June 1919, when the final fifty internees departed. In September 1916 it held 1,357 men, of whom thirty-five had served in the German navy. Another 457 nominally attached to Leigh found themselves employed in working camps connected to it. By this time the accommodation consisted of seven dormitories. Social activities here included gardening, two theatre companies, two orchestras, handball and bowling, while both Roman Catholic and Protestant services took place. As elsewhere the prisoners assisted with the cooking. A report in the *Manchester Guardian* from July 1916 described Leigh as 'a military camp for the German rank and file'. It claimed that 'the prisoners seem to thrive' on the rations available and that 'in a camp where the great majority of the men were captured in the earlier stages of the war, and presumably belonged to the first line, the physique was of high standard'. Although they came from 'all parts of Germany', they included 'many Brandenburgers', while 'the average age would perhaps work out to 28' with 'probably not more than a dozen' over forty.[92]

Pattishall (or Eastcote) camp, which lay between Pattishall and Eastcote near Towcester in Northamptonshire, appears to have opened by the end of 1914 and survived until 1919. Its origins remain obscure, but the living quarters consisted of standard huts. It appears to have initially held civilians until 1916, but at some stage during late 1916 it also held military internees, and by the following year it had become a military camp, when it also changed

Figure 3.5 Pattishall. This was a long-lasting camp, near Towcester in Northamptonshire, which would become a primarily military establishment and also the headquarters for several working camps connected to it.

its name from Eastcote to Pattishall. Although just 660 civilians lived here in February 1916, the number of soldiers totalled 4,509 in May 1919, including 1,000 non-commissioned officers. It was eventually divided into four compounds. Because of its longevity, it developed a wide range of social, cultural, religious and sporting activities.[93] By 1917 it had become a parent camp to thirty working camps spread throughout the Midlands and beyond, and it continued to serve this function into 1918 and 1919.[94]

The camp at Brocton in Staffordshire, which first opened in April 1917, utilized the site of an old factory and received much criticism from German sources. It held around 5,000 prisoners during 1918 and 1919. During its existence it served both as a transit point for those awaiting repatriation or transfer to a neutral state and as a parent camp for other working establishments in the area. It also had an important hospital attached to it. The complaints focused upon the poor quality of the housing and a draconian commandant.[95]

Another long-standing camp emerged in Jersey, initially opened in March 1915 for combatant prisoners and then closed in September 1917 when the prisoners faced transfer to England. It re-opened in April 1918, when it held German non-commissioned officers. One United States Embassy report from 27 April 1916 asserted that the 'camp seemed to be almost a model of its kind and the men appeared to be in extraordinary good physical condition'. The visitor commented on the availability of work, internal organization and social activity. At this time it held 1,197 German prisoners, 314 of them from the navy. In February 1919 the camp numbered 1,098 Germans. A Swiss Embassy report commented: 'Not a single complaint was brought forward while the prisoners spontaneously expressed their appreciation for the way in which they were being treated and the general conditions of this camp.'[96]

'Donington Hall is the most-talked-of all the internment camps', and to 'go by all we read about it for weeks in English papers it should have been Paradise', although 'none of this was true'.[97] Sections of the press and parliamentary opinion, however, focused upon the apparent luxury enjoyed by the officers who spent time in this camp near Derby,[98] opened in February 1915. One of the reasons for this assertion was the fact that it consisted of a large stately house set in 900 acres of countryside, 600 of which the prisoners could use. Although many lived in the house itself, others found themselves in huts in the grounds, which held sixteen or seventeen officers each. Those living within the stately home shared the bedrooms, which held between two and twelve officers each in May 1917; at this time the camp contained approximately 300 internees, although by 1919 the total number had reached over 500. A range of ranks lived here. In April 1918, the German internees included eighteen naval lieutenants, five majors, ten captains and 342 lieutenants from the army and one medical captain, together with thirteen Austrian military lieutenants and one Turkish naval commander. In addition, 117 'orderlies' lived here. During the course of the war this worked out to a ratio of about one servant to five officers. The officers paid these men, presumably out of the four shillings per day they could receive from the British government under the Hague Convention, which also meant that they could purchase superior food and drinks from the canteen.

Although the objective comments on Donington Hall made by those who visited it did not describe it as luxurious,[99] most observers regarded it as superior to the nearby officers' camp in Kegworth in Derbyshire. This lay just six miles away and utilized 'a collection of structures, built solidly and substantially of brick', originally intended for an agricultural college. It held 531 officers and 142 orderlies in April 1918.[100]

The officers' camp in Holyport, Berkshire, utilized a disused boys' military boarding school near Maidenhead from some stage in 1915. Together with the officers, orderlies also lived here, totalling 125 and 42 respectively in December 1915, and 517 and 150 in June 1919. Some of the officers shared bedrooms in the house, while others lived in huts erected outside; huts also served as accommodation for orderlies, although they remained separate. Both visitors and residents commented positively on Holyport, particularly on the sporting activity available and the quality of food which officers could purchase. Gunther Plüschow, who spent some time here between stays in Dorchester and Donington Hall, wrote that 'the treatment in the camp was good'. The food, however, 'was purely English' and therefore 'hardly palatable to the majority of Germans'. But he liked 'the bi-weekly appearance of an excellent tailor' and a haberdasher.[101]

The first officers' camp was Dyffryn Aled in North Wales, which utilized an old country house and held fewer than 100 officers, together with their orderlies. A Swiss Embassy report of January 1918 commented favourably on conditions, although some of those who stayed here earlier criticized the treatment they endured. Dr Kirsche of the German navy, held here from 2 September 1914 to 26 June 1915, commented on the bad hygiene and claimed that urine leaked from the toilets into a dining room below. Another prisoner who spent eleven months here during 1915 and 1916 focused especially upon the commandant, whom he described as 'a complete German hater' who took every opportunity to cause problems for the internees.[102]

Three officers' camps also emerged in North Yorkshire in the latter stages of the war, in Ripon, Colsterdale and Skipton. The first of these used concrete huts containing twenty-eight prisoners each and housed a total 675 German officers and 219 of their compatriots as orderlies in February 1919. Conditions remained cold and wet within the huts, while complaints emerged about the hygiene. Forty-five officers died as a result of influenza. Those who spent time here included J. Machner, who described the sophisticated social activities which developed. Arriving here on 6 October 1918, he did not depart until the very end of December 1919.[103] The camp in Colsterdale opened in April 1917 and utilized huts. Covering an area of 31 hectares, it was 'surrounded as usual by barbed wire'. In June 1917 370 officers and 143 privates, including orderlies, lived here. Colsterdale was divided into a north camp and a south camp, which remained separate from each other.[104] Some of those held here were transferred to a newly established camp in Skipton, which had previously served several regiments in the British army and therefore had ready-made huts. It began to take German officers and their subordinates in January 1918. Those who arrived here included Fritz Sachse and Paul Nikolaus Cossmann, who described the layout of the camp and the construction of the huts. They would remain until October 1918, during which time a rich social life would develop. In June 1918 the camp held 300 German officers and 109 soldiers who acted as their servants.[105]

Clearly a vast number of camps held German soldiers and officers in First World War Britain. While some of these emerged from civilian establishments that opened at the start of the conflict, others came into existence from scratch in the final two years of the war. Despite the claims of luxury put forward by the British press about officers' camps, especially Donington Hall, most of those who lived in converted schools and stately homes and shared rooms and accommodation, admittedly with people of their own class, and did not experience the sort of bourgeois and upper-class privacy which characterized their lives before 1914. Most officers lived in huts, even in places such as Donington Hall, Holyport and Sandhill Park near Taunton, another stately home, which held officers during 1917 and 1918 but which received much criticism from inmates.[106] But these officers did live in relative luxury, especially in comparison to the men they commanded, whom they used as their servants. The fact that they received payment alleviated their position further.

Military hospitals

All camps had access to a doctor, and those which held a significant number of prisoners or which lasted for any length of time also contained infirmaries, which essentially treated those prisoners who became ill while in Britain, although a hospital at the camp in Brocton contained 1,000 beds and also treated those who sustained injuries on the battlefield.[107] In addition, several hospitals looked after Germans wounded in France. A German report of 1916 listed twenty-eight places of internment which contained hospitals, including some of those which had existed in camps such as the ships moored off the south coast, which no longer operated. The list also pointed out the faults of each of these hospitals.[108] A German Red Cross report from January 1916 listed ten military hospitals in use at the time, focusing upon London and the south of England.[109] They included the two about which most information has survived, Lower Southern Hospital in Dartford and the Nell Lane Hospital in Manchester. Other important establishments which cared for German prisoners included the Belmont Hospital in Surrey, which had space for 875 patients in July 1917, and the Fulham War Hospital, with beds for 318 in May 1917.[110]

The hospital for prisoners in Dartford appears to have begun operating in the early stages of the war and initially took in all wounded German soldiers, who found themselves in hospital with Englishmen. In March 1916 civilian internees also went to Dartford. The hospital utilized huts made out of corrugated iron, which had originally been used for patients following a smallpox outbreak fifteen years previously. By 1917 the hospital had grown to thirty wards and could take 1,036 patients serviced by 16 doctors, 2 matrons, 45 nurses, 2 masseuses and 152 British attendants. The seventy-four deaths which occurred from June 1916 until February 1917 resulted largely from wounds sustained on the battlefield. The number of people admitted increased as the war progressed, totalling 3,726 in all by 17 July 1917. Soldiers, officers and privates had separate wards. Although the Swiss Embassy reporters wrote positively about conditions in Dartford, many of those who spent time here subsequently produced critical accounts. Lieutenant Bötefür, who came here in December 1915, wrote of the poor quality of the food; the inadequate heating, which meant that the temperature of his room fell to around 5 degrees Centigrade; the weak lighting; and the medical treatment, focusing upon the lack of availability of the doctor and the handling of those with wounds and further detailing the experience of a soldier with a burst appendix. A report in the *Frankfurter Zeitung* criticized the hygiene here. A Lieutenant Beck claimed that the doctors operated on him on fifteen different occasions, leading to the removal of his right shoulder joint, which meant that he could no longer move his right arm. These types of complaint seem to have ceased towards the end of the war, suggesting that conditions in Dartford had improved.[111]

The Nell Lane Military Hospital in Didsbury, Manchester, lay on the site of a former workhouse and infirmary and began to take in prisoners of war in August 1916. In June 1917 they had sixty-six wards set aside for them with accommodation for 1,665 patients. Most patients came here for surgery. Swiss Embassy reports commented favourably upon conditions, although a staff surgeon who had spent time here and returned to Berlin in 1919 commented particularly unfavourably upon the treatment of 'mental patients'.[112]

German prisoners also received treatment in Lewisham Hospital, which before the war 'was a regular civilian hospital' but began to take in casualties from the middle of 1917. The number of Germans held here remained small and never seems to have exceeded 160. Officers and privates used separate wards. Although Swiss Embassy reports about conditions here painted a positive picture,[113] one German wrote that 'unbelievable dirtiness ruled'. He also claimed that the attendants mistreated the patients and stole from them.[114]

Working camps

As the number of military prisoners of war increased towards the end of the war, the British government, through the Ministry of National Service, utilized the labour power of rank and file troops, who were allowed to work under the Hague Convention, unlike civilians and officers. In the autumn of 1916 the Prisoners of War Employment Committee came into existence to facilitate and coordinate this task. The numbers working increased from the 3,832 of September 1916 to 27,760 by December 1917, reaching a peak of 66,853 (including 1,356 civilians) in December 1918 and falling back to 34,000 by August of the following year.[115] Because they worked in a wide variety of occupations, especially in agriculture, from 1917 Germans spent time in small camps scattered throughout the country, rather than in the larger establishments which may have existed for years. These developed rapidly, in many cases emerging from camps made up of bell tents, which were followed by the standardized huts used throughout the country, often constructed by the prisoners. They often had a short life as some of them simply accommodated prisoners carrying out a particular task which needed an immediate supply of labour. Working camps usually had an affiliation to one of the established places of internment, such as Stobs, Dorchester, Brocton and Pattishall. Frongoch had a total of twenty working camps attached to it in June 1919 employing 1,111 people, together with another 228 prisoners affiliated to it as 'migratory gangs', who were essentially involved in agricultural work.[116]

Stobs also had a large number of working camps. Although most of these lay in Scotland, others as far away as Lincolnshire also seem to have had a relationship with it. Thus a Swiss Embassy report pointed out that Belton Park, near Grantham, had opened in April 1917 and was 'dependent upon Stobs'. Prisoners in this short-lived camp lived in bell tents and were 'employed by the Government in constructive and quarrying work'.[117] Some of the other working camps affiliated to Stobs lay closer to it in the Scottish Borders and County Durham, but most were situated in Scotland.[118] These included Kinlochleven, opened in spectacular highland countryside in September 1916 'in a valley in the hills at the head of Lochleven'. The prisoners here originally lived in Handforth before being transferred to Stobs and subsequently to Kinlochleven. Probably because of the hard physical nature of the work, the internees complained about food rations, clothing and bathing facilities. By the following summer Kinlochleven had become a more permanent structure housing 890 men in wooden huts, with well-developed bathing facilities and a kitchen committee, although the prisoners still complained about the rations. The men worked for Balfour Beatty in 'constructing an additional water plant for the British Aluminium Co', which involved heavy digging.[119] Stobs also had a relationship with a camp on the Isle of Raasay, next to Skye, opened in June 1916. Most of the 280 prisoners here carried out iron ore mining, of which 100 had previous experience, and they lived in thirty-three concrete houses, surrounded by barbed wire, formerly inhabited by British civilian miners. The prisoners did not depart until the middle of 1919.[120]

Dorchester had a whole series of agricultural camps affiliated to it from 1916. For example, three opened in late 1918 and early 1919 at Cumnor in Berkshire and Charlbury and Enstonne in Oxfordshire. These indicate the scale and nature of many of the places which now held Germans, utilizing farmhouses and holding between thirty and forty prisoners.[121] Other camps affiliated to Dorchester existed in Blandford, Milldown, Louds Hill,

Stowell, Glastonbury, Itton, Usk, Abergavenny, Bwlch, Brecon, Talgarth, Abbeydore and Churchdown, in an area stretching from south-west England to South Wales. These again were small camps employing people in agricultural work.[122] The prisoners in Witney in Oxfordshire lived in the 'eight rooms of various sizes on the second and third floors' of the Fleece Hotel, while those in nearby Woodstock occupied 'the premises of the local drill hall, a large concrete building of recent construction, admirably suited to its present purpose'; the 'prisoners' beds are arranged in two parallel rows down one side of the hall while tables and benches occupy the other'. Internees in both camps 'were employed as ploughmen by farmers of the district'.[123]

Brocton also had significant numbers of camps affiliated to it as far away as Cambridgeshire. Kelham, Carlton-on-Trent, Ossington and Halam in Nottinghamshire all opened in the spring of 1918 and, a year later, held 127 prisoners between them. The accommodation varied: Kelham used 'an old brick factory', Carlton-on-Trent 'a disused malting factory', and Ossington 'the stable buildings of Ossington Hall', while Halam 'formed part of Halam House, a pleasant country residence'.[124] One Swiss Embassy report of 25 June 1919 commented on the camps at Plumtree, Eastlake, Woodborough, Papplewick and Norton.[125] Another from 11 February 1919 mentioned Hallowell Grange and Guilsborough in Northamptonshire and Ilston Grange and Thorpe Satchville in Leicestershire.[126] Kilburn Hall in Derbyshire, previously 'a pleasant country residence . . . is well situated in open country surrounded by pasture land, large orchards, pleasure grounds, kitchen garden'. The sixty prisoners here at the end of 1917 lived in outhouses and 'were employed by the Tarmac Company Limited in breaking up slag for road making', although others subsequently carried out agricultural work.[127] Meanwhile the 107 prisoners at a camp in Burton-on-Trent were 'employed in finishing the construction of a factory and in general labour', although this establishment also served as the 'headquarters' for five other camps.[128]

Finally, Pattishall also acted as a parent site for numerous other camps in Northamptonshire, Bedfordshire, Buckinghamshire, Kent, Sussex, Surrey, Essex, Norfolk and Lincolnshire.[129] Once again, many of these were farms which employed small numbers of Germans to carry out agricultural work, such as those at Horsham, Wisborough Green and Midhurst, all in Sussex, and Cranleigh in Surrey, which housed respectively 25, 40, 40 and 50 military internees in accommodation which did 'not fall short of the high standard almost invariably found in agricultural camps'. Despite the small numbers of people involved in most of the working camps, including these, they included an interpreter who came from among the prisoners.[130] A much larger camp in Kenninghall in Norfolk held 394 prisoners 'employed on agricultural work, cleaning rivers, timber felling, in gravel pits and on engineering work under the Royal Engineers'.[131] Even larger was the 'temporary camp' at Richborough in Kent, which held 1,459 military and twenty-two naval prisoners in September 1917 and was 'situated in flat lowland country on the left bank of the river Stour, two miles north of the town of Sandwich and about 1 mile west of the sea'. The flatness of the land caused problems with drainage. Virtually all of the men here lived under canvas, with ten or eleven in each tent. Conditions here were 'camp style' when it came to sanitation, drinking water and cooking. The prisoners were 'employed by the "Inland Water and Docks Department" of the Royal Engineers, in general work "pertaining to hut and camp construction"'.[132] Meanwhile, Rochford in Essex opened in June 1917 for non-commissioned officers from Pattishall who had volunteered for agricultural work 'because they could no longer bear the idleness of Pattishall and because they were engaged by the month'.[133]

Hundreds of other working camps which seem to have been independent also emerged in the latter stages of the War. Many of these consisted of bases for agricultural labourers, often in farmhouses of various sizes or in standard huts. A Swiss Embassy report of 19 June 1918 covered seventeen different establishments in Norfolk, which were visited in three different groups. The first group consisted of Lakenham, which occupied 'part of the premises of an old disused mill', Long Stratton and Aldborough, which used 'a large Temperance Hall'. They held 22, 40 and 20 German prisoners respectively, while a description of Honig wrote of 11 German military prisoners in a 'migratory gang', which also became a common phenomenon. 'The headquarter camp at Lakenham provides the rations for the prisoners of war and the escort guard which consist of 2 men. The prisoners, however, come from Burnham Market', another place of incarceration in Norfolk.[134] Graycombe House near Pershore in Worcestershire held 100 German soldiers in December 1917. The prisoners lived in the building and several outhouses 'situated in a large compound surrounded by fields, orchards, kitchen garden'. The eight dormitories held between six and sixteen men. 'The prisoners are employed in agricultural work by the farmers and fruit growers of the district.'[135]

But prisoners also found employment in numerous non-agricultural tasks and lived in accommodation near their place of work. Rothwell in Northamptonshire started off as a camp providing agricultural labourers, but some of the prisoners here worked in an ironstone quarry. They lived in wooden huts.[136] Meanwhile, the 343 prisoners held in Banbury in October 1918 carried out a large variety of tasks including the laying of rail tracks, the making of bridges, quarrying and farming. Those in Stanhope in County Durham worked in limestone quarrying, while prisoners in Orfordness in Suffolk found themselves constructing an aerodrome.[137]

The extent of the camp system

During the First World War Britain developed a vast and complex system of internment camps, which incarcerated hundreds of thousands of civilians and combatants. The geographical spread of these camps meant that no corner of Britain remained untouched, from the Isle of Raasay and Kinlochleven to the Isle of Man and on to the south and east coasts. While some of the older camps may have lasted for four or five years, the numbers of places incarcerating Germans increased dramatically during the latter stages of the war, reflecting the growth in the total prisoner population as a result of German defeats in France, but also the fact that these new military prisoners also provided much needed labour power. Consequently, camps of all sizes sprang up throughout the country in both urban environments and also, more usually, in rural areas. While Knockaloe essentially became a town without women which would hold 20,000 men for almost five years, some of the smaller rural camps which emerged in the closing stages of the war and its immediate aftermath held just a few dozen Germans for a short period of time.

The existence of hundreds of concentration camps required a large bureaucracy. At the top a whole range of government ministries became involved, including the Home Office, War Office, Foreign Office and Ministry of National Service, while quangos also emerged to specifically focus upon prisoners of war. At the same time humanitarian organizations and the United States and Swiss Embassies helped to ensure the fair treatment of the German prisoners. The thousands of British government files which have survived bear testimony to the extent of the camp system. However, relatively few Britons found themselves employed in the internment bureaucracy, either at central government level or on the ground. Part of the reason for this lies in the fact that the camps remained fairly autonomous entities, which, as the example of Knockaloe indicates, could run themselves and did not require large numbers of Britons to become involved. The smaller institutions simply required a commandant, or even a shared commandant and a few guards. Even the 20,000 prisoners at Knockaloe never required more than 300 British personnel.

Notes

1 Paul Cohen-Portheim, *Time Stood Still: My Internment in England* (London, 1931), pp. 68–9.

2 Zygmunt Bauman, *Modernity and the Holocaust* (Cambridge, 1989); Götz Aly and Susanne Heim, *Architects of Annihilation: Auschwitz and the Logic of Destruction* (London, 2003).

3 For a general picture see contributions to Ian F. W. Beckett and Keith Simpson, eds, *A Nation at Arms: A Social Study of the British Army in the First World War* (Manchester, 1985).

4 See, for instance, Trevor Wilson, *The Myriad Faces of War: Britain and the Great War, 1914–1918* (Cambridge, 1986), pp. 215–42, 533–6.

5 Charity and humanitarianism are considered in Chapter 7 below.

6 NA/WO162/341, Report of the Prisoners of War Information Bureau.

7 Ronald F. Roxburgh, *The Prisoners of War Information Bureau* (London, 1915), pp. v, 1–2, 12–15, 18.

8 Richard B. Speed III, *Prisoners, Diplomats, and the Great War: A Study in the Diplomacy of Captivity* (London, 1990), pp. 19–25.

9 The reports have survived in three locations in particular: NA/FO383, BA/R67 and BA/R901.

10 NA/HO45/11025/410118, Report of the Directorate of Prisoners of War, September 1920, p. 5.

11 Ibid., pp. 5–6; NA/FO383/471, War Cabinet, Co-ordination of Work Connected with Prisoners of War, Memorandum by the Secretary of State for War, 5 August 1918; NA/WO32/5376, Précis for the

Army Council No. 483; Hampden Gordon, *The War Office* (London, 1935), p. 313.

12 See, for example, *Hansard* (Commons), fifth series, vol. 70, col. 832, 3 March 1915.

13 B. E. Sargeaunt, *The Isle of Man and the Great War* (Douglas, 1922), pp. 59–79; NA/HO45/11025/410118, Report of the Directorate of Prisoners of War, September 1920, p. 42; MNH/MS1062, List of Camp Staff at Knockaloe and Douglas Alien Detention Camp; MNH/B115/70f, Government Circular No. 581; NA/HO45/10946/266042/1a; NA/HO45/10946/266042/120.

14 IWM, German Prisoners of War in Great Britain, 1914–1918.

15 Gordon, *War Office*, p. 313.

16 The reports can be found in NA/FO383, BA/R67 and BA/901.

17 Tighe Hopkins, *Prisoners of War* (London, 1914), p. 108.

18 British Red Cross Archive, London, Verzeichnis der Kriegsgefangenenlager und Lazerette in Frankreich, Großbritannien, Italien, Russland und Japan, Abgeschlossen am 1. Mai.

19 J. Köhler, ed., *Karte von Grossbritannien, Italien u. den überseeischen Ländern, in denen Kriegs- und Zivilgefangene befinden* (Hamburg, 1917).

20 NA/ADM137/3868, List of All Prisoners of War Camps in England and Wales (with Postal and Telegraphic Addresses).

21 NA/WO162/341, Report of the Prisoners of War Information Bureau.

22 See Chapter 6 below.

23 Köhler, ed., *Karte*.

24 Frederick Lewis Dunbar-Kalckreuth, *Die Männerinsel* (Leipzig, 1940), pp. 160–79.

25 NA/ADM137/3868, List of All Prisoners of War Camps in England and Wales (with Postal and Telegraphic Adresses).

26 Jill Drower, *Good Clean Fun: The Story of Britain's First Holiday Camp* (London, 1982).

27 Rudolf Rocker, *The London Years* (1956; Nottingham, 2005), pp. 149–53; Panikos Panayi, *The Enemy in Our Midst: Germans in Britain during the First World War* (Oxford, 1991), pp. 99–100; *Manchester Guardian*, 20 August 1914.

28 Panayi, *Enemy*, p. 100; *Kölnische Zeitung*, 12 November 1914; Hopkins, *Prisoners*, p. 114; Vereinigung Wissenschaftlicher Verleger, *Deutsche Kriegsgefangene in Feindesland* (Leipzig, 1919), pp. 13–14; BA/R901/83066, Swiss Embassy Visit to Frith Hill, 1 June 1918.

29 Panayi, *Enemy*, p. 100; *Die Eiche*, July 1914.

30 *Daily Mirror*, 22 August 1914.

31 *Scotsman*, 26 August 1914; Stefan Manz, 'Civilian Internment in Scotland during the First World War', in Richard Dove, ed., *'Totally*

un-English'? Britain's Internment of 'Enemy Aliens' in Two World Wars (Amsterdam, 2005), p. 85.

32 Panayi, *Enemy*, pp. 101–2; *Hansard* (Commons), fifth series, vol. 71, cols 385–6, 22 April 1915; Rocker, *London Years*, pp. 154–73; NA/FO383/81, Intercepted Letter from E. G. Müller, Prisoner of War at Wakefield; Speed, *Prisoners*, pp. 98–9; Karl von Scheidt and Fritz Meyer, *Vier Jahre Leben und Leiden der Auslandsdeutschen in den Gefangenenlagern Englands* (Hagen, 1919), pp. 27–34.

33 Panayi, *Enemy*, pp. 106–7; BL, Rudolf Rocker, 'Alexandra Palace Internment Camp in the First World War'; Janet Harris, *Alexandra Palace: A Hidden History* (Stroud, 2005), pp. 63–118; Otto Schimming, *13 Monate hinter dem Stacheldraht: Alexandra Palace, Knockaloe, Isle of Man, Stratford* (Stuttgart, 1919), pp. 7–17; Scheidt and Meyer, *Vier Jahre*, pp. 32–73.

34 Panayi, *Enemy*, pp. 103–4; Cohen-Portheim, *Time Stood Still*, pp. 25–7. See also the complaints about this camp in NA/FO383/163.

35 Panayi, *Enemy*, p. 111; NA/MEPO2/1633; *The Times*, 28 September 1915.

36 NA/FO383/164, US Embassy Visit of 20 October 1916; BA/R901/83106, Swiss Embassy Visits of 13 March and 10 July 1917.

37 Panayi, *Enemy*, p. 102; NA/FO383/31, M. L. Waller to Under Secretary of State, Foreign Office, 20 August 1915.

38 *Manchester Guardian*, 21 August 1914.

39 BA/R67/779, Der Reichkommisar zur Erörterung von Gewaltätigkeiten gegen deutsche Zivilipersonen in Feindesland, 'Vergleich der Berichte des Genfer Roten Kreuzes über die englischen und französischen Sammellager mit den Feststellungen des Reichkommissars', pp. 3–4.

40 See pp. 102–3 below.

41 F. E. Heusel, *Handforth through the Ages* (Chester, 1982), p. 43; Wilhelm Kröpke, *Meine Flucht aus englishcher Kriegsgefangenschaft 1916: Von Afrika über England nach Deutschland zur Flandern-Front* (Flensburg, 1937), p. 21; *National Zeitung*, 4 July 1915; NA/FO383/107, translated extract from *Zürcher Zeitung*, 30 December 1914.

42 *Wakefield Express*, 26 September, 24 October 1914; NA/FO383/163, US Embassy Reports on Wakefield, 25 March, 12 June 1916; NA/FO383/423, Swiss Embassy Reports on Wakefield, 9 March, 24 September 1918; Cohen-Portheim, *Time Stood Still*. pp. 104–9; Peter Wood, 'The Zivilinternierungslager at Lofthouse Park', in Kate Taylor, ed., *Aspects of Wakefield 3: Discovering Local History* (Barnsley, 2001), pp. 97–9; Henning Ibs, *Hermann J. Held (1890–1963): Ein Kieler Gelehrtenleben in den Fängen der Zeitläufe* (Frankfurt, 2000), pp. 38–40; NA/FO383/505, Report on the Transfer of those at

Lofthouse Park Camp near Wakefield Yorkshire to the Isle of Man; Albrecht Hermann Brugger, *Meine Flucht aus dem Kriegsgefangenen-Lager Lofthouse-Park* (Berlin, 1937), pp. 9–11.

43 Panayi, *Enemy*, p. 104; *Scotsman*, 2 November 1914; Judith Murray, 'Stobs Camp, 1903–1959', *Transactions of the Hawick Archaeological Society* (1988), 12–25.

44 BA/R901/83150, Swiss Embassy Report on Stobs, 6 November 1918.

45 NA/HO45/10948/267603; Peter Southerton, *Reading Gaol* (Stroud, 2003), pp. 87–8; NA/FO383/177, US Embassy Report on Brixton, 31 November 1916.

46 Panayi, *Enemy*, p. 112; Tammy Proctor, *Female Intelligence: Women and Espionage in the First World War* (London, 2003), pp. 33, 47–50.

47 Rocker, *London Years*, p. 199.

48 *Daily Express*, 31 July, 18 August 1916.

49 Panikos Panayi, *German Immigrants in Britain during the Nineteenth Century, 1815–1914* (Oxford, 1995), p. 174.

50 NA/HO45/11006/264762; *Reports of Visits of Inspection Made by Officials of the United States Embassy to Various Internment Camps in the United Kingdom* (London, 1916), pp. 17–18; NA/FO383/163, US Embassy Report on Libury Hall, 20 June 1916; NA/FO383/276, Swiss Embassy Report on Libury Hall, 11 May 1917.

51 See, for instance, Robert Jan von Pelt and Deborah Dwork, *Auschwitz: 1270 to the Present* (London, 1996), especially pp. 354–78.

52 Matthew Stibbe, *British Civilian Internees in Germany: The Ruhleben Camp, 1914–18* (Manchester, 2008), pp. 163–83.

53 Drower, *Good Clean Fun*, pp. 7–41.

54 Ibid., p. 41.

55 *Isle of Man Weekly Times*, 26 September 1914.

56 MNH/MS06465/1, Douglas Camp Journal.

57 See Chapter 4 below.

58 NA/FO383/276, Swiss Embassy Report on Douglas, 29 May 1917; MNH/MS06465, Douglas Camp Journal.

59 NA/FO383/276, Swiss Embassy Report on Douglas, 29 May 1917.

60 'British Treatment of Enemy Prisoners: Journalists Visit Manx Camps', *Manx Quarterly*, vol. 17 (October 1916), 73–4. See also *Manchester Guardian*, 19 July 1916.

61 *Reports of Visits of Inspection*, pp. 17–18; NA/FO383/432, Swiss Embassy Report on Knockaloe and Douglas, 11 September 1918; Margery West, *Island at War: The Remarkable Role Played by the Small Manx Nation in the Great War 1914–1918* (Laxey, 1986), p. 90.

62 NA/FO383/432, Swiss Embassy Visit to Knockaloe and Douglas, 11 September 1918.

63 LMA/Acc/2805/4/4/7, 'Committee for the Supply of Kosher Food to Interned Jews: Précis of Present Position', 20 September 1915.
64 LMA/Acc/2805/4/4/19, James John Wolf to E. S. Montefiore, 5 May 1916.
65 Derek Winterbottom, 'Economic History', in John Belchem, ed., *The New History of the Isle of Man*, vol. 5, *The Modern Period, 1830–1999* (Liverpool, 2000), p. 237.
66 MNH/MS09310, Isle of Man Constabulary Archive, Box 5, Daily Return of Prisoners Interned; Pat Kelly, *Hedge of Thorns: Knockaloe Camp, 1915–19* (Douglas, 1993), p. 5.
67 *Daily Express*, 30 May, 9 July 1919.
68 NA/HO45/10947/266042, James Cantlie, Report upon the Conditions of the Internment Camps at Knockaloe, Isle of Man.
69 BA/MA/RM3/5391, Statement by Carl Lausch Hermann, 15 June 1916.
70 Cohen-Portheim, *Time Stood Still*, pp. 33, 47–9, 60–1.
71 *Manchester Guardian*, 19 July 1916.
72 Scheidt and Meyer, *Vier Jahre*, pp. 68, 130.
73 MNH/MS12028, Diary of Karl Berthold Robert Schonwalder, pp. 1–10.
74 NA/FO383/277, Swiss Embassy Report on Knockaloe, 29 November 1917.
75 Scheidt and Meyer, *Vier Jahre*, pp. 70, 73.
76 West, *Island at War*, p. 92.
77 NA/HO45/10947/266042, James Cantlie, Report upon the Conditions of the Internment Camps at Knockaloe, Isle of Man; *Manchester Guardian*, 19 July 1916.
78 NA/FO383/276, Swiss Embassy Report on Knockaloe, 30 May 1917.
79 NA/FO383/163, US Embassy Report on Knockaloe, 18 May 1916.
80 *Reports of Visits of Inspection*, 1916, p. 20.
81 Adolf Vielhauer, *Das englische Konzentrationslager bei Peel (Insel Man)* (Bad Nassau, 1917), p. 2.
82 NA/FO383/432, Swiss Embassy Report on Knockaloe and Douglas, 11 September 1918.
83 BA/MA/MSG200/2277, Schilderungen eines Lederfachmannes.
84 'British Treatment of Enemy Prisoners', p. 73.
85 *Reports of Visits of Inspection*, p. 20; NA/FO383/432, Swiss Embassy Report on Knockaloe and Douglas, 11 September 1918; NA/FO383/162, US Embassy Report on Knockaloe, 8 January 1916; BA/MA/MSG200/2071, Annual Report on the Organization, Functions and Activities of the Committees formed by the Prisoners of War Interned at Camp 4, December 1916; MNH/B115/43q, Final Report

and Statistical Record on the Internal Administration of the Prisoners of War Camp No. IV, 1915–1919.

86 See the full list of those which existed in January 1919 in NA/WO162/341.

87 NA/FO383/185, Correspondence regarding Rouen and Le Havre from June and July 1916; Peter Scott, 'Captive Labour: The German Companies of the BEF, 1916–1920', *Army Quarterly Defence Journal*, vol. 110 (1980), 319–38; Heather Jones, *Violence against Prisoners of War in the First World War: Britain, France and Germany, 1914–1920* (Cambridge, 2011), pp. 231–8.

88 *Scotsman*, 19 November 1914; Bruno Schmidt-Reder, *In England kriegsgefangen! Meine Erlebninsse in dem Gefangenenlager Dorchester* (Berlin, 1915).

89 *Dorchester Mail*, 24 December 1915; BA/R901/83053, US Embassy Visit, 28 February 1916; NA/FO383/276, Swiss Embassy Report, 2 April 1917; NA/FO383/507, Swiss Embassy Report, 7 April 1919.

90 NA/FO383/106, Note of Visits to Prisoners Camps, 2 February 1915.

91 BA/R901/83075, Swiss Embassy Report on Handforth, 27 April 1917; NA/FO383/506, Swiss Embassy Report on Handforth, 18 March 1919; L. Bögenstätter and H. Zimmermann, *Die Welt hinter Stacheldraht: Eine Chronik des englischen Kriegsgefangenlagers Handforth bei Manchester* (Munich, 1921), pp. 3, 26, 30, 32, 34; Vereinigung Wissenschaftlicher Verleger, *Deutsche Kriegsgefangene*, p. 14.

92 Leslie Smith, *The German Prisoner of War Camp at Leigh, 1914–1919* (Manchester, 1986); *Manchester Guardian*, 21 July 1916; NA/FO383/164, US Embassy Report on Leigh, 19 September 1916; BA/R901/83098, Swiss Embassy Report on Leigh, 16 April 1917.

93 Richard Moss and Iris Illingworth, *Pattishall: A Parish Patchwork* (Astcote, 2000), pp. 80–5; NA/FO383/162, US Embassy Report on Eastcote, 14 February 1916; BA/R901/83057, US Embassy Report on Eastcote, 14 April 1916; NA/FO383/276, Visit by R. H. D. Acland to Donington, Kegworth and Pattishall Camps, 16 August 1917; NA/FO383/507, Swiss Embassy Report on Pattishall, 3 May 1919.

94 NA/FO383/277, Swiss Embassy Report on Pattishall, 29 October 1917. Reports on the camps dependent upon Pattishall can be found in BA/R901/83128, BA/R901/83129 and BA/R901/83132.

95 Vereinigung Wissenschaftlicher Verleger, *Deutsche Kriegsgefangene*, pp. 16–20; NA/FO383/432, Swiss Embassy Report on Brocton, 16 March 1918; NA/FO383/431, Swiss Embassy Report on Brocton, 22 January 1918; NA/FO383/507, Swiss Embassy Report on Brocton, 3 April 1919; BA/R67/561, Arthur Weber über den Kriegsgefangenenlager Brocton.

96 T. E. Naisk, 'The German Prisoners of War Camp at Jersey during the Great War, 1914–1918', *Bulletin of the Société Jersiaise*, vol. 15 (1955), 269–80; BA/R901/83081, US Embassy Report on Jersey, 27 April 1916; NA/FO383/505, Swiss Embassy Report on Jersey, 7 February 1919.

97 *Manchester Guardian*, 20 July 1916; Gunther Plüschow, *My Escape from Donington Hall* (London, 1922), p. 178.

98 See Chapter 7 below.

99 *The Times*, 20 July 1916; NA/FO383/164, Response of US Embassy to German Note Verbale of 30 September 1916; NA/FO383/276, Visit by R. H. D. Acland to Donington, Kegworth and Pattishall Camps, 16 August 1917; BA/R901/83052, Swiss Embassy Visit to Donington Hall and Kegworth, 8 August 1918.

100 BA/R901/83095, US Embassy Report on Kegworth, 24 October 1916; BA/R901/83052, Swiss Embassy Report on Donington Hall and Kegworth, 8 August 1918.

101 *Observer*, 19 December 1915; *New York Herald*, 19 December 1915; Plüschow, *Escape*, pp. 171–2; NA/FO383/508, Swiss Embassy Report on Holyport, 1 July 1919.

102 BA/R67/253, DRK, Interner Bericht 69, 10 June 1916; BA/MA/RM3/5377, Bericht des Marine-Assistentarztes Dr Kirsche, 20 July 1915; NA/FO383/431, Swiss Embassy Report on Dyffryn Aled, 17 January 1918.

103 NA/FO383/506, Swiss Embassy Report on Ripon, 19 March 1919; J. Machner, *Gefangenen in England: Erlebnisse and Beobachtungen* (Hildesheim, 1920); Vereinigung Wissenschaftlicher Verleger, *Deutsche Kriegsgefangene*, pp. 26–30.

104 BA/R67/1343, Bericht des Leutenants d. R. Schön; NA/FO383/277, Swiss Embassy Report on Colsterdale, 26 June 1917: BA/R901/83045, Swiss Embassy Report on Colsterdale, 9 October 1918; Fritz Sachse and Paul Nikolaus Cossmann, *Kriegsgefangen in Skipton: Leben und Geschichte deutscher Kriegsgefangenen in einem englischen Lager* (Munich, 1920), pp. 28–34.

105 Geoffrey Rowley, *The Book of Skipton* (Buckingham, 1983), p. 117; Sachse and Cossmann, *Kriegsgefangenen*; BA/R901/83146, Swiss Embassy Report on Skipton, June 1918.

106 NA/FO383/277, Swiss Embassy Report on Sandhill Park, 5 June 1917; NA/FO383/505, Swiss Embassy Report on Sandhill Park, 6 December 1918; BA/R67/1215, Auszugsweise Abschrift eines Berichte des Majors Bek.

107 NA/FO383/277, Swiss Embassy Report on Brocton, 20 June 1917.

108 LBWHS/M1/8/220, Bericht der freiwilligen Krankenpflege über die Vernehmungen bei Gelengenheit des Gefangenenaustausches am 9. Februar 1916 in Aachen.

109 BA/R67/1282, DRK, England, Interner Wochenbericht No. 59, 19 January 1916.
110 NA/FO383/276, Swiss Embassy Report on Fulham War Hospital, 27 April 1917; NA/FO383/276, Swiss Embassy Report on Belmont Hospital, 26 July 1917.
111 NA/FO383/163, Conditions at Lower Southern Hospital, Dartford, 17 August 1916; NA/FO383/276, Swiss Embassy Report on Lower Southern Hospital, 3 February 1917; NA/FO383/277, Swiss Embassy Report on Lower Southern Hospital, 30 July 1917; NA/FO383/432, Swiss Embassy Report on Lower Southern Hospital, 8 March 1918; *Frankfurter Zeitung*, 2 May 1915; BA/R901/84678, Bericht des Kapitänleutenants d. Res. Bötefür über die Erlebnisse während seiner Gefangenschaft, 31 March 1916.
112 BA/R901/83121, Swiss Embassy Report on Nell Lane, 13 June 1917; NA/FO383/506, Swiss Embassy Report on Nell Lane, 19 March 1919; NA/FO383/506, Conditions at the Manchester Military Hospital for German Prisoners, 12 February 1919.
113 NA/FO383/276, Report on Lewisham Military Hospital, 22 May 1917; NA/FO383/277, Report on Lewisham Military Hospital, 4 October 1917; NA/FO383/431, Report on Lewisham Military Hospital, 2 January 1918.
114 See BA/MA/RM3/5399, pp. 53–60.
115 For full details on employment and further information on working camps see Chapter 6 below.
116 NA/FO383/508, Swiss Embassy Report on Frongoch, 27 June 1919.
117 BA/R901/83033, Swiss Embassy Report on Belton Park, 7 June 1917.
118 See the reports in NA/FO383/164 and NA/FO383/277.
119 NA/FO383/164, US Embassy Report on Kinlochleven, 15 September 1916; NA/FO383/277, Swiss Embassy Report on Kinlochleven, 27 June 1917.
120 Laurence and Pamela Draper, *The Raasay Iron Mine: Where Enemies Became Friends* (1990; fifth printing Dingwall, 2007), pp. 15–18, 31; BA/R901/83150, Swiss Embassy Report on the Isle of Raasay, 30 June 1917.
121 NA/FO383/506, Swiss Embassy Report on Cumnor, Charlbury and Enstone, 19 March 1919.
122 See the Swiss Embassy Reports dated 30 April 1919 in NA/FO383/506. See a report of 2 January 1919 in NA/FO383/505 for details of other small camps affiliated to Dorchester.
123 BA/R901/83054, Swiss Embassy Report on Witney and Woodstock, 17 May 1918.
124 NA/FO383/506, Swiss Embassy Report, 24 March 1919.
125 NA/FO383/506.

126 NA/FO383/505.
127 NA/FO383/431, Swiss Embassy Visit to Kilburn Hall, 18 December 1917; NA/FO383/506, Swiss Embassy Report on Kilburn Hall and Denby, 24 March 1919.
128 NA/FO383/506, Swiss Embassy Report on Burton-on-Trent, 21 March 1919.
129 See the reports on camps affiliated to Pattishall in BA/R901/83130.
130 BA/R901/83130, Swiss Embassy Report, 24 May 1918.
131 BA/R901/83130, Swiss Embassy Report on Kenninghall, 10 June 1918.
132 NA/FO383/277, Swiss Embassy Report on Richborough, 4 September 1917.
133 NA/FO383/277, Swiss Embassy Report on Rochford, 4 September 1917.
134 The report on all these camps, dated 19 June 1919, can be found in NA/FO383/507.
135 NA/FO383/431, Swiss Embassy Report on Graycombe House, 4 January 1918.
136 BA/R67/813, Swiss Embassy Report on Rothwell, 19 March 1918.
137 See the Ministry of National Service Reports on these camps in NA/NATS1/1330.

4

Barbed wire disease and the grim realities of internment

> Wer es nicht durchgemacht hat, kan es nict fassen: vier Jahre eingesperrt in einem maessigen Geviert, auf dem weder Grass noch Baueme wachsen, auf dem kein Vogel sein Nest baut, auf dem schwarze Huetten den einzigen Schatten und das einzige Regendach bieten. Vier Jahre Leben erwachsene Männer mit Geisen und Knaben, bunt durcheinander gewürfelt, ohne Unterschied der Bildung, des Standes, der Erziehung, der religiosen and politischen Überzeugung. Vier Jahre ist die Frau aus unserer Kreise verbannt.[1]

Barbed wire disease

Once they arrived in an internment camp German prisoners would have to face the grim realities of internment, which, apart from loss of freedom, included boredom, an all-male society, basic accommodation and repetitive food. Captives reacted in varying ways to their new environment. Those who found the experience most difficult included older middle-class civilians used to their own personal space, who faced some of the longest spells behind barbed wire. Such individuals also had no need to work, which made the passage of time appear slower. Their ability to pay for some luxuries may have alleviated their situation in some ways, but it did not solve the issue of boredom. In contrast, younger working-class Germans, especially those who had grown up in inner-city tenements and had been captured on the battlefield, perhaps coped best with their new situation.[2] Not only did imprisonment in Britain take them away from the conflict zone and place them in living conditions superior to those on the western front, but they could also work, which meant that the issue of boredom did not arise, although separation from families and the all-male society remained.

Many of the civilian internees did not fall into the boredom and subsequent depression consequent upon incarceration because they created a 'prison camp society', to use a phrase coined by John Davidson Ketchum, a professor of psychology at the University of Toronto writing decades after his First World War confinement in Ruhleben. Ketchum asserted that after the British 'settled' there, they took part in a range of activities and formed associations which essentially created a community structure. We might suggest that, although Ketchum also pointed out the deprivations faced by the 'Ruhlebenites', he took a basically positive view of their experience of internment, as they collectively managed to survive it through creating community, a point also emphasized more recently by Matthew Stibbe.[3]

Ketchum tackled the physical health of the prisoners, partly in statistical terms, pointing out that sixty of them in all died out of an average population of 3,500, which meant a low death rate.[4] He also looked at the mental condition of the prisoners. In fact, he devoted just six out of 355 pages to their psychological well-being, pointing to forty-seven breakdowns, three suicides and three attempted suicides. Ketchum divided the prisoners into two types, with Type I consisting of those aged over fifty, for whom depression was 'more or less inevitable under the circumstances', while for those in Type II, mostly aged thirty and under, it 'should have been preventable'.[5]

Ketchum's account concentrates especially on the first two years of the war. His basically positive perspective, explained by his social psychological background and his distance from the events he describes at the time of writing, contrasts with most of the classic accounts of internment in First World War Britain. Ketchum does not deal with the concept of barbed wire disease, which began to circulate in 1917. Dr A. L. Vischer, one of the Swiss Embassy officials who visited the British camps holding Germans, popularized it in a book on the subject, originally published in German in 1918, but subsequently appearing in English in 1919.[6] The explanation for the name of the disease lies in the fact that barbed wire represented a symbol of the prisoner's confinement and unhappiness. 'More than anything else, the barbed wire winds like a thread through his mental processes. With hypnotic gaze his mind's eye is fixed on this obstacle.'[7] A Knockaloe internee emphasized this in a letter of July 1916: 'It is two years now since I am looking through the barbed wire, a stress which sometimes feels unbearable'.[8] Vischer saw psychosis everywhere, claiming that 'very few prisoners who have been over six months in the camp are quite free from the disease'.[9] He recognized that it affected different types of prisoner in varying ways. Civilians felt it most acutely, although he found it 'in military and civilian camps, both amongst officers and men; on the whole, reservists suffer more than regulars'. He claimed that migrants 'with self-reliant characters' who had 'emigrated in order to strike out a new career and develop unrestricted their own individuality' suffered the most. 'To such people restraint comes very much harder than to officers and men who by their barrack life are prepared to some extent to a cramped and herded existence'. At the same time, 'the military prisoner, who loses his liberty in the stress of battle, finds in captivity a rest from his toil'. Vischer also asserted that the 'most favourable conditions are certainly those of the labour camps, where the men are not so thickly aggregated and are engaged in agriculture'.[10] Similarly, Rudolf Rocker's unpublished account of his time in Alexandra Palace, written at the request of the camp sub-commandant, Major Mott, in 1917, included a section on 'camp psychology', where he recognized that the 'social standing of the prisoners before internment' and 'occupations during internment' played a central role in determining their mental condition.[11] Cohen-Portheim, meanwhile, referring to his time in Wakefield, declared that 'Time here really had to be *killed*, for it was the arch-enemy, and everyone tried to achieve this as best he could and according to his nature.'[12] Rocker also pointed to a series of other factors which influenced the mentality of the internees, including food, 'the general camp conditions and treatment of the prisoners', contact with the outside world, especially women, and the duration of captivity.[13]

Vischer identified symptoms of the disease including 'an increased irritability, so that patients cannot stand the slightest opposition and readily fly into a passion'. The internees also had 'difficulty in concentrating on one particular object', which led to restlessness. Vischer also pointed to loss of memory, 'especially as regards names of people and of places with incidents occurring shortly before the outbreak of war'. Those affected 'brood for three or four days without uttering a single word'. Furthermore, they had 'a dismal outlook and a pessimistic view of events around them'. They were 'also inordinately suspicious' and many experienced sleeplessness.[14]

These symptoms do not seem to differ significantly from those of any other form of depression, and it seems tempting to suggest that Vischer was trying to label a new form of psychosis in the age when psychoanalysis had established itself,[15] as most clearly symbolized by the recognition of shell shock.[16] Perhaps in the same way as shell shock became the symbol of those traumatized by First World War conflict, barbed wire disease played the same role for men who could not cope with confinement. Leslie Baily, the biographer of J. T. Baily, who helped to alleviate conditions on the Isle of Man on behalf of the Society of Friends, described the symptoms as 'moroseness, avoidance of others, and an aimless promenading up and down the barbed-wire boundary of the compound, like a wild animal in a cage. The consequences might be insanity, perhaps suicide.'[17]

Vischer did not operate in a vacuum, as several other sources focus upon depression and even use the phrase 'barbed wire disease'. Vischer based many of his conclusions on visits to Knockaloe.[18] The concept of 'Stacheldrahtkrankheit' circulated as early as 1916, indicated by the title of an article which appeared in an internment newspaper published in Wakefield.[19] A letter from a missionary held in Knockaloe, dated 30 September 1916, pointed to 'the serious inroad that the internment has caused on the intellectual powers of many of us'. He wrote of 'the camp disease' and claimed that those who attempted to escape from the Isle of Man suffered from it because anyone 'in his full mental vigour must be aware that he would not have the slightest chance to get away from this island and reach the shores of a friendly country, and knowing the harsh sentences inflicted in the past he would give it thorough consideration before running the risk of still further aggravating his position'.[20] In May 1917 those held in Islington wrote to the Swiss ambassador to bring his attention to 'the rapidly increasing effect of mental depression bordering on desperation which the long and seemingly endless internment is having on the innocently interned civilians', which in some cases had 'resulted in mental derangements, attempts at suicide and worse'.[21] Another unnamed prisoner, who appears to have spent time in Stobs, produced a handwritten account of 'Die Stacheldrahtkrankheit' in 1919, in which he acknowledges the work of Vischer.[22]

Paul Cohen-Portheim produced the most damning and incisive account of barbed wire disease. His narrative stresses the frustrations of a middle-class internee interned for years without trial in an all-male environment with little personal space. He particularly focused upon Wakefield, where he spent the most time.

> There is nothing like it to be found anywhere else. Monks retire to their cells, soldiers have their days or weeks off; here it continues for ever, and the longer it continues the more you suffer from it. No privacy, no possibility of being alone, no possibility of finding *quietude*. It is inhuman, cruel and dreadful to force people to live in closest community for years; it becomes almost unbearable when that community is abnormally composed like that of a prisoners' camp. There are no women, no children, there is no old age and next to no youth there, there is just a casual rabble of men forced to be inseparable. Try to imagine – though it is impossible really to understand without having experienced it – what it means, *never* to be *alone* and *never* to know *quiet*, not for a minute, and to continue for years, and you will begin to wonder that there was no general outbreak of insanity, that there yet remained a difference between lunacy and barbed wire nerves.[23]

In this last sentence, Cohen-Portheim, like other writers both at the time and subsequently, suggests the existence of a collective mood within camps, often influenced by events occurring outside. On a visit to Knockaloe in November 1917, Vischer asserted that 'The mentality varies according to external influences.' For instance, during this visit, 'the prisoners were cheered' by the release of about 800 individuals. 'The sight of packing and repairing trunks and other preparations for departure reminded the remaining prisoners that their own captivity would come to an end one day, and, to a certain extent, raised their depressed spirits.'[24] On the other hand, the raising of hopes of release led to depression if they were not realized. In 1917 the 'Chief Captains' of Knockaloe Camp III wrote to the Red Cross in Geneva declaring: 'Nearly a year ago the hope was aroused in us that the exchange idea would materialise. The long months of the third year of imprisonment passed by and brought disappointment after disappointment and in their train despair and despondency.'[25] The November 1918 armistice understandably had a negative effect upon internees.[26] Two prisoners held in the military camp at Skipton wrote:

> On the morning of the Armistice day of 11 November as, from outside the camp gate, the sound of the jubilation of the English guards rang above the barbed wire and everywhere on the English

> accommodation huts the flags fluttered in the wind, the pain and sorrow struck our German souls with almost outlandish hardness. One genuinely saw strong men cry like children.[27]

The arrival of post and contact with wives in particular also played a significant role in the collective mood of the camp.[28]

Mental and physical health

Despite the depressing nature of internment and the evolution of the concept of barbed wire disease by the end of the First World War, statistics point to a generally sound mental and physical condition among the prisoners, especially in comparison with the population as a whole and with casualty rates on the western front. To deal first with figures for mental health, a report by the Destitute Aliens Committee on the Isle of Man camps in October 1916 claimed an insanity rate of 1.6 per cent per thousand, which 'is markedly less than the pauper lunacy incidence in the general population in 1914 – for males of the same ages', although the report mentioned 'milder forms of mental derangement', whose incidence the investigators could not establish.[29] Other statistics for diagnosed mental illness remain patchy. The 1,020 prisoners held at Nell Lane Hospital on 21 February 1919 included '43 patients under treatment for mental disorder'.[30] On 21 July 1917 the 3,000 patients held at the London County Asylum in Colney Hatch included forty-four German prisoners of war.[31] A Swiss Embassy report on the military camp in Loch Doon in Ayrshire from July 1917 pointed to '3 cases of insanity in this camp since it opened 3 months ago, and one man will now be sent to the asylum for observation. Thus, insanity cases would seem to amount to more than 1 per cent per annum'.[32]

Another possible way of measuring insanity is to study suicide attempts, which certainly occurred on the Isle of Man, although the suicide rate here did not exceed that outside. In 1910–14 the figures stood at 22 per 100,000 in Germany and 26 per 100,000 in England. In Germany the figures declined to between 15 and 20 per 100,000 during the First World War, and in the period 1919–30 the suicide rate there stood at 28 per 100,000, while the figure for England was 13.[33] Paul Francis, who trawled through the *Ramsey Courier* and the *Isle of Man Weekly Times*, listed just five prisoners who killed themselves in Douglas and Knockaloe, which seems a low rate considering the tens of thousands of men who passed through the camps, although it would match figures quoted above.[34] My own research has discovered other suicides, although they would not significantly affect the statistics. They included Johannes Juchstock, who hung himself in January 1917 after facing capture on a Danish steamer in Kirkwall in November 1916,[35] and Wolfgang Dorfer, arrested in the Cameroons in December 1914, who cut his wrists and throat after arriving in Knockaloe in July 1916.[36] An inquest into the death of Paul Waldemar at Knockaloe in September 1918 decided that 'The deceased while of unsound mind did kill himself by hanging in the washouse [sic] of compound 2, Camp 3.'[37] A wealthy prisoner at Douglas, fifty-two-year-old Frederick Braubauer, who had his own valet, wrote a letter to the commandant before committing suicide, declaring:

> The agonies before me in my death struggle will be nothing compared to what I suffer mentally in my internment, and what I should have to go through if I submitted to the repatriation order. I am stone deaf and unable to walk unassisted and the long journey will reduce me to such a condition that I shall arrive absolutely helpless with nobody to look after me. I will be better dead and at rest.[38]

At least one prisoner, Hans Erkart, unsuccessfully tried to kill himself. Erkart took some embrocation from a bottle marked 'poison', while in a cell in Knockaloe awaiting trial for another misdemeanour, but now found himself charged with attempted suicide.[39]

It proves difficult to come to any conclusions about the relationship between these suicides and incarceration. Despite the tragedy involved in each individual case, the suicide rate among German prisoners remained similar to that of the English and German populations overall. This does not change the reality of the depressing psychological consequences of internment for many years, leading to the concept of barbed wire psychosis, which, as Vischer pointed out, had many symptoms. However widespread this malady may have become, perhaps even affecting most prisoners at least temporarily, it did not lead to suicides on any significant scale.

Prisoners who died in captivity usually did so as a result of physical rather than mental ailments, although overall death rates also remained relatively low in comparison with those of the population

Table 4.1 Causes of death of German prisoners in Britain

Cause of death	Number who died	Percentage of sample
Battlefield injuries	81	43.8
Influenza	26	14.0
Pneumonia	21	11.4
Tuberculosis	12	6.5
Heart disease	7	3.8
Accident	4	2.1
Suicide	3	1.6
Other	31	16.8
Total	185	100.0

Sources: BA/R67/852, BA/R67/1038, BA/R67/1039.

as a whole, certainly in civilian camps. By April 1917 only 105 alien enemies had died in camps controlled by the Home Office, which meant an annual death rate of about three per thousand. The situation had changed little a year later when James Cantlie of the British Red Cross Society, after visiting Knockaloe, pointed out that the death rate there averaged about 2.5 per thousand, whereas that for the Isle of Man as a whole stood at 15.7 per thousand.[40] A higher death rate may have existed among military prisoners, although this largely finds explanation in the fact that some arrived in Britain already wounded, while a few became victims of accidents as a result of physical work which they carried out.

A series of files in the Bundesarchiv in Berlin contain death certificates of both military and civilian prisoners who perished in British hands.[41] Approximately 644 of these died on British soil, while numerous other injured soldiers did not even travel beyond France. The 644 consisted overwhelmingly of Germans, together with some members of other nationalities. Not all of these certificates give a cause of death, but we can utilize three of the files which do to come to some conclusions about the causes of death of German prisoners of war in Britain, which are summarized in Table 4.1.

The most obvious cause of death here was clearly injuries sustained on the battlefield. In addition, dozens of prisoners died as a result of the influenza outbreaks which affected several camps in particular during 1918 and 1919 rather than spreading throughout the country. Some of the deaths from pneumonia probably also had a connection with the influenza epidemic, which had a global reach and which killed about 250,000 people in Britain.[42] Five of those who died as a result of heart disease were civilians. The other causes of death included cancer, brain haemorrhage and kidney disease.

Several types of source provide examples of individuals who died in internment as a result of the causes listed above.[43] One of the camps hardest hit by influenza was Skipton. A Swiss Embassy report of March 1919 mentioned the fact that, out of the 530 German officers and 125 orderlies in the camp on the day of the visit (24 February), 279 of the former and 28 of the latter 'were reported sick on that day. 15 officers and 15 orderlies were under treatment at Keighley Hospital, of the latter 5 died . . . Two large huts were occupied by re-convalescent cases and the more acute cases were received in the wards of the camp hospital.' Nevertheless, it would appear that the number of deaths as a result of influenza in Skipton increased further during the course of the summer, as is indicated by the publication of a pamphlet for the relatives of forty-seven men buried in Keighley by May of 1919.[44] Other camps which suffered particularly as a result of the influenza outbreak included Raasay, where twelve of the fourteen men who died perished as a result of the disease.[45] In Pattishall 'a bad flu epidemic in 1918 . . . soon spread around the camp and especially in the crowded conditions'.[46]

Most of the deaths which occurred on the Isle of Man were reported in the local newspapers. Prisoners died from a variety of natural causes. Those who perished as a result of heart failure at Knockaloe included Ludwig Lembke, Leonard Fuchs and Anton Roesch.[47] Frederick Williams, who had changed his name from Fritz Wihlelm and had lived in England for thirty-six years, suffered from bronchial asthma and was admitted to the hospital of Camp IV in Knockaloe on 25 August 1916. He actually died as a result of heart failure.[48] Albert Peter also died in the hospital in Camp IV at Knockaloe. After he was admitted initially suffering from 'gastritis', doctors discovered that he had a 'malignant growth on his liver', which caused his death.[49] Meanwhile those who fell victim to tuberculosis in Knockaloe included Peter Kusper and Henri Hoffmann.[50] Elsewhere, although it does not seem to have resulted in any deaths, an outbreak of scurvy occurred in Raasay in the autumn of 1917; the commandant appears to have dealt with this by adjusting the rations, and especially preparing the meat more carefully.[51]

Some prisoners, particularly those involved in manual work,

died as a result of accidents. Four soldiers perished near Farnham when 'their motor-lorry laden with timber' fell into a ditch and turned over after passing another vehicle, crushing all of them.[52] Meanwhile, two prisoners died together with a farmer in Wiltshire when overcome by fumes while 'cleaning a small whey tank'.[53] Bernhard Schneider perished 'on the 28th day of August, 1915, at Dorchester, from carbolic poisoning accidentally administered by carbolic acid being put into a hot bath for purposes of disinfection, in which bath the deceased bathed himself'.[54]

Killings also occurred in the camps when guards fired upon captives. The most notorious example occurred in Douglas in November 1914,[55] but individual shootings happened throughout the war, especially as a result of escape attempts or refusal to obey orders. On one occasion in Catterick a 'Court of Enquiry' decided that 'the evidence of the German prisoners was unreliable' and 'considered that Private Keys carried out his orders in firing at the prisoner after calling and signalling to him to get away from the wire, and gave him a sufficient opportunity to obey his challenge before firing'. The court decided to attach no blame to Keys, even though this seems to have been a case of overreaction.[56] A similar overreaction appears to have caused the shooting of Wilhelm Karl Schmidt in Leigh for crossing a boundary. 'The deceased was found on the top of the boundary of his dormitory, a very high partition close to the glass roof, and he was warned not once but four times to come down. He disregarded the warnings, whereupon the sentry Thompson fired upon and killed him.'[57] On another occasion a sentry shot dead a prisoner at Oswestry when he climbed to the top of a roof and started throwing biscuits to prisoners below.[58]

Although in such cases medical personnel could do little to save individual prisoners with bullets through them, most of the larger camps had hospitals to deal with those who fell victim to disease. These supplemented the military hospitals, which dealt primarily with those soldiers who had sustained injuries in France. Knockaloe had an infirmary in each of its four sub-camps. In total eight doctors looked after the patients in each camp, together with forty German attendants. At the end of April 1916 they held a total of 146 patients between them.[59] The individual hospitals appear to have had different tasks, and patients certainly moved from one to another. Those in Camps II, III and IV 'are intended for cases of a chronic nature and for minor ailments. More serious ailments are transferred from Camps II, III, and IV to the Main Hospital Camp I.' An isolation hospital for all the sub-camps, connected to Camp III and 'with its own staff in a separate wired enclosure', contained 'cases of venereal, tuberculosis and other troubles'. In addition, 'out-patients are examined and treated during certain daily visiting hours at each of the four camp hospitals. The average numbers are 700 to 900 per week – that is about 100–130 per day – at each dispensary.'[60]

Elsewhere, Handforth contained a hospital with sixty beds. A Swiss Embassy report of 1917 claimed: 'The average of illness is quite low, now being about 0.5 per cent in-patients and 1 per cent out-patients.' The two deaths here had resulted from tuberculosis and pneumonia, while 'four cases of lunacy have been recorded'.[61] United States and Swiss Embassy reports commented positively upon the hospital in Leigh, which in April 1917 had a British doctor 'aided by a British dispenser, 6 British and 3 German hospital orderlies, a British and a German dentist'. It contained fifty beds. Seven prisoners had died here since its opening, 'one of Tuberculosis, 4 of Typhoid Fever, one was shot while trying to escape, 1 died of heart disease'.[62]

Cases of disease, some of them fatal, clearly existed in the internment camps which developed during the Great War, as the individual examples given above suggest. While each case carried its own personal tragedy, a statistical approach points to the fact that German prisoners in Britain actually remained quite healthy in comparison to the population as a whole. Excluding those already injured in France, death rates remained low, although even the inclusion of wounded soldiers would probably still suggest a generally healthy population. Part of the reason for these statistics lies in the fact that all the prisoners were aged between seventeen and fifty-five, excluding older and potentially less healthy males. Similarly, despite the apparent epidemic of barbed wire psychosis, the numbers of suicides and admissions into mental institutions suggest that, while many prisoners may well have suffered from bouts of melancholy, sadness or depression, these did not become serious.

Rules, regulations and routine

Lack of routine became problematic for many of the prisoners, especially those who did not have any employment.

Cohen-Portheim wrote that 'Each day began, of course, by a parade', which was largely for the purpose of counting the prisoners. 'Then one dressed . . . Then came breakfast – and then came nothing.' Cohen-Portheim regarded the social activities as futile attempts to kill time.[63] Rudolf Rocker described the initial trauma which prisoners felt upon entering Alexandra Palace and the period of meditation and gradual realization of the realities of internment which followed. Prisoners tried to find ways 'to overcome the monotony of the creeping hours, days, and weeks. Unfortunately, however, the facilities offered . . . are of such a poor and limited nature, that only a fraction of the prisoners are able to satisfy the ongoing necessity for some kind of occupation.'[64]

Military camps had a more structured routine, which helped to prevent the type of disillusionment, frustration and development of barbed wire disease described by Cohen-Portheim and Rocker. A Swiss report on the officers' camp at Sandhill Park provided a precise routine revolving mainly around meals.

Breakfast	8 to 9 am
Parade	10 am
Dinner	12.45 pm
Supper	6 pm
Parade	7 pm
'Lights Out'	10.30 pm after roll call in rooms[65]

Fritz Sachse and Paul Cossmann, interned in Skipton during 1918 and 1919, described their day in the following way: the trumpet sounded at 8 a.m.; the prisoners drank coffee at 9.15; at 10.00 they walked outside the camp; they returned at midday for their lunch; they received their post at 2.00 p.m.; and they ate their supper at 7.30.[66] Similarly, another internee described his day in the working camp in Grantham (dependent upon Brocton) in a letter of June 1917. The prisoners woke up at 5.30 a.m. when the sun began to shine. They made their beds and cleaned their cells until they heard a whistle. They then had their breakfast and subsequently passed out of the large gate in three groups to begin work. This consisted of constructing a road, which meant both laying it and gathering the necessary stones. Lunch took place at 12.30 p.m., when some of the prisoners went back to the camp. A whistle sounded at 5.00 and all work ceased. At the end of the day the prisoners took part in a range of social activities including reading and playing cards.[67] In Handforth the wake-up call sounded at either 6.00 or 6.30 a.m. depending on the time of year, at which time life stirred only in the kitchens, while a few early risers made their way to the bath. However, in this camp, which contained a mixture of officers and privates, the signal to get up consisted of the sound of breakfast crockery. Many of those here had no employment and therefore spent time as they wished until a coffee break at 10.30 a.m., which was followed by a parade. There then followed preparation of food, and lunch at 12.30 p.m. 'Until about 2 pm a deep silence reigned.' Another count occurred between 5.00 and 7.00 p.m. depending on the time of year. Prisoners (presumably officers) filled their days and evenings here with games, sports, gymnastics, studying and walking. Lights went out at 10.00 p.m.[68]

Every camp developed a routine, although some civilians found the adjustment to it more difficult than the regimented and militarized soldiers did. All places of internment also became subject to rules and regulations that were dependent partly upon the Hague Convention. These controlled many aspects of the lives of prisoners and could change during the course of the conflict in retaliation against the German treatment of British prisoners. On 4 August 1914 a royal warrant entitled 'Maintenance of Discipline among Prisoners of War' was published. These regulations covered virtually every aspect of the prisoners' lives. A military court could impose sentences which included death. Prisoners had to 'comply with all rules and regulations deemed necessary for their safety, good order and discipline'. There then followed a series of subheadings. 'Organization' focused upon the way in which prisoners became divided into 'companies, huts, tents, messes', each of which would have an elected captain. 'Routine' included instructions for mustering and roll-call, as well as instructions to clean huts twice a week. Other subheadings included 'Admission of Strangers', which needed the prior permission of the commandant; 'intoxicating liquors', which were allowed automatically only to officers; smoking; 'correspondence'; and diet. The royal warrant also contained several pages on punishment. Although this document ran to fifty-five pages in length,[69] prisoners knew of its contents through English and German summaries of between one and three pages.[70]

Housing conditions

Military discipline, following the Hague Convention, essentially allowed the British government and military authorities to keep control of camps and prisoners in a basically humane way. At the same time, the routine which emerged allowed most internees to make sense of their lives in their new environment. Nevertheless, while internment may have become tolerable for the majority of prisoners, fundamental problems remained. These emerged in publications produced by those returning home, letters to relatives and complaints to United States and Swiss Embassy visitors. One of the key areas of concern was the living conditions. In the immediate aftermath of the war publications appeared which focused upon these poor conditions, with claims that the unsatisfatory accommodation at the beginning of the conflict did not significantly improve, partly as a result of the increase in numbers of military prisoners as the conflict progressed.[71]

Middle-class prisoners in particular focused upon the lack of space and privacy within their new environment. Once again, Cohen-Portheim provided one of the most damning accounts of his life at Wakefield, highlighting 'the monstrous, enforced, incessant community', which he viewed as one of the main causes of barbed wire disease.

> The space allotted to a prisoner in a hut was exactly six feet by four (a coffin is six feet by two) . . . In your own space you were as far removed from the next man as you can be in the hut and that is a few feet. Nearly all people enclosed their space as time went on, converting it into a crucible for one or possibly for more, but even then you naturally heard every sound through the thin matchboards which formed the partitions . . .[72]

Rocker also pointed to the lack of solitude in Alexandra Palace,[73] while another internee emphasized the lack of space.[74]

Most of the complaints from internees about their housing conditions focused upon the condition of the accommodation, rather than the lack of space. The acceptance of the 'enforced' community finds explanation in the fact that many working-class prisoners lived in cramped conditions before the war, while many captured soldiers would have preferred life behind barbed wire to spending years in a trench.[75]

Figure 4.1 The sleeping hall at Alexandra Palace. This photograph perfectly illustrates the problems of lack of space resented by many internees, especially those from middle-class backgrounds. Those writing on the subject of barbed wire disease regarded the absence of privacy as an important factor in development of this ailment.

The most vocal and enduring discontent emerged in Knockaloe, partly because of the length of time which some individuals spent here. One Swiss Embassy report pointed out, 'Perhaps no complaints have been so persistent on the part of the prisoners as those in regard to the conditions of the huts.'[76] Discontent about accommodation here surfaced early, focusing upon the poor construction of the huts and the grounds, which was aggravated by the dampness of the climate and the strong winds for much of the year. Some of the problems emerged because of the rapidity with which Knockaloe had come into existence. United States and Swiss Embassy reports regularly confirmed the poor conditions of the huts and their surroundings. 'In Camps II, III & IV the hut walls are made of thin horizontal boards, creocoted but not tarred, each board overlapping the one below. Many of these walls were not weather-proof.' Every hut had walls which 'were black with damp or grey with mould' and had 'many spots at which the rain had blown in'. Furthermore, 'luggage, boots, and clothing were entirely covered with mildew' while bed covers 'were in many instances damp'. A prisoner returning home to Germany confirmed this picture, pointing out that the huts were 'completely wet through so that bread becomes covered with mould in a day and all clothes become rotten. Therefore one sits freezing by the insufficient oven during bad weather.' During a visit in December 1915 United States Embassy inspectors pointed out that 'almost the entire six acre area of every compound was covered with mud and rain water'. A Swiss Embassy report on Camp I from May 1917 pointed out that 'the dust and sand in the air is a feature of the camp. Some of the walls leak. The huts are overcrowded, not only on account of the number of men, but owing to the fact that luggage and washing are stored in them.' Furthermore, several reports commented on the insufficient nature of the latrines and the bathing facilities in Knockaloe.[77]

Complaints about housing also emerged in numerous other camps throughout the country during the course of the war as well as in official German publications at the end of the war.[78] Some of the complaints came from locations which held predominantly middle-class educated internees and may find explanation in their ability to publicize their plight. This was partly true of Stratford, one of the worst camps, where a variety of documents, especially those produced by released Germans, point to the poor conditions within it. One United States Embassy report actually 'found the camp in excellent order, and everything in a satisfactory condition', although there was little elaboration of any sort in this one-page portrait.[79] Those Germans who spent time here pointed to the problems with Stratford. Hans Erich Benedix spoke of 'Terrorism in Stratford' and 'Modern Slaves', focusing his ire especially upon the senior personnel of the camp, who, he claimed, worked on the maxim that 'A prisoner has absolutely no rights.'[80] A Herr Bötefür, previously 'Director of Customs in the Cameroons', concentrated on 'the so-called hospital', a former factory where, he claimed, the 'roof does not meet the walls. The intervening space is partly stopped up with paper and rags but allows plenty of room for wind and rain to enter.' Mirroring Benedix's claims, Bötefür also criticized the administrative staff of the camp and made strong claims against the commandant, 'who was said to be in the habit of punishing anyone who came to him with a complaint during his rounds or otherwise came into contact with him by having them placed in solitary confinement', although Bötefür did not provide any evidence.[81]

Meanwhile, a returning doctor who had spent time in Stratford confirmed Bötefür's negative impressions of the hospital.[82] Other prisoners complained about a series of issues including the roof and the heating, which the commandant, F. A. Heygate Lambert, dismissed after carrying out an investigation. He admitted that the roof 'has never been rainproof' but stated that it had 'been constantly under repair . . . but the leakages are of comparatively small importance'. He also pointed out that 'steam heating' maintained the temperature at 59 degrees Fahrenheit, which seems rather low. He investigated eleven cases of punishment by imprisonment but claimed that in most of these the prisoners were simply 'admonished'.[83] Despite the robust defence of Stratford put up by Heygate Lambert, it seems clear that conditions remained poor, while his reputation as a disciplinarian seems to have contained truth.

Complaints also emerged in Wakefield, although as a privilege camp this contained some of the most highly literate and articulate prisoners, who had 'really nothing to do and no way of occupying their time except by dwelling upon the hardships of imprisonment', according to a United States Embassy report from March 1916. One concrete grievance which existed related to the water supply, which caused shortages at 'certain times of day'. In addition, some concern focused upon the condition of the paths in winter. However, these seem relatively minor irritants, particularly when compared with the situation at Knockaloe or Stratford.[84]

Officers' camps also generated a whole series of complaints, again perhaps because of the educated nature of many of the prisoners held within them. Captain Theodore Schlagintweit, the German consul in Manchester at the outbreak of war,[85] spent time in Dyffryn Aled and made a statement under oath describing conditions there when he returned home to Freising on 12 May 1915. He claimed that when the camp first opened there were no wash basins or towels and that prisoners had to eat out of tins with their fingers. In addition, they could not drink the water. They found themselves confined to three rooms. He then described how some of the initial problems had been resolved during the autumn of 1914.[86] However, in September 1915 the United States Embassy received a long list of grievances written by the 'Naval Captain and Senior German Officer of the Concentration Camp for prisoners of war at Dyffryn Aled', who signed himself Wallis. This nineteen-page document included complaints about the following issues: accommodation, heating, lighting, bathing arrangements, 'household arrangements', 'danger of fire', 'disposition of the rooms', exercise, hours, walks, 'physical situation of the camp', visits, 'retention of objects', the method of dealing with parcels, letters and the commandant.[87] Complaints continued about Dyffryn Aled until the end of the war. These focused especially upon the commandant, who was described as 'Germanophobic' and 'an absolute German hater' who dealt with minor misdemeanours by imposing strict penalties such as suspending post for up to six weeks. Furthermore, complaints also emerged about the condition of the accommodation and the lack of space available.[88]

Visiting embassy staff made sure that they picked up any concerns about accommodation by talking to prisoners. Some reports detailed problems in a frank manner. When Edward Lowry visited Stobs in February 1916, discontent focused upon a range of issues, including the fact that prisoners had to use second-hand boots, the electric lighting, 'the fragile "Abestos" lining in many of the huts', which had 'broken and permitted draughts and rain to come through the outside wall of the hut', the 'leaky roofs' and the food. Prisoners also requested walks in the countryside.[89] In January 1919, when Gaston Carlin visited an officers' camp at Redmires, near Sheffield, the inmates bombarded him with complaints. They 'concerned chiefly the non-arrival of bedsteads', which, however, appeared on the day of his visit. Other officers mentioned that the 'washhouses outside the huts were without doors and consequently very draughty', while complaints also emerged 'that the recreation rooms were overcrowded'. Nevertheless, on this occasion, Carlin concluded, 'On the whole I was favourably impressed with my visit to Redmires Camp.' He also spoke positively about the commandant and his efforts to deal with complaints.[90] But Carlin wrote in frank terms about the camp in Marshmoor Siding in Hertfordshire in early 1918: 'Owing to the total absence of practicable roads and paths in and approaching Marshmoor Siding Camp, the soft clay ground is in a hopeless condition, and the sticky wet mud is carried throughout the camp, annihilating all efforts to maintain cleanliness.' However, he anticipated a resolution to these issues.[91]

Although the British authorities may not have deliberately mistreated German internees between 1914 and 1919, many resented their confinement, as became apparent in the constant complaints which emerged. These became most serious in Knockaloe, where some men spent years surrounded by fellow Germans and Austrians in leaking prefabricated huts, where, to use Cohen-Portheim's phrase, quietude became an impossibility, especially in the limited space in which they found themselves. Educated middle-class internees, whether civilians or officers, complained most readily, because of the contrast between their current living conditions and those which they had experienced before the war.[92] At the same time, these two groups, who were not required to work under the Hague Convention, also had the most time to think about their situation. The issue of accommodation certainly formed part of the propaganda war, as evidenced both in the constant flow of complaints made by returning internees and in the publications that appeared during and after the war. Despite the qualifications, conditions clearly remained difficult for many prisoners.

Food

Food became one of the most contentious issues of all during the course of the conflict as prisoners fired off complaints about its quantity and quality. Rocker regarded the 'alimentary conditions of the prisoners' as one of the issues which influenced their psychology, perhaps because, in many cases, meals formed the focal point of their day, especially for those who had little else to do with their time.[93] The Army Council set the daily food ration, which changed during the course of the conflict owing to the scarcity of some items as a consequence of German submarine activity. The changes also proved important in prisoner psychology, representing yet another way in which they lost control of their lives. Prisoners could supplement their rations by the receipt of parcels or the purchase of additional food from canteens. In virtually all camps internees cooked the food themselves, which in an establishment of the size of Knockaloe became an enormous logistical exercise.

The official ration dictated that prisoners should receive three meals a day, breakfast, dinner and supper, with the midday meal providing the most food and nourishment. During the first two years of the war the daily ration looked as follows:

Bread, 1lb. 8oz, or biscuits, 1lb.
Meat, fresh or frozen, 8oz., or pressed, 4oz.
Tea, ½oz. or coffee, 1oz.
Salt, ½oz.

Sugar, 2oz.
Condensed milk, 1/20th tin (1lb).
Fresh vegetables, 8oz.
Pepper, 1/72oz.
Cheese, or butter or margarine, 1oz.
Peas, beans or lentils, or rice, 2oz.[94]

As the conflict progressed, however, the ration altered. At the start of 1916, bread went down to 1 lb, although flour appeared at 6 oz. Cheese also seems to have disappeared.[95] By the end of 1918 the ration looked considerably different, with bread at 9 oz, supplemented by 4 oz of broken biscuit, while the meat consisted of beef or horseflesh on three days per week, Chinese bacon on two days and salt-cured, smoked or pickled herrings on the other two days. By this time potatoes had made an appearance at 20 oz per day, together with rice, oatmeal and split peas or beans, the last of which seems to have taken the place of some of the fresh vegetables.[96] The quantities changed during the course of 1919 as a result of the cessation of hostilities, although horseflesh became the norm on five days per week, while 'pork and beans' also made an appearance.[97] Throughout the conflict those involved in physical work received higher rations than other internees. In fact, in the latter stages of the war, those not employed obtained only 5 oz of bread per day, less rice or oatmeal and less cheese, margarine or maize than those who were employed. In addition, those working 'on heavy manual' tasks received slightly higher rations of Chinese bacon or margarine, but this was in lieu of cheese or fat.[98]

Lists of rations appeared within the individual camps. In some cases, they were virtual duplications of the War Office documents, as in the case of the Dorchester list in 1919, which mentioned pork and beans, horseflesh, bacon and various types of herring.[99] On the Isle of Man, the 'Dietary' of the two detention camps did not go into such graphic detail, although prisoners would have known what type of meat they ate.[100] A 'Scale of Rations' from the camp at Jersey in 1916 simply listed ten available items, together with their quantities, consisting of bread, meat (fresh, frozen or preserved), tea or coffee, salt, sugar, condensed milk, fresh vegetables, pepper, margarine and peas, beans or oatmeal.[101]

In other camps details of the way in which the local staff cooked the ingredients have survived, suggesting limited variety in the meals served. In Oswestry, for example, the breakfast consisted of tea or coffee, bread and margarine every day, while the evening meal contained tea, bread and margarine, although if food remained from lunch, this could be made into soup. The midday meal had some variation, although it always included bread, potatoes, vegetables and beans, but no indication survives of the way in which these items were cooked. The variation came in the meat or fish element of the meal, which consisted of smoked fish on Monday and Friday, boiled meat on Tuesday and Saturday and 'meat' on Wednesday, Thursday and Sunday.[102] 'Menus' from the compounds in Camp I of Knockaloe for the week ending 27 May 1916 provide slightly more detail. In compound 2, for example, dinner consisted of corned beef, potatoes and suet pudding on Monday, clear soup, turnips, beef and potatoes on Thursday and clear soup, beef, potatoes and dumplings on Saturday. Although this diet appears monotonous, with the prisoners eating beef on every day of this week,[103] it probably represented an improvement on the working-class diet of the early twentieth century.[104] This applied even more to the 'Bill of Fare' for the ordinary sub-camp in Douglas in the week ending 18 December 1915, in which variety also existed. The items available here included roast beef on Sunday, Irish stew on Monday, Wednesday and Saturday, 'Königsberger Klops' on Tuesday, scouse on Thursday and 'Hamburg Steaks' on Friday. Furthermore, the document concluded with 'second helpings when asked for'. The privilege camp in Douglas served bacon, eggs and marmalade for breakfast, while the midday meal could include beef, mutton or pork. 'Tea' could include cold meat, fish and cakes.[105]

Prisoners cooked the food in virtually all of the camps. Dyffryn Aled had ten cooks and ten waiters at the start of the war, while Frith Hill employed 'twelve cooks, all German' in September 1916.[106] A Swiss Embassy visit to Alexandra Palace in May 1915 described the kitchens as 'bright, airy and clean' and 'presided over by German cooks. A Committee of Prisoners prepare their own Menus.' The visitor from the United States Embassy 'inspected the meat', which he found 'sweet and good', while the 'quantity of food prepared seemed ample'.[107] The American officials who visited the officers' camp in Kegworth in October 1916 provided a glowing account of the kitchens.

> There are 2 British cooks, 2 German cooks, and 6 German assistant cooks.

> The kitchen is spacious, airy and possesses a range, a Richmond cooker for roasting, baking and steaming, 3 boilers for soups and broths, a steamer for vegetables, 3 porcelain sinks, and apparently every sort of kitchen utensil, all in good order. Adjoining the kitchen on one side is a serving room provided with a steam hot-table to keep viands and dishes warm while serving, and on the other are 3 store-rooms respectively for vegetables, bread and meat, besides a fourth for general stores.[108]

Meanwhile, Douglas had three kitchens, one each for the ordinary and special camps and another for the Jewish internees.[109] The largest cooking operation existed in Knockaloe. A. B. Crookhill looked after the 'messing arrangements' here and had a contract to provide the required amount of food, while Joseph Garside became the 'messing superintendent' responsible for 'the issue of all rations to the kitchens', as well as for listening to any complaints about the quality of food issued.[110] Each compound had its own kitchen.[111]

In addition to the official ration, many prisoners obtained food in the parcels they received, while each camp had its own canteen where internees could buy additional food. In July 1916 a total of 29,590 parcels arrived in Knockaloe, 21,266 of them from Germany and over 800 from the United States. The largest parcels came from Austria and contained a variety of articles including sausage, rye bread, dried fruit and tobacco. But the average parcel from Germany did not provide more than a day's provisions.[112] As the war progressed and rationing tightened its grip on Germany[113] the contents became more basic. According to Archibald Knox, a censor in Knockaloe, 'for two years every German parcel was of first rate quality of food . . . That changed and during 1918 the contents were almost without variation bread – a loaf or stick – or biscuits and potatoes.'[114] The food items available in canteens were mostly processed or dried food including dried fruits, cheese, pickles and rice.[115] The camps which held officers or internees who paid for extra rations appear to have had the canteens with the widest range of products. Journalists who visited Donington Hall in July 1916 commented upon the 'American Bar', whose shelves included hock and claret.[116]

Despite some of the positive comments about the food and kitchens made by journalists and United States and Swiss Embassy officials, prisoners regularly complained about the quantity and quality of their food. In the summer of 1916 a survey of the Knockaloe diet pointed out that internees received an average of 2,535 calories per day. Despite this they wanted more bread and the same standard and amount of food obtained in camps elsewhere in Britain.[117] Two years later the Knockaloe internees complained to Gaston Carlin that 'the food restrictions are becoming more and more stringent and must lead to starvation'.[118] Prisoners' letters also reveal concern about the amount of food obtained. One internee writing to his mother from Kegworth in April 1918 complained: 'I have received so little to eat that I am virtually starving. In the space of four weeks I have lost 8 pounds. I shall soon become only skin and bones.' He also claimed that the he could not afford the food available in the canteen. 'It is impossible to speak of being full up. One wakes up hungry and goes to bed hungry.' He asked his mother to send him more food including bread, marmalade and apples.[119] The type of food which the prisoners ate also caused concern. For instance, at the end of 1915 Knockaloe internees complained that they did not receive haricot beans or rice, despite the fact that they should have done according to the menu, and instead obtained cabbage or turnips.[120] In January 1916 Lieutenant Bötefür complained that in Dartford Hospital the meat was 'bad and smelt', and he had similar comments about the fish, while 'the whole meal was almost always cold'.[121] Lieutenant Wollenhaupt wrote in a similar manner about the food he received in the military hospital in Belmont in 1917. He commented on the thin soup, the meat and the vegetables, which were 'very often bad and unenjoyable'.[122] The 'substitution of horseflesh for ordinary meat in the beef rations issued to prisoners of war' in 1918 caused 'great discontent in certain Civilian Internment Camps'.[123]

Apart from obtaining food from the parcels and canteens, internees used various methods to supplement their food rations. Rocker remembered that on his first day in Alexandra Palace he lost his appetite and could not eat his meal. 'The man sitting next to me saw that and asked me if he could have my food; without waiting for an answer he snatched my plate and ate greedily.'[124] Cohen-Portheim, meanwhile, mentioned the existence of bartering in Wakefield, where money had 'become as good as useless, for people only wanted food, and that money could not buy . . . If you still possessed two tins of sardines, you might exchange one for chocolate, half your bread ration might buy an apple.'[125] Those members of the German navy held at Scapa Flow in 1919 caught fish until the shoals migrated at the end of April. Attempts to shoot seagulls failed,[126] although Knockaloe internees appear to have had more success in catching some of the thousands of birds which hovered around the camp, which was situated close to the coast.[127]

Despite the complaints made by the prisoners about food, they usually received enough calories to keep them quite healthy, as the low death and disease rates would suggest. Nevertheless, the prisoners 'were far more strictly limited in food than the general population, and felt acutely . . . the sudden change in conditions'. Despite its calorific value the food 'was monotonous and ill-balanced'.[128] The lack of control over the food they consumed also irked the prisoners.

Post

This last point also applies to the post, which represented the key contact with the outside world for most prisoners and played a central role in the mood of the camps. As Gunther Plüschow wrote of his experience in Holyport, 'The post was the Alpha and Omega of our existence. We divided our whole day according to its delivery, and the temper of the camp was regulated by it.'[129] Similarly, a diary kept by Karl Schonwalder in Knockaloe gradually came to focus almost entirely upon his correspondence and consequent contact with the outside world, providing little other information. For example, his entries for the first two weeks of July 1917 run as follows:

3. Sent 20/- home. Letters from home.
4. Wrote to Mrs Hands. Received.
   Parcel from home. 2 P.C. from Rosa.
6. Letters from home.
7. Letter from home. Wrote home.
8. Wrote to Mr Hammond.
9. Letter from home. Letter from Mrs Hands.
10. Sent 10/- home.
11. Wrote to Mr Clark. Letter from Max.
    Letter from home.
12. Letter from Mr Hands . . .
13. Parcel from home + 2 letters
    Wrote home
14. Letters from home.[130]

Figure 4.2 Distribution of letters at Brocton. Contact with the outside world became one of the most important factors in maintaining the mental health of the prisoners, and for military prisoners, as well as most civilians on the Isle of Man, the post became the only way to make contact with relatives in Germany.

Despite the desire of many prisoners to continue with their external contacts as best they could, regulations, based on the Hague Convention, controlled correspondence. Prisoners could send two letters per week to a maximum of twenty-three lines each on specially devised official writing paper and in clearly legible handwriting and plain language referring simply to private affairs and business matters. No limit existed on the number of letters which prisoners could receive. Postage remained free for letters up to 2 oz. The internees could also receive parcels of up to 5 kilograms, which could not include spirits or weapons but often contained items of food. They could also receive cash from relatives. During the course of the war some short-term reprisals were implemented as a result of actions taken by the German government against British prisoners. For example, between 14 February and 10 July 1915, German prisoners could not receive books, as the German authorities had imposed a similar restriction upon British internees.[131] Letters were censored by the prisoner-of-war branch of MI9. If they contained 'passages about poor treatment', they 'were returned to the Commandant, with a covering form, for action'. Most of the reading of letters happened centrally, and it seems that over 250 people found themselves employed in this task.[132]

Despite the level of control exercised over the correspondence of prisoners, vast amounts of this mail passed into and out of Britain. Because of the number of internees held at Knockaloe, a post office opened there. In 1918 alone a total of 4,714,090 items of mail came into UK camps, while 7,550,350 left them. Archibald Knox claimed that 'from the day I started work Nov 9 1914 until I left Oct 25 1919: 1,207,000 parcels passed through my department'. The number of parcels which arrived daily, according to Knox, increased from about 2,500 to around 5,000 at Whitsun and Christmas, which suggests that each prisoner received an average of one every fortnight. As well as the letters and parcels which internees received from friends and families, German charities sent them further provisions.[133]

Because of the situation of total war, sending and receiving mail did not prove a straightforward process. Letters from Germany arrived irregularly, about once a fortnight for several years and then once every ten days from the middle of 1918, although mail sent from within Britain came much more often.[134] In 1918 prisoners held in Colsterdale drew up a table for the Swiss Embassy to demonstrate that, during December, all letters had an average transit time of more than thirty days, with 37 per cent taking over fifty-three days.[135] Meanwhile, the camp leader at Seer Green in Buckinghamshire, 'who is certain that his wife writes to him every week', informed a Swiss Embassy inspector that 'he had not received a line from home during the past seven months', which clearly caused much anxiety.[136] An article in the Stobs prisoners' newspaper pointed out that while 'a letter sometimes flew over the barbed wire' from Germany or from an 'English home', 'What we wanted to know is not contained within. Of course not.' When something valuable came in a parcel, the censor handled it.[137]

Nevertheless, many letters point to the joy of receiving either a parcel or correspondence. For instance, Max Gottshalt, when writing to his wife Thekla from Knockaloe, almost invariably began by expressing joy and gratitude for the parcel or letter he had received, as well as demonstrating concern about correspondence which he had sent out and which had gone missing.[138] Similarly, Hans Rinteln began a letter to his wife as follows:

> My dearest little wife,
> This week too sunshine again:- Two dear, dear letters of the 8th. and 10th. November (56/7) and so much sweetness in it about our child, which likes to run about and get into trouble.[139]

Men without women

Although letters and parcels from the outside world proved central for morale among prisoners of war, they could not make up for one of the most fundamental problems which they faced: the absence of women. Many of those who either visited the camps or spent time within them stressed this point. Rocker emphasized the position of those men who had families, for whom 'sudden and long-continued segregation . . . must cause a corresponding reaction in their psychology'.[140] Cohen-Portheim contrasted the position of internees with that of soldiers, observing that 'all armies recognized the need of making some sort of provision for the satisfaction of the sexual needs of the troops'.[141] J. T. Baily displayed concern about the 'sexual perversities of an all-male society'.[142] In contrast, Vischer elaborated upon the prisoners' sex lives (or lack of them). 'Two essential facts must be realised – the prisoners are deprived of normal sexual intercourse, and they live solely in association with men.' He hinted at masturbation when he pointed out that the prisoners 'initially try with all their might to keep the recollection of their womenfolk alive, and by this means obtain some relief. This is in reality an effort towards a substitute for normal sexual intercourse.' He pointed to the presence of 'suggestive pictures'. He also wrote: 'Homosexual practices are probably not as frequent as may be imagined. Mutual self-abuse would be more likely to be indulged in.' He further asserted: 'It is not uncommon for two friends to associate like lovers' and that in a few camps he 'was informed of homosexual epidemics', especially during the early part of internment but not in the third or fourth year. He claimed that 'the image of woman is gradually suppressed into the subconsciousness.' The first meeting with a woman after release 'is for many a soul stirring-experience', while one prisoner told him that 'the first time he spoke to a woman . . . he was indescribably moved and became embarrassed and confused'.[143] Cohen-Portheim claimed that 'sexual acts' between two men in the camps where he stayed were 'extremely infrequent' and that he 'knew of none at all', partly because 'the camp offered no possibility of isolation'.[144] Rocker, meanwhile, claimed that the suppression of sexual instincts resulted 'in the "moodiness" of the younger, idealistic or cultured men, as well as the critical remarks and jests of the sexual "blasé"'.[145]

Empirical evidence about sex and sexuality remains, with a few exceptions, largely absent. In fact, some internees did have contact with their wives through visits, especially those who lived in London and found themselves interned in either Alexandra Palace or Cornwallis Road in Islington. Those in the latter were 'allowed to see their wives and children regularly and often' but by 1917 still complained about the 'long separation from wife and children'.[146] Pál Stoffa, meanwhile, who spent time in Alexandra Palace, stressed 'the emotional importance of fortnightly visits to which every prisoner who had no black mark against him was entitled'. He continued:

> It was pathetic to watch the painful excitement of the men whose visitors were due in the afternoon: suddenly oblivious of the existence of their comrades, they were a prey to subdued suspense all the morning and as soon as the mid-day was over they started their preparations, each man deliberately anxious to look his best. Long before 3 o'clock, which was the appointed hour for visitors, they assembled with their little bunches of flowers and toys for the children, and were then marched off to the visiting rooms.
>
> I was once allowed to assist and shall never forget the scene: the men sitting at one side of a long table and the visitors filing in to sit down opposite; here a father with a child on his lap timidly peering into the face of the strange man, there an elderly couple hardly

Figure 4.3 Sexual fantasies. Most accounts of internment devote little attention to sexuality among prisoners in Britain, with some suggesting that it would become suppressed during the course of the war. These illustrations from the Holyport *Faschingszeitung* of 1919 suggest that sexual images circulated in the camps.

> speaking, just looking and looking at one another with an intensity of longing that words cannot express. Elegant young women with engagement rings on their fingers, poor working women with a bevy of half-starved children, a grim looking solicitor with a pile of papers in front of him – visitors from another world bringing solace to some and tearing open the wounds of others. It made me feel almost glad that I could have no visitors: it seemed cruel to allow the poor wretches to have their world so near to them only to be snatched away after a few moments.[147]

Military internees never had the opportunity to see their relatives, although, in the absence of visits, letters developed an increased importance. Somewhere in between the situations of the military prisoners and those who lived near their families in London lay that of those held on the Isle of Man, who could receive visitors. But in addition to the costs of travelling there, which would have prohibited many working-class women, wives had to go through a complicated procedure to receive a permit to visit. Once on the island, they had to register with the Douglas police station and obtain permission to travel more than five miles. They 'could only remain on the Island seven days and three visits during that time was the limit; there could be no further permit for three months. In certain approved cases British born and non-enemy born wives were permitted to reside on the island and to visit fortnightly.'[148] During 1917 and 1918 between thirty and forty women with interned husbands lived in Douglas.[149] If women broke any of these regulations, they faced a fine, as in the case of 'two aliens – well to do ladies, who were on a visit to their husbands who are interned at Knockaloe'. They failed to register and travelled more than five miles without a permit. On another occasion two visiting women, together with their landlord, faced charges of falsely filling in the forms for permits.[150]

Some liaisons with women, perhaps involving sex, occurred both on the Isle of Man and on the mainland.[151] On some occasions, sexual intercourse may have taken place between internees and their partners, as revealed in a court case on the Isle of Man in 1918 which reached the press. It involved a Russian woman and a French woman. The former, Pauline Bock, had 'obtained permission to visit her sweetheart', a prisoner named Jacobson, while Madeleine Blau had resided on the island since June. Both women appear to have planned the events of 24 August 1918 on previous visits to their partners. The charge actually consisted of 'interfering with the discipline of the Douglas Internment camp', although the main witness, police sergeant George Edward Cowley, gave evidence which suggested some sort of sexual liaison. The partners of the two women belonged to a working party employed at Groudle Glen. Cowley, observing events from a distance with field glasses, stated:

> About noon the aliens knocked off work for lunch. At that time I saw a lady come down the main road, which leads to the shore. She got into the plants and one of the guards turned his back. He followed Bock up to the corner but after he had gone, she went back to the top of the allotments, and got in among some shrubs. I saw an alien come down along the wall to the place where the woman was. He then got into the ditch and went into the shrubbery. I then lost sight of them.

Cowley subsequently went to the spot in question and 'found Miss Bock sitting on the ground with her mackintosh coat and hat off'. Cowley saw Blau speaking to her husband and stated that they 'were not doing anything'. Both women faced a fine or a short prison sentence. The extract above suggests that liaisons outside camps probably occurred often, especially as one of the guards turned his back.[152]

On only one occasion did the Isle of Man newspapers bring to light what would appear to have been a homosexual act committed 'in the cinema theatre' of the Douglas camp. The two men involved faced prosecution at a criminal court outside the camp. They consisted of Alfred Krahanan and Karl Kiesbauer. Before the war Krahanan 'was a master in an English Grammar School', while 'Kiesbauer was not of such good social standing as his fellow prisoner, but was a young workman'. They faced a charge of 'committing an act of gross indecency'. The evidence 'was of such a disgusting character as to be unfit for publication'. The jury found the men guilty. The judge 'took into account the trying circumstances under which the prisoners lived and sentenced them each to one month's imprisonment with hard labour'.[153]

It seems difficult to come to conclusions about the way in which long-term internees dealt with the absence of women. Cohen-Portheim and Vischer suggest that sex became suppressed, while few stories of any sexual activity survive either in the press or in official papers. Such stories might suggest that sexual acts, whether homosexual or heterosexual, occurred more widely, but the evidence remains too limited to come to any conclusions. The importance of contact with wives and girlfriends, whether this consisted of the receipt of letters or visits, seems more evident. Both events caused great excitement, and the failure to maintain contact could cause great anxiety on the part of prisoners.

Crime

Crime represented part of everyday life in an internment camp, especially in an artificial situation with numerous rules and regulations. Whether the fact of internment made crime more likely than it was elsewhere seems difficult to establish. To turn again to Vischer and Cohen-Portheim, these writers suggest that it did. The former wrote: 'The barbed wire provokes opposition. The prisoner feels compelled to kick against it. He puts himself on the defensive and starts to repine and complain, not only against the camp routine and the authorities, but also against his friends and relations.' However, Vischer did not specifically claim that this led to criminal actions.[154] Cohen-Portheim, meanwhile, wrote about the hatred which years of confinement caused among the inmates towards each other, leading to a poisoned atmosphere in which 'mutual dislike, suspiciousness, meanness, hatred . . . becomes almost tangible. Desperate quarrels break out for the most improbable motives.'[155] On some occasions serious injuries or even death occurred. As Vischer suggests, the prisoners faced numerous regulations, which may have made criminality more likely, although no figures exist to measure it. In Knockaloe, Vischer claimed, 'on an average one prisoner is sent to trial each week for an offence against common law, such as stealing government property or robbing a fellow prisoner'. The reporting of criminal activity in the Isle of Man newspapers, which regularly focused upon events in Douglas and Knockaloe, would suggest that this represents a significant exaggeration. In a population of about 30,000 living within the two camps at their height, it seems unlikely that illegal acts exceeded the level in society as a whole. Vischer blamed law-breaking in Knockaloe partly on 'a certain number of criminals and, in fact, all disreputable elements from other civilian camps find their way to Knockaloe'. He claimed that they numbered over 1,000 and that 'these bad characters must have a most deteriotative influence on their fellow prisoners'.[156]

It seems most useful to divide the crimes committed in camps into non-violent and violent. Those in the former category include perhaps the most common misdemeanour for which prisoners faced punishment, escaping.[157] Vischer also displayed much concern about gambling in Knockaloe, although this was not a crime in itself. He accused the criminal elements here of 'starting gambling dens . . . where "card sharping" and similar practices are not uncommon'. Some of those who received external funds 'cannot resist the temptation of passing their time by gambling'.[158]

The Isle of Man newspapers, together with a few other sources, help us to document the type of everyday crime outlined by Vischer. In the first place, forgery occurred. For instance, in February 1917 both Frank Moss, interned at Douglas, and Walter Jack, in Knockaloe, faced conviction for 'feloniously altering and forging an order payment of money dated 28th October 1915, and drawn on Lloyds Bank, Ltd, Horfield, for the sum of £18 15s. with intent thereby to defraud'.[159] Meanwhile, two Knockaloe internees, Otto Bensch and Georg Hubner, received a sentence of six months' hard labour after they 'forged a bank deposit of receipt for £4. 10s and raised money against it at the camp'.[160]

Theft certainly occurred, both on the Isle of Man and elsewhere. In one case, John Immer, a kitchen superintendent at Alexandra Palace, went to jail for twelve months with hard labour for stealing 234 lb of rice and 'a quantity of tea' from the camp stores and then selling it to a contractor outside the camp, who faced the same sentence.[161] Similarly, five prisoners in Knockaloe faced a charge of 'breaking and entering a warehouse . . . and stealing goods to the value of £66', while August Dittmer stole tobacco from a 'lock-up shop' in the same camp.[162] Other internees robbed their fellow inmates. For instance, 'George Bauer, an alien prisoner of war from Knockaloe Camp, was charged with having, on March 22nd and 23rd [1917] feloniously stolen a pair of patent, leather boots, the property of another prisoner'. Paul Oswald faced a sentence of six months' hard labour for 'stealing letters and money with which he was entrusted as a postman to deliver to fellow prisoners interned at Knockaloe Detention Camp'.[163] Despite Vischer's claims about thefts occurring once a week, the Isle of Man press does not confirm this.

Similarly, violent crime and murder remain rare. A handful of such incidents occurred on the Isle of Man. For instance, in

December 1915 Kurt Bruder went to jail for two months with hard labour for stabbing Henry Stocker in the head during an argument in Knockaloe. This appears to have been the culmination of a series of quarrels dating from Stocker's arrival on 21 October.[164] In January 1916 Ferdinand Neske faced charges of cutting William Kern's wrist in Douglas because Kern had moved Neske's chair when climbing on to his bunk bed.[165] In the autumn of 1916 Wilhelm Pinhammer went to court for attacking Edward Lhendorf in Knockaloe following an argument over who should sweep a room, with Pinhammer striking Lhendorf on the head with a brush, resulting in instant death. At the trial the jury unanimously agreed on manslaughter.[166] Such incidents appear to confirm Cohen-Portheim's analysis of the 'desperate quarrels' which broke out among prisoners over petty issues. It is possible that they formed the tip of an iceberg and came to court because of their seriousness. Nevertheless, the death of Lhendorf appears to have been the only example of the killing of a fellow prisoner on the Isle of Man, which seems a remarkably low incidence in view of the tens of thousands of people who went through Douglas and Knockaloe.

On two occasions, events described as mutinies broke out on the island. The second and less serious of these occurred in the autumn of 1916, when Georg Coller faced trial for 'making a speech, which incited the crowd so that a state of mutiny existed, with the result that three hut captains were assaulted in Knockaloe'. Those involved in the disorder were prosecuted. The incidents occurred in compound 3 of Camp III and, again, violence broke out because of simmering resentments, on this occasion over internal administration.[167]

The other 'mutiny' occurred in Douglas on 19 November 1914, at the beginning of the internment process and resulted in the deaths of five prisoners. The spark for the events of this day appears to have been the quality of the food, which had caused resentment over several weeks. Underlying this was the rapid expansion of the camp, with the prisoners finding themselves in poor accommodation in which tents were collapsing. A disciplinarian commandant, Colonel Henry Madoc, who had previously worked in the Transvaal police force, added to the charged atmosphere, which partly manifested itself in the internees defiantly singing patriotic songs in the days leading up to the riot. At the same time, some co-ordination of the events which led to the shootings of 19 November appears to have taken place involving the internees passing messages to each other. At 2.00 p.m. on that day prisoners started throwing tables, chairs, crockery and cutlery across the dining room. The unsupervised guards began shooting in the air but then at the prisoners, causing the deaths of five of them and the wounding of nineteen others. The inquest held after the event found that the soldiers had acted correctly in order to maintain military discipline.[168]

The riot at Douglas remained quite unusual in the history of First World War internment in Britain. Guards shot other individual prisoners on a handful of occasions, but violence among internees appears to have been uncommon according to archival and newspaper sources. Perhaps, as Cohen-Portheim suggests, quarrels took place on a regular basis because of the intensity of the irritation, caused by confinement for many years, which some prisoners felt towards each other. On the other hand the fact that archives and newspapers reveal only one killing of a prisoner by another in any British camp seems quite remarkable in view of the numbers of people who found themselves behind barbed wire and in view of the slaughter a few hundred miles away in France, which the military prisoners had witnessed. Perhaps internment offered an escape from the brutality of the western front. Even excluding the reality of First World War conflict, which civilian internees would not have faced, the single killing seems remarkable.

Despite the relatively low level of violence, many prisoners found their spell behind barbed wire unbearable, as the accounts of Vischer and Cohen-Portheim stress. Some did suffer from depression, as both these authors suggest. Nevertheless, a range of factors contributed to the extent to which individuals became victims of barbed wire disease, including class and the extent to which they 'killed' time, to return to Cohen-Portheim. Prisoners like him, who were used to their bourgeois living space, found the conditions intolerable. On the other hand, many working-class prisoners, used to cramped living and working conditions, did not feel their confinement to such an extent and found numerous ways to pass their time in what became prison camp societies.

Notes

1 'Whoever has not lived through it cannot comprehend it: four years confined in a measured square upon which neither grass nor trees

grow, upon which no bird builds its nest, upon which black huts offer the only shade and the only shelter. For four years grown men lived with adolescents and boys, jumbled up together without any differentiation of nurture, class, education or religious or political conviction. For four years woman has been banned from our circle.' BA/MA/MSG200/1831, 'Stimmungsbilder aus dem Knockaloe-Lager (Isle of Man)', *Welt am Montag*, June 1918.

2 For an introduction to pre-war German housing see Adelheid von Soldern, 'Im Hause zu Hause: Wöhnen im Spannungsfeld von Gelegenheiten und Aneigungen', in Jürgen Reulecke, ed., *Geschichte des Wohnens*, vol. 3, *1800–1918: Das bürgerliche Zeitalter* (Stuttgart, 1997), pp. 145–332.

3 John Davidson Ketchum, *Ruhleben: A Prison Camp Society* (Toronto, 1965), pp. 153–4; Matthew Stibbe, *British Civilian Internees in Germany: The Ruhleben Camp, 1914–18* (Manchester, 2008), pp. 79–110.

4 Ketchum, *Ruhlaben*, p. 164.

5 Ibid., pp. 167–73.

6 The two versions are *Die Stacheldraht-Krankheit: Beiträge zur Psychologie des Kriegsgefangenen* (Zurich, 1918) and *Barbed Wire Disease: A Psychological Study of the Prisoner of War* (London, 1919).

7 Vischer, *Barbed Wire Disease*, p. 31.

8 HHC/LDBHR/1/1/21, August Schauffer to C. Ross (Hohenrein), 30 July 1916.

9 Vischer, *Barbed Wire Disease*, p. 53.

10 Ibid., pp. 55–6.

11 BL, Rudolf Rocker, 'Alexandra Park Internment Camp in the First World War', p. 4.

12 Paul Cohen-Portheim, *Time Stood Still: My Internment in England* (London, 1931), p. 91.

13 BL, Rudolf Rocker, 'Alexandra Park Internment Camp in the First World War', p. 4.

14 Vischer, *Barbed Wire Disease*, pp. 50–1.

15 See, for instance, Daniel N. Robinson, *An Intellectual History of Psychology*, 3rd edn (London, 1995), pp. 297–329.

16 See, for example, Peter Leese, *Shell Shock: Traumatic Neuroses and the British Soldier in the First World War* (Basingstoke, 2002).

17 Leslie Baily, *Craftsman and Quaker: The Story of James T. Baily, 1876–1957* (London, 1959), p. 93.

18 See especially his reports on Knockaloe dated 30 May and 29 November 1917 in NA/FO383/276 and NA/FO383/277 respectively.

19 BA/MA/MSG200/1878, *Lager-Bote*, 15 February 1916.

20 NA/FO383/293, E. Arndt to the Sub-Commandant, Camp IV, Knockaloe, 30 September 1916.
21 NA/FO383/294, Inmates at Islington Internment Camp to President of Swiss Legation, 21 May 1917.
22 This can be found in BA/MA/MSG200/1587.
23 Cohen-Portheim, *Time Stood Still*, p. 85.
24 NA/FO383/277, Swiss Embassy Report on Knockaloe, 29 March 1917
25 NA/FO383/306, Chief Captains of Knockaloe Camp III to the International Committee of the Red Cross, 15 June 1917.
26 L. Bogenstätter and H. Zimmermann, *Die Welt hinter Stacheldraht: Ein Chronik des englischen Kriegsgefangenenlager Handforth bei Manchester* (Munich, 1921), p. 88.
27 Fritz Sachse and Paul Nikolaus Cossmann, *Kriegsgefangen in Skipton: Leben und Geschichte deutscher Kriegsgefangenen in einem englischen Lager* (Munich, 1920), p. 123.
28 See pp. 146–54 below.
29 NA/HO45/10946/266042/199.
30 NA/FO383/506, Swiss Embassy Report on Nell Lane Hospital, 19 March 1919.
31 NA/FO383/277, Swiss Embassy Report on London County Asylum at Colney Hatch, 31 July 1917.
32 BA/R901/83105, Swiss Embassy Report on Loch Doon, 6 July 1917
33 Christian Goeschel, *Suicide in Nazi Germany* (Oxford, 2009), pp. 207–9.
34 Paul Francis, *Isle of Man Twentieth Century Military Archaeology*, part 1, *Island Defence* (Douglas, 1986), pp. 169–72.
35 *Mona's Herald*, 10 January 1917; *Isle of Man Weekly Times*, 6 January 1917; *Isle of Man Examiner*, 6 January 1917.
36 *Isle of Man Weekly Times*, 3 February 1917.
37 See his death certificate in BA/R67/1039.
38 *Isle of Man Weekly Times*, 4 May 1918.
39 *Peel City Guardian and Chronicle*, 13 October 1917.
40 *Manchester Guardian History of the War*, vol. 4 (Manchester, 1916), p. 215; *Hansard* (Commons), fifth series, vol. 92, col. 1135, 3 April 1917; NA/HO45/10947/266042/307.
41 BA/R67/852; BA/R67/909; BA/R67/1038; BA/R67/1039; BA/R67/1040; BA/R67/1041.
42 Howard Phillips and David Killingray, 'Introduction', in Howard Phillips and David Killingray, eds, *The Spanish Influenza Pandemic of 1918–19: New Perspectives* (London, 2003), pp. 3–12.
43 Those who died as the result of battlefield injuries have already received attention in Chapter 2 above.

44 NA/FO383/506, Swiss Embasy Report on Skipton, 21 March 1919; BA/MA/MSG200/2221, 'Den Angehörigen unserer lieben Verstorbenen', Offiziere und Mannschaften des Lagers Skipton, June 1919.
45 Laurence and Pamela Draper, *The Raasay Iron Mine: Where Enemies Became Friends* (1990; fifth printing, Dingwall, 2007), p. 20.
46 Richard Moss and Iris Illingworth, *Pattishall: A Parish Patchwork* (Astcote, 2000), p. 80.
47 *Isle of Man Examiner*, 4 September, 13 November 1915, 1 January 1916.
48 *Peel City Guardian and Chronicle*, 16 September 1916.
49 Ibid., 2 December 1916.
50 *Isle of Man Examiner*, 14 August, 11 September 1915.
51 BA/R67/1356, letter of 10 October 1917.
52 *Daily Mirror*, 10 December 1918.
53 Ibid., 29 August 1918; *Scotsman*, 29 August 1918.
54 *Dorchester Mail*, 3 September 1915.
55 See pp. 156–7 below.
56 BA/R901/83042, Swiss Embassy Report on Catterick, 10 October 1918.
57 *Daily Telegraph*, 1 June 1915.
58 *Manchester Guardian*, 15 July 1919.
59 NA/FO383/163, US Embassy Report on Knockaloe, 18 May 1916.
60 NA/FO383/162, US Embassy Report on Knockaloe, 8 January 1916.
61 BA/R901/83075, Swiss Embassy Report on Handforth, 27 April 1917.
62 BA/R901/83098, Swiss Embassy Report on Leigh, 6 April 1917.
63 Cohen-Portheim, *Time Stood Still*, p. 90.
64 BL, Rudolf Rocker, 'Alexandra Park Internment Camp in the First World War', pp. 11–12.
65 NA/FO383/277, Swiss Embassy Report on Sandhill Park, 5 June 1917.
66 Sachse and Cossmann, *Kriegsgefangen*, pp. 92–7.
67 The letter is contained in BA/R67/210, DRK, England, Interner Wochenbericht No. 97, 13 October 1917.
68 Bogenstätter and Zimmermann, *Die Welt hinter Stacheldraht*, pp. 37–42.
69 NA/WO32/5367, Royal Warrant, 'Maintenance of Discipline among Prisoners of War', 4 August 1914.
70 NA/HO45/10948/267603, Regulations as to the Treatment of Alien Prisoners Confined in Reading Prison under Orders of Deportation or Expulsion or Internment; IWM, Vorschriften für Kriegsgefangene.
71 Vereinigung Wissenschaftlicher Veleger, *Deutsche Kriegsgefangene in Feindesland* (Leipzig, 1919), pp. 5–7.

72 Cohen-Portheim, *Time Stood Still*, p. 85.
73 BL, Rudolf Rocker, 'Alexandra Park Internment Camp in the First World War', p. 7.
74 BA/MA/RM3/5378, 'Meine Flucht aus England. Von Kapitän Schmidt-Klafleth'.
75 See, for example, John Ellis, *Eye-Deep in Hell: The Western Front, 1914–1918* (London, 2002).
76 NA/FO383/432, Swiss Embassy Report on Knockaloe and Douglas, 11 September 1918.
77 NA/FO383/162, US Embassy Report on Knockaloe, 8 January 1916; NA/FO383/276, Swiss Embassy Report on Knockaloe, 30 May 1917; BA/R67/1437, Einiges über Knockaloe.
78 NA/FO383/202, *Sonderabdruck aus der Deutschen Medizinischen Wochenschrift*, 1916; Vereinigung Wissenschaftlicher Veleger, *Deutsche Kriegsgefangene*.
79 NA/FO383/33, US Embassy Report on Stratford, 22 May 1915.
80 Hans Erich Benedix, *In England interniert* (Gotha, 1916), p. 26.
81 NA/FO383/163, Note Verbale, Berlin, 25 May 1916.
82 NA/FO383/202, Dr Zum Busch's last letter from England.
83 NA/FO383/163, Prisoners of War 'Camp' at Stratford – Complaints, 20 February 1916.
84 NA/FO383/163, US Embassy Reports on Wakefield, 16 March, 12 June 1916; NA/FO383/432, Swiss Embassy Report on Wakefield, 11 February 1918; NA/FO383/432, Note Verbale, 20 April 1918.
85 Panikos Panayi, *German Immigrants in Britain during the Nineteenth Century, 1815–1914* (Oxford, 1995), p. 188.
86 BA/MA/RM3/5375, Das erste Internierungslager deutscher kriegsgefangener Offiziere in 'Dyffryn Aled'.
87 NA/FO383/34, Letter from Wallis, 14 September 1915.
88 BA/R67/1283, DRK, England, Interner Wochenbericht No. 102, 4 March 1918.
89 NA/FO383/162, US Embassy Report on Stobs, 17 February 1916.
90 NA/FO383/505, Swiss Embassy Report on Redmires, 4 February 1919.
91 NA/FO383/431, Swiss Embassy Report on Marhsmoor Siding, 1 February 1918.
92 See, as an introduction to such issues, David Blackbourn and Richard J. Evans, eds, *The German Bourgeoisie: Essays on the Social History of the German Middle Classes from the Late Eighteenth to the Early Twentieth Century* (London, 1991).
93 BL, Rudolf Rocker, 'Alexandra Park Internment Camp in the First World War', p. 4.
94 NA/HO45/11025/410118, Report of the Directorate of Prisoners of War, September 1920.

95 NA/FO383/237, Army Council Instruction No. 103 of January, 1916, Amended Scale of Rations for Prisoners of War.
96 NA/FO383/499, Army Council Instruction No. 1203 of 1918, Prisoners of War, Amended Scale of Rations.
97 NA/HO45/11025/410118, Report of the Directorate of Prisoners of War, September 1920; NA/FO383/543, Army Council Instruction No. 194 of 1919, Prisoners of War, Amended Scale of Rations.
98 NA/FO383/499, Army Council Instruction No. 1203 of 1918, Prisoners of War, Amended Scale of Rations; NA/FO383/543, Army Council Instruction No. 194 of 1919, Prisoners of War, Amended Scale of Rations.
99 NA/FO383/507, Swiss Embassy Report on Dorchester, 7 April 1919.
100 MNH/MS09377/5, Catering Records of Knockaloe, Dietary Circulars.
101 BA/R901/83081, US Embassy Report on Jersey, 27 April 1916.
102 BA/R901/8130, Swiss Embassy Report on Oswestry, 18 September 1918.
103 MNH/MS0937/7, Catering Records of Knockaloe Alien Detention Camp, Menus.
104 See, for example, Alf Lüdtke, *Eigen-Sinn: Fabrikalltag, Arbeitererfahrungen und Politik vom Kaiserreich bis in den Faschismus* (Hamburg, 1993), pp. 194–209; and Linda Bryder, 'The First World War: Healthy or Hungry', *History Workshop*, vol. 24 (1987), 141–57.
105 NA/FO383/162, US Embassy Report on Douglas, 10 January 1916.
106 BA/MA/RM3/5375, Das erste Internierungslager deutscher kriegsgefangener Offiziere in 'Dyffryn Aled'; NA/FO383/164, Swiss Embassy visit to Frith Hill, 12 September 1916.
107 NA/FO383/33, US Embassy Report on Alexandra Palace, 26 May 1915.
108 BA/R901/83095, US Embassy Report on Kegworth, 24 October 1916.
109 NA/FO383/276, Swiss Embassy Report on Douglas, 29 May 1917.
110 B. E. Sargeaunt, *The Isle of Man and the Great War* (Douglas, 1922), p. 69.
111 NA/FO383/276, Swiss Embassy Report on Knockaloe, 30 May 1917.
112 NA/FO383/164, Knockaloe Diet Survey, 25 September 1916.
113 See, for instance, Hans-Jürgen Teuteberg, 'Food Provisioning on the German Home Front, 1914–1918', in Ina Zweiniger-Bargielowska, Rachel Duffett and Alain Drouard, eds, *Food and War in Twentieth Century Europe* (Farnham, 2011), pp. 59–72.
114 MNH/MS09954, Archibald Knox to Mrs Holding, 17 November 1919.
115 NA/FO383/276, Swiss Embassy Report on Knockaloe, 30 May 1917; NA/FO383/431, Swiss Embassy Visit to Black Park, 1 February 1918.

116 *Manchester Guardian*, 20 July 1916.
117 NA/FO383/164, Knockaloe Diet Survey, 25 September 1916.
118 NA/FO383/432, Swiss Embassy Report on Knockaloe, 21 May 1918.
119 BA/R67/1188, Abschrift, Kegworth, 9 April 1918.
120 NA/FO383/162, US Embassy Report on Knockaloe, 8 January 1916.
121 BA/R901/94678, Bericht des Kapitänleutnants d. Res. Bötefür über die Erlebnisse während seiner Gefangenschaft, Berlin, 31. März 1916.
122 BA/R67/1437, Abschrift des Berichts von Leutnant Wollenhaupt.
123 NA/FO383/432, Swiss Embassy Letter, 25 June 1918.
124 Rudolf Rocker, *The London Years* (1956; Nottingham, 2005), p. 150.
125 Cohen-Portheim, *Time Stood Still*, p. 165.
126 Friedrich Ruge, *Scapa Flow 1919: The End of the German Fleet* (London, 1973), pp. 87–9.
127 Pál Stoffa, *Round the World to Freedom* (London, 1933), pp. 240–1.
128 Anna Braithwaite Thomas, *St Stephen's House: Friends Emergency Work in England, 1914 to 1920* (London, 1920), p. 51. As an introduction to rationing in Britain see, for example, John Burnett, *Plenty and Want: A Social History of Food in England from 1815 to the Present* (London, 1989), pp. 243–53.
129 Gunther Plüschow, *My Escape from Donington Hall* (London, 1922), p. 173.
130 MNH/MS12028, Diary of Karl Berthold Robert Schonwalder.
131 NA/FO383/20, War Office to Foreign Office, 21 October 1915; NA/FO383/193, Army Council Instruction No. 359 of 1916; Graham Mark, *Prisoners of War in British Hands during WW1: A Study of their History, the Camps and their Mails* (Exeter, 2007), pp. 13–19; BA/R67/80382, Bestimmungen über den Verkehr mit in England und den engl. Kolonien befindlichen Zivil und Kriegsgefangenen; MNH/MS09954, Archibald Knox to Mrs Holding, 17 November 1919.
132 Mark, *Prisoners of War*, pp. 23–4.
133 MNH/MS09954, Archibald Knox to Mrs Holding, 17 November 1919; Charles Field, *Internment Mail on the Isle of Man* (Sutton Coldfield, 1989), p. 4; Mark, *Prisoners of War*, pp. 24, 28; Hilfe für Kriegsgefangene Deutsche, Landesausschuss für Anhalt, *Arbeitsbericht 1914 bis 31. März 1917* (Dessau, 1917), p. 6; BA/R67/774, Ausschuss für deutsche Krigesgefanene in England, Richtlinien für die Versorgung der deutschen kriegs- und Ziviligefangenen in England mit Einheitspaketen, Mai 1917.
134 Mark, *Prisoners of War*, p. 24.
135 NA/FO383/431, Senior Officer of Colsterdale, South Compound, to Swiss Legation, 23 January 1918.
136 BA/R901/83130, Swiss Embassy Report on Seer Green, 6 November 1918.

137 *Stobsiade*, 5 September 1915.
138 MNH/MS08562, Letters from Max Gottshalt to his Wife.
139 NA/ADM137/3855, H. Rinteln to his Wife, 5 December 1915.
140 BL, Rudolf Rocker, 'Alexandra Park Internment Camp in the First World War', p. 52.
141 Cohen-Portheim, *Time Stood Still*, p. 126.
142 Baily, *Craftsman and Quaker*, p. 93.
143 Vischer, *Barbed Wire Disease*, pp. 40–3.
144 Cohen-Portheim, *Time Stood Still*, p. 128.
145 BL, Rudolf Rocker, 'Alexandra Park Internment Camp in the First World War', p. 53.
146 NA/FO383/34, US Embassy Report on Cornwallis Road, 18 September 1915; NA/FO383/294, Letter from Captain's Committee, Islington Internment Camp, to Swiss Legation, 21 May 1917.
147 Stoffa, *Round the World*, pp. 194–5.
148 MNH/MS10417/4, Papers of J. T. Baily, Scrapbook No. 8, p. 593.
149 See the lists of 'Alien Enemies Residing on the Isle of Man' in MNH/MS09845.
150 *Mona's Herald*, 12 May, 22 September 1915.
151 See also Chapter 8 below.
152 *The Times*, 27 August 1918; *Mona's Herald*, 28 August 1918; *Isle of Man Weekly Times*, 31 August 1918.
153 *Peel City Guardian and Chronicle*, 10 June 1916; *Isle of Man Weekly Times*, 10 June 1916.
154 Vischer, *Barbed Wire Disease*, p. 32
155 Cohen-Portheim, *Time Stood Still*, p. 89.
156 NA/FO383/311, A. L. Vischer to R. Vansittart, 4 December 1917; NA/FO383/277, Swiss Embassy Report on Knockaloe, 29 November 1917.
157 See Chapter 8 below.
158 NA/FO383/311, A. L. Vischer to R. Vansittart, 4 December 1917; NA/FO383/277, Swiss Embassy Report on Knockaloe, 29 November 1917.
159 *Peel City Guardian and Chronicle*, 3 February 1917.
160 *Isle of Man Weekly Times*, 12 August 1916.
161 *Daily Express*, 10 October 1917; *Daily Mirror*, 10 October 1917; *Scotsman*, 10 October 1917.
162 *Mona's Herald*, 29 December 1915, 1 August 1917.
163 *Isle of Man Weekly Times*, 27 November 1915, 12 May 1917.
164 Ibid., 4 December 1915.
165 *Isle of Man Examiner*, 15 January 1916.
166 Ibid., 23 September, 2 December 1916; *Peel City Guardian and Chronicle*, 30 September 1916.

167 *Peel City Guardian*, 28 October 1916; *Mona's Herald*, 25 October 1916; NA/HO45/10947/266042, Lt. Col. Panzera to Government Secretary, 6 October 1916.

168 Much primary and secondary information survives on this event, including Margery West, *Island at War: The Remarkable Role Played by the Small Manx Nation in the Great War 1914–1918* (Laxey, 1986), pp. 82–7; Robert Fyson, 'The Douglas Camp Shootings of 1914', *Proceedings of the Isle of Man Natural History and Antiquarian Society*, vol. 11 (April 1997–March 1999), 115–26; Jill Drower, *Good Clean Fun: The Story of Britain's First Holiday Camp* (London, 1982), pp. 45–6; *Manchester Guardian*, 16 December 1914; *Isle of Man Examiner*, 5 December 1914; *Isle of Man Weekly Times*, 28 November, 19 December 1914; *Mona's Herald*, 25 November, 2, 23 December 1914; *Peel City Guardian and Chronicle*, 28 November, 5, 19 December 1914; MNH/MS06465/1, Douglas Camp Journal; MNH/MS09845, H. W. Madoc to Government Secretary, Isle of Man, 20 November 1914; *Disturbance at the Aliens Detention Camp at Douglas on Thursday November 19th, 1914: Inquiry by the Coroner of Inquests on Friday, November 20th, and Friday, November 27th, 1914* (Douglas, 1914).

5

Prison camp societies

> As the months lengthened into years the prisoners sorted out their own civilization: there were theatres, there were camp orchestras with players whose names had been well-known in pre-War London, there were football leagues and tennis matches, there were classes of every description from art to political economy.[1]

Introduction

Although German internees in Britain faced problems of separation and isolation from families, which led some of them into bouts of depression, their experience away from the trenches and zones of direct conflict meant that they escaped the most brutal of First World War experiences. Military prisoners may have already fought on the western front, but many civilians, especially those in Britain, would not have faced a single day of combat. Nevertheless, they had become subject to the Aliens Restriction Act and would have come face to face with the realities of First World War British Germanophobia and perhaps even with rioters attacking their shops in the peak of anti-German hatred which followed the sinking of the *Lusitania* in May 1915. At the same time, for many of the civilians four years of confinement behind barbed wire represented one of the worst periods of their lives.

A full understanding of First World War internment experiences needs to take into consideration the lives of different groups within them and of individuals within these groups. Those who resented confinement most and who became some of the worst victims of barbed wire disease were middle-class immigrants used to having control of their own lives, who suddenly found themselves taken away from their families and having to spend years in an all-male environment with no privacy. In contrast, as Vischer pointed out, military prisoners viewed internment as an escape from experiences on the western front. Furthermore, under the Hague Convention, governments which captured servicemen could also put them to work, which the British government did *en masse* during the second half of the war, meaning that these prisoners had less time than many middle-class civilians to contemplate their plight and to experience the frustrations. The same exception from working applied to officers, although the accounts which they kept do not reveal the same level of frustration as some civilian memoirs, perhaps because of the feeling of escape from conflict that they experienced and perhaps because their confinement tended to last for a shorter period. Because of their pre-war housing, many of the working-class civilian internees would not have experienced quite the shock of internment faced by those higher up the social scale. Like their bourgeois compatriots, they had no need to work, but they do not appear to have faced the same sense of frustration. Although the pre-war German community came from a variety of social backgrounds, the majority originated in occupations at the lower end of the social scale. Some were self-employed bakers, butchers and barbers. By the Edwardian years a large percentage of the German community in Britain also found itself employed in the restaurant trade, especially as waiters. The geographical distribution of the German community before 1914, especially in London, also demonstrates its working-class credentials, being focused especially upon the East End and a community in the West End. Unlike their middle-class counterparts they had become used to living in small spaces,[2] which may have meant that the internment camp experience did not differ significantly from their pre-war lives in this sense, even though they would have felt the same wrench and separation from family. But like their middle-class countrymen they could not legally work under the terms of the Hague Convention.

Many civilians did actually work, whether by becoming involved in camp administration or by continuing their pre-war trades behind barbed wire, as in the case of tailors, cobblers and barbers, for instance. At the same time, some camps developed employment schemes, including Douglas, Knockaloe, Hackney Wick and Islington.[3] Nevertheless, in some camps the majority of prisoners found little useful employment, which meant that they had to develop other ways of passing their time.

This led to the evolution of 'prison camp societies', to use Ketchum's phrase, which we can interpret in various ways. Ketchum referred partly to the basically positive interaction which developed between the civilians who found themselves interned in Ruhleben, who had never previously met each other. The vast majority of Ruhlebenites became part of this society, although class distinctions survived.[4] Ketchum pointed out that some of the communities which emerged here partly did so from the basic proximity with other prisoners with whom individuals had become familiar in their accommodation,[5] a situation which would almost certainly have developed in the various divisions of sub-camps and compounds in Knockaloe. Nevertheless, class also played a central role in the British camps, both civilian and military, owing to the distinctions which existed between officers and men and the development of privilege camps, whether self-standing, such as that at Wakefield, or within the Douglas camp. Ketchum focused much attention upon the sporting, educational and cultural activities of the prisoners, which had two major functions.[6] First, they helped to foster community, both between prisoners of the same social group, who would have participated in similar activities, but also between different classes, as educational activity would suggest, with the teachers and lecturers who found themselves within Knockaloe, for instance, interacting with less educated internees. At the same time, the mass of activity which developed in all of the civilian and officers' camps had another crucial function in that it allowed prisoners to pass their time and to give further structure to their existence beyond the meal times and parades. Those military prisoners who spent most of their days working did not develop the same level of social and cultural activity as they had only their evenings and part of their weekends in which to 'kill time'.

Despite the development of barbed wire disease and the feelings of isolation which some internees felt, the vast majority participated in the educational, social and cultural activity which developed in the camps. This took a variety of forms, including religion; reading, writing and learning; high culture; and sport. In one week in April 1916 Frederick Lewis Dunbar-Kalckreuth recounted the range of activities available in Douglas: on Tuesday, a dancing class; on Wednesday, a 'football world championship'; Thursday was a training day for the sports club; Friday was a day of prayer for Jewish internees; Saturday offered Bible study and a film; and a theatre performance took place on Sunday.[7] The backgrounds of individual prisoners, especially their class, level of education and religion, helped to determine the community and activity in which they became involved. External organizations helped in these processes, especially the Society of Friends, the Red Cross, the Markel Committee and the YMCA.[8]

Religion

Cohen-Portheim claimed that 'religion played an astonishingly small part in the men's life' although he did point to the availability of services.[9] While his first assertion may contain some truth, so does his second. Religious life in the camps reflected the denominational make-up of both the German population and the German community in Britain before the war, with a majority Protestant community, a significant group of Roman Catholics and a small minority of Jews. Whether inside or outside the camps, religion played a role not simply in satisfying the spiritual needs of Germans, but also in cementing their identity as Protestants, Catholics or Jews.[10] Within the concentration camps the most obvious manifestation of religion, apart from the holding of services, consisted of the celebrations of the major religious festivals, above all Christmas, which remained the most important day in the calendar.

Religious services became one of the first forms of communal activity following the initial establishment of a place of internment and took place in even the most basic of camps because of the efforts of local British churches and German clergymen in Britain. For instance, in a small camp which opened in Hendon in June 1917 a Pastor Scholten held a Protestant service by September, while 'Dr Shut, a Dutch priest of St. Joseph's College, Mill Hill, Hendon, holds Roman Catholic Services once a week'.[11] In November 1917 a report into complaints about the lack of religious services in a variety of camps throughout the country concluded that such assertions remained 'without foundation' as 'services had been held at each of these camps'. Nevertheless, at Yatesbury 'services are held once every two months'. At Nethybridge a Roman Catholic priest 'attends about once a month', while a 'Protestant Chaplain visited this camp until want of attendance by the prisoners of war forced him to discontinue his ministrations'.[12]

Long-lasting camps developed more regular services over the

years. By January 1919 in Bramley, which opened in 1917 and held 2,470 soldiers, 'Protestant and Roman Catholic Services were held every Sunday and . . . even during the week there were services amongst the prisoners – on Tuesday for the Protestants and on Thursday for the Roman Catholics.' The Swiss Embassy official who visited the camp at this time did not comment on any other social or cultural activities.[13] In March 1917 Pastor Scholten was conducting Lutheran services 'frequently' in Dorchester, while two Catholic priests visited 'once a week or once a fortnight . . . spending enough time in the camp to talk privately to those who wish to ask their advice'.[14] Similarly, by August 1917 a Lutheran service took place in Holyport 'every second Thursday', and an 'English Roman Catholic priest visited the camp once, and a priest from Oxford, Father Martindale, who speaks German', had arranged to hold confession.[15] In Stobs, Roman Catholic services initially took place only once every two weeks if the priest from Hawick could make the journey. However, an internee took over with permission from the Bishop of Edinburgh and the commandant in the summer of 1915, resulting in two masses being held on Sundays and holy days. A Roman Catholic choir also developed in Stobs, but this broke up in April 1917 when most of its members went to working camps. Protestant services took place at the same time as the Catholic ones.[16] In Alexandra Palace both denominations used the same room every Sunday but the Catholics began at 9.30 a.m. while the Protestants started at 10.45. Members of both groups attended religious lectures on Tuesday and Thursday evenings respectively. Jewish services also took place here.[17] In Douglas, Anglican services occurred on a weekly basis, while 'Roman Catholic Services are held regularly and religious festivities are provided for the large Jewish community'.[18] Prisoners from Knockaloe who had not already moved to the Jewish camp in Douglas could attend these.[19]

As the largest and longest-lasting camp, Knockaloe developed the most complex religious activities. Each of the individual camps here appears to have held services for both Roman Catholics and Protestants. In Camp I a large theatre in compound 2 served as the church for both. By 1916 three Roman Catholic priests held services in both Douglas and Knockaloe. At one stage the same German pastor, Rudolf Hartmann, who had taken up a position with the German Lutheran Church in Birmingham in 1913, appears to have held services in both Camps II and III, while a clergyman from Peel led those in Camp IV. Hartmann actually held overall responsibility for all those interned here. In addition to the services, Bible classes and religious lectures also occurred in Knockaloe. By 1918 the Protestant service in Camp I occurred in compound 1 on Sundays at 11.15 a.m. and each compound had an individual who took responsibility for religion. Internees had access to religious books here. Bible classes took place every week in five of the six compounds in Camp I. In addition the YMCA held a weekly meeting, while prisoners could also speak to the pastor.[20]

Some figures exist to demonstrate the extent to which prisoners participated in organized religious activity. Although they do not lead to definite conclusions, they tend to suggest a fairly low rate of attendance at services. The Home Office believed that the Isle of Man camps contained 'about 9,000 baptised Roman Catholics . . . of whom about 2,000 avail themselves of the opportunity to receive the Sacrament every month'.[21] A survey of Camp IV listed four different types of service held every Sunday: Protestant, Roman Catholic, 'Old Catholic' and 'Low Church'. It claimed that the average attendance stood at 80–100, 100–130, 30–40 and 40–50 respectively. Between 80 and 100 men also participated in the Bible classes here.[22] Such figures would suggest that a minority of prisoners participated in organized religious services and might confirm Gerald Newton's assertion that most men held at Knockaloe had become 'kirchenfremd', or strangers to church attendance.[23] Even an article on religious activity written by a pastor who regularly corresponded with his colleagues in England suggested that a minority of prisoners participated in religious activity and preferred, instead, secular pastimes.[24] Roman Catholics may have had a higher attendance rate on the Isle of Man. Attending church could facilitate contact with former acquaintances. George Kenner 'looked in vain' for his brother at the Roman Catholic services in Knockaloe, but 'met former comrades . . . when of course, a mutual joyful conversation followed'.[25]

Several groups helped to establish religious activity in the camps. In the first place, English churches, both Roman Catholic and Protestant, assisted in this process by providing clergymen. Some priests and pastors came from among the prisoners themselves, while the German Protestant churches which had emerged in Britain during the Victorian and Edwardian years provided others. In addition to Hartmann these included Albert Rosenkranz, who

Figure 5.1 *Deutsche Zeitung*, Brocton, Easter 1919. This drawing illustrates the importance for prisoners of the key religious festivals.

had worked at the German Church in Liverpool but returned to Germany in June 1915. During the early stages of the war he had looked after the camps at Lancaster and Dyffryn Aled as well as holding services in Douglas and Knockaloe. Members of the German YMCA, which had emerged in London during the nineteenth century, also helped to establish religious activities in a variety of places of internment. The Anglican Bishop Bury, who helped to look after the spiritual needs of German prisoners in Britain, worked with both the YMCA and American organizations. Prisoners also received Bibles and other religious reading material from the Evangelische Blättervereinigung für Soldaten and Kriegsgefangene Deutsche, which looked after both German soldiers and prisoners of war throughout Europe. In addition, a wide range of German-based Roman Catholic organizations assisted the prisoners.[26]

Although a minority of prisoners may have participated in organized religious activity, many more appear to have celebrated the key festivals of the year, whether Jewish, Catholic or Protestant. One of the highpoints for the Jewish camp in Douglas was Passover, which the 500 Jews who found themselves confined here celebrated annually.[27] Christian prisoners also commemorated the key festivals of their religious calendar. These included New Year's Eve, *Fasching* (the carnival before the beginning of Lent) and Whitsun. Such festivals received attention in a wide range of camp newspapers, which either produced special issues when they occurred or printed poems or articles at these times of year. Many of these publications and the pieces within them took time to reflect upon the situation in which the prisoners found themselves, often by contemplating the religious significance of the particular moment or festival. For instance, at New Year in 1918 a poem appeared in a special newspaper issued at Skipton in which the author pondered his situation as a prisoner and asked 'When will the day of freedom come?' At Easter 1919 the Brocton *Deutsche Zeitung* appeared in a special edition which included a poem by Goethe and an essay entitled 'Easter Hopes', as well as a picture on the front in which a prisoner gazes at a girl beyond the barbed wire, who appears to offer him an olive branch. Meanwhile, a Knockaloe newspaper which carried the title of *Die Hunnen* published an article by Pastor Hartmann for 'Whitsun' 1917 in which he contemplated its religious meaning and its significance before the outbreak of the war, as well as asking the prisoners to take the opportunity to look forward to a period of peace and brotherhood. On the other hand a *Faschingzeitung* from Holyport in 1919 carried pictures and articles reflecting this time of year, including sexual images and pieces on themes of partying and celebration.[28]

By far the most important festival for the overwhelmingly Christian population among the German internees was Christmas, reflecting the growth and increasing secularization of this festival in both Britain and Germany from the Victorian years onwards.[29] It became a key festival among the German armed forces during the Great War, as reflected both in the conflict zones[30] and among prisoners. Christmas behind barbed wire raised mixed feelings of reflection, joy and longing for freedom, family and childhood. Hans Erich Benedix recalled that, when interned in Alexandra Palace, although many of the prisoners looked forward to their second Christmas in captivity, others became bitter when thinking about it and claimed that they would go to bed early on Christmas Eve.[31] Such contradictory feelings find reflection in some of the articles appearing in the camp newspapers. A 1917 Christmas edition of the Douglas *Unter Uns* claimed that little appetite had existed for Christmas in the weeks that preceeded it, but that the arrival of numerous presents had changed the atmosphere. An article from *Stobsiade* of 24 December 1915 looked back to the time 'when we were free' when 'the sun shone more warmly, the light shone more brightly, the flowers smelt sweeter'. It then reflected on the duty to fight for the Fatherland which had brought the prisoners to Stobs, while others with wives and children remained separated from their Anglo-German homes. Christmas, or *Weihnachten*, 'the German festival', presented an opportunity to look forward to longer days and a brighter future. Two years later, an article in the same journal looked back to 'the celebration of our blissful childhood', but claimed that Christmas 1917, which had just passed, 'was really sad and gloomy', partly because of the lack of post, although the same article detailed the events which took place.[32] Similarly, a piece in the Douglas *Lager-Laterne* of Christmas 1916 by Pastor Oskar Goehling, entitled 'Christmas in Exile', reflected that 'to proper Christmas festivities belong', among other things, 'children shouting, joyous glancing women's eyes . . . delightful pines from the German forest, nuts and mushrooms, carp and bratwurst' as well as a 'brightly lit church'. He continued: 'And now? Christmas in exile! Everything that is prepared for a Christmas party is really only a poor effort, a substitute; thoughts wander to those who love us far away with whom we would like to be united.' He looked forward to a future Christmas outside the camp.

Figure 5.2 A Knockaloe Christmas card. As in the outside world, Christmas became the most important festival for internees. Although they celebrated this event collectively, many simply desired to spend this time with their family. Presents and Christmas cards represented one way to maintain contact.

Despite the complex emotions caused by Christmas behind barbed wire without women and children, it still represented the highpoint of festivities during the year.[33] Much planning went into the events of 24 and 25 December, which included putting money aside and preparing rooms and cooking.[34] The arrival of parcels and Christmas cards, which maintained the link with relatives outside, formed a key part of the approach to Christmas. In Dorchester, thousands of parcels arrived every week during December 1915, while in Frongoch in the same year 'Christmas brought some 4000 letters from home and friends, besides parcels innumerable, and these made their substantial contribution towards good spirits'.[35] Prisoners also received financial help with the preparation for Christmas, as well as presents from external charities and other agencies. Baron Schroeder, one of the leading philanthropists of German origin in Britain, provided two Christmas trees for festivities in Frongoch in 1915 'together with sixpence per head for sundry festivities'. Prisoners celebrating Christmas in Alexandra Palace in 1916 also received help from Schroeder, as well as from the Markel Committee together with cigarettes, pipes and tobacco from the United States Embassy.[36] As in a German Christmas outside the barbed wire, the festivities lasted for several days, climaxing on 24 and 25 December and 31 December and 1 January. Accounts of events in the camps focus upon the food in particular, while others also mention the staging of special plays. A service on Christmas Eve preceded communal Christmas meals on the same evening and the following day. Accounts from both newspapers and individual prisoners which focus upon the festivities themselves, unlike those which reflect on the meaning of Christmas behind barbed wire, invariably paint a positive picture.[37]

Reading, writing and learning

Christmas represented a highpoint for prisoners, as well as an event in which all seem to have become involved, no matter what their level of religious adherence. In contrast, attendance at religious services appears low, despite their wide availability in all camps. Religious practice offered just one way of escaping the monotony of life behind barbed wire. The other serious pursuits were reading, writing and learning.

The presence of significant numbers of middle-class educated Germans, including teachers and academics, some of whom came from the German community in Britain,[38] facilitated such activities. While some of the educational events took the form of informal lectures, all types of schools and even universities emerged on a sophisticated and significant scale, especially in the large and long-lasting camps on the Isle of Man, as well as in the predominantly bourgeois Lofthouse Park. The Swiss Embassy officials in London contacted the Prussian Ministry of Education via the German Foreign Office in order to define the curriculum for military prisoners and to formalize the issue of certificates for those who successfully completed courses to use after the war.[39]

Formal educational activity therefore emerged in a wide variety of camps, both military and civilian. As early as November 1914 a 'school and lecture room' already existed in Dorchester.[40] In Handforth 1,600 prisoners participated in fifty-six courses in 1917, while other informal lectures also took place.[41] Stobs developed quite sophisticated educational activities during the course of 1915 and 1916 supported by the commandant. By January 1916 twenty-two teachers taught 611 pupils in a range of subjects and levels, encompassing maths, 'lessons for businessmen', 'lessons for farmers, gardeners, foresters' and languages, together with a range of other subjects. A special educational hut allowed prisoners to study for two hours in the morning and two and a half hours in the afternoon.[42] Alexandra Palace held 'a large proportion of excellent teachers upon all kinds of subjects'. The commandant here provided 'three rooms for studying purposes', which meant that 'there developed in a very short time, a rich mental life'. The subjects available included a range of sciences and languages, with 700 students becoming involved. However, 'the undertaking suffered a great blow' when some of the teachers were transferred to the Isle of Man during the course of 1915. The school did not recover until the end of the following year, and another 'calamity awaited it' when some of the internees went back to Germany. Further problems over the use of the rooms meant that by December 1917 the classes had 'practically ceased'.[43]

Alexandra Palace's loss became the Isle of Man's gain as Douglas and Knockaloe developed the largest and most sophisticated range of educational activities. The school in Douglas opened in January 1915, thanks largely to the efforts of Paul Keppler. At this stage it offered instruction in a range of subjects, particularly languages and during its first term about 256 pupils attended per day.[44] In the years that followed Bruno Kahn appears to have become the leading light in the school. He kept a wide range of statistical information, including registers that point to both the range of subjects offered and the number of pupils who attended. Languages remained important, but other subjects also took off, including arithmetic, drawing, physics and chemistry. In early 1916 as many as 1,000 students attended classes every day, representing a large minority of the Douglas prisoners. By the following January the number of pupils attending daily had fallen but still averaged between 500 and 1,000.[45]

Thanks to the number of prisoners held at Knockaloe, educational activity became even more extensive and diverse there. Each of the sub-camps appears to have developed its own institutions. In Camp I activity began in early 1915 through the efforts of Pastor Hartmann and several teachers who lived here. Education took place within the different compounds, with thousands of pupils attending classes every week by September 1917. Within Camp I a series of specialist institutions emerged, including a commercial school and a textile school.[46] The school in Camp III compound 5 formally took in pupils from September 1915, and by the autumn of 1917 the focus of education lay in languages, commerce and technology.[47] In Camp IV education became centralized, with the establishment of a school board as part of an overarching committee structure which existed here from 1915. By the end of 1917 a total of 389 pupils attended classes run by fifty-one teachers. A reorganization took place in early 1918 which set up nine different schools including a high school aimed at younger internees preparing for the 'War Examinations' instituted by the German government. Others focused upon engineering, agriculture and commerce. A hotel school was aimed at the large numbers of Germans employed in hospitality before the war. There was also a nautical school and an industrial school, while general schools emerged in compounds 1, 3 and 6. As well as this formal schooling, Camp IV had a Literary and Scientific Society which organized regular lectures.[48]

Some of the camps including Knockaloe and Holyport, held academics. In the former a Professor Albers directed the school in Camp IV,[49] while a Professor Kohlsbutter had 'done excellent astronomical research during his imprisonment at Holyport'. The school here was 'presided over by University professors and scientific men with blackboards covered with maps, designs, and tables'.[50] The largest concentration of academics, however, appears to have lived in Wakefield, which held sixty-seven. They initially ran informal classes but their presence led to the development of university-level education with at a Camp College, which opened to students on 1 October 1917. About 650 internees listened to lectures, which remained well attended until Christmas, but repatriation of internees in the following year caused disruption, although the institution survived until the autumn. Cohen-Portheim, in keeping with his cynical tone, described the idea of a university at Wakefield as 'a pathetic delusion'. Nobody seems to have graduated but those lecturers who attempted to make the idea work did so in good faith, including Hermann J. Held, who had found himself in Cambridge at the outbreak of war.[51]

The development of so much educational activity meant that the camps needed a ready supply of books, which they obtained from a variety of charitable sources. For example, the Deutsche Dichter Gedächtnis Stiftung, which took an interest in supplying books to smaller libraries, provided almost 650,000 volumes to German troops and internees all over the world between August 1914 and December 1917, of which 10,681 went to German prisoners in Britain. Individuals also appear to have received books from the Evangelische Blättervereinigung für Soldaten and Kriegsgefangene. Those prisoners held in Handforth obtained books from at least eight different sources, mostly charities and foundations, but also including publishers.[52]

The ready supply of books led to the development of significant libraries. By August 1917, for instance, the catalogue in Handforth listed 2,692 volumes.[53] The largest collections, as we would expect, lay in Knockaloe, where each of the sub-camps had its own central library together with others in the compounds. In April 1916 each camp held approximately 4,000 books, 'of which 40 per cent are in constant circulation. A penny per month is charged for books lent to men who can afford to pay for it'.[54] By the end of the war the number of volumes held in Camp IV alone had reached 18,080, divided in the following way:

Classification of Books	
Scholastic Books	1,130
Classical Books	1,531
Technical Books	2,327
German Novels	5,015
English Novels	2,312
French Novels	442

Other languages	318
German Popular Editions (Reklam)	1,224
Illustrated Periodicals	1,486
Religious Books	2,295
Total	18,080[55]

Such a large number and diversity of books point to a prisoner population which devoted a significant amount of its time to reading as well as to a literate and multilingual group of internees. Many of the volumes, especially those described as scholastic, technical and literary, had connections with the educational activities. Such books covered a large range of subjects ranging from history and philosophy to commerce, transport and mathematics.[56]

As well as reading, many prisoners became involved in writing. Although some authors produced accounts of their experiences behind barbed wire after returning to Germany, many had already begun doing this while still in Britain. At least one internee appears to have written an academic monograph while interned in Alexandra Palace, using the limited number of books available in the camp library as well as obtaining others from outside.[57] At the same time, at least one volume of poetry appeared in Knockaloe, focusing on the realities of everyday life.[58]

In fact, much more poetry appeared in what became the main literary vehicle for internees during the Great War, in the form of the prisoner-of-war newspaper, which, as Rainer Pöppinghege has demonstrated, became a phenomenon among German, English and French internees held in camps throughout the world during the conflict. These evolved in co-operation with camp censors and necessitated the existence of some form of printing press. Those who ran them invariably came from educated middle-class backgrounds. In Britain such newspapers became formalized during the course of 1915, reflecting the development of more permanent camps during that year. Pöppinghege has pointed out that, while these publications initially devoted space to events beyond the barbed wire, they focused increasingly upon the camps themselves. One of their key functions consisted of providing information on social and educational activities within individual camps, although they also allowed prisoners to express their feelings about internment, especially through literary sketches and poems. They had an overarching aim of creating community within specific camps.

Many prisoners sent editions, which might have a print run of several thousands, to their relatives, and these kept them informed about camp life.[59] Jennifer Kewley Draskau, using the newspapers produced upon the Isle of Man, has focused upon their function in creating a sense of *Heimat*, fuelled by the feeling of alienation which the prisoners felt on being transferred here and encouraged by the overwhelmingly German male environment in which they found themselves.[60]

Pöppinghege has identified a total of thirty-two different camp newspapers published in Britain during the Great War, including four at Douglas, five at Handforth and seven at Knockaloe, although their numbers point to the fact that they tended to remain short-lived. Those at Handforth had a circulation of 250–300 while *Stobsiade* reached 4,000 and the Knockaloe *Lager-Zeitung* 4,500.[61] Although most newspapers such as the Dorchester *Deustche Blätter* and the Wakefield *Lager-Bote* (both from 1916)[62] followed Pöppinghege's pattern of concentrating upon events within the camps which they serviced, the handwritten *Deutsche Zeitung* published in Brocton in 1918 devoted much more attention to military events outside.[63] *Stobsiade* first appeared on 5 September 1915 and survived, intermittently, until early 1919, when Stobs became a purely military camp. The editorial team then moved to Knockaloe, where they established the *Lager-Zeitung*. The prisoners typeset *Stobsiade* and then checked it. In all the publication process took about one week.[64] The first article in the first edition focused upon some of the key aspects of internment life.

Some of the newspapers published in Knockaloe came from specific camps, while others attempted to serve a specific constituency, including one aimed at gymnasts.[65] The earliest effort here was *Werden*, edited by Pastor Hartmann, which seems to have appeared only twice in April and May 1915 and mostly provided information on forthcoming events. *Quousque Tandem* ran to just one edition of nine pages in October 1915. It also contained much information on events within Knockaloe as well as the camp itself and the internees, together with three poems. *Lager-Echo*, which appeared intermittently from 1916 until 1918 and serviced Camp III, devoted much of its space to pieces contemplating the internment experience.[66] A poem from 15 November 1917 entitled 'Am Winterabend', for instance, did not simply focus upon the anonymous writer's current condition but also looked back to the years he had spent with his wife, as well as his connection to his Fatherland. The *Lager-Zeitung* first appeared in September 1916 through the efforts of H. Beckmann, E. Behrens and F. Oberdorfer, who had previously edited *Stobsiade*. It described its purpose as the promotion and recording of activities within the camp and 'to show relatives abroad that the inmates of the camp were making the best of circumstances'. There were twenty-six issues with an average circulation of 2,500, of which 750 went abroad. This newspaper carried a wide range of articles including those which informed readers of artistic and sporting activities within Camp IV, together with literary pieces. It regularly published poems on a variety of subjects including life within the camp, weather, climate and the seasons, the surrounding countryside, imprisonment and 'In der Heimat'.[67]

High culture

The literary pieces which appeared in the newspapers form part of what we might describe as a high culture which emerged in the camps, being developed by many of the middle-class internees. While some of the activities, such as painting and sculpting, were relatively solitary, much that took place behind barbed wire involved the development of community, including music and, above all, theatre, which brought together significant numbers of people as directors, performers and spectators. Despite this, we should still remember that high cultural activities, like the celebration of Christmas, served as a substitute for real-life and events outside in an attempt to construct pre-war realities. Theatrical performances even created substitute women because of the necessity for male internees to dress up for female parts.

Having been an artist before the war, Paul Cohen-Portheim could continue his painting within Wakefield, where, although he had to readjust to his new surroundings, he managed to paint on a variety of themes, some of them in response to commissions. Some of his fellow internees, meanwhile, carried out wood-carving.[68] Similarly, a report on Holyport mentioned both these of activities among the prisoners held there.[69] The Isle of Man inmates used all sorts of materials to create artistic objects.[70] Although there 'was an acute shortage of sheet metal . . . there was no shortage of empty bully-beef tins. These were cut up, flattened into sheets, made into mugs, cake tins, baking pans, pastry cutters, funnels, scoops, boxes, candlesticks, ashtrays, footlights, and suits of armour for theatrical productions'. At the same time:

> Imprisoned sculptors, for want of better material, carved the meat-bones discarded by the cook-houses. The bones were first boiled to remove fat, marrow and gristle, then bleached with soda or bleaching powder. Long leg bones were transfigured into slender flower vases decorated with carvings of roses, tulips, lilies, or a human figure. The shorter bones were made into pincushions, ashtrays, match and cigarette stands, table cruets, napkin rings, paper knives, and brooches, very delicately carved.[71]

In Alexandra Palace, 'Woodworking, carving ox bones into ornaments, marquetry, toy-making and art (paintings, drawing etc.) all flourished.' But the available workspace here proved 'wholly inadequate' for the number of men who wished to carry out such activities, and so they moved them to their bedsides. However, the constant sound of 'hammering, sawing, filing and so on . . . was extremely detrimental to the mental health of the prisoners, especially during the long winter months, when forced to remain indoors by bad weather and early head counts'.[72] Some of the art and craftwork actually found buyers.[73] The camps also held exhibitions displaying the efforts of the prisoners. In September 1917 Lofthouse Park held its second exhibition in the west camp, with 500 paintings on display.[74] In Ripon an exhibition took place in June 1919, with an accompanying booklet, which featured the work of only one prisoner, Georg Wörlen.[75] In Stobs, meanwhile, the prisoners held two exhibitions in 1915 which included model ships in bottles, model aeroplanes and zeppelins and portraits of prisoners, together with landscapes, woodcarvings and musical instruments made from available materials.[76]

In fact, music became an important part of camp life, reflecting both the importance of this art form in pre-war Germany[77] and the presence of large numbers of musicians in London before 1914, who ranged from players in the leading British orchestras to members of marching brass bands.[78] Margery West, commenting on the Isle of Man, wrote that 'Concerts were an important feature of . . . life behind barbed wire', as they 'were needed to keep up morale and were a necessary outlet for those alien prisoners with talent going to waste'.[79]

Ensembles of various sizes emerged to perform concerts in camps throughout Britain, especially those which lasted longest, although even temporary establishments developed a musical life. On board the *Ascania*, for instance, which held internees for a few months in late 1914 and 1915, an Ascania orchestra developed which performed popular pieces on at least two occasions, while the prisoners also held a carol service during Christmas 1914.[80] Wakefield had developed a musical society in all three of its sub-camps by 1916 and arranged all types of concert. For example, a concert in the north camp on 4 February 1916 featured one of Beethoven's trios for violin, cello and piano. In Dorchester music became a feature of life with the arrival of the first prisoners. A string orchestra focused upon the symphonies of Haydn, Mozart and Beethoven, although the camp also featured chamber and solo performances.[81] Handforth held internees who could play all of the major instruments, which allowed the development of an orchestra. On 26 June 1917 music played a large role in a variety evening which included acrobats and 'Hebrew Comedians'. The music included choral and orchestral pieces, trios and ragtime.[82] Alexandra Palace also developed 'a strong and well-trained orchestra . . . in fact, it was said at that time in London the finest orchestra was . . . to be found' here made up of 'many talented musicians' and 'industrious amateurs'.[83] This orchestra came into existence in September 1915 and initially performed weekly concerts on Sunday evenings using instruments provided by Dr Markel's Committee. As the war progressed concerts took place several times a week until the closure of the camp.[84]

A sophisticated musical life developed in the camps on the Isle of Man, as analysed by Jutta Raab Hansen. She has pointed to symphony orchestras, choirs and ensembles as well as music critics and the use of music in religious festivities and plays.[85] One of the most significant groups in Douglas was the Gleitsmann Orchestra, named after its director, Friedrich Gleitsmann-Wolff, and performing regularly during 1916 and 1917.[86] A choir existed in Douglas from the early stages of the war, but was dissolved in July 1916 owing to disagreements among its members. Nevertheless, a new one held over 100 performances in the year that followed.[87] In Knockaloe each of the four camps had both a string orchestra and a brass band. Although these sometimes accompanied theatrical performances, they also regularly performed purely instrumental

Figure 5.3 The band at Dorchester. Music became an important activity for both civilian and military internees, helping prisoners to pass their time as well as creating community among band members and their audiences.

concerts.[88] Whitsun 1917 witnessed a concert given by 'Mr Sterbal and his new symphony orchestra' in compound 2 of Camp I which included pieces by Liszt and Tchaikovsky. A positive review of this event written in German in one of the Knockaloe camp newspapers began and ended with the English quotation 'Iron bars do not a prison make'.[89] In June 1918 compound 5 of Camp III held a series of concerts with a diverse programme which focused upon opera and included overtures and extracts from Wagner's *Rienzi* and Puccini's *Madame Butterfly*, as well as pieces by Weber and Donizetti.[90] Subscription concerts also appear to have developed, as witnessed by four which took place during a third concert cycle in May and June 1917. The event on 9 May included ten fairly short pieces which began with Rossini's overture to *Semiramide* and the Adagio from Weber's Clarinet Concerto performed by a Mr Degen. In fact, excerpts, rather than complete pieces, appear to have been the norm.[91] Those who attended these events had high praise for them. James Baily regularly received invitations and 'had not heard anything elsewhere to surpass them . . . Among the conductors and artists were men whose names were well known in musical circles.'[92] Similarly, A. L. Vischer 'was present at a string band concert in compound 4 of Camp IV. The programme consisted chiefly of classical music and it was an impressive sight to watch the audience of several hundred prisoners, most of whom were seamen and working men by profession, listening to music with the greatest attention.'

Vischer's November 1917 report on Knockaloe continued, 'Nearly every night some dramatic performance is given',[93] pointing to the fact that theatre became as important as music in the camps throughout Europe, as recognized by several authorities. As early as 1933 Hermann Pörzgen examined the importance of theatre for German prisoners during the Great War, viewing it as an escape from the monotony of captivity which they faced and a development which could prevent barbed wire disease. It helped to divert attention from the everyday realities of internment, provided an intellectual stimulus and allowed the development of a communal life by serving as a meeting point for new interests which brought prisoners together.[94] More recently Alon Rachamimov, focusing upon those interned in Russia, has pointed to the power of performance 'to combat physical and mental decay'.[95] Rachamimov has also studied the cross-dressing actors who played female roles on the stage, arguing that they helped to keep the idea of women alive in the camps and also allowed those who felt uncomfortable in normal gender boundaries to express themselves. He points out that some actors developed a following characteristic of actresses outside the camps.[96] In Camp IV of Knockaloe several 'female impersonators' gained 'well merited success'.[97] Jennifer Kewley Draskau, focusing upon the Isle of Man, has summed up the various roles of female impersonators as follows:

> Whether cherished as a skilful illusion that added zest to the internment experience, as a wistful chimera, an erotic interest, or a reassurance that somewhere outside the wire another, more familiar desirable reality continued to exist despite the forces of destruction, the drag artistes on the prison stage . . . played an important role in the social and psychological resilience of heterogeneous all-male societies within the internment camps.[98]

In this sense, the cross-dressers added an extra and perhaps crucial dimension to the more general social activity in the camps which

Figure 5.4 Theatre rehearsal at Handforth. Theatre became one of the most important leisure activities among prisoners throughout the world during the First World War, and most of the long-established camps in Britain developed their own. Theatre helped to bring prisoners together but also kept the image of woman alive as a result of cross-dressing actors.

had the role of relieving boredom and depression. Nevertheless, like much else which existed in First World War camps, they represented substitutes, in this case for real women. As Cohen-Portheim recalled of those who played female roles in Wakefield: 'When I look at some of the snapshots I possess, the "leading ladies" look rather absurd to me now, but they did not look so at the time.'[99]

Pörzgen calculated that 69 camp theatres existed in Britain, including 9 for officers, 27 for privates and 33 for civilians.[100] One of the most well-developed military theatre groups emerged in Brocton in July 1917, shortly after the camp came into existence and sustained by the thousands of people who found themselves interned here. In its first season it performed 40 pieces on 81 evenings and in the second year 31 on 61 evenings, encompassing a wide repertoire.[101] The theatre society at Dorchester, meanwhile, staged a wide range of plays during 1918 and 1919.[102] Similarly, the civilian theatre which existed in Wakefield continued when combatants replaced civilians at the end of 1918.[103]

A sophisticated threatre culture developed in the Isle of Man camps. An article in one of the Douglas newspapers stated that the maintenance of two theatres for 2,000 people represented a significant cultural achievement.[104] A series of programmes which have survived help us to establish some of the key personalities here, who included Walter Wollanke and W. Schmieder. Both of these individuals also took many of the leading roles, with Wollanke invariably playing women.[105] In Knockaloe, theatre, along with education, probably became the most important social activity, with performances taking place not only in each of the individual camps, but also in many, if not all, of the compounds. A total of twenty separate theatres seem to have existed here.[106] In Camp IV seven independent theatres emerged, each with its own stage and even orchestral pit, pointing to the numbers of people involved in such activity. The individual companies 'toured' the other compounds. In total, 170 actors lived in Camp IV, together with seventy-four people connected with theatrical activity as stage hands and dressmakers, scenery painters and electricians. Between October 1915 and March 1919 a total of 1,125 'theatrical plays' were 'produced' here together with 84 variety shows, 220 concerts and 102 'festivals, social evenings etc.', making a 'total number of entertainments of 1,532'.[107] A similar situation existed in Camp I, where some of those who had spent time in Alexandra Palace ended up in compound 1 and resurrected the theatrical activity which they had created at their previous camp. In addition to giving evening performances, the actors spent much of the day releasing.[108] In Camp I each of the six compounds also developed its own theatre. The one in compound 2 even produced its own history.[109] It could cater for 350 spectators.[110] The theatres produced a large range of plays, most of them in German.[111]

The presence of theatre in the camps acted against the arrival of the most important form of popular culture at the time, the cinema.[112] The latter, as a more passive form of entertainment, would have deprived many of those involved in the theatre of their occupation. At the same time, problems of censorship also existed. Nevertheless, by the end of the war contemporary films, excluding those with war themes, did make an appearance in the camps as cinemas began to function, as evidenced by experiences in Knockaloe. Between 24 June 1917 and 14 March 1918 seventy-four showings of English-language films took place in compound 4 of Camp II. The cinema in Camp IV employed twenty-three men.[113]

Sport

The other major form of popular culture which became part of everyday life in the camps consisted of sport and exercise, which may have involved more people than theatre activity through the range of games which the prisoners developed, both competitive and non-competitive and encompassing English and German sports. Once again, although such activities emerged in both the military and civilian camps, they became most sophisticated in the settled and long-standing civilian camps, with the development of of competitive leagues. An article in one of the Knockaloe newspapers summed up the role of sport by stating the obvious: 'A healthy body means a healthy mind.'[114] Some naval prisoners interned at Oswestry found that talking about football acted as a useful icebreaker for communicating with their guards and even improving their English.[115] We can also contextualize sporting activity in the camps against the background of its importance during the Great War, as Tony Mason and Eliza Riedi have demonstrated with regard to the British army.[116] In a different context Charles Korr and Marvin Close have focused upon the importance of football for anti-Apartheid prisoners on Robin Island in South Africa during the 1960s, suggesting that the league they established allowed the prisoners to 'gain more control over their day-to-day lives'.[117]

The British authorities recognized the value of sport and exercise by providing recreational facilities in most of the camps, irrespective of their size. The seventy-two combatants held at Rosyth in Scotland, who worked for nine and a half hours per day in the local brickworks in June 1917, had access to a 'sports field outside the camp . . . every evening, where the prisoners have a bowling alley and a football ground'.[118] Similarly, the 231 combatants interned in Lentran in Scotland, employed in 'cutting wood and working a steam saw mill' for eight hours per day, could use a sports field outside the camp during the evening.[119] The more established places of internment, whether military or civilian, developed more sophisticated sporting facilities. Leigh, for instance, had three recreation grounds, although these partly acted as sites for 'military and physical drill'.[120] In Jersey the prisoners 'have an exercise field 310 yards long and 120 yards wide, where they play football and other games. They also take route marches of between five and six miles, two or three times a week, 300 men going each time, weather permitting.'[121] Furthermore, as the camp lay not far from the sea, during the summer 'the neighbouring beach offers facilities for sea-bathing', which the prisoners of war utilized 'in relays of about 400', which suggests a coastal idyll.[122] In Colsterdale a 'large lawn and two tennis courts offered opportunities to participate in sporting activity' including football, handball, rounders and gymnastics.[123] Facilities in the civilian camps became perhaps most sophisticated, although few would have had access to open-air bathing like those held in Jersey. Wakefield had several sports fields, while the men 'are taken for route marches three or four times a week'. Furthermore, a total of eight tennis courts existed here for the predominantly middle-class prisoners, together with 'a gymnasium, fitted with all the usual gymnastic appliances'.[124] Those held at Douglas had access to two recreation fields totalling over ten acres by the spring of 1916, at least five tennis courts, a football field and a running track.

> The interned men have opportunity for Tennis, Football, Fistball, Skittles, for which a fine new alley has been built, Running, Dancing, Boxing, Wrestling and Swimming. They have two Billiard Tables and a ping-pong table. There is also a very large gymnastic class in connection with the Upper Camp and a small one, mostly for Swedish Drill, in the Lower Camp. There is a Swimming Pool in the Lower Camp.[125]

Knockaloe provided a similar range of facilities including a 'large recreation field open to each compound as a rule twice a week, alternately morning and afternoon', while each compound also had its own hall of 150 by 30 feet.[126]

The prisoners took full advantage of the facilities available. In Camp IV in Knockaloe they participated in gymnastics, athletics, cricket, football, tennis and golf (based on three holes). As many as 180 people played cricket, pointing to the Anglicization of many of the internees. Football proved most popular, with 36 teams in existence between 1915 and 1919 and playing 600 matches, including 64 between different compounds and 25 between the sub-camps.[127] The gymnastics society of Camp I compound 6 produced an annual report on its activities during 1916 which stated that it had 90 members, '75 active and 15 inactive', but worked out that 7,425 people had used the available equipment.[128] Meanwhile, prisoners at Oswestry established an athletic club whose activities alternated

Figure 5.5 Gymnastics society in Knockaloe. This is a photograph of one of several such organizations which existed in this enormous camp.

with football because of the availability of just one sports field.[129] As we have previously seen, sport also became especially important in Jersey, where activities included handball, athletics, gymnastics and football.[130]

While physical activity became part of the everyday lives of prisoners, sporting festivals also characterized the camps, perhaps representing an occasion to relieve monotony. On 15 August 1915 the military sports committee in Stobs organized its third festival. The event began with a gymnastics exhibition; this was followed by a pentathlon competition consisting of stone throwing, high jump, triple jump, hurdling and gymnastics, which was won by a junior military officer called Schneider. Other athletics events also took place, together with a football world championship between a *Blücher* and infantry team, which the former won by two goals to one.[131] Meanwhile, in August 1917 a *Heimat* festival occurred in Camp I at Knockaloe, which involved a range of activities including sport but also theatre and foreign-language presentations. Preparations for this event took place through May, June and July and included negotiations with the commandant of Knockaloe and qualifying tournaments for the tennis and football competitions. The event lasted for a whole week. In addition to the competitions which took place during the day, plays and concerts followed in the evenings.[132] Other events focused upon specific sports, such as the tennis tournament in Douglas in July 1915. Meanwhile, on 13 August 1916 a boxing tournament was held in Douglas to decide upon the camp champion.[133] Similarly, a gymnastics festival in Camp IV at Knockaloe on 15 August 1916 began at 8.00 a.m. with music sounding throughout the camp.[134]

Prison camp societies or substitute societies?

These sporting festivals represented an attempt by confined men to continue with the normalities of everyday life, as did the educational, religious and theatrical activities. The available sources point to the success of such activities, as indicated by the scale of the events taking place, although part of the explanation lies in the amount of spare time which prisoners had, especially in the long-standing civilian camps. There seems no doubt that theatre, sport and the celebration of festivals of various types, whether religious or sporting, both relieved the boredom of internment and created a sense of camaraderie or positive mental unity.

In view of the slaughter taking place in Europe, from which the military prisoners had escaped and which the civilian internees had never experienced, spending time playing football, learning foreign languages, listening to top-class musicians playing the music of Beethoven and Mozart or regularly attending the theatre seemed almost the ideal masculine existence during the Great War. Rather than risking their lives on the European battlefields, internees in Britain remained safe and comfortable.

Yet if we scratch below the surface and dissect the activities in which the prisoners participated, everything lends itself to interpretation as an illusion. The men found themselves held against their will in an all-male environment away from any members of their families, especially their wives, daughters and other females. All of the events which they constructed represented a substitute for their previous lives. While issues such as lack of space and privacy may have affected middle-class internees more than those with working-class backgrounds, events such as Christmas brought home to all their separation from families and the fact that they found themselves spending the ultimate family time in an all-male environment. What they experienced essentially constituted a substitute

Christmas. In fact, life behind barbed wire really represented a substitute for their lives before the war. The educational, sporting and cultural activities certainly did keep prisoners together and many clearly enjoyed them. Yet we can write of all types of substitutes for life outside the camps: substitute food, substitute sport, substitute festivals, substitute education and substitute theatre, which contained the ultimate illusion in the form of substitute women made up of men who dressed up and helped to keep the outside world alive. These cross-dressers symbolized everything about the internment camp experience. The prisoners needed them to keep their image of womanhood and perhaps sexual desire alive (although they appear to have remained untouchable), yet they were ultimately substitute women, an illusion, necessary for surviving years behind barbed wire.

Notes

1 Leslie Baily, *Craftsman and Quaker: The Story of James T. Baily, 1876–1957* (London, 1959), p. 100, describing Knockaloe.
2 Panikos Panayi, *German Immigrants in Britain during the Nineteenth Century, 1815–1914* (Oxford, 1995), pp. 90–129.
3 See Chapter 6 below.
4 John Davidson Ketchum, *Ruhleben: A Prison Camp Society* (Toronto, 1965), pp. 35–57.
5 Ibid., pp. 104–7, 129–32.
6 Ibid., pp. 192–311.
7 Frederick Lewis Dunbar-Kalckreuth, *Die Männerinsel* (Leipzig, 1940), p. 193.
8 The activities of these groups receive attention in Chapter 8 below.
9 Paul Cohen-Portheim, *Time Stood Still: My Internment in England* (London, 1931), p. 93.
10 For religion in Germany in the Kaiserreich see, for example, Olaf Blaschke and Frank-Michael Kuhlermann, eds, *Religion im Kaiserreich: Milieus – Mentalitäten – Krisen* (Gütersloh, 1996). Religion among the German community in Britain is covered by Panayi, *German Immigrants*, pp. 149–70.
11 NA/FO383/277, Swiss Embassy Report on Hendon, 27 September 1917.
12 NA/FO383/432, Replies to Statements of Complaints Transmitted with Note Verbale No. III B. 45841/160005/ Dated November 12th 1917.
13 NA/FO383/505, Swiss Embassy Report on Bramley, 21 January 1919.

14 NA/FO383/276, Swiss Embassy Report on Dorchester, 2 April 1917.
15 BA/R901/83077, Swiss Embassy Report on Holyport, 9 August 1917.
16 *Stobsiade*, October 1917.
17 Otto Schimming, *13 Monate hinter dem Stacheldraht: Alexandra Palace, Knockaloe, Isle of Man, Stratford* (Stuttgart, 1919), p. 12.
18 NA/FO383/277, Swiss Embassy Report on Douglas, 29 November 1917.
19 NA/HO45/10947/266042, Civilian Prisoner of War Camp No. IV, Knockaloe, I.O.M.
20 Adolf Vielhauer, *Das englische Konzentrationslager bei Peel (Insel Man)* (Bad Nassau, 1917), p. 5; F. Siegmund-Schultze, 'Die Gefangenenseelsorge in England', *Die Eiche*, vol. 6 (1918), p. 319; MNH/B115/xf, Bericht über die Evangelische Kirchengemeinde des Kriegsgefangenen Lagers Knockaloe; NA/FO383/181, Home Office to Foreign Office, 29 May 1916.
21 NA/FO383/181, Home Office to Foreign Office, 29 May 1916.
22 NA/HO45/10947/266042, Civilian Prisoner of War Camp No. IV, Knockaloe, I.O.M.
23 Gerald Newton, 'Wie lange noch? Germans at Knockaloe, 1914–18', in Gerald Newton, ed., *Mutual Exchanges: Sheffield Münster Colloquium II* (Frankfurt, 1999), p. 111.
24 Siegmund-Schultze, 'Die Gefangenenseelsorge', p. 349.
25 MNH/MS11425, Sketches of a German Interned Civilian Prisoner in England (1914–1919).
26 Siegmund-Schultze, 'Die Gefangenenseelsorge', pp. 318, 324–6, 337–9, 343–4, 346; *Arbeitsbericht der Evangelische Blättervereinigung für Soldaten and Kriegsgefangene Deutsche, Bad Nassau (Lahn) über das Tätigkeitsjahr 1917/1918* (Bad Nassau, 1918); *Stobsiade*, October 1917; Sophie McDougall Hine, *Bishop Bury: Late Bishop of North and Central Europe* (London, 1933).
27 BA/MA/MSG200/703, Pesach, 1917.
28 BA/MA/MSG200/2225, *Deutsche Zeitung* (Brocton), Ostern 1919; BA/MA/MSG200/1837, *Die Hunnen*, 1 June 1917; BA/MSG200/1878, *Sylvester Zeitung*, Skipton, 1918; BA/MA/MSG200/2219, *Faschingzeitung*, Holyport, 1919.
29 Mark Connelly, *Christmas: A Social History* (London, 1999); Joe Perry, *Christmas in Germany: A Cultural History* (Chapel Hill, NC, 2010).
30 Perry, *Christmas in Germany*, pp. 93–138.
31 Hans Erich Benedix, *In England interniert* (Gotha, 1916), p. 69.
32 *Stobsiade*, January–February 1918.
33 J. Machner, *Gefangenen in England: Erlebnisse and Beobachtungen* (Hildesheim, 1920), p. 190.

34 Benedix, *In England interniert*, pp. 69–70.
35 *Scotsman*, 18 December 1915; BA/R67/805, William Whiting, 'Christmas and New Year at Frongoch'.
36 Benedix, *In England interniert*, p. 70; BA/R67/508, William Whiting, 'Christmas and New Year at Frongoch'.
37 See, for instance. Benedix, *In England interniert*, pp. 70–3; *Stobsiade*, January–February 1918; Machner, *Gefangen in England*, pp. 186–90.
38 Panayi, *German Immigrants*, pp. 134–8, 191–2.
39 NA/FO383/304, Camp Schools for German Prisoners of War.
40 *Scotsman*, 19 November 1914.
41 L. Bogenstätter and H. Zimmermann, Die *Welt hinter Stacheldraht: Eine Chronik des englischen Kriegsgefangenlagers Handforth bei Manchester* (Munich, 1921), pp. 165, 174.
42 NA/FO383/162, US Embassy Report on Stobs, 17 February 1916.
43 BL, Rudolf Rocker, 'Alexandra Park Internment Camp in the First World War', pp. 15–19.
44 MNH/MS09379/3, Bruno Kahn, 'Abbreviated Report on the First Year's Working of the Camp-School established at Douglas Alien's Camp', October 1915.
45 The registers can be found in the Bruno Kahn Papers in MNH/MS09379/1 and MNH/MS09379/2.
46 Ludwig Meyn and Wolfgang J. Mörlins, eds, *Knockaloe Aliens Detention Camp, 1914–1917: Drei Jahre Schul-Arbeit* (Knockaloe, 1917); Textil-Fach-Schule, Zivilgefangenen Lager Knockaloe, Insel Man, England, Lager I, Compound 4, *Jahres-Bericht, 1917–1918* (Knockaloe, 1918); Handels-Schule, Camp I, Compound IV, *Bericht über des Winterhalbjahr 1916/1917 und Lehrplan für das Sommerhalbjahr 1917* (Knockaloe, 1917).
47 MNH/B115/xf, Lager-Schule Compund 5 gegründet 10 September 1915, Stundenplan für das 5. Halbjahr Winterhalbjahr 1917/18.
48 MNH/B115/43q, Camp IV, Knockaloe, I. O. M., Final Report and Statistical Record on the Internal Administration of the Prisoners of War Camp No. IV, 1915–1919.
49 NA/FO383/163, US Embassy Report on Knockaloe, 18 May 1916.
50 *Scotsman*, 20 December 1916.
51 Cohen-Portheim, *Time Stood Still*, pp. 92–3; Peter Wood, 'The Zivilinternierungslager at Lofthouse Park', in Kate Taylor, ed., *Aspects of Wakefield 3: Discovering Local History* (Barnsley, 2001), pp. 97–107; Henning Ibs, *Hermann J. Held (1890–1963): Ein Kieler Gelehrtenleben in den Fängen der Zeitläufe* (Frankfurt, 2000), pp. 34–48.
52 F. W. Brepohl, ed., *Briefe unserer Gefangenen* (Bad Nassau,

1916), pp. 13–14; Bogenstätter and Zimmermann, *Die Welt hinter Stacheldraht*, p. 169; *Verzeichnis der Knockaloe-Bücherei* (Hamburg, 1918), p. 2.
53 Bogenstätter and Zimmermann, *Die Welt hinter Stacheldraht*, p. 169.
54 NA/FO383/163, US Embassy Report on Knockaloe, 18 May 1916.
55 MNH/B115/43q, Camp IV, Knockaloe, I. O. M., Final Report and Statistical Record on the Internal Administration of the Prisoners of War Camp No. IV, 1915–1919.
56 *Verzeichnis der Knockaloe-Bücherei*, p. 7.
57 Henry S. Simonis, *Zum alten jüdischen Zivilrecht* (Berlin, 1922).
58 Karl Knauft, *Die schwarze Stadt: Knockaloe vom Morgengrauen bis Mitternacht* (Knockaloe, 1918).
59 Rainer Pöppinghege, *Im Lager unbesiegt: Deutsche, englische und französische Kriegsgefangenen-Zeitungen im Ersten Weltkrieg* (Essen, 2006), pp. 183–294.
60 Jennifer Kewley Draskau, 'Relocating the Heimat: Great War Internment Literature from the Isle of Man', *German Studies Review*, vol. 32 (2009), 83–106.
61 Pöppinghege, *Im Lager unbesiegt*, pp. 318–20.
62 See BA/MSG200/1831.
63 BA/MSG/200/2224.
64 Julie M. Horne, 'The German Connection: The Stobs Camp Newspaper, 1916–1919', *Transactions of the Hawick Archaeological Society* (1988), 26–32.
65 Pöppinghege, *Im Lager unbesiegt*, pp. 320–1.
66 Ibid.
67 Draskau, 'Relocating the Heimat', p. 86; MNH/B115/43q, Camp IV, Knockaloe, I. O. M., Final Report and Statistical Record on the Internal Administration of the Prisoners of War Camp No. IV, 1915–1919.
68 Cohen-Portheim, *Time Stood Still*, pp. 138–45.
69 BA/R901/83077, Swiss Embassy Report on Holyport, 9 August 1917.
70 Yvonne Cresswell, 'Behind the Wire: The Material Culture of Civilian Internees on the Isle of Man in the First World War', in Richard Dove, ed.,*'Totally un-English'? Britain's Internment of 'Enemy Aliens' in Two World Wars* (Amsterdam, 2005), pp. 46–61.
71 Baily, *Craftsman and Quaker*, p. 100.
72 Janet Harris, *Alexandra Palace: A Hidden History* (Stroud, 2005), pp. 99–101.
73 See Chapter 6 below.
74 SBB, Kriegsgefangenenlager Lofthouse Park.
75 BA/MSG200/1961.
76 *Stobsiade*, 5 September, 1 December 1915.

77 As an introduction see Celia Applegate and Pamela Potter, 'Germans as the "People of Music": Genealogy of an Identity', in Celia Applegate and Pamela Potter, eds, *Music and German National Identity* (London, 2002), pp. 1–35.

78 Panayi, *German Immigrants*, pp. 126–30; Stefan Manz, *Migranten und Internierte: Deutsche in Glasgow, 1864–1918* (Stuttgart, 2003), pp. 111–24.

79 Margery West, *Island at War: The Remarkable Role Played by the Small Manx Nation in the Great War 1914–1918* (Laxey, 1986), p. 88.

80 BA/MA/MSG200/2384, Internierten-Schiff 'Askania' [sic], Drei Programme von Veranstaltungen auf der Askania.

81 BA/MSG200/1878, *Lager-Bote*, 15 Februray 1916; *Deutsche Blaetter*, 24 December 1916.

82 Bogenstätter and Zimmermann, *Die Welt hinter Stacheldraht*, p. 232; BA/R67/218, DRK, Interner Wochenbericht No. 98, 27 October 1917

83 Pál Stoffa, *Round the World to Freedom* (London, 1933), p. 194.

84 Harris, *Alexandra Palace*, pp. 97–8.

85 Jutta Raab Hansen, 'Die Bedeutung der Musik für 26.000 internierte Zivilisten während des Ersten Weltkrieges auf der Isle of Man', in Dove, ed., *'Totally un-English'?*, pp. 63–81.

86 Ibid., p. 68; *Die Lager Laterne*, 13 August 1916; *Unter Uns*, 2 September 1917; *Das Schleierlicht*, 18 June 1916.

87 BA/MA/MSG200/845, Lagerchor Douglas, 'Jahres Bericht 1916/17'.

88 NA/FO383/163, US Embassy Report on Knockaloe, 18 May 1916.

89 *Die Hunnen*, 1 June 1917.

90 *Lager-Echo*, 25 August 1918.

91 BA/MA/MSG200/1973, Dritte Konzert-Zyklus.

92 MNH/MS10417/4, Papers of James T. Baily, Scrapbook No. 8, pp. 595–6.

93 NA/FO383/277, Swiss Embassy Report on Knockaloe, 29 November 1917.

94 Hermann Pörzgen, *Theater ohne Frau: Das Bühnenleben der kriegsgefangenen Deutschen, 1914–1920* (Königsberg, 1933), pp. 5–6.

95 Alon Rachamimov, 'The Disruptive Comforts of Drag: (Trans) Gender Performances among Prisoners of War in Russia, 1914–1920', *American Historical Review*, vol. 111 (2006), 372.

96 Ibid., pp. 375–82.

97 MNH/B115/43q, Camp IV, Knockaloe, I. O. M., Final Report and Statistical Record on the Internal Administration of the Prisoners of War Camp No. IV, 1915–1919.

98 Jennifer Kewley Draskau, 'Prisoners in Petticoats: Drag Performance

and its Effects in Great War Internment Camps on the Isle of Man', *Proceedings of the Isle of Man Natural History and Antiquarian Society*, vol. 12 (April 2007–March 2009), 202.

99 Cohen-Portheim, *Time Stood Still*, p. 148.

100 Pörzgen, *Theater ohne Frau*, p. 166.

101 BA/MA/MSG200/1966, Festschrift zur Feier des 2. jährigen Bestehens des Deutschen Theaters Broctonlager.

102 BA/MA/MSG200/1957, Dorchester Theater Verein.

103 Cohen-Portheim, *Time Stood Still*, pp. 146–58; Pörzgen, *Theater ohne Frau*, p. 187.

104 *Die Lager Laterne*, 14 May 1916.

105 See the relevant programmes in MNH/B115/2xf, Internment Scrapbook; and BA/MA/MSG200/1967.

106 Franz Bauer, *1915–1918: Mein Erinnerungsbuch zum dreijährigen Bestehen des Camp Theaters Compound 2, Camp 1, am. 20. März 1918, zu gleich ein Überblick über die Tätigkeit aller anderen Bühnen des Lager 1* (Knockaloe, 1918), p. 2.

107 MNH/B115/43q, Camp IV, Knockaloe, I. O. M., Final Report and Statistical Record on the Internal Administration of the Prisoners of War Camp No. IV, 1915–1919.

108 Karl von Scheidt and Fritz Meyer, *Vier Jahre Leben und Leiden der Auslandsdeutschen in den Gefangenenlagern Englands* (Hagen, 1919), pp. 90–4.

109 Bauer, *1915–1918*.

110 R. Hartmann, *Bilder aus dem Gefangenenlager Knockaloe in England* (Bad Nassau, 1918), p. 18.

111 Bauer, *1915–1918*, pp. 26–51.

112 See, for instance, David A. Welch, 'Cinema and Society in Imperial Germany, 1905–1918', *German History*, vol. 8 (1990), 28–45.

113 Bauer, *1915–1918*, p. 52; MNH/B115/43q, Camp IV, Knockaloe, I. O. M., Final Report and Statistical Record on the Internal Administration of the Prisoners of War Camp No. IV, 1915–1919.

114 *Werden*, May 1915.

115 Friedrich Ruge, *Scapa Flow 1919: The End of the German Fleet* (London, 1973), p. 130.

116 Tony Mason and Eliza Riedi, *Sport and the Military: The British Armed Forces, 1880–1960* (Cambridge, 2010), pp. 80–111.

117 Charles Korr and Marvin Close, *More than Just a Game: Football v Apartheid* (London, 2008), p. 72.

118 NA/FO383/277, Swiss Embassy Report on Rosyth, 29 June 1917.

119 NA/FO383/277, Swiss Embassy Report on Lentran, 9 July 1917.

120 NA/FO383/164, US Embassy Report on Leigh, 19 September 1916.

121 BA/R901/83081, US Embassy Report on Jersey, 27 April 1916.

122 BA/R901/83081, US Embassy Report on Jersey, 4 November 1916.
123 BA/R67/1343, Bericht des Leutenants d. R. Schön von Gren. Regt. über Lagerverhältnisse und Verfugung im englischen Lager Colsterdale.
124 NA/FO383/163, US Embassy Report on Wakefield, 12 June 1916.
125 NA/FO383/163, US Embassy Report on Douglas, 18 May 1916.
126 NA/FO383/162, US Embassy Report on Knockaloe, 8 January 1916.
127 MNH/B115/43q, Camp IV, Knockaloe, I. O. M., Final Report and Statistical Record on the Internal Administration of the Prisoners of War Camp No. IV, 1915–1919; *Lager-Ulk*, 7 November 1917.
128 Turnverein Knockaloe Compound 6, Gefangenenlager Knockaloe Insel Man, Camp I, *Turnberict über das Jahr 1916* (Knockaloe, 1916).
129 Ruge, *Scapa Flow*, p. 130.
130 BA/R67/800, Report by W. Persow.
131 *Stobsiade*, 19 September 1915.
132 Scheidt and Meyer, *Vier Jahre*, pp. 98–105.
133 *Die Lager Laterne*, 30 July 1915, 27 August 1916.
134 *Lager-Zeitung*, 7 October 1916.

6

Employment

> Unser Lager liegt an einem Abhang; im Tale zieht sich ein grosser See hin, umgeben von hohen, kahlen Bergen. Wir wohnen in Hütten, die kleiner sind als die in Stobs, immer nur zwölf Mann zusammen. Unsere Arbeitszeit beträgt täglich acht Stunden; die Arbeit besteht in Wege-, Waserleitungs- and Strassenbau.[1]

Introduction

Most internees who had enough spare time to participate in the range of social activities available in the internment camps either did so or helped to create the prison camp societies which emerged. While such activity occurred in most of the camps, it became fundamental in those which held civilians, where, as a result of international agreements about their utilization for employment, a large percentage of the internees did not work. Some civilians appear to have enjoyed the whole range of social opportunities available, while others, as encapsulated especially in Cohen-Portheim's narrative, simply viewed them as a way of 'killing time' and stood aside as far as they could. Cohen-Portheim may have represented the most extreme example of the cynicism which some prisoners felt towards internment, but many of the accounts produced from within the camps, especially in the newspapers which emerged, pointed to their longing for the outside world of the past which they had left behind, either in Germany or among the German community in Britain, in which their families played a central role. For many internees the sham prison camp societies simply represented a passing phase of their lives which they wanted to end as soon as possible.

A few did so by committing suicide,[2] while far more attempted to escape, almost always unsuccessfully.[3] The latter included people in work parties, which contained some of the most contented prisoners according to some contemporary commentators. A. L. Vischer pointed out that work provided the most effective remedy for boredom and the consequent development of barbed wire disease: 'The most favourable conditions are certainly those of the labour camps, where the men are not so thickly segregated and are engaged in agriculture. I attribute this well-being chiefly to the fact they are engaged in productive work.'[4] Similarly, Rudolf Rocker, focusing upon Alexandra Palace, asserted that 'the more the prisoner finds opportunity to satisfy his active instincts, the more he is helped to overcome the monotony of the creeping hours, days, and weeks'.[5]

Prisoners were employed during the course of the First World War both within Britain and on the continent. They had previously been employed in Britain during the Revolutionary and Napoleonic Wars,[6] but during the First World War and the twentieth century as a whole, the process became more organized and formalized, legitimized by article 6 of the Annex to the Hague Convention of 1907.[7] As Gerald Davis pointed out, 'When soldiers surrender they take their muscles and brains with them.'[8] For the German war economy in particular, prisoner-of-war labour became central, and by 1 August 1916 it utilized 1.6 million captives, working in both agriculture and industry and seized from the range of enemies which fought against Imperial Germany, especially Russia and France.[9] Meanwhile, a similar number of prisoners found themselves working for the Tsarist Empire at the height of its employment of captives during the First World War.[10] The utilization of prisoner labour continued into the Second World War, especially in the case of the German economy, which in 1944 employed 1,831,000.[11] Similarly, the British state used German and Italian captives both during and immediately after the Second World War.[12]

Davis divided the employment carried out by prisoners into two categories, 'service work for the armed force detaining the prisoners' and 'contract employment in agriculture and industry'.[13] First World War Britain utilized prisoners in both of these senses, although those working for the British forces laboured in the conflict zone in France[14] rather than in mainland Britain. Our main concern lies with those who found themselves working in industry and agriculture. The industrial work included a vast range of activity from coal mining and quarrying to brick making, road surfacing and factory work. Davis focused upon combatants, although more recent scholars have dealt with prisoners of war as part of a larger system of forced labour which included foreign workers either recruited or forced to toil for war economies, as recognized especially in the German case by Ulrich Herbert for both World Wars[15] and, more recently, by Matthew Stibbe in the context of the Great War.[16] Thus, to the 1.8 million prisoners of war employed in Germany in 1944 we need to add 5,295,000 civilians, overwhelmingly forced workers: these two groups constituted 19.9 per cent of the German labour force in 1944.[17]

Although Second World War Britain recognized the usefulness of prisoner-of-war labour and therefore utilized Italians from the early stages of that conflict,[18] the British state demonstrated reluctance to do this during the Great War. Part of the reason for this lay in the fact that the Hague Convention forbade civilians, who made up the bulk of prisoners in the early stage of the conflict, from working, 'except for carrying out routine fatigue duties at their camps. Most were, however, prepared to work to help support their families, to be able to buy extra food or other items from the camp canteen, or simply to help combat the monotony of camp life.'[19] Several camps, especially in London, had factories attached to them, while even Knockaloe internees worked in a variety of occupations outside the camp. Other civilians, such as barbers and bakers, could carry out their trades behind barbed wire because of the demand for their services. The other group which did not work consisted of officers, who also received pay which allowed them to employ servants, meaning that they had the most idle of experiences, spending their time in leisure activities. As most spent relatively short periods of time in camps they do not seem to have become the main victims of barbed wire disease. The most important group of workers therefore consisted of combatants, many of whom spent virtually all of their time in Britain in a working camp, usually for a short spell in the closing stages of the war. While they may have played some role in the First World War economy, their relatively small numbers in comparison with the number of captives in the other belligerent states, or in Britain and other countries during the Second World War, meant that this did not prove decisive.

Employment policy

The employment of combatant prisoners took off during the second half of the Great War with the increasing need for labour and the growing numbers of captives within the country. MPs began asking questions about the employment of both civilian and military internees at the end of 1915.[20] By 13 July 1916 between 3,000 and 4,000 enemy aliens 'are employed on work which is to the public advantage, without counting those engaged in performing ordinary camp fatigues'.[21] Some military and naval prisoners also worked by this time, including those who 'are employed in the immediate neighbourhood of their camps', while others 'are employed in making mail bags'.[22] Those in the former category included people 'employed in works of public utility, such as labouring on farms and road making'.[23] *The Times* asked why 'more effective use should not be made of the 15,000 Germany military and 32,000 alien civilians who are at present interned in this country', while 'between 900,000 and a million prisoners are employed in some capacity' in 'Prussia alone'.[24]

Despite a spate of questions in the House of Commons during 1916 about the employment of prisoners, the numbers working remained small. A Cabinet memorandum of September 1916 gave a series of reasons for this situation, some of which had more credibility than others. The least credible included the density of population in Britain compared with that of those working for the British army in northern France. More persuasive 'is the feeling of the people against the Germans' which exploded in the *Lusitania* riots of May 1915. However, a total of 3,892 combatants were working throughout Britain by this time, in tasks which included mining, forestry and road making. 'Another thing that has to be contended with is the Labour Party. A short time ago proposals were made for employing the prisoners at the docks in London, but this had to be dropped on account of the feeling of the Labour Party.' More general trade union opposition had also proved problematic.[25]

Apart from the increasing numbers of German prisoners and a public opinion questioning the fact that they did not work, the other driving force behind the change of policy at the end of 1916 was the labour shortages, especially in agriculture, where the number of aliens and women employed increased during the course of the conflict but was not enough to meet demand, especially as the government wanted to increase the amount of land cultivated.[26]

In December 1916 the Prisoners of War Employment Committee therefore came into existence with the task of considering 'all applications for the employment of prisoners of war, and to decide whether they should be adopted'.[27] It included representatives from the Board of Agriculture and Fisheries, the Home Office, the War Office, the Ministry of National Service and the Ministry of Munitions. During the period of its existence, until November 1918, it met thirty-four times 'for ordinary purposes'.[28] It was dissolved following the armistice, 'and the allocation of prisoners of war to various forms of labour was vested in the War Office, which acted in close accord with the Department of Civil Demobilization and Resettlement of the Ministry of Labour'.[29]

Prisoner employment became a complex operation which involved numerous rules and regulations. In the first place, only combatant men and non-commissioned officers were eligible in theory, although all of those employed had to volunteer. These included civilians, despite the technical problems involved in utilizing them as a result of the Hague Convention and objections from the German government. By early 1918 '1,847 civilians are employed outside their parent camps'. Prisoners could not work with 'civilian British or civilian Alien labour'. In addition, 'no application could be put forward until the resources of the local labour exchange have been exhausted'.[30] Those prisoners who worked received payment, which averaged at about 1½*d* per day. They also obtained higher food rations of 2,700 calories per day, whereas those not employed received 2,000 calories. The 'scientific adviser' of the Ministry of Food also recommended that prisoners 'engaged on such work as quarrying, agriculture, land reclamation, and other similar work should receive a ration of not less than 3,300 calories'.[31]

Agriculture was a significant area of employment. The prisoners carried out a wide range of tasks between 1917 and 1919 and played a role in securing the harvest. Most performed their jobs effectively, although some worked slowly because they had limited experience and received inadequate food supplies. A local bureaucracy became important in employing them, in which the Board of Agriculture and County War Agricultural Committees played a role. Both of the these needed to consider the availability of guards and accommodation. Farmers wanting to employ prisoners had to apply to the County War Agricultural Committee; prisoners employed in other jobs could be released temporarily for the harvest. The Board of Agriculture tried to secure those prisoners who had previous agricultural experience.[32] We can see the operation of this bureaucracy in operation in Bedfordshire during the course of 1918; the Food Production Department was also involved because of its role in the maintenance of agriculture and food supplies. As a result of representations by the Bedfordshire War Agricultural Committee to the Food Production Department, twenty camps came into existence in the county for migratory gangs, which supplemented the fifty-one other places which held prisoners here.[33]

This insight into Bedfordshire provides an indication of the way in which the process of prisoner employment actually operated, usually through the establishment of work camps affiliated to parent camps, and the use of migratory gangs, although some employment, including that involving civilians, took place within some of the long-standing places of internment. As well as being used in agriculture, prisoners became engaged in a vast range of other tasks, carrying out their duties either in an established camp or an affiliated work camp, which often lay right next to their place of employment. Occupations included forestry; land reclamation; building work; road and railway construction and maintenance; dock work; brick making; quarrying; brush making; aerodrome construction; thermometer making; navvy work; and mail bag making. In cases of non-agricultural work employers applied to the Ministry of Labour.[34]

Some of the problems associated with the employment of prisoners of war before 1917 remained, including the hostility which they faced, fuelled by the all-encompassing Germanophobia which characterized Britain during the Great War. However, this needs consideration against the background of positive interaction between those who found employment on the land and Britons.[35] The negative reactions to the employment of prisoners focused upon three issues. In the first place, Lord Lamington complained in the House of Lords that the German prisoners did not carry out strenuous enough work compared with their British equivalents in Germany, where many 'are employed in both coal and salt mines'.[36] At the same time complaints arose about the quality of work carried out on the land, with prisoners described as 'idle', 'insolent', 'independent' and 'obdurate'.[37] Most commonly, local workmen objected to the employment of prisoners, either because of Germanophobia or because they viewed them as a threat to their wages. In one Cheshire village workmen threatened to withdraw their labour.[38] In Port Talbot complaints arose about the fact that Germans had found employment 'on the construction of the new steel works while at the same time local workmen are unemployed and receiving unemployment donation benefit'.[39] Similarly, in Mundham, near Chichester, English labourers claimed that they had 'been denied the opportunity of earning extra money by working the customary piece work' and had 'been sent home whilst German prisoners have been kept on working overtime'. Meanwhile, at Climping, near Littlehampton, a farmer had apparently 'threatened the women workers that if they asked for increased wages they would not be allowed to work, and that the German prisoners would be set on to do their work'.[40] Protests of various types materialized against German labour. For instance, in January 1918 'Mr Winston Churchill, Minister of Munitions, received a deputation from the Executive of the Miners' Federation of Great Britain with reference to the employment of German prisoners during a strike of mine workers on the island of Raasay'.[41] In Newport Town Council a 'strong protest' occurred 'against the employment of German prisoners in building operations at Chepstow while British trade union men were being discharged'.[42] Similarly, a 'crowded meeting of ex-servicemen' took place in the Victoria Hall in Leighton Buzzard in July 1919 to complain against the fact that German prisoners worked 'on farms and in other occupations for a small pittance', which 'was responsible to a great extent for the unemployment among returned soldiers'. The meeting passed a resolution 'calling upon the Government to withdraw the German prisoners or to occupy their time until their return to Germany was due with employment that was not the means of keeping discharged soldiers out of work'.[43]

Despite these examples of hostility, and as this animosity suggests, the number of working prisoners increased gradually from 1917 to 1919. Thus by February 1918 a total of close to 25,000 prisoners had found employment. By July of that year the total figure had increased to 50,585, including 17,100 in agriculture, while the total at the armistice stood at 64,250. In the following March the total remained high at 62,500, including 26,000 in agriculture. As repatriation took place the numbers declined, falling to

31,595 (including 22,416 in agriculture) by July 1919 and to just 3,132 by October 1919.[44]

Civilian employment

Despite the fact that the Hague Convention stipulated that civilian prisoners should not work, many of those who found themselves behind barbed wire for years welcomed the opportunity to carry out some type of useful employment and some did so from the early stages of the war. Such work can be divided into three types. First were general camp duties, with some internees, such as bakers, barbers and tailors, simply carrying on their previous jobs. At the same time, several specialist camps, especially in London, employed civilians for specific firms. Finally, some internees, particularly on the Isle of Man, became engaged in work outside the camps. In Knockaloe thousands of men refused to work. Whereas those 'whose day is filled with useful work are contented . . . those who lead an idle life are invariably discontented and their health sooner or later suffers in consequence'. They presented 'a pitiful sight' and many passed their time 'gambling, smoking or quarrelling'.[45]

A United States Embassy report on Douglas from May 1916 claimed that about 85 per cent of the prisoners worked, as follows:

> Waiters and Stewards in the Privilege Camp, working for their fellow prisoners, roughly about 100.
> Clerks in the Quartermaster's store, purser's office, censor's and parcels office and requisition office.
> Camp Cleaners (mostly lavatory work), two or three bath attendants, and masseur.
> Private tailors.
> Barbers.
> Men who wash clothes for other men, of whom there are a considerable number.
> Watchmakers.
> Jewellers.
> Dentists.
> One Doctor.
> Hospital Orderlies.
> Librarians.
> Assistants in Cunningham's Kitchen, etc, for the Privilege Camp, which takes quite a number of men.
> Workers in the gardens about the camp, and the fowl-run . . .

> Members of the two bands, string and brass.
> Artists, who are able to work in the studios found for them.
> A large number of inmates go out every day as labourers to the neighbouring farms and do regular work, the number of which is nearly a hundred.[46]

It seems unclear how many of these internees actually received payment; for civilian prisoners performing work 'connected with the ordinary routine of the camp, such as cooking, cleaning, fatigue and ordinary sanitary work' obtained 'no pay from public funds'.[47] Some internees in Douglas advertised their services in the camp newspapers, among them 'Clucas's Laundry' and Philip Shimmin, 'Baker and Confectioner'.[48] In Alexandra Palace some internees worked 'in the kitchens, stores and offices; others look after the cleaning of lavatories, baths, ablution rooms, etc.; others again are engaged as coal carriers'. Rocker claimed that they received 'a small wage of a few shillings a week', which may have come from contributions made by wealthier internees. Prisoners in Alexandra Palace originally carried out these jobs on a permanent basis, but because increasing numbers wished to do them, especially among the poorer internees, who welcomed the opportunity to earn a few shillings, those carrying out the tasks changed every six weeks.[49] Cohen-Portheim found that at Knockaloe the supply of barbers and shoe shiners outstripped demand.[50] A United States Embassy report of 1916 claimed that 72 per cent of Knockaloe internees 'are at work', including 'bootmakers, tailors, cap workers, plumbers, woodworkers, gardeners, latrine men, police, coal and railway workers, quarry workers, post-office workers, and parcel-post workers'.[51]

This report enumerated a variety of activities in order to reach an employment rate of 72 per cent. One of these was the cultivation of vegetables, an outdoor activity which resembled sport in terms of its health benefits. In Knockaloe, 'There are "plots" everywhere, both in and around the Camp, where the prisoners can cultivate their own food.'[52] Much planning went into the improvement of the soil here, as well as the drawing-up of a timetable of planting and the distribution of crops.[53] The gardeners here had success and even held agricultural shows.[54]

Many internees also became involved in the internal administration of the camps, in tasks which would have remained unpaid and essentially represent attempts to find employment for as many men as possible. The most elaborate structures appear to have developed in Douglas and in Camp IV at Knockaloe. Internees in Douglas left a record of the bureaucracy which evolved. In January 1918 W. E. Schulz, the head captain of the upper camp, produced an account of the administration of Douglas from April to December 1917, with the former date serving as a starting point for the development of the participation of the prisoners in the administration of Douglas.[55] Camp IV at Knockaloe developed a complex internal bureaucracy. At first a military system evolved which involved the election of hut captains in each compound as well as head captains, who were ultimately answerable to the commandant and played a role in the implementation of routine, discipline and cleanliness. Separately from this there evolved a system of internal administration which had responsibility for organizing the social activities of the prisoners. This became centralized with a camp secretary at its head, assisted by a central committee board. This interacted with the chairman of a series of groups responsible for the social activity of the camp, whether sporting, literary or industrial, for example. On the one hand we might see this structure as playing a significant role in the organization and financial administration of the wide range of activities in which the prisoners participated. On the other hand, it helped to keep minds occupied. Certainly, the individuals who produced the reports on administration spent many man-hours in drawing them up.[56] Cohen-Portheim, as usual, provided a cynical, but perhaps accurate, view of the camp administration at Wakefield, describing it as 'a true *Beamtenstaat*: everyone was administering and there was very little to administer'.[57]

Some productive work did, however, take place in the civilian camps. Hackney Wick, for example, which opened on 1 June 1916, housed sixty-five prisoners in October 1916, of whom fifty-three were 'skilled volunteer mechanics' gathered from other places of internment and employed by Vickers for the purpose of 'fashioning tools, fixtures and gauges for the manufacture of sewing machines'. The rest of the prisoners 'are occupied in the kitchen, laundry, barber's shop and in camp fatigue work generally'. By July 1917 the number of internees had reached 134. They worked fifty-four hours per week and received a weekly wage of 45 shillings. The prisoners held here could also see their wives and children once a week.[58] The internees held at the camp in Cornwallis Road in Islington found themselves employed in a variety of paid tasks during the course of the war. In March 1916 a total of 600 out of 714 men worked here, of whom 500 received wages totalling up to 15 shillings per week. The tasks at this stage included making artificial limbs and other equipment for the Red Cross, which some of them had done before they arrived, while others made international mail bags and prison clothing. In January 1917 the Home Office, which controlled this camp, reached an agreement with a brush-making firm, Strachan and Co., which gave employment to 250 prisoners, who could earn up to 30 shillings per week.[59] In Douglas, meanwhile, internees became involved in the manufacture of pipes, watches and, above all, brushes. Contractors established a brush-making factory here which sold its products to government departments and to the public. In August 1918 it employed 734 prisoners.[60]

A variety of schemes, in which the Society of Friends Emergency Committee for the Assistance of Germans, Austrians and Hungarians in Distress (FEC)[61] played an important role, attempted to make use of the labour power available in Knockaloe, as well as in some of the other civilian camps. The FEC provided tools and equipment and helped to organize the industrial committees established by the prisoners. It also tried to sell the goods which internees manufactured. Camp III in Knockaloe, for example, held four professional basket makers, leading to the establishment of a basket-making industry here where these four instructed sixty-five others. James Baily, who worked here on behalf of the Society of Friends and eventually became part of the Manx government as industrial superintendent, initially sourced supplies of willow from Lancashire and Nottinghamshire, but subsequently made use of locally available material, which involved the men making trips outside the camp to gather it. During the course of the war these craftsmen manufactured nearly 65,000 baskets. In Camp IV meanwhile, internees found themselves employed in a variety of tasks, including the manufacture of boots, suits, tables and cupboards.[62]

Other civilians worked outside the camps, particularly on the Isle of Man, even before the establishment of the Prisoners of War Employment Committee at the end of 1916. In fact, by the summer of that year civilians could 'with their consent, be employed on behalf of the state or by private individuals'. Employers would pay 'the standard rate in the district in which the prisoner is employed'.[63] As early as March 1916 the Isle of Man government had already instituted a scheme for the use of internees for agricultural work whereby farmers would apply to the commandant for permission to recruit them; work parties would leave at 7.00 a.m. and return at 7.00 p.m.[64] Although this scheme was initially confined to agriculture, during the course of 1916 the Manx government devised others. One of these schemas reclaimed waste land on the island. Each gang of prisoners, from either Douglas or Knockaloe, would have the following members:

> 1 experienced alien farmer to take charge of the gang. He will be paid 1/6 daily.
> 3 experienced alien farmers to assist in supervision and to be paid 1/- each daily.
> 87 men, provided with spades, to be paid 3d. each daily.
> 4 men, provided with picks.
> 4 men, provided with axes.
> 1 cook, to be paid 8d. daily.

This provided a total of 100 men. The Manx government outlined two areas on the island where the prisoners would carry out their tasks.[65] Also in November 1916 Isle of Man internees became involved in quarrying and road making in gangs of fifty.[66]

A United States Embassy report of August 1916 had already outlined the range of employment activities in which Knockaloe and Douglas internees participated. Interestingly, although it states that '75 per cent of interned aliens at Knockaloe are occupied in some form or another', it continued, 'many of them are occupied in Schools, but for the most part their occupation is of such a nature that it requires but little of their time'. Nevertheless, the main focus of this report was the 'War Working Stations' on the Isle of Man, which it proceeded to list and describe: a site in 'the near neighbourhood of the camp' where 100 men found employment constructing a new sewage system; a quarry 'within a five minute walk of Camp IV' where 'about 150 men are employed in stone-breaking'; Tynwald Hill, about two miles from Knockaloe, where another 150 broke stones; and Poortown Quarry, where a further 150 carried out the same task. In addition, 200 men worked in the canalization of the Sulby river, about fifteen miles from Knockaloe. These men 'greatly enjoy their work'; in fact, a 'great demand is being made to the Camp authorities for permission to join the working party for this particular district, and the men returning from their work, seemed happy and contented'. The working stations connected with Douglas were a site near the top of Snaefell mountain, about seven miles from Douglas, where 'a detachment of 100 men are employed in the cutting, stacking and drying of peat'. Another group of fifty worked on quarrying about a mile from Douglas.[67] The internees employed outside this camp added to those working in the brush factory although their totals did not generally exceed 600, according to the diary of the commandant, with the vast majority employed in the factory.[68] There also appear to have been other schemes for using the internee labour on the Isle of Man. Farmers utilized prisoner labour. Joseph Cunningham, who owned the holiday camp which acted as the site for Douglas camp, built Ellerslie Farm (which provided fresh produce to holidaymakers after the war) with the labour power of internees.[69]

Some civilians clearly found employment, although the United States Embassy reports on the Isle of Man camps which suggest that the vast majority did, seem inaccurate and refer to all of the activities in which the internees involved themselves, including education. Most civilians remained basically idle in terms of paid employment, and it was precisely this situation which led them to social and educational activities. The camps in Islington and Hackney Wick were unique among those which held civilians because they were essentially work camps similar to those which held military internees in the latter stages of the war. Those who earned money, carrying out either craft work, skilled engineering tasks or physical labour outside the camps, appear to have enjoyed their employment.

The employment of military prisoners of war

Most military internees tended not to endure the type of boredom and consequent barbed wire disease which characterized the life of many civilians because they started working almost immediately upon their arrival in Britain during the course of 1917 or 1918. In fact, the reason for their transfer from France was the need to fill labour shortages. While a significant percentage worked in rural locations in agricultural work, many others found themselves employed in other forms of physical labour including mining, quarrying and road making.

Many military prisoners enjoyed their work in the way that

civilians did, particularly those who found themselves in picturesque locations far away from French battlefields. One Swiss Embassy report on a working camp in Wasdale Head in Cumberland, for example, which held thirty-six prisoners, described the 'wild and imposing scenery' in which this camp lay, 'surrounded by lofty mountains'. The prisoners lived in a farmhouse. 'There is not a yard of barbed wire about the place to spoil the effect of the beautiful and peaceful scenery.' The prisoners worked for fifty-four hours a week 'in river work making a new bed for the river Irt'. The Swiss Embassy inspectors commented that 'the outward appearance' of the internees 'speaks for their well being'.[70] An article in *Stobsiade*, describing prisoners going out to work in forestry, romanticized the whole experience, with an evocation of the winter morning, the waking-up routine, the trip into the wood and the work carried out, which are described in a poetic manner, as the following extract indicates:

> Die Arbeit beginnt. Klingend hallen die harten Axtschläge durch den Winterwald, das Ritsch-ratsch der grossen Baumsägen vermischt sich mit dem Gekrach der stürzenden Bäume. Dort hat man eben eine Edletanne vorgenommen, einen alten Herrn von ungefähr 20 Meter; seine dichten, hängenden Zweige haben sicher schon manches Geschlecht heranwachsen und ins Grab sinken sehen.[71]

Nevertheless, other sources point to discontent among German prisoner labour. One post-war account mentioned mistreatment in the camp in Larkhill, focusing upon the cold and the Germanophobic guards.[72] Mrs H. Stahlschmidt wrote to the Swiss Embassy complaining that some men, including her husband, had left Alexandra Palace for a working camp in Coventry where their employment as carpenters and bricklayers involved 'building Aeroplane Assembly Sheds', to which they objected; they faced consequent transfer to the Isle of Man despite the fact that all 'are married with English wives residing in London, and they volunteered to help their wives in their financial trouble'.[73]

Some internees went on strike because of their working conditions. For instance, in June 1918, 'A squad of thirty German prisoners engaged on land work at Cranleigh, Surrey, have struck work. They have a grievance because three of their party have been punished.'[74] In September 1918, a strike took place in Frodsham in Cheshire, where about 250 men 'have been engaged on a big drainage scheme on the River Birkett'. They objected to the fact that 'some of the men were taken off the drainage work and lent in gangs to neighbouring farmers. Harvesting is far preferable, in the prisoner's mind, to cutting and scouring ditches.' Farm workers could also obtain 'a copper or two a day extra money and the chance of a little extra food from the farmer'. The two-day strike essentially constituted 'a protest on the part of those left behind on the marshes against the favoured treatment of the harvesters' as well as 'an all-round demand for a higher allowance'.[75]

While some prisoners welcomed the chance to work, others resented the conditions in which they found themselves labouring. Officers who did not have to work under the Hague Convention found other ways of passing their time, usually through social activity. Officers even received payment, which, by 1918, stood at 6*d* per day for those below the rank of captain and a shilling per day for captains and higher ranks.[76] Captured medical personnel also obtained payment on condition that they carried out hospital duties.[77] The latter group would clearly have worked in their normal occupations. On the other hand, officers used the money which they received to pay servants, which increased their leisure time even further. For instance, in Holyport in May 1916 the 118 military and naval prisoners 'have no work to do for themselves as they have their servants to attend to them'; the number of servants totalled forty-seven. The officers passed their time 'chiefly in study and reading, and in attending to the gardens allotted to them'. In addition, they could take daily walks and had access to tennis courts and other sporting activities.[78] Officers, while having an easy life, should, however, have fallen victim to barbed wire disease, although United States and Swiss Embassy reports do not bring this out in the way that they do in the case of the Isle of Man camps in particular. Perhaps, to recall Vischer, they appreciated the escape from the toils of battle. At the same, their acceptance of a regimented military life may have meant that they could accept the routine of an internment camp more easily than could the independent immigrants who were caged in on the Isle of Man for up to five years. But this represents something of a generalization. Gunther Plüschow, who successfully escaped from Donington Hall, wrote: 'In time, captivity became unbearable. Nothing relieved my gloom – neither letters, parcels forwarded from home by loving hands, the company of my friends, not even the hockey, to which I devoted myself so strenuously that in the evenings I used to drop asleep, half-dead from fatigue.'[79]

While officers may not have worked, the vast majority of military and naval captives did so, particularly in agriculture but also in a wide range of other activities. The employment of prisoners in agriculture evolved gradually during the course of 1917 and 1918; eventually they found themselves located in either working camps or migratory gangs. Initially seventy-five prisoners were available to each County War Agricultural Committee, and any further workers would arrive in batches of seventy-five. These men lived in depots and would go out to work in the vicinity under guard in groups of at least five.[80] At the beginning of 1918 'the Government decided that a large number of German prisoners, selected as being skilled ploughmen, should be sent to England to assist in the ploughing and subsequent cultivation of' additional land needed for the 1918 harvest.[81]

In June 1918 migratory gangs of ten men each worked as harvesters, and 370 of these gangs still existed by December of that year, scattered throughout the country. They could live under canvas and 'solved the difficulty of getting men quickly to any place where labour was urgently required'.[82] Each had an attachment to a nearby head camp or working camp; these camps were described as depots in much of the contemporary government and academic literature. The expansion in the number of camps during the course of 1918 caused a headache for the army, which was responsible for guarding and administering them, and the Food Production Department, which identified the areas which needed labour. One of the main problems was the difficulty of securing suitable accommodation. For instance, a house at Haywards Heath 'was rejected by the War Office because the occupants of the adjoining houses were ladies who objected to having German prisoners near them'. It was also difficult to secure guards, who could amount to 50 per cent of the prisoners employed.[83]

Despite these problems, the number of working camps and the number of prisoners employed increased significantly during the course of 1918. Although agricultural workers found themselves spread throughout the country, some concentration occurred in the south and Midlands during the early stages of agricultural employment.[84] In the case of Handforth,

> Every day 26 guards, armed only with their walking canes, take from the camp over 200 prisoners (last Saturday the number was 213) and distribute them at 96 different farms within a radius of three miles. The guards go each with six to 10 prisoners and drop them like postmen dropping letters, one at one farm, three at another, and so on. If there are over three and up to six the guard (one man) remains with them; otherwise they are left on the farms all day without guards, and the guards go the same route in the evening and pick them up again. If a farmer wishes to keep his prisoners later he is allowed to do so provided he sees them back to camp and hands them over to the provost sergeant on duty.

In addition, 'under the group system' 145 prisoners 'are distributed to three places' with seven guards and a sergeant 'and supply farms within a three mile radius of their location'. Furthermore, the 'gang system provides 17 gangs of 10 prisoners each', who were accompanied by two private soldiers. 'The 17 gangs go to 14 different places.'[85] Another long-standing camp which became the centre of a whole system of sub-camps and depots was Pattishall. By April 1919 it had become 'the Parent Camp for 161 Working Camps including the Agricultural Groups and Depots with a total of 14,537 Prisoners of War'.[86] In the autumn of 1917 the agricultural camps dependent upon Pattishall included Linton; the agricultural depot at Dunmow; Kedington, where seventy-five prisoners lived in a workhouse and worked for local farmers for 2*d* per hour; Rothwell, where seventy-five prisoners laboured on nearby farms for 1*d* per day; Hemel Hempstead, where forty prisoners lived in a 'private house in the High Street' and 'are engaged in work on 7 farms in the district, and go out in parties of 5 men'; South Ockendon, where the 'men are employed by local farmers in agricultural work' and 'go out in parties of 5 to 10 men'; Hatfield; Sompting, where the seventy-four military captives lived in tents of eight men each and worked for local farmers; and Kenninghall, where the 'prisoners are housed in a substantial building which was originally erected as a home for inebriates' and worked in agriculture and timber felling.[87] Pattishall continued to have a large number of camps affiliated to it, both agricultural and non-agricultural, throughout 1918 and 1919.[88] The importance of this camp is confirmed by the fact that, despite its location in Northamptonshire, the camps dependent upon it stretched as far away as Norfolk by the summer of 1919. The relationship lies in the fact that Pattishall provided the initial labour for the places of incarceration in Norfolk, to which the prisoners might return.[89]

Several other long-standing places of internment acted as central administrative and labour supply headquarters for smaller agricultural establishments at the end of the war. Dorchester, for instance, in the primarily agricultural county of Dorset (and the south-west of England as a whole) had a series of agricultural camps connected to it, including Devizes, Wootton Bassett, Wookey, Frome, Ramsbury and Hatherleigh.[90] Similarly, five camps in Leicestershire, located in Loughborough, Ashby de la Zouch, Ragdale, Narborough and Normanton Hall, had an affiliation to Brocton.[91] Finally, the following extract from a Swiss Embassy report on camps affiliated to Frongoch gives an excellent indication of the way in which the whole agricultural labour supply of prisoners operated:

	Soldiers	*Sailors*	*Total*
Beaumaris	84	16	100
Deganwy, Llandudno	187	10	197
Penarth	49	1	50
Pembrey Agric. Group	21	–	21
Brecon Agric. Depot:-			
Brecon Agric. Group	55	1	56
Talgarth Agric. Group	48	1	49
Llandebie Working Group	41	–	41
Towyn Agric. Depot:-			
Towyn Agric. Group	55	3	58
Llanfarian Agric. Group	43	–	43
Machynlleth Agric. Group	32	7	39
Lampeter Agric. Group	29	–	29

	Soldiers	*Sailors*	*Total*
Cilian Agric. Group	16	–	16
Welshpool Agric. Group	77	1	78
Caersws Agric. Group	55	–	55
Caernarvon Agric. Depot:-			
Port Madoc Agric. Group	36	–	36
Maltrenth March Agric. Group	40	10	50
Llanbedy Agric. Group	61	1	62
Llanengan Agric. Group	38	1	39
Ruthin Agric. Group	64	3	67
Denbigh Agric. Group	31	–	31

Migratory Gangs Affiliated:-

	Soldiers	*Soldier Airmen*	*Sailors*	*Total*
Ruthin Depot	96	–	8	104
Caernarvon Depot	44	2	4	50
Brecon Depot	39	–	1	40
Towyn Depot	17	–	2	19
Penarth	15	–	–	15[92]

Prisoners employed in agriculture worked mostly as ploughmen and harvesters to secure the harvest, 'helping to produce the corn and other articles the country needs so badly'.[93] In March 1918, in the camp at Blairfield House near Chichester, where prisoners were 'employed as ploughmen by the farmers of the district', they started 'work at 7am and are conveyed to and fro by horse vehicles'.[94] Prisoners focused upon the gathering of hay, corn and potatoes.[95] They also became involved in fruit picking; seventy-five were employed in the Toddington orchards and fruit farms in Gloucestershire.[96]

Those prisoners working in agriculture appear to have played an important role in food production during the final few years of the war. But a report from 1918 stated that although they worked methodically they remained slow in comparison with their English counterparts. Although part of the explanation for this might lie in the fact that they had no real desire to help their enemies, unfamiliarity with the work may have played a bigger role.[97]

As well as carrying out work for farmers, those prisoners of war employed as part of the agricultural labour schemes could find themselves performing other tasks. Of the 4,279 prisoners working in agriculture at the beginning of February 1918, 3,587 laboured in 'general agriculture', with 282 in market gardening and fruit picking, 251 in land reclamation and 159 in drainage.[98] Those employed in the latter two tasks included prisoners held at Snettisham in Norfolk 'engaged in drainage work and land reclamation on the sea front'.[99] Prisoners went from Stobs to a camp in Dallmellington, where the main task consisted of improving the water supply and involved transporting stones from a lake and redirecting the watercourse.[100] Meanwhile, over 325 prisoners found themselves draining and improving the river Ouse and its tributaries the Flitt and Ivel in Bedfordshire in the spring of 1919.[101] Such activity had become widespread by this time, as was recognized in an article in the *Daily Express* entitled 'The Hun as River Cleaner'. This stated that the War Office had lent prisoners 'to various county councils free of charge, for river cleaning', which meant that they 'are doing something to improve the areas that are flooded year by year'. The article concluded:

> Now, as though by way of a parting gift to the country he proposed to overrun and enjoy, the Hun is cutting down and dragging away the pollard willow and other useless timber on the banks of many a little river. He is digging out the cores and pulling out the marshes that have grown so deep in the mud. Ropes are passed round the trees that lie athwart the stream, and they are pulled to the bank; these banks, in their turn, are shelved and shaped. Already you may find little rivers that were once as sluggish as aldermen after a banquet assuming the faces and spirits of first youth.[102]

Although forestry was not strictly regarded as agricultural work, in that those who carried it out did not form part of the scheme for employing prisoners in the countryside, many Germans also worked on various forestry schemes. By April 1918, for example, a letter from the Controller of Timber Supplies pointed out that his 'Department' was utilizing over 3,000 prisoners 'distributed in 17 working camps'.[103] One of these was Bwlch in South Wales, where '92 men work in the forest, 8 of whom drive the lumber wagons'.[104] Meanwhile, prisoners held at Eartham, near Chichester, 'are employed at lumber work'. When their working hours went up to ten per day they went on strike, which resulted in a reduction to nine.[105] In the Scottish Highlands prisoners found themselves employed in 'felling trees' in several camps including Lentran and Nethybridge by the autumn of 1916.[106]

Despite the importance of agriculture for the employment of prisoners of war, most appear to have worked in non-agricultural activities. A breakdown from July 1918, which listed 50,585 prisoners who worked, gave a figure of just 17,100 in agriculture, together with 4,500 in timber. The total also included 5,300 in 'R.E.'[107] services; 4,370 constructing aerodromes and seaplane stations; 4,020 in mining and quarrying; 2,000 in roads; 3,000 in the erection of munitions stores concentrated at Bramley; 2,850 in shipyard construction; and 1,300 employed on camp duties. In addition, the list mentioned sixteen other occupations in which prisoners worked.[108] Another breakdown from the end of February 1918 indicated the involvement of government ministries in the employment of prisoners, pointing to their role in the war effort, whether direct or indirect. Thus, 2,338 worked for the Admiralty in 'waterworks for Rosyth' in the Glendevon camp; 'brick and tile making for the Admiralty' at Inverkeithing; and shipyard construction in Beachley. A total of 5,430 prisoners in twenty camps found themselves under the Ministry of Munitions, mostly in various types of quarrying. The twelve camps under the War Office employed 3,750 people in aviation. Meanwhile, 3,070 prisoners worked under the Royal Engineers works in eleven camps.[109]

An analysis of a few individual camps demonstrates the specific types of work carried out by prisoners. First of all was construction, as described poetically in an article in *Stobsiade* focusing upon Kinclochleven, where the prisoners found themselves laying water pipes, which involved digging 'with spades and picks' as well as deep drilling. At midday the prisoners ate their lunch while 'hungry seagulls' sailed above. The prisoners continued until 4.30 p.m.[110] A prisoner interned in a working camp involved in road construction

Figure 6.1 German prisoners employed in quarrying. Military internees found themselves working in a whole variety of tasks, of which quarrying was just one.

in Grantham painted a less romantic picture, describing the labour carried out by individual groups including stone breakers.[111] Nevertheless, both of these accounts indicate the routine involved and point to the way in which work structured the day, after which the prisoners could retire to their leisure activities in the evening, in contrast to many of the interned civilians who resented their lives of leisure. The account of the work in Grantham points out that the prisoners enjoyed their hobbies during the evening, whether they consisted of reading, card playing or gymnastics.

Quarrying represented hard work similar to that involved in construction and, as the figures indicate, thousands of men laboured for a range of firms securing a variety of raw materials. Thus at Glendon camp near Kettering the men 'work in an ironstone quarry, about 100 yards west of the camp' for 'Kettering Iron Smelters' for 1*d* per hour.[112] Meanwhile, at Frampton 500 prisoners found themselves 'employed in excavating gravel required in bulk for use on urgent war jobs in the South of England and also required by the Admiralty for the national shipyards, while a proportion of the prisoners are employed in making concrete brickworks for walling, etc., to take the place of brickwork, owing to the scarcity of both bricks and men to lay them'.[113] In the camp in Eastgate in County Durham the prisoners 'were employed by the Weardale Iron, Steel, Coal and Coke Co. in quarry work . . . The work is in open quarries with horizontal ledges from which the men break off silica stone called ganister and also limestone.' They laboured for forty-eight hours per week.[114] Meanwhile, a total of 250 Germans eventually found themselves working in the Raasay iron mine; most had appropriate experience, especially as miners, but they also included joiners, masons and electricians. They toiled mainly in the mine, crusher, kilns and pier, although a few worked as cooks or on nearby farms.[115]

Numerous prisoners worked in general labouring work in a variety of locations. Among them were Germans employed in Chepstow shipyard, which displeased the Monmouthshire Labour Party.[116] In Bulford in Wiltshire 191 civilians, most of whom had families in Great Britain, had 'volunteered to work in order to make money'. The prisoners 'are employed by the Road Board and the Royal Engineers in painting, plumbing, blacksmith work, carpentry and bricklaying, in connection with camp hut construction'.[117] Those prisoners involved in brick making at the camp in Rosyth worked for nine and a half hours per day on weekdays and seven on Saturdays and were divided into three working groups. 'The first group is digging the clay, loading it on small railroad cars and bringing it into the factory. The second group attend to the machinery, to the kneading apparatus and brick "presses". The third dries the bricks and places them into the furnaces.'[118]

The importance of prisoner work

German prisoners in Britain, especially military captives, found themselves involved in a variety of tasks at the end of the First World War. Although the largest group, but not the majority, worked in agriculture, tens of thousands of others found employment in a range of areas, which, like planting and harvesting, assisted the British war effort. Prisoner labour did not, however, have the type of importance to the British economy in the First World War which it would do in the Second. In the former conflict, the government did not get hold of a substantial supply of prisoners until the latter stages of the war, while it also faced hostility towards their employment both in the early stages of the conflict and after Germans started carrying out work, although public opinion remained divided on this issue. Even when Germans did start playing a role in the economy, their numbers remained too small to matter to any significant degree, and were certainly not on the scale of the German war economy's dependence on Allied prisoners in both world wars. The 50,000 prisoners employed in Britain at the end of the First World War remained of limited importance. 'The Board of Trade estimated that the output of prisoners labour was from 55 to 60 per cent that of pre-War English labour but that when skilled men were employed in their trades under proper supervision the quality was high. The Ministry of Munitions found that the voluntary, well paid, labour of civilian prisoners was about 85 per cent that of English labour.'[119] Reports by the Ministry of National Service broke down the number of prisoners employed in individual locations together with their tasks. Thus the largest proportion of those in Banbury, who included people in quarrying and railway construction, consisted of labourers.[120] Similarly, while eighty-nine bricklayers and seventy-two carpenters in Bovington in September 1918 were involved in building their own camp, 252 prisoners were described as 'miscellaneous'.[121] From the descriptions provided by Swiss Embassy staff it appears that many prisoners carried out heavy labouring tasks in quarrying and construction and many worked long hours. While the Board of Trade may have criticized their efforts, the internees certainly worked hard.

Despite the toughness of the tasks which many of them carried out, prisoner employment helped to relieve the boredom, monotony and consequent depression caused by living behind barbed wire. Some opposition surfaced to the treatment which workers faced, especially in the form of strikes. At the same time some instances of depression remained. In a camp at Hermitage in South Wales a prisoner who refused to work 'was found to be suffering from "barbed wire disease" . . . and has been sent to another camp'. One of the reasons for this diagnosis lay in the fact that he demanded £1 per day for working.[122] Meanwhile, at a working camp at Port Talbot, 'Two men tried to escape but both were recognised as being mentally unbalanced. One tried to climb the fence, but fortunately the guard, instead of shooting, spoke to him, and discovered that his mind was not sound. Both are now in a lunatic asylum.'[123] Despite such diagnoses of mental illness, accepted in both cases by F. Schwyzer, the Swiss Embassy visitor, other sources point to the value of work. These include the reports of Schwyzer's colleague

Vischer, but also the pages of *Stobsiade*, which carried numerous articles romanticizing and poeticizing the tasks which prisoners employed in the working camps connected to Stobs peformed. These articles focused not only on employment which was linked with a rural idyll, such as forestry, but also on road construction. At the same time, as both *Stobsiade* and other sources indicate, work provided the type of routine which many civilians lacked, meaning that leisure time became precisely that during the evening rather than forming the reason for getting up every morning.

Despite the hard physical work which many prisoners carried out, reflecting both the needs of the British war economy and the number of people involved in manual labour at the start of the twentieth century,[124] their employment may have proved more important for the men themselves than for the British war effort. Prisoners played some role in securing the 1918 harvest. Some of the other tasks they carried out also indirectly helped the war effort, yet, as the article on 'Hun' river cleaners in the *Daily Express* indicated, many of the jobs which prisoners performed appear to have improved local environment and infrastructure, as the road-building and water supply work would also suggest. In essence, prisoner labour, certainly in comparison with other twentieth-century instances of its utilization, remained too small to matter to any great extent. Despite the long hours and hard physical nature of the work involved it may have proved more important in maintaining routine and fending off the onset of barbed wire disease.

Notes

1 Description of a prisoner-of-war working camp in Dalmellington from *Stobsiade*, June 1917: 'Our camp lies on a slope; in a valley including a large lake, surrounded by high, bare mountains. We live in huts, which are smaller than those in Stobs, always containing twelve men. Our hours of work total eight per day; the work consists of path, aqueduct and street construction.'

2 See Chapter 4 above.

3 See Chapter 8 below.

4 A. L. Vischer, *Barbed Wire Disease: A Psychological Study of the Prisoner of War* (London, 1919), p 56.

5 BL, Rudolf Rocker, 'Alexandra Park Internment Camp in the First World War', p. 11.

6 Heinz-Peter Mielke, *Kriegsgefangenen Arbeiten aus zwei Jahrhunderten* (Viersen, 1987), pp. 12–29.

7 For the full text see Hague Convention (IV) respecting the Customs of War on Land and its Annex: Regulations Concerning the Laws and Customs of War on Land, 18 October 1907, ANNEX TO THE CONVENTION: Regulations Respecting the Laws and Customs on Land # Section I: On Belligerents # Chapter II: Prisoners of War, at www.icrc.org/ihl.nsf/full/195 (accessed 27 March 2012).

8 Gerald H. Davis, 'Prisoners of War in Twentieth Century Economies', *Journal of Contemporary History*, vol. 12 (1977), 623.

9 Jochen Oltmer, 'Unentherbliche Arbeitskräfte: Kriegsgefangene in Deutschland 1914–1918', in Jochen Oltmer, ed., *Kriegsgefangene im Europa des Ersten Weltkrieges* (Paderborn, 2005), pp. 67–96.

10 Alon Rachamimov, *POWs and the Great War: Captivity on the Eastern Front* (Oxford, 2002), p. 108.

11 Edward L. Homze, *Foreign Labour in Nazi Germany* (Princeton, NJ, 1967), p. 195.

12 Lucio Sponza, *Divided Loyalties: Italians in Britain during the Second World War* (Frankfurt, 2000), pp. 183–317; Inge Weber-Newth and Johannes-Dieter Steinert, *German Migrants in Post-War Britain: An Enemy Embrace* (London, 2006), pp. 63–6.

13 Davis, 'Prisoners', p. 626.

14 Peter Scott, 'Captive Labour: The German Companies of the BEF, 1916–1920', *Army Quarterly Defence Journal*, vol. 110 (1980), 319–38.

15 Ulrich Herbert, *A History of Foreign Labour in Germany, 1880–1980: Seasonal Workers/Forced Laborers/Guest Workers* (Ann Arbor, MI, 1990), pp. 87–119; Ulrich Herbert, *Hitler's Foreign Workers: Enforced Labour in Germany under the Third Reich* (Cambridge, 1997).

16 Matthew Stibbe, 'Introduction: Captivity, Forced Labour and Forced Migration during the First Word War', *Immigrants and Minorities*, vol. 26 (2008), 1–18.

17 Homze, *Foreign Labour*, p. 195.

18 Sponza, *Divided Loyalties*, pp. 205–34.

19 J. C. Bird, *Control of Enemy Alien Civilians in Great Britain, 1914–1918* (London, 1986), p. 280.

20 *Hansard* (Commons), fifth series, vol. 74, cols 7–8, 14 September 1915.

21 *Hansard* (Commons), fifth series, vol. 84, col. 523, 13 July 1916.

22 *Hansard* (Commons), fifth series, vol. 80, col. 1526, 8 March 1916.

23 *Hansard* (Commons), fifth series, vol. 82, cols 5–8, 3 May 1916.

24 *The Times*, 2 June 1916.

25 NA/CAB42/20/7, The Employment of Prisoners of War, 12 September 1916. See also NA/ADM1/889/109, Memorandum by the Secretary of the Admiralty, 16 December 1916; NA/HO45/11025/410118, Report of the Directorate of Prisoners of War, September 1920, p. 13.
26 P. E. Dewey, 'Farm Labour in Wartime: The Relationship between Agricultural Labour Supply and Food Production in Great Britain during 1914–1918, with International Comparisons' (Ph.D. thesis, University of Reading, 1978), p. 242; Pamela Horn, *Rural Life in England in the First World War* (Dublin, 1984), pp. 140–4.
27 NA/NATS1/1332, Prisoners of War Employment Committee, First Interim Report, 1918.
28 NA/WO32/3099, Prisoners of War Employment Committee, Final Report, 1918.
29 NA/HO45/11025/410118, Report of the Directorate of Prisoners of War, September 1920, p. 51.
30 NA/NATS1/1332, Prisoners of War Employment Committee, First Interim Report, 1918.
31 NA/HO45/11025/410118, Report of the Directorate of Prisoners of War, September 1920; NA/NATS1/570, Rations for Prisoners of War, 1918.
32 Dewey, 'Farm Labour', pp. 249–50, 253; J. K. Montgomery, *The Maintenance of the Agricultural Labour Supply in England and Wales during the War* (Rome, 1922), pp. 42–3, 46; Horn, *Rural Life*, p. 161.
33 BLARC/WW1/AC/R/1, War Agriculture Eastern Committee, Drainage, Clearing of Waterways etc., Report of the Bedfordshire Agricultural Executive Committee Made Pursuant of the Cultivation of Land Order (No. 2), 1918.
34 NA/HO45/11025/410118, Report of the Directorate of Prisoners of War, September 1920, pp. 54, 118.
35 For this positive interaction see Chapter 7 below.
36 *Hansard* (Lords), fifth series, vol. 31, col. 972, 31 October 1918.
37 *Hansard* (Commons), fifth series, vol. 105, col. 980, 24 April 1918; Dewey, 'Farm Labour', pp. 249, 250.
38 Horn, *Rural Life*, p. 148; *Hansard* (Commons), fifth series, vol. 116, col. 1831, 3 June 1919.
39 *Hansard* (Commons), fifth series, vol. 113, col. 2110, 19 March 1919.
40 *Hansard* (Commons), fifth series, vol. 109, col. 29, 29 July 1918.
41 *Scotsman*, 11 January 1918.
42 *Daily Express*, 3 March 1919.
43 *Luton and Bedfordshire Advertiser*, 17 July 1919.
44 NA/NATS1/1332, Prisoners of War Employment Committee, 'First Interim Report', 1918; NA/NATS1/571, 'Details of Prisoners of War

Week Ended 14.7.18'; War Office, *Statistics of the Military Effort of the British Empire during the Great War, 1914–1920* (London, 1922), p.636; *The Times*, 28 March 1919; *Hansard* (Commons), fifth series, vol. 117, cols 1795–7, 9 July 1919; *Hansard* (Commons), fifth series, vol. 120, col. 649, 29 October 1919.

45 NA/FO383/432, Swiss Embassy Report on Knockaloe and Douglas, 11 September 1918.

46 NA/FO383/163, US Embassy Report on Douglas, 18 September 1916.

47 NA/FO383/237, Army Council Instruction No. 1280 of 1916, Grant of Working Pay to Interned Civilians, 27 June 1916.

48 *Das Schleierlicht*, 18 June 1916.

49 BL, Rudolf Rocker, 'Alexandra Park Internment Camp in the First World War', p. 12.

50 Paul Cohen-Portheim, *Time Stood Still: My Internment in England* (London, 1931), p. 44.

51 *Reports of Visits of Inspection Made by Officials of the United States Embassy to Various Internment Camps in the United Kingdom* (London, 1916), p. 22.

52 NA/HO45/10947/266042, James Cantlie, Report upon the Conditions of the Internment Camps at Knockaloe, Isle of Man.

53 MNH/MS10417/2, Prisoners of War Camp Knockaloe, I. O. Man, Garden Planning, Abhandlung ueber Gemuesebau.

54 MNH/MS10417/2, Results of the Agricultural Show.

55 BA/MA/MSG200/704, Ein Rueckblick auf unsere Lagerverwaltung seit ihrer Enstehung im April bis Ende 1917.

56 BA/MA/MSG200/2071, Internal POW Administration Camp IV, 30 March 1917; MNH/B115/43q, Camp IV, Knockaloe, I. O. M., Final Report and Statistical Record on the Internal Administration of the Prisoners of War Camp No. IV, 1915–1919.

57 Cohen-Portheim, *Time Stood Still*, p. 94.

58 NA/FO383/164, US Embassy Visit of 20 October 1916; BA/R901/83106, Swiss Embassy Visits of 13 March and 10 July 1917.

59 *Reports of Visits of Inspection*, p. 5; *Scotsman*, 21 July 1916; NA/MEPO2/1633.

60 Panikos Panayi, *The Enemy in Our Midst: Germans in Britain during the First World War* (Oxford, 1991), pp. 118–19.

61 See Chapter 7 below.

62 Panayi, *Enemy*, pp. 117–18; Leslie Baily, *Craftsman and Quaker: The Story of James T. Baily, 1876–1957* (London, 1959), pp. 104–5; NA/FO383/405, Industrial Department, Camp III, Knockaloe to Swiss Legation, German Division, 16 April 1918; *Lager-Zeitung*, 10 May 1917; MNH/MS10417/1, Papers of James T. Baily, 'FEC 1915–19, Isle of Man'.

63 NA/FO383/237, Army Council Instruction No. 1280 of 1916, Grant of Working Pay to Interned Civilians, 27 June 1916.
64 MNH/MS09845, Government Circular No. 188, Alien Labour on Farms, 21 March 1916; Government Circular No. 211, Alien Labour on Farms, 14 July 1916.
65 MNH/MS09845, Government Circular No. 240, Reclamation of Waste Land by Prisoner of War Labour, 24 November 1916.
66 MNH/MS09845, Government Circular No. 246, Quarrying and Road Making by Prisoner of War Labour, 27 November 1916.
67 NA/FO383/163, US Embassy Report on Prisoners of War Working Stations, Isle of Man, 28 August 1916.
68 MNH/MS06465/2, Douglas Camp Journal, vol. 2.
69 Margery West, *Island at War: The Remarkable Role Played by the Small Manx Nation in the Great War 1914–1918* (Laxey, 1986), p. 91; Jill Drower, *Good Clean Fun: The Story of Britain's First Holiday Camp* (London, 1982), p. 50.
70 NA/FO383/508, Swiss Embassy Report on Wasdale Head, 23 June 1919.
71 'And so the work begins. Ringing sound the hard axe cuts through the winter wood, the ritch-ratch of the big pruning saw combines with the crack of the tumbling trees. A noble spruce has been decided upon, an old gentleman of about 20 metres; his dense hanging branches have certainly seen many generations rise and sink into the grave.' *Stobsiade*, February 1917.
72 Albin Eckhardt and Kurt Maul, *Was wir in englischer Kriegsgefangenschaft erlebten und erlitten* (Frankfurt, 1922), pp. 126–7.
73 NA/FO383/279, Mrs H. Stahlschmidt to Swiss Ambassador, 2 September 1917.
74 *Daily Express*, 24 June 1918.
75 *Manchester Guardian*, 11 September 1918.
76 NA/FO383/543, Army Council Instruction No. 17 of 1919, Enemy Prisoners of War, Pay of Officers, 5 January 1919.
77 NA/FO383/409, Army Council Instruction No. 991 of 1918, Enemy Prisoners of War, Pay of Medical Personnel Officers, 4 September 1918.
78 BA/R901/83077, US Embassy Visit to Holyport, 25 May 1916.
79 Gunther Plüschow, *My Escape from Donington Hall* (London, 1922), p. 184.
80 Montgomery, *Maintenance*, p. 42; NA/HO45/11025/410118, Report of the Directorate of Prisoners of War, September 1920, p. 52.
81 Montgomery, *Maintenance*, pp. 43–4.
82 NA/HO45/11025/410118, Report of the Directorate of Prisoners of War, September 1920, p. 52.

83 NA/NATS1/1331, Notes by the Food Production Department as to the Present System of Employing Prisoners of War.
84 Horn, *Rural Life*, p. 152.
85 *The Times*, 29 August 1918.
86 NA/FO383/507, Swiss Embassy Report on Pattishall, 3 May 1919.
87 Swiss Embassy reports on all of these camps for September and October 1917 exist in BA/R901/83128. Further reports on camps dependent upon Pattishall covering late 1917 and early 1918 can be found in BA/R901/83129.
88 See the 1918 Swiss Embassy reports in BA/R901/83130.
89 See, for instance, the Swiss Embassy Report on North Elmham, Gressenhall, Shouldham, Wereham and King's Lynn of 2 June 1919 in NA/FO383/507.
90 BA/R901/83055, Swiss Embassy Report on Lulworth, Swanage and Hatherleigh, 10 December 1918; NA/FO383/505, Swiss Embassy Report on Lulworth, Swanage, Hatherleigh, Woodford, Wookey, Frome, Binegar, Devizes, Wootton Bassett and Ramsbury, 2 January 1919.
91 FO383/506, Swiss Embassy Report on Loughborough, Ashby de la Zouch, Ragdale, Narborough and Normanton Hall, 25 March 1919.
92 NA/FO383/508, Swiss Embassy Report on Frongoch and Affiliated Working Camps and Agricultural Depots, 27 June 1919.
93 *The Times*, 19 November 1917.
94 BA/R901/83129, Swiss Embassy Report on Blairfield House, 12 March 1918.
95 Montgomery, *Maintenance*, p. 47.
96 *Manchester Guardian*, 26 March 1917.
97 Horn, *Rural Life*, p. 153–4; Dewey, 'Farm Labour', pp. 249–53.
98 Dewey, 'Farm Labour', pp. 248–9.
99 BA/R901/83129, Swiss Embassy Report on Snettisham, 25 March 1918.
100 *Stobsiade*, August 1917.
101 BLARC/WW1/AC/R/1, Chief Executive Officer to J. Blofeld, 13 March 1919.
102 *Daily Express*, 25 March 1919.
103 NA/NATS/1331, Controller of Timber Supplies to Director, Prisoners of War, 20 April 1918.
104 NA/FO383/277, Swiss Embassy Report on Bwlch, 10 October 1917.
105 BA/R901/83129, Swiss Embassy Report on Eartham, 16 March 1918.
106 NA/FO383/164, US Embassy Visit to Nethybridge, 13 September 1916; US Embassy Visit to Lentran, 13 September 1916.
107 Probably referring to Royal Engineers.
108 NA/NATS1/571, Details of Prisoners of War – Week Ended 14.7.18.

109 NA/NATS1/1332, Prisoners of War Employment Committee, First Interim Report, 1918.
110 *Stobsiade*, August 1917.
111 BA/R67/210, DRK, Interner Wochenbericht No. 97, 13 October 1917.
112 NA/FO383/277, Swiss Embassy Report on Glendon, 10 October 1917.
113 NA/NATS1/1331, Memorandum on Employment of Prisoners of War, 12 June 1918.
114 BA/R901/83061, Swiss Embassy Report on Eastgate, 18 June 1917.
115 Laurence and Pamela Draper, *The Raasay Iron Mine: Where Enemies Became Friends* (1990; fifth printing, Dingwall, 2007), p. 16.
116 *Daily Express*, 7 April 1919.
117 NA/FO383/277, Swiss Embassy Report on Bulford, 6 October 1917.
118 NA/FO383/277, Swiss Embassy Report on Rosyth, 29 June 1917.
119 NA/HO45/11025/410118, Report of the Directorate of Prisoners of War, September 1920, p. 53.
120 NA/NATS1/1330, Visit to Banbury, 21 and 22 October 1918.
121 NA/NATS1/1330, Visit to Bovington, 13 September to 9 October 1918.
122 NA/F0383/277, Swiss Embassy Report on Hermitage, 10 October 1917.
123 NA/F0383/277, Swiss Embassy Report on Port Talbot, 10 October 1917.
124 As an introduction to German working-class life, see, for example, Alf Lüdtke, *Eigen-Sinn: Fabrikalltag, Arbeitererfahrungen und Politik vom Kaiserreich bis in den Faschismus* (Hamburg, 1993).

7

Public opinion

> Fresh home after nineteen months in Ruhleben, I have made it my business to inform myself as to the conditions at the Alexandra Palace, where the London Germans are interned.
>
> I am amazed at the descriptions given me of the comfort and brightness of everything after the poverty and the suffering of the unhappy prisoners of the Huns.[1]

Huns and relatives

Prisoners became an important theme in the Anglo-German propaganda war, with both sides claiming that the other mistreated captives. Both countries developed sophisticated publicity machines in which the vilification of the enemy became a key theme. For the British, the main foe was the Germans, despite the fact that they also fought against other nation states. The beastly and brutal Hun loomed above all other discourse about the enemy against which the country fought as Britain became saturated with Germanophobia, leading to the ethnic cleansing of traces of the country from British society.[2] On the German side, although the propaganda machines focused upon several enemies, the British became a key focus.[3]

Prisoners formed a key element in the propaganda ammunition of both states, which involved official opinion, the press and Parliament. In the British case much newspaper attention focused upon the experiences of civilians in Ruhleben, contrasting them with the apparently comfortable lifestyle faced by those on the Isle of Man and elsewhere. Both press and parliamentary opinion also compared the working conditions of those British military captives labouring on the eastern front with the apparently easier employment experiences of Germans working in Britain. Official opinion also backed this picture of mistreated British prisoners, both before and immediately after the war.

On the German side regular articles appeared in a variety of newspapers, often sparked off by the return of an individual prisoner who told his story of mistreatment in a British camp, although much of the press and Reichstag opinion focused upon the experiences of military captives in France and Russia, which held greater numbers of Germans than Britain. Similar to the British one, the German propaganda machine, backed up by official material, claimed that the British mistreated working prisoners, in this case behind the lines in France.[4]

This mistreatment of prisoners by the enemy offers one insight into the way in which public opinion in both Britain and Germany understood this issue. Behind the headlines about the evils of the enemy in the press of both countries, more subtle movements developed which took different views of military and civilian internees. Independent charities, which managed to stand above the nationalistic hatreds thrown up by the Great War, continued to carry out their work, including the Red Cross and the Society of Friends, together with the Markel Committee, which had been established by a long-standing naturalized German resident in Britain. Such groups focused their attention upon both the internees and their families who had been left to fend for themselves. We may partly view this as a survival of internationalism, particularly in the case of the Quakers (or Friends), whose history in the early twentieth century remained pacifist and concerned with helping victims of war.[5] On the other hand, the Markel Committee points to the importance of a link with the prisoners.

This becomes more obvious when we examine the captives about whom British and German public opinion really cared, in the form of their relatives held by the enemy, reflecting the importance of family during the Great War as recently stressed by Michael Roper in his study of the emotional survival of British soldiers during the conflict, facilitated by contact through letters and gifts.[6] As well as keeping in touch with relatives by sending letters, German families also played a role in the establishment of local committees which formalized assistance to prisoners in Britain, France and Russia. These groups usually came under the umbrella of the Red Cross. Heather Jones has suggested that humanitarianism during the First World War operated upon self-interest rather than internationalism and even formed part of the war effort, especially in the case of the Red Cross, whose local and national committees primarily cared, among the prisoners of war, for nationals interned abroad.[7]

Nevertheless, among all this self-interest for country or family, some genuine traces of positive attitudes towards the enemy also existed. While the official and unofficial British propaganda machine pumped out the imagery of the brutal Hun, by the end of the war Britons increasingly came into contact with the growing number of German prisoners, especially those who worked beyond the barbed wire, particularly upon farms. In such cases familiarity did not breed contempt but understanding, sympathy and attraction, as romanticized in Hall Caine's *The Woman of Knockaloe.* No evidence exists of a suicide pact between doomed lovers, although those women and men who displayed sympathy or affection for prisoners could face fines or imprisonment. The importance of human contact in breaking down prejudice towards prisoners has found reflection throughout the twentieth century. In Second World War Britain, women entered into relationships with both Germans and Italians.[8] Even in Nazi Germany, which racialized and completely marginalized prisoners and foreign workers, acts of kindness became normal and relationships sometimes developed, despite the draconian sentences which those who entered into them could face, some of which would survive the war.[9]

Public opinion therefore needs analysis along national lines because of the fact that, like all else in the Great War, extreme nationalism tainted attitudes towards any aspect of relationships with the enemy. On the one hand British public and official opinion focused upon the Hun as the central image of Germans. However, this formed only one aspect of attitudes towards Germans, because humanity survived even in this most brutal of conflicts, meaning that some individuals and organizations continued to show compassion, particularly when they came into contact with real human beings. In Germany, press and official opinion painted the reverse picture of the one which existed in Britain, focusing upon the mistreatment of the prisoners of war held by the enemy. At the same time, the driving force in attitudes towards those interned in England consisted of relatives, desperate to keep in touch. These desires played a key role in the actions of the German-based humanitarian organizations concerned with those interned in Britain.

Britons and German prisoners

A dissection of British attitudes towards the enemy within appears to reveal a dichotomy in which, on the one hand, a hostile press constantly vilified prisoners, while, on the other hand, those who actually came into contact with them treated them humanely. We should not, however, overestimate the level of positive feeling towards and interaction with internees. During the First World War Britain became saturated with Germanophobia, and for those fighting the war at home,[10] the main focus of their hatred was the 'enemy in our midst'. The hatred manifested itself in anti-German movements and organization, social boycotts and, following the sinking of the *Lusitania* in May 1915, the most widespread riots in modern British history. Such public actions went hand in hand with the official measures which the government introduced, including confiscation of German property, deportation and internment.

Figure 7.1 Anti-German riot in London. Attacks upon German property occurred on several occasions during the course of the First World War, peaking in May 1915. This influenced the government's decision to introduce wholesale internment.

The internment campaign in Britain, part of the overall expression of hatred of Germany at this time, had two key elements: the demand for wholesale incarceration; and the issue of the positive treatment of German prisoners, especially in contrast to Britons held in Germany. Large sections of the press played a key role. The few organs which did not become victim to such views included the liberal *Manchester Guardian*, the *Nation* and the *New Statesman*. Virtually all other local and national newspapers in First World War Britain peddled, either constantly or intermittently, extreme Germanophobia, and the internment campaign played a key role in this. At the same time, a group of radical right-wing politicians, including William Joynson-Hicks and Lord Charles Beresford, took every opportunity to bring the attention of Parliament to the issue of internment. As the war progressed several extreme right-wing Germanophobic organizations came into existence with wholesale internment as a key element of these beliefs, including the British Empire Union, the Vigilantes and the National Party.[11]

The demand to intern all males of military age surfaced regularly throughout the war. It operated against the background of an ideology fuelled by both the newspapers and several novelists about the potential damage which male enemy aliens at liberty could inflict upon the British war effort. This ideology initially surfaced as 'spy-fever', an obsession with and fear of German espionage, which had its origins in the Edwardian years, and subsequently developed into a conspiracy theory which suggested that Germans were controlling the British establishment as a result of sexual blackmail and were preventing British victory on the continent.[12]

Demands for wholesale internment began to emerge in the autumn of 1914 following a peak of anti-German feeling in the middle of October as German armies rapidly advanced through Belgium, resulting in a peak of 'spy-fever', a campaign against German waiters and anti-German riots in Crewe and Deptford.[13] On 22 October the *Daily Express* published an article commenting upon a round-up of Germans but also calling for the sacking of all German hotel and restaurant employees in the country. On 12 November the first major debate on internment policy occurred in the House of Commons, initiated by William Joynson-Hicks, who attacked the Home Secretary, Reginald McKenna, upon all aspects of his policy.[14] Although the issue surfaced occasionally in the House of Commons during the course of the winter of

1914–15,[15] the next major debate took place on 3 March, again led by Joynson-Hicks, who moved a motion which asked that 'the whole administration of the Acts and regulations concerning Aliens and suspected persons during the War should be concentrated in the hands of one Minister who should be responsible to this House'. His opening address concentrated upon the 'spy peril' and the number of Germans at liberty in Britain, and contrasted this with the numbers of Britons free in Berlin.[16]

The sinking of the *Lusitania* led to the highest peak of First World War Germanophobia in Britain, which manifested itself most obviously in the riots following this event, caused largely by the press reaction which painted Germans as inhuman. Horatio Bottomley's *John Bull* even called for the extermination of Germans in Britain.[17] More sober opinion focused upon the need for thorough internment and deportation. On 13 May, the morning on which Asquith announced the decision to implement wholesale internment for males of military age,[18] with anti-German riots raging, *The Times* declared, 'Internment the Only Remedy'. After focusing upon the 'numerous inhuman acts committed by the enemy' the editorial suggested that 'segregation on a large scale will become desirable for the safety and protection of the Germans themselves just as much as for the preservation of order'. Asquith made similar assertions in the Commons.[19] *The Times* followed with a self-righteous article declaring: 'The Government have at last decided to do what they should have done nine months ago. They propose to make a clean sweep of enemy aliens.'[20]

Despite the decision to introduce wholesale internment, critics in Parliament and the press focused upon those who remained at liberty. Just as the campaign calling for wholesale internment had previously reached its peak at times of heightened Germanophobia in October 1914 and May 1915, this correlation continued later in the war. Another high point occurred in June 1916, following the death of Lord Kitchener when the ship upon which he was travelling to Russia hit a mine on 5 June, and this resulted in a new outbreak of anti-German riots, on this occasion confined to London.[21] Eight days later a meeting organized by the British Empire Union in Hyde Park, attended by over 1,000 people, declared 'that all Germans, naturalised and unnaturalised, shall be interned forthwith . . . Lord Kitchener's death was the culminating point in a long string of events that went to indicate that this country had been betrayed through an elaborate system of German espionage.'[22] On 29 June Joynson-Hicks launched another attack on the internment policy of a new Home Secretary, Herbert Samuel, in which he declared that 'the desire of the people is that every alien enemy should be interned or repatriated unless there are some really stringent reasons in the public interest why he should be allowed to be free'. There followed a lengthy debate on the issue.[23] On the same day a similar discussion took place in the House of Lords, initiated by Lord Meath, during which Beresford asked why 22,000 enemy aliens remained 'uninterned', including 6,756 males. He continued:

> What are they here for? What do we want them here for? Surely they are a danger to us and ought to be locked up. I do not wish to be hard on them, but I would put the whole lot behind barbed wire and keep them there until the war is over. Any leniency that we show to these people is not treated with gratitude in Germany, but with contempt. They think we are afraid and dare not lock them up as we should.[24]

Joynson-Hicks launched yet another debate on internment policy in the Commons on 17 December 1917 in which he declared that 'no man should be allowed to remain uninterned except for definitely national as opposed to personal reasons'.[25]

The final peak in the internment campaign arrived in the summer of 1918, caused by a series of factors including the partially successful Ludendorff offensive, which pushed back Allied forces on the western front and raised the spectre of possible German victory. At the same time war-weariness had become widespread.[26] Finally, a new star of the radical right, Pemberton Billing, who had entered Parliament as a result of a by-election in April 1916 and represented a party called the Vigilantes, heightened the Germanophobic atmosphere. The demands for wholesale internment took place against the background of a final intense peak of hostility towards Germans in Britain. Its manifestations included the trial of Billing for libel in connection with claims he had made about a hidden hand which controlled the British establishment as a result of sexual misdemeanours by 47,000 people.[27] At the same time several newspapers began to stress the enemy alien danger from early June. The summer of 1918 also witnessed a series of meetings calling for stricter measures against alien enemies. Furthermore, local councils throughout the country passed resolutions against Germans.[28] On 24 August 1918 a Hyde Park meeting adopted a petition calling for the internment of all enemy aliens. The 1,250,000 million signatures subsequently went to Downing Street.[29] The intensity of the pressure which faced the government led to a re-examination of internment policy by the Cabinet on 24 June and a statement by the Home Secretary at the time, Sir George Cave, to the Commons on 11 July announcing that those enemy aliens who still found themselves free would have their cases re-examined by a reconstituted Aliens Advisory Committee.[30]

The Home Office, Home Secretaries, and other departments charged with internment found themselves under constant pressure to re-examine policy in order to ensure that every enemy alien who ought to find himself behind barbed wire did so. A hostile public opinion, measured through press and parliamentary views, as well as the actions of rioters, ensured that this issue never remained far from frontline domestic politics in Britain throughout the Great War. The call to 'lock them up' formed part of a wider Germanophobia which would result in wholesale deportation in 1918 and 1919.

Even when the German-haters had managed to force government to adopt wholesale internment and deprivation of liberty, they did not rest there, as both military and civilian prisoners became the focus of a different campaign criticizing the humane treatment which they received, especially in contrast with that meted out to Britons who found themselves behind barbed wire in Germany.

This remained a key theme in the aftermath of the war, when an article entitled 'Great Britain's Humane Treatment of German Prisoners of War' in volume 12 of a publication called *The Great War* opened with the following sentence: 'No one who knew the British people at all well would believe that their treatment of prisoners of war, German or otherwise, was cruel and barbarous, or was in any way like that which British prisoners of war suffered at the hands of the Germans.'[31] During the course of the conflict Ruhleben in particular became synonymous with German military actions and mistreatment during the Great War, and in the immediate aftermath an exhibition took place in Westminster Hall to commemorate the experiences of internees held there.[32] For much of the war the British press and parliamentary opinion stressed the mistreatment of internees in Ruhleben and other camps in Germany, often noting the contrast with the situation in Britain. A letter to *The Times* dated 28 April 1915, from a released prisoner who had just returned from Germany, claimed that some captives had found themselves tied to posts. 'One prisoner, whom I knew well, saw in February three men taken down from these posts to which they were in all weathers crucified. It should be remembered that the cruelties suffered in these camps, especially by the British prisoners, were continuous and cumulative in their effect.' The edition which published this letter carried another directly underneath it on the same page from a J. F. Williams, who had read a copy of the Douglas *Camp Echo* and declared: 'At the same time when British prisoners have suffered so much in Germany, we may take pride in the fact that we treat German prisoners in England with the liberality of which the mere existence of this journal is evidence.'[33] Meanwhile, a piece in the *Isle of Man Weekly Times* contrasted the position of German internees on the Isle of Man with those in Germany: 'While British prisoners in Germany are being starved, ill-treated, and imprisoned, aliens in the Manx camps are having a high old time. While English Tommies are labouring at the dirtiest and heaviest work, the enemy aliens are kept idle, and their idleness is relieved by games and by walks in the country.'[34] On 5 July 1916 an editorial in *The Times* entitled 'British and German Prisoners', citing a wide variety of sources, asserted that the treatment of Britons in Germany 'has varied in different camps at different times, but on the whole their condition is most pitiable'. In contrast, Germans released in Switzerland 'bore ready witness to the excellent treatment, material and moral, they had met with when interned in this country'. Other newspapers also played this game of contrast. The *Weekly Dispatch* compared Alexandra Palace with Ruhleben using the evidence of a former internee of the latter who had visited the former. A column on Alexandra Palace carried the subheadings 'Hundreds of Washing Basins' and 'Food Cost 1s. 7d. Per Man', while the juxtaposed subheadings for Ruhleben read 'One Water Tap to 150 Men' and 'Food Cost 7d. Per Man'.[35] The *Daily Express* suggested cutting the rations of Alexandra Palace internees.[36]

The same theme of the differing treatment of British and German prisoners surfaced in parliamentary debates. In the spring of 1915, for instance, Beresford 'asked whether the time has arrived when the German Government should be given to understand that unless British prisoners of war, both military and civil, received better treatment in Germany than they do at present, steps will be taken by His Majesty's Government to treat German prisoners in this country in a less lenient manner'.[37] Two days later Beresford asked Asquith 'whether he is aware that British prisoners in Germany are treated as convicts, while German prisoners in this country are treated as if they are an honourable foe'.[38] During a Commons debate on the treatment of Britons held in Germany, the Unionist Donald Macmaster pointed to 'the comforts of the German prisoners in this country'.[39] A year later Sir John Butcher, Unionist MP for York, suggested that German prisoners who died in England should no longer have 'funerals with processions, flowers and military honours . . . in view of the frequent brutal treatment of our prisoners in Germany'.[40] A final Commons debate on prisoners on 29 October 1918 again made the contrast.[41]

Not all press and parliamentary opinion compared the treatment of British and German prisoners, although those which focused simply upon the position of the latter worked against the background of public assumptions about German actions. An article in the *Daily Mirror* from as early as 22 August 1914 carried the title 'Prison De Luxe for Germans: Captives of War Who Eat and Waltz at Cardiff'. Even this mentioned the German situation in its opening paragraph: 'In contrast to the treatment of English people in Germany, who have been classed spies, placed in prison and generally shown no consideration, is the treatment accorded to the German prisoners in Cardiff.' On 15 May 1915 the *Isle of Man Weekly Times* carried a piece from a Belgian which began: 'We Belgian refugees in England are surprised at the splendid manner in which the German prisoners of war are treated . . . Here at Douglas the Teutons are like masters amongst us. They take their walks to the sound of beautiful joyous music. They whistle and sing and march along the seafront and admire the beauty of the country.' When the War Office and Home Office allowed some journalists to visit the Isle of Man camps in July 1916 predictable headlines followed. The *Daily Express*, for instance, stated: 'Where Huns Are Well Fed. In Prison Camps in England. Cakes, Music, Jam, and Sausage.' The *Manchester Guardian* and *The Times* took a more sober tone, although the latter similarly began its article on 'Germans in British Camps' by stating: 'The painful revelations as to the conditions under which our fellow-countrymen are interned or imprisoned in Germany render it particularly desirable that the facts concerning our own treatment of aliens and prisoners of war should be generally known.'[42]

Attention focused upon one camp in particular, Donington Hall, which became synonymous with luxury, despite the fairly basic conditions which officers endured here, as was eventually revealed by journalists who visited in July 1916.[43] Questions in the Commons focused upon the furnishings, alcoholic beverages, transport to the camp by motor car and expenditure by the government. Once again a reference was made to 'the starvation of British prisoners in Germany'.[44] The focus upon Donington Hall even led to allegations by the *Globe* that Asquith's wife sent food and other items to prisoners here, which led her to launch a successful libel action against the paper.[45]

The negative coverage which German prisoners received actually led to physical attacks upon them. For instance, 'Charles Ridge, a seaman, was bound over and ordered to pay 4s. costs at Long Ashton . . . for knocking down a German prisoner, one of a party who was being marched to work on the land.'[46] Nevertheless, this type of occurrence remained something of a rarity, and those who appeared in court for interacting with prisoners usually did so because they had broken an aspect of military law by assisting them in some way. Despite the image of 'the Hun' perpetuated by the press and parliamentary opinion, when ordinary people came into contact with prisoners they usually displayed acts of kindness and even love, rather than hostility. While we should not forget the mass rioting against Germans in Britain which peaked in May 1915, those who met prisoners during the latter stages of the war tended to behave positively towards them. When considering this dichotomy, we should also remember that some sections of British society carried out charitable activities for German internees.

Some of those who faced charges for interacting with German prisoners did so because they had provided them with food and other gifts. For example, William Barratt 'was sentenced to three months hard labour . . . for giving a box of food to German prisoners of war'.[47] In August 1919 Dr Frederick Horseman faced a fine of £25 for giving fruit to prisoners 'engaged in filling trenches at Whitley' after asking the guard 'if there would be any harm in giving them a few bananas'. After the sentry replied that 'no persons were allowed to give articles to the prisoners', Horseman decided to 'risk it' and 'returned in a motor car in which he had a box of apples and commenced to throw the apples to the prisoners'. This caused them to congregate around him, and the sentries 'had a hard time of half an hour in restoring order'. When he appeared in court Horseman stated that he 'thought it best to let bygones be bygones' and 'what we wanted was brotherly love'.[48] In a similar case, although without the appeal for Anglo-German reconciliation, a rector in Yorkshire faced a fine of three guineas for giving cigars to German prisoners in a station waiting room.[49]

The press devoted more attention to cases which involved captives having contact with British women. Like male Britons, some women simply displayed acts of kindness towards Germans. In October 1918 Jane Deeming 'was charged under the Defence of the Realm Regulations by interfering with the discipline of a prisoner of war in supplying him with bread'. The sole witness claimed that he saw her meeting a German prisoner in Whittington Lane in Grendon with a loaf of bread which she handed over. She denied the charge and claimed that she had simply spoken and waved to the prisoners. 'The girl, who had a bad character, was sentenced to one month's hard labour.'[50] In a similar case twenty-year-old Gladys Hall and twenty-two-year-old Mary Elizabeth Gordon, both members of the Women's Royal Air Force, faced fines of three guineas each for giving cigarettes to German prisoners in Cove in Hampshire. They had also received a letter from one of the prisoners thanking them for the cigarettes. According to another member of the corps, Gordon had described the Germans as 'fine looking boys' and 'real men'.[51] In both the Grendon and the Cove cases there appears to have been some element of sexual attraction, although no real indication of any relationship. In 1917 Ann Radcliffe went to jail for one month for harbouring two escaped prisoners, Jon Voigt and Otto Rohreig, in Ramsay on the Isle of Man, and not reporting their presence in her house to the police. Radcliffe met the escapees in an inn, where she had some drinks with them. She claimed she thought they were Welsh, as they had told her. They subsequently went to her house, where they had something to eat in the presence of two other women. When the police came to her house, by which time she had worked out their nationality, she did not admit to their presence, which added to her crime. A series of conflicting accounts came to light at the trial but Radcliffe probably told the truth. Her husband spoke in her support and she fainted when hearing the sentence was passed upon her.[52]

Further cases surfaced of British women writing to German prisoners. In September 1915 Mary Hayes and her domestic servant,

Alice France, received fines of £10 and £2 respectively for communicating with internees. Mary Hayes's house faced the recreation ground of the camp; one of the guards became suspicious when he saw the two women waving to prisoners, and they consequently received a warning. 'Suspicions, however, continued to be aroused, and eventually a cunningly concealed secret post office was discovered outside the barbed wire barrier of the compound, from which it was found later that letters were passing between the women and the prisoners.'[53] In a similar case Lily Fleet and Bridget McHugh, who worked as domestic servants in a house in Groveland Avenue in Wallasey, received sentences of 'three months imprisonment on charges of transmitting to a prisoner of war cigarettes, tobacco and flowers, which acts were likely to interfere with the discipline of a place of detention'. Fleet had visited the camp at Leasowes Castle a dozen times and received letters on standard prisoner-of-war writing paper commencing, 'My Dear Betty'. One prisoner at the camp had a letter from Fleet, together with a picture of her. Meanwhile the billiard room in the house at Groveland Avenue contained photographs of German prisoners.[54] The most bizarre case involved Elizabeth Gibb, 'wife of the licensee of an hotel at Wadhurst', who 'was sentenced to three months' imprisonment with hard labour for 'sending uncensored letters and cigarettes to a German prisoner of war at a camp in Sussex'. The prosecuting solicitor stated that Gibb 'wrote impassioned and abandoned letters to the German which were never censored. Not only was this done without the knowledge of the husband, but the woman had never even spoken to the man. She had corrupted the corporal of the guard of the camp by paying him a 10s Treasury note for every letter he delivered.'[55] Finally a case came to court as a result of two teenagers, fifteen-year-old Nellie Ware and eighteen-year-old Lily Meyers, loitering on government grounds next to a prisoner-of-war camp in Hounslow. It seems that Ware and Meyers managed to get through some hedges and fences, as other girls had done previously. They 'were found crouching behind bushes near the German camp'.[56]

When British people came into contact with prisoners they tended to ignore the press stereotypes of Germans as murderers and the regulations which forbade contact and fraternization.[57] Many of these cases involved women, and, although sexual attraction played a role, none of the instances outlined above provide strong evidence of any type of relationship. Examples of interaction simply involved attraction or kindness to the enemy.

Most of the British charities which helped prisoners came from outside the mainstream of British society. The most important of those focusing specifically upon prisoners was the Markel Committee, established by a naturalized German in Britain. The FEC grew from a pacifist religious group, the Quakers. Much of the charity work which this and other organizations carried out was actually aimed at those women whose German husbands found themselves interned behind barbed wire, who also received assistance from the British government.[58]

The Markel Committee bore the name of its founder, Dr Emil Markel, a chemist born in Hesse to a German father and an English mother in 1860 who had moved in 1865 to Britain, where he became naturalized, married an English wife and subsequently established several chemical factories. Markel appears to have played the leading role in establishing and financing the Prisoners of War Relief Agency in his own house near Hyde Park in October 1915, and it continued its activities until 1919. The Markel Committee provided equipment for the social activities of prisoners in camps, including musical instruments, tools for trades and books, together with medicines, and it also established dental stations in the larger camps. By early 1918 it was spending £4,500 a month. The funding came from Englishmen who had ties with Germany as well as from Germans and Americans. Markel also made efforts to help British prisoners in Germany.[59] The Markel Committee and its branches appear to have remained distinct from the Prisoners Aid Societies in terms of the tasks they carried out. Some documentation does not appear to distinguish between the two. By 1916 they both existed, as either the same entity or separate entities, in most camps.[60] The most significant appeared in Knockaloe. Here each sub-camp had a Prisoners Aid Society with its own chairman, deputy chairman and secretary, together with 'a general Committee comprising members from each compound'. Leland Littlefield and W. H. Buckler of the United States Embassy in London outlined its four main aims. First, it gave advice to prisoners on a variety of issues which had arisen as a consequence of their internment. Second, it helped to trace missing personal belongings. Third, it directed prisoners to the proper agencies which could help their families if they were suffering as a consequence of internment. Finally, it could write letters on behalf of uneducated prisoners and those who did not have a sufficient command of English.[61] In Camp I the Prisoners Aid Society received financial help from both the German and Austro-Hungarian governments, as well as from Dr Markel. During its first year it dealt with 1,380 cases. By the end of 1918 the Prisoners Aid Society in Camp IV in Knockaloe had assisted 2,656 people.[62] Meanwhile, the Markel Committee here, 'which closely collaborates with the Prisoners of War Relief Agency (Dr. Markel)', had distributed a wide variety of 'comforts' including clothing, 'educational utensils', books and money. It also represented the German Red Cross and other benevolent societies.[63]

The FEC came into existence just after the outbreak of war, on 7 August 1914. Its executive consisted of prominent Quakers, but it received support from public figures including the Archbishop of Canterbury and Lord Haldane. Much of its activity focused upon those enemy aliens who remained at liberty, but it also made efforts to assist internees.[64] Its work overlapped with that of the Markel Committee, as it included providing prisoners with items which they requested. The FEC also played a major role in looking after and maintaining links between civilians and their families.[65] One of its most significant activities consisted of providing work for internees, especially in Knockaloe.[66] Although most of its efforts focused upon helping members of the pre-war German community in Britain, it also assisted military prisoners. For instance, some of the working camps 'were visited once or twice by our representatives, but the main or parent camps at Stobs, (Scotland), Leigh, Handforth, Frongoch (Wales), Brocton, Catterick, Oswestry, Pattishall, Dorchester, Blandford, Feltham and Jersey' also had 'local visitors' attached to them 'during part or the whole of their history'. The work it carried out for civilian and military prisoners also differed because the FEC 'were not in direct touch with the families of military prisoners'. But the committee sometimes dealt with messages from relatives abroad and also sent information to them in Germany by working with the Prisoners of War Information Bureau. In addition, the FEC sometimes took flowers to wounded prisoners in hospitals, which 'brought the purest joy to many a broken and lonely man'. Furthermore, 'when death came to end an internment it was sometimes possible to send a parcel or letter from the visitor to the wife or mother in Germany, telling of the care given during the last illness, or enclosing a photo of the grave in some lovely English Churchyard'.[67]

German public opinion

The efforts of the Quakers and Dr Markel, who remained outside mainstream British society, helped to alleviate the position of internees. At the same time, when ordinary Britons came into contact with German prisoners, they often displayed acts of kindness towards them, while some women felt an attraction and may even have entered into relationships with them. Despite these positive acts, perceptions of the German prisoner in England remained dominated by the press and parliamentary view that the enemy interned in Britain remained well treated in comparison with the plight of those Englishmen who were suffering at the hands of the Germans in Ruhleben and elsewhere.

German public opinion focused upon almost the reverse of the issues which worried the British. The main concern of official and unofficial circles consisted of pointing to the mistreatment which prisoners received in Britain. Newspapers, books and semi-official publications played this game. In addition to constructing the negative images of the Englishman,[68] German mainstream public opinion devoted attention to alleviating the plight of the prisoners who found themselves on British soil, a movement driven by the concerns of relatives working together with a range of humanitarian organizations.

German public opinion focused upon the mistreatment of its prisoners by the enemy in the same way as the British did, although, while the main concern in Britain was Germany, the British formed one strand which devoted much attention to the plight of German prisoners in France and Russia. The main reason for this lies in the fact that the Germans, in contrast with the British, fought three equally powerful enemies, who all captured and interned their soldiers and civilians.[69] At the same time, Britain also meant the British Empire. When the Reichstag discussed the issue of the plight of German prisoners, speakers often focused upon experiences in more than one country. This certainly happened in the longest debate on prisoners, which took place on 2 November 1916. Those who contributed focused, as in debates in the House of Commons, upon the plight of both foreign prisoners of war in

Germany and Germans abroad. Heinrich zu Schoenaich-Carolath, referring to 'the position of the German prisoners abroad', spoke about 'a prisoner of war camp in India' where 800 internees who wished to return to Europe faced bad conditions. Schoenaich-Carolath then looked at French camps before speaking about prisoners in Germany. Some of the debate which followed focused upon negotiations over exchange and release between the German government and the Allied states, although speakers also made specific allegations about individual camps in France and Russia.[70] Similarly, on 13 June 1918, Theodor Held spoke about prisoners in a stable in France and then moved on to paraphrase from a letter he had received from a German officer held in England who feared he would be shot. He then played the game of comparison by suggesting that 'the treatment of prisoners on the land by us, I would like to say, is excellent'.[71] Such sentiments found replication in the press. Thus an article in the *Hamburger Fremdenblatt* of 10 June 1918, entitled 'The Condition of the German Prisoners in England', began, 'Extraordinary need determines the position of the German prisoners in England' and then declared that the position of the 'imprisoned English in Germany is going well'.

On other occasions, Reichstag debates focused simply upon the treatment of Germans in one particular nation state or even in one camp. For instance, on 5 July 1918 Dr Ludwig Haas declared that 'extraordinarily bad news' had come from Brocton, quoting the *Hamburger Fremdenblatt*. He commented upon the accommodation and claimed that the prisoners here suffered from hunger, while the camp authorities ignored the complaints of the internees. In fact, stories about Brocton had appeared earlier in the year, and on 20 February reports on the German wireless had claimed that 'there is a brutal and money taking commandant in command, and miserable conditions arise which are a disgrace to England, who nevertheless is so proud of her treatment of prisoners of war'.[72]

This type of reporting characterized German media reports on British camps throughout the course of the war. Press articles often appeared when a prisoner returned home and told his story, or even when a relative of an internee gained information about treatment in Britain.[73] Some newspaper stories remained fairly objective, but others simply had the aim of stressing mistreatment. Those in the latter category sometimes began with an attack on Britain and often contrasted it with the more humanitarian situation which they claimed existed in Germany. In June 1915 an article in the *Hamburger Fremdenblatt* entitled 'Germans in English Imprisonment' began by stating that there was no point in trying to negotiate with enemies about humanitarianism and harked back to the Boer War, when Britain had first used concentration camps. The article then quoted a letter from the brother of one the newspaper's readers in which he described conditions on the *Royal Edward*, moored off the coast at Southend. Meanwhile, an article in the *Frankfurter Zeitung* of 2 May 1915 began by launching an attack on the reporting of the English newspapers, which focused upon the treatment of British internees in Germany, and proceeded to provide an account of conditions at the military hospital in Dartford in order to prove that the British constituted the real villains in dealings with prisoners. A flurry of articles appeared in the summer of 1918, linked with the increasing numbers of returning internees, which focused upon their mistreatment.[74] Most starkly the *Kieler neueste Nachrichten* of 15 June 1918 carried the headline 'English Brutality' and began: 'It is generally accepted in Germany that the English treat our prisoners in a chivalrous or at least good manner. In particular one is led to believe that, at the very least, England fittingly treats those defenceless wounded officers in need of care from the army and navy who fall into its hands in this manner.' However, the article proceeded to suggest that experiences of returning exchanged prisoners contradicted this image, using the example of four officers who pointed out 'how inadequate care and accommodation was in many military hospitals and how brutally and roughly the staff carried out their duties'.

At the end of 1916 an article appeared in the *Deutsche medizinische Zeitschrift* entitled 'Englische Leichtfertigkeit und englischer Dünkel'. Following the pattern of many stories in both the British and German newspapers of this time, it pointed to the brutal actions of the foe and the relative humanity of the homeland in its prosecution of the war. Much of the piece focused upon a rebuttal of claims found in British newspapers about the actions of the German army in Belgium and the condition of British prisoners in Germany. The article also devoted much time to the experience of German internees in Britain, concentrating upon the mistreatment which they faced and quoting several personal accounts. It concluded with the full text of a letter written by Dr J. P. zum Busch, who had worked for twenty years as chief surgeon at the

German Hospital in east London, entitled 'Mein Letzter Brief aus England', which had also appeared in the *Kölnische Zeitung*, in which he made a series of allegations investigated and disputed by the British government. Like other negative German accounts, it devoted much attention to conditions at Stratford.[75]

An earlier peak of indignation had arrived in the spring of 1915 over the treatment of German submarine crews. On 27 April the First Lord of the Admiralty, Winston Churchill, had declared: 'No special conditions are applied to German submarine prisoners because they fight in submarines; but special conditions are applied to prisoners who have been engaged in wantonly killing non-combatants, neutrals, and women on the high seas', which, however, remained 'in every respect humane'.[76] Nevertheless, this statement and the decision to separate thirty-nine members of submarine crews led to a flurry of diplomatic activity and a decision by the German government to treat thirty-nine British officers similarly until the British government backed down.[77] In addition, a series of indignant articles surfaced in German newspapers during the spring and summer of 1915.[78] The issue of the treatment of submarine crews continued to appear intermittently throughout the war.[79]

In addition to the highly critical approach which German newspapers took to the treatment of prisoners in Britain and elsewhere, official and semi-official bodies also made similar allegations. For example, the Reichskommisar zur Erörterung von Gewaltätigkeiten gegen Deutsche Zivilpersonen in Feindesland issued a couple of reports, although their circulation appears to have been confined to official circles. In 1915 a series of allegations about internees in Britain emerged. For instance, some prisoners mentioned 'torn and inadequate clothing' which did not keep out the cold, and those held at Queensferry complained about accommodation, food and toilet facilities. The report also carried information about the ships moored off Ryde, Southend and Gosport, which received universal condemnation. The information came from a variety of sources including United States Embassy and Red Cross reports.[80] A similar report from 1916, dealing with violence against Germans throughout Europe, carried sections on physical attacks on Germans, confiscation of property and internment in Britain.[81]

Similarly, the German Red Cross's committee for German prisoners published weekly reports for internal consumption on the treatment of the people it cared for throughout the world, including the entire British Empire. The information they contain remains largely objective and was taken from a variety of sources, especially United States and Swiss Embassy reports, but also from accounts provided by returning prisoners as well as letters written home to relatives and newspaper articles. Internal report 69 of 10 June 1916 carried information on the Dyffryn Aled officers' camp, about which complaints had emerged throughout the war, perhaps because the educated prisoners here had spread their stories upon their return. On this occasion, a former inmate commented upon the condition of the buildings, as well upon as the commandant, who was described as 'an absolute German hater', a phrase suspiciously used again in report 102 of 4 March 1918.[82] Report 27 of 14 June 1915 provides an example of the objectivity of these documents with a commentary on Handforth. It carried a précis of a positive article written by a Danish author in the Copenhagen newspaper *Politiken* and commented: 'Although he is inclined to be a friend of England and to see everything through rose tinted spectacles, one must nevertheless accept that he endeavours to judge things impartially.' Another account in report 33 stated that while the committee had previously had doubts about the impartiality of the Danish author, an account by the sister of an internee held in Handforth confirmed many of his assertions.[83] On the other hand a report of March 1918, by which time a variety of negative comments about the treatment of German prisoners in England had begun to appear in a range of sources, summarized a series of such stories.[84]

Demand for personal accounts of wartime experiences meant that some of those who returned home published their experiences as books.[85] These may well have played a role in the Anglo-German propaganda war, which stressed domestic humanity over the brutality of the enemy, but this did not form the main purpose of the volumes. The main selling point of many of these books was the excitement of wartime experiences. In many cases the process which actually led to internment takes up much of the narrative. D. W. Pult, for example, does not begin his account of sixteen months of imprisonment in England until page 16.[86] Similarly, the first thirty-five pages of Bruno Schmidt-Reder's story of life in Dorchester focus upon his journey there, which involved arrest upon the *Potsdam* while sailing from New York to Germany in

August 1914.[87] The same is true of those accounts by individuals who spent time in English camps after initial arrest in British and German colonies. Experiences before arriving in Britain form the main basis of these stories, as adventures in the Tropics provided more opportunities for narrative than everyday life in a British concentration camp.[88]

Many of the books on experiences of life behind barbed wire remained matter-of-fact rather than sensationalist, as for example the volume published in 1919 by Karl von Scheidt and Fritz Meyer on the life and 'suffering' of Germans in England.[89] Those who spent much time on describing their eventual journey to a camp described internment experiences fairly mundanely. D. W. Pult, for instance, captured in France, provided sober details of life in Portsmouth, Holyport and Leigh.[90] Bruno Schmidt-Reder devoted space to simply describing the dimensions of Dorchester.[91] Similarly, Otto Schimming, a German missionary in Togo, who spent time in both Alexandra Palace and the Isle of Man, provided a useful narrative of both of these camps, which complements many of the other sources that have survived about life within them.[92] Interestingly, perhaps as a reflective man of God, Schimming concluded: 'I would not like to have missed the last few years in Africa and in English imprisonment. They were difficult times, hard and humiliating at the same time. They were not without gain.'[93] R. Hartmann, meanwhile, who had worked as a pastor in Knockaloe, provided an objective account of everyday life there.[94]

Some of these personal stories, however, leave readers in no doubt about the brutality of the British. One of the most overt attacks came from another man of God, Georg Wagener, the first pastor of the German Protestant community in Cape Town, who eventually found his way to Alexandra Palace and then Stratford. Towards the end of his narrative he launched a full-scale attack on the English: 'Anyone who has even a reasonable knowledge of English history and, in particular, the history of the English colonies, must also know that the English always and everywhere act with bloody cruelty and unbridled ruthlessness.' After describing English missionaries as political instruments in the colonies he eventually turns to Stratford, where he remained 'only 9 days, thank God'. He pointed out that the reputation of this camp had already reached the attention of those in Alexandra Palace and, like virtually every other writer on Stratford, painted a bleak picture of life there.[95] Other narratives published during the war attacked the British and their internment policy. For instance, Gotthilf Vöhringer's account, originally given as a lecture and mainly focusing upon experiences in Cameroon and the journey to Europe, ends in a nationalistic crescendo and criticizes conditions in Handforth, especially the cold. However, he describes the 'treatment' which the prisoners received as 'faultless, because we had the entire camp administration – order, cleanliness, cooking, post and even office work – in our own hands'.[96]

The personal narratives demonizing Britain which appeared during the Great War played some role in the propaganda struggle between Britain and Germany, although we need to remember the fairly objective nature of some of these accounts in comparison with the press reports, which tended to focus more heavily upon the mistreatment of German prisoners. Publications form one aspect of German public opinion, representing an attempt to inform the entire country of life behind barbed wire.

In addition, we need to recognize the German humanitarian groups which made efforts to assist prisoners in Britain. These operated on a variety of levels, from the international to the national and the local. While the stories coming out of Britain, France and Russia provided some of the motivation for these groups, so did the wishes of relatives. Assistance from the homeland helped to alleviate the plight of German internees, providing a pattern which other nation states also followed.[97] Heather Jones views the First World War as 'a watershed in the professional development of humanitarian action: mass killing was paradoxically accompanied by an outpouring of aid'.[98]

The Red Cross saw a significant development in its activity during the course of the Great War. This included a concern with prisoners of war. On the one hand, the International Committee of the Red Cross operated upon a transnational basis by visiting the prisoners' camps throughout Europe and trying to ensure an equality of treatment of both military and civilian internees in all belligerent states. However, national committees established in individual states almost became part of the war effort too and played a central role in providing assistance for their own citizens held by the enemy.[99]

This becomes clear through an examination of the German Red Cross, which, at the end of 1914, centralized all of its work concerning the 'Search for the Missing' and the 'Relief for German Prisoners of War' in Hamburg and Frankfurt-am-Main, with the former concentrating upon the activities of north and east Germany and the latter on the south and the west.[100] It also appears that the Hamburg branch increasingly dealt with prisoners in Russia during the course of the war while Frankfurt focused upon France and Britain and its colonies. Despite the apparent logic of this division, another committee appears to have come into existence in Cologne in 1915 which devoted its attention to German combatant and civilian prisoners in England, the English colonies and Japan.[101]

The work of the German Red Cross for prisoners of war focused upon several issues. In the first place, it gathered information on Germans held throughout the world from a range of official and unofficial sources, which it brought together in its weekly reports, issued jointly by the Frankfurt and Hamburg committees for internal consumption.[102] It also concerned itself with the search for missing German soldiers and dealt with enquiries about individuals, for which it devised a card index which held details of the plight of soldiers killed or captured, totalling 160,000 cases by the end of 1915. An enquiry office in Frankfurt dealt with soldiers who had fought against Allied forces. It also dealt with over 3,000 letters on a daily basis by this time. Another key task of the German Red Cross consisted of supplying German prisoners with gifts and money, gathered through donations, especially at Christmas. Dr Markel's organization played a key role in distributing these presents in Britain. The German Red Cross also made enquiries about missing enemy soldiers. By late 1915 the Frankfurt office employed 311 people, including 218 volunteers.[103]

Despite the centralization of German Red Cross efforts, local branches at both city and regional levels continued to carry out their own efforts on behalf of local people.[104] In Worms, for example, a district committee for missing and imprisoned Germans had come into existence by the end of 1914 with responsibility for both Worms and nearby Alzey because of the concerns of relatives; it also worked with a similar organization responsible for Hesse, as well as with the headquarters in Frankfurt. By 1917 it had records of 114 men from Worms and Alzey held as military prisoners in Britain, together with five civilians. This branch also devised a card index, which totalled 3,460 cases by this time. It sent 427 parcels to England and its colonies for Christmas 1916.[105] The Giessen branch of the Red Cross carried out a similar range of activities.[106] Regional organizations included the Schleswig-Holstein subcommittee for German prisoners of war, based in Kiel. Its annual report from 1916 stated: 'We have so far searched for 3,250 sons of our province. Of these 1,130 found themselves as prisoners in enemy territory while 262 were found to be dead.' During the course of 1915 it dealt with 5,048 enquiries. Like the other local and regional groups it also sent gifts to internees from its locality.[107] The Anhalt branch, established at the end of 1914, carried out similar activities to that in Schleswig-Holstein.[108]

The Protestant Church also devoted some attention to helping prisoners of war in a variety of ways. At the end of 1914 a Help Committee for the Spiritual Welfare of Prisoners came into existence,[109] although limited documentation has survived on its activities. One of its main tasks consisted of working with German pastors caring for internees in Britain.[110] The Evangelische Blättervereinigung für Soldaten and Kriegsgefangene Deutsche devoted most of its attention to sending Bibles and other religious reading material to prisoners.[111] It issued one volume of letters from prisoners, most of which consisted mainly of thanks for the books received.[112] Local churches also provided parcels for internees from their locality, as the example of Pastor Buchholz of Bastenburg indicates. During the course of 1918 he received letters from prisoners held in camps throughout England thanking him for the presents they had received.[113]

Elisabeth Rotten's Auskunfts- und Hilfstelle für Deutsche im Ausland und Ausländer in Deutschland carried out similar work to the FEC in Britain, with which it co-operated. This group emerged out of the pacifist and women's movements, with which it had connections. Although much of its work focused upon the plight of foreigners in Germany, it also searched for missing relatives, a task it carried out with the help of the Red Cross and other international organizations, although it needed to communicate with the various British-based organizations for the assistance of Germans.[114] A letter dated 29 April 1916 dealt with the case of Fritz Lowenstein, interned in Douglas and described as being 'in a very low state of health, mentally and physically, and appears to a great extent incapable of doing anything for himself'.[115] Internees in Britain also contacted Dr Rotten's organization for information about their relatives in Germany. On 1 April 1918 the Knockaloe

Prisoners Aid Society of Camp I sought information 'on behalf of our Secretary, Mr Walter Tennhard', who had 'received yesterday news from home, saying that his father had died on February 7th last'. The letter from the chairman of the committee expressed concern about the plight of Tennhard's mother and asked if 'some philanthropic person or institution' could forward Tehnard 1,500 Marks to enable him to look after his mother.[116]

Conclusions

Between 1914 and 1918 internment became a key issue in the propaganda war between Britain and Germany. Each side essentially played the same game, accusing the enemy of mistreating the prisoners which it held while claiming that it dealt fairly with the internees in its hands. Such accusations received support from stories told by men returning home, as well as from official reports, including those produced by the United States and Swiss Embassies. Both sides picked and chose what they believed. The press played the central role in this propaganda war, publishing selected accounts which revealed the enemy in a negative light. In Britain a small group of MPs focused upon the mistreatment of prisoners by Germany and the conditions in British internment camps, while also clamouring for the incarceration of all Germans in Britain. Some books published by returning Germans during the war provided an objective account of their experiences, although others simply banged the nationalist drum and condemned the actions of Britain and its empire.

A few individuals raised their heads above the parapet of hatred. This becomes clear in the acts of some British people who came into contact with Germans in the latter stages of the war, whose behaviour contrasted with the actions of those rioters who had destroyed property in the early stages of the conflict. In addition, a few charities in Britain assisted prisoners in a more organized manner, although they remained outside the mainstream of British society: the Markel Committee, founded by an Anglo-German with family connections in both Britain and Germany, and the Society of Friends.

Elisabeth Rotten's charity work in Germany resembled the work of the FEC, with which it had connections. However, other groups had a nationalistic agenda, especially the German Red

Cross, despite the humanitarian anti-war origins of this body.[117] Nevertheless, as the local German Red Cross committees demonstrate, the main motivation of many individuals who became involved in this group was to assist their family members who were interned in camps all over Europe.

Notes

1 Alexander Ross, 'Bitter Contrast of Two Internment Camps', *Weekly Dispatch*, 25 June 1916.

2 Cate Haste, *Keep the Home Fires Burning* (London, 1977); Gary S. Messinger, *British Propaganda and the State in the First World War* (Manchester, 1992); John Ramsden, *Don't Mention the War: The British and the Germans since 1890* (London, 2006), pp. 91–133; Michael Saunders and Philip M. Taylor, *British Propaganda during the First World War, 1914–18* (London, 1982); Panikos Panayi, *The Enemy in Our Midst: Germans in Britain during the First World War* (Oxford, 1991).

3 Matthew Stibbe, *German Anglophobia and the Great War, 1914–1918* (Cambridge, 2001).

4 Heather Jones, *Violence against Prisoners of War in the First World War: Britain, France and Germany, 1914–1920* (Cambridge, 2011), pp. 29–69; Matthew Stibbe, *British Civilian Internees in Germany: The Ruhleben Camp, 1914–18* (Manchester, 2008), pp. 3–4.

5 Thomas C. Kennedy, *British Quakerism, 1860–1920: The Transformation of a Religious Community* (Oxford, 2001), pp. 237–431.

6 Michael Roper, *The Secret Battle: Emotional Survival and the Great War* (Manchester, 2009).

7 Heather Jones, 'International or Transnational? Humanitarian Action during the First World War', *European Review of History*, vol. 16 (2009), 697–713.

8 Lucio Sponza, *Divided Loyalties: Italians in Britain during the Second World War* (Frankfurt, 2000), pp. 211–17; Inge Weber-Newth and Johannes-Dieter Steinert, *German Migrants in Britain: An Enemy Embrace* (London, 2006), pp. 56–63.

9 See, for example, Jill Stephenson, *Hitler's Home Front: Württemberg under the Nazis* (London, 2006), pp. 265–90.

10 Gerhard Fischer, 'Fighting the War at Home: The Campaign against Enemy Aliens in Australia during the First World War', in Panikos Panayi, ed., *Minorities in Wartime: National and Racial Groupings in Europe, North America and Australia during the Two World Wars* (Oxford, 1993), pp. 263–86.

11 Panayi, *Enemy*.
12 Panikos Panayi, '"The Hidden Hand": British Myths about German Control of Britain During the First World War', *Immigrants and Minorities*, vol. 7 (1988), 253–72. For the reality of German espionage activity in First World War Britain see Thomas Boghardt, *Spies of the Kaiser: German Covert Operations in Great Britain during the First World War* (Basingstoke, 2004).
13 Panayi, *Enemy*, pp. 75–6, 198, 225–9.
14 *Hansard* (Commons), fifth series, vol. 68, cols 81–122, 12 November 1914.
15 See, for instance, ibid., cols 1379–1402, 26 November 1914.
16 *Hansard* (Commons), fifth series, vol. 70, cols 834–916, 3 March 1915. On this last point see Matthew Stibbe, 'A Question of Retaliation? The Internment of British Civilians in Germany in November 1914', *Immigrants and Minorities*, vol. 23 (2005), 1–29.
17 Panayi, *Enemy*, pp. 229–53; Nicoletta F. Gullace, 'Friends, Aliens and Enemies: Fictive Communities and the Lusitania Riots of 1915', *Journal of Social History*, vol. 39 (2005), 345–67; Ben Braber, 'Within our Gates: A New Perspective on Germans in Glasgow during the First World War', *Journal of Scottish Historical Studies*, vol. 29 (2009), 94–6; Gerald Newton, 'Germans in Sheffield, 1817–1918', *German Life and Letters*, vol. 46 (1993), 86–92.
18 *Hansard* (Commons), fifth series, vol. 71, cols 1841–6, 13 May 1915.
19 Ibid., col. 1649, 12 May 1915.
20 *The Times*, 14 May 1915.
21 Panayi, *Enemy*, pp. 253–6.
22 *The Times*, 14 June 1916.
23 *Hansard* (Commons), fifth series, vol. 83, cols 1047–94, 29 June 1916.
24 *Hansard* (Lords), fifth series, vol. 22, col. 471, 29 June 1916.
25 *Hansard* (Commons), fifth series, vol. 100, col. 1658, 17 December 1917.
26 Trevor Wilson, *The Myriad Faces of War: Britain and the Great War, 1914–1918* (Cambridge, 1986), pp. 545–747.
27 Panayi, *Enemy*, pp. 176–80, 209–12.
28 Ibid., pp. 217–20.
29 Michael MacDonagh, *In London during the Great War* (London, 1935), p. 309; *Daily Mirror*, 26 August 1918.
30 Panayi, *Enemy*, pp. 91–5; *Hansard* (Commons), fifth series, vol. 108, cols 522–605, 11 July 1918.
31 Robert Machray, 'Great Britain's Humane Treatment of German Prisoners of War', in H. W. Wilson and J. A. Hammerton, eds, *The Great War*, vol. 12 (London, 1919), pp. 401–14.

32 Stibbe, *British Civilian Internees*, pp. 3, 167.
33 *The Times*, 29 April 1915. In fact, similar newspapers appeared in Ruhleben, for which see which see ibid.
34 *Isle of Man Weekly Times*, 1 May 1915.
35 Alexander Ross, 'Bitter contrast of Two Internment Camps', *Weekly Dispatch*, 25 June 1916.
36 *Daily Express*, 26 July 1916.
37 *Hansard* (Commons), fifth series, vol. 70, col. 249, 1 March 1915.
38 Ibid., col. 793, 3 March 1915.
39 *Hansard* (Commons), fifth series, vol. 71, cols 623–90, 27 April 1915.
40 *Hansard* (Commons), fifth series, vol. 82, cols 2554–6, 30 May 1916.
41 *Hansard* (Commons), fifth series, vol. 110, cols 1311–90, 29 October 1918.
42 *Daily Express*, 19 July 1916; *Manchester Guardian*, 19 July 1916; *The Times*, 19 July 1916.
43 *The Times*, 20 July 1916; *Manchester Guardian*, 20 July 1916.
44 *Hansard* (Commons), fifth series, vol. 70, cols 557–9, 1 March 1915; vol. 83, cols 1217–18, 3 July 1916.
45 *Globe*, 21 December 1915, 21 March 1916; *Daily Mirror*, 18 December 1915; *Manchester Guardian*, 22 March 1916.
46 *Daily Express*, 1 June 1918; *Daily Mirror*, 1 June 1918.
47 *Daily Express*, 2 October 1918.
48 *Manchester Guardian*, 28 August 1919.
49 *The Times*, 2 January 1919.
50 Ibid., 14 October 1918; *Atherstone Express*, 17 October 1918.
51 *The Times*, 9, 13 August 1918; *Daily Express*, 13 August 1918; *Daily Mirror*, 9 August 1918.
52 *Mona's Herald*, 8 August 1917; *Isle of Man Weekly Times*, 11 August 1917; *Peel City Guardian and Chronicle*, 11 August 1917.
53 *Manchester Guardian*, 15 September 1915.
54 *Daily Mirror*, 30 July 1918.
55 *The Times*, 28 August 1918.
56 *Chiswick Times*, 6, 13 September 1918; *The Times*, 2 September 1918; *Observer*, 1 September 1918.
57 'Assisting Prisoners of War and Interned Persons', *Defence of the Realm Regulations Consolidated and Revised, January 31st 1917* (London, 1917), p. 51.
58 Help for the wives and families of civilian internees receives full consideration in Panayi, *Enemy*, pp. 259–70.
59 Ibid., p. 273; 'Karl Emil Markel', *Der Auslandsdeutsche*, vol. 15 (November–December 1932), 317–19.

60 *Reports of Visits of Inspection Made by Officials of the United States Embassy to Various Internment Camps in the United Kingdom* (London, 1916).
61 NA/FO383/162, Leland Littlefield and W. H. Buckler, 18 February 1916.
62 MNH/B115/43q, Camp IV, Knockaloe, I. O. M., Final Report and Statistical Record on the Internal Administration of the Prisoners of War Camp No. IV, 1915–1919.
63 BA/MA/MSG200/2071, Annual Report on the Organization, Functions and Activities of the Committees Formed by the Prisoners of War Interned in Camp 4, December 1916.
64 Panayi, *Enemy*, pp. 266–70.
65 Ibid., p. 271.
66 See Chapter 6 above.
67 Anna Braithwaite Thomas, *St Stephen's House: Friends Emergency Work in England, 1914 to 1920* (London, 1920), p. 64.
68 Stibbe, *German Anglophobia*.
69 See Chapter 1 above.
70 *Stenographische Berichte über die Verhandlungen des deutschen Reichstages*, session 72, pp. 1979–2000, 2 November 1916.
71 Ibid., session 174, pp. 5480–1, 13. June 1918.
72 Ibid., session 184, pp. 5831–3, 5 July 1918; NA/FO383/464, Prisoners of War Notes.
73 See, for example, *Kölnische Zeitung*, 12 November 1914; *National Zeitung*, 19 July 1916; *Berliner Tageblatt*, 13 December 1916.
74 *Kölnische Volkszeitung*, 4 June 1918; *Vossische Zeitung*, 18 June 1918.
75 The article and the correspondence about zum Busch's allegations can be found in NA/FO383/202. For Stratford see Chapter 4 above. For the German Hospital see Panikos Panayi, *German Immigrants in Britain during the Nineteenth Century, 1815–1914* (Oxford, 1995), p. 175.
76 *Hansard* (Commons), fifth series, vol. 71, cols 572–3, 27 April 1915. See also Chapter 2 above.
77 *Manchester Guardian History of the War*, vol. 4, *1915–16* (Manchester, 1916), p. 218.
78 See, for instance, *Hamburger Nachrichten*, 10 April 1915; *Vossische Zeitung*, 12 March 1915; *Frankfurter Zeitung*, 5 June 1915.
79 See, for instance, *The Times*, 15 November 1916; NA/FO383/464, Prisoners of War Notes.
80 BA/R67/779, Reichskommisar zur Erörterung von Gewaltätigkeiten gegen deutsche Zivilpersonen in Feindesland, *Vergleich der Berichte des Genfer Roten Kreuzes über die englischen und französischen*

Sammellager mit dem Feststellungen des Reischskommissars (Berlin, 1915).

81 *Bericht des Reichskommisars zur Erörterung von Gewaltätigkeiten gegen deutsche Zivilpersonen in Feindesland über seine Tätigkeit bis zum. 1. Januar 1916* (Berlin, 1916).

82 BA/R67/253, DRK, England, Interner Wochenbericht No. 69, 10 June 1916; BA/R67/1283, DRK, England, Interner Wochenbericht No. 102, 4 March 1918.

83 BA/R67/215, DRK, England, Interner Wochenbericht No. 27, 14 June 1915; Interner Wochenbericht No. 33, 31 July 1915.

84 BA/R67/1283, DRK, England, Interner Wochenbericht No. 102, 4 March 1918.

85 See also Chapter 1 above.

86 D. W. Pult, *Siebzehn Monate in englischer Kriegsgefangenschaft* (Siegen, 1917).

87 Bruno Schmidt-Reder, *In England kriegsgefangen! Meine Erlebnisse in dem Gegangenenlager Dorchester* (Berlin, 1915).

88 See for example, Gotthilf Vöhringer, *Meine Erlebnisse während des Krieges in Kamerun und in englischer Kriegsgefangenschaft* (Hamburg, 1915); Georg Wilhelm Wagener, *Meine Gefangenschaft in Südafrika und England vom 15. Sept. 1914 bis 18. Juni 1916* (Brunswick, 1917); J. Maue, *In Feindes Land: Achtzehn Monate in englischer Kriegsgefangenschaft in Indien und England* (Stuttgart, 1918).

89 Karl von Scheidt and Fritz Meyer, *Vier Jahre Leben und Leiden der Auslandsdeutschen in den Gefangenenlagern Englands* (Hagen, 1919).

90 Pult, *Siebzehn Monate*, pp. 47–109.

91 Schmidt-Reder, *In England kriegsgefangen!*, p. 35.

92 Otto Schimming, *13 Monate hinter dem Stacheldraht: Alexandra Palace, Knockaloe, Isle of Man, Stratford* (Stuttgart, 1919), pp. 7–28.

93 Ibid., p. 31.

94 R. Hartmann, *Bilder aus dem Gefangenenlager Knockaloe in England* (Bad Nassau, 1918).

95 Wagener, *Meine Gefangenschaft*, pp. 91–7.

96 Vöhringer, *Meine Erlebnisse*, p. 21.

97 Alon Rachamimov, *POWs and the Great War: Captivity on the Eastern Front* (Oxford, 2002), pp. 161–90.

98 Jones, 'International or Transnational?', p. 697.

99 Ibid., pp. 700–3; Matthew Stibbe, 'The Internment of Civilians by Belligerent States during the First World War and the Response of the International Committee of the Red Cross', *Journal of Contemporary History*, vol. 41 (2006), 5–19; John F. Hutchinson, *Champions of*

Charity: War and the Rise of the Red Cross (Oxford, 1996), pp. 279–319; NA/FO383/162, Rapport de MM. Ed. Naville et J. Martin sur leur seconde visite aux camps de prisonniers en Anglettere.

100 BA/R67/136, The Frankfurt Red Cross: Special Relief Committee for Prisoners of War.

101 BA/R67/1554, Verein vom Roten Kreuz Frankfurt Main, Ausschuß für deutsche Kriegsgefangene, Bericht vom 1. Januar 1916; BA/MA/RM3/5396, Ausschuß für deutsche Kriegsgefangene in England, Fürsorge für die deutschen Kriegs- und Zivilgefangenen in England, den englischen Kolonien und Japan, Bericht über die Tätigkeit des Ausschusses, 1915–1917.

102 These survive in two main locations. First, they are scattered in the papers of the Frankfurt committee of the Red Cross held in the Bundesarchiv, Berlin-Lichterfelde, under R67. There is also a chronological selection covering 1914–16 in the Staatsbibliothek zu Berlin.

103 BA/R67/136, The Frankfurt Red Cross: Special Relief Committee for Prisoners of War; BA/MA/RM3/5396, Ausschuß für deutsche Kriegsgefangene in England, Fürsorge für die deutschen Kriegs- und Zivilgefangenen in England, den englischen Kolonien und Japan, Bericht über die Tätigkeit des Ausschusses, 1915–1917; BA/R67/1265, Ausschuß für deutsche Kriegsgefangene in England, Fürsorge für die deutschen Kriegs- und Zivilgefangenen in England, den englischen Kolonien und Japan, Rundschreiben Nr. 27, 10. Januar 1918; BA/R67/1554, Verein vom Roten Kreuz Frankfurt Main, Ausschuß für deutsche Kriegsgefangene, Bericht vom 1. Januar 1916.

104 Bezirk-Ausschuss Gießen für Vermißte und Kriegsgefangene Deutsche, Abteilung d. Zweigvereins Gießen von Roten Kreuz, *Erster Bericht* (Gießen, 1917), p. 3.

105 Zweigverein Worms E.V. d. Hessischen Landesvereins vom 'Roten Kreuz': Bezirksausschuß f. Vermißte u. Kriegsgefangene Deutsche, *Drei Jahre Vermissten-Ermittlung und Gefangenenfürsorge* (Worms, 1917).

106 Abteilung des Zweigvereins Gießen vom Roten Kreuz, *Zweiter Bericht des Bezirks-Ausschusses Giessen für Vermißte und kriegsgefangene Deutsche* (Gießen, 1918).

107 LBWHS/M1/8/220, Provinzialverein vom Roten Kreuz für Schelswig-Holstein, Jahresbericht des Unterausschusses für kriegsgefangene Deutsche, March 1916.

108 Landesausschuss für Anhalt, *Hilfe für kriegsgefangene Deutsche: Arbeitsbericht 1914 bis 31. März 1917* (Dessau, 1917).

109 EZA/1/788, Hilfs-Ausschuss für Gefangenen-Seelsorge, Protokoll über die Begründung, 11 December 1914.

110 F. Siegmund-Schultze, 'Die Gefangenenseelsorge in England', *Die Eiche*, vol. 6 (1918), 315–49.

111 *Arbeitsbericht der Evangelische Blättervereinigung für Soldaten and Kriegsgefangene Deutsche, Bad Nassau (Lahn) über das Tätigkeitsjahr 1917/1918* (Bad Nassau, 1918).

112 F. W. Brepohl, ed., *Briefe unserer Gefangenen* (Bad Nassau, 1916).

113 These letters survive in BA/MSG200/1483.

114 Matthew Stibbe, 'Elisabeth Rotten and the "Auskunfts- und Hilfstelle für Deutsche im Ausland und Ausländer in Deutschland"', in Alison S. Fall and Ingrid Sharp, eds, *The Women's Movement in Wartime: International Perspectives* (Basingstoke, 2007), pp. 194–210; EZA/45/37, Auskunfts-und Hilfstelle für Deutsche im Ausland und Ausländer in Deutschland, Bericht über die bisherige Tätigkeit, January 1915.

115 EZA/51/cIII,l,3,2, Sent to Dr Rotten, 29 April 1916.

116 EZA/51/c/I/7/1, Knockaloe Prisoners Aid Society Camp I to Auskunfts- und Hilfstelle für Deutsche im Ausland und Ausländer in Deutschland, 22 June 1918.

117 Dieter Riesenberger, *Für Humanität in Krieg und Frieden: Der Internationale Rote Kreuz, 1863–1977* (Göttingen, 1992), pp. 14–82.

8

Escape, release and return

> As weeks and months go by, you must know, dear that I grow more anxious about you. If you are still alright and your strength has returned and you have written to me, I have never received a line. I have been waiting for this instruction letter you promised me from Spalding and were looking forward to a reunion with you in Germany. What is a family without a father? Walter is nearly 13 years of age and all his hopes are concerning his dear clever father, he thinks nobody got such a good daddy like he has. The other children are all growing up all want daddy to come home again.[1]

German prisoners spent varying periods of time behind barbed wire in Britain. Civilians endured the longest periods of captivity, which, in theory, could have lasted for over five years, from the late summer of 1914 until the end of 1919, when the last internees faced liberation. Most experienced shorter spells. Soldiers captured in France and arriving in significant numbers in 1917 and, more especially, 1918 faced relatively short spells of time imprisoned in Britain. A series of schemes had also emerged throughout the war which allowed the repatriation and exchange of a variety of groups, including religious functionaries, doctors and invalids. Meanwhile, thousands of prisoners tried to end their captivity through flight, which became part of everyday camp reality in Britain, although only a handful succeeded in getting back to Germany, with the rest facing recapture, trial and punishment.

The end of internment meant new challenges in view of the consequences of the First World War for both Britain and Germany. Soldiers who returned home found a transformed society and economy suffering from the consequences of four years of total war. Along with millions of other demobilized soldiers, they tried to integrate into a devastated country in which mass unemployment had become the norm,[2] as well as attempting to resume their pre-war family relationships after years of separation. The plight of civilian internees proved even worse. The virulence of the Germanophobia which had affected Britain in these years meant that anyone who had owned small businesses before the war would have had them destroyed by rioters. Worse still, the state confiscated all German-owned businesses in Britain, no matter what their size, and even used them as part of the reparations payments under the Treaty of Versailles.[3] A return to pre-war family relationships proved difficult if not impossible. German women, including those with interned husbands, had faced deportation. At the cessation of hostilities this ethnic cleansing reached its peak with the deportation of most of the released civilians. In some cases internees went to Germany with their families, including those born in Britain, but in others the internee left alone. The end of internment may have resulted in freedom from confinement, depression and barbed wire disease for tens of thousands of men, but it threw up new difficulties which they could not have foreseen while contemplating their captivity and subsequent liberty. In virtually all cases a return to pre-1914 lives proved impossible for either returning German soldiers or released civilians.

Escape

Despite the uncertainties which might face them outside, hundreds, and perhaps even thousands, of German prisoners took the issue into their own hands by trying to escape. Largely because of the impossibility of crossing the North Sea, the English Channel or the Irish Sea (in the case of those on the Isle of Man), only three appear to have made succeeded in getting back to Germany: Wilhelm Kröpke, Johannes Schmidt-Klafleth and, most famously, Gunther Plüschow. The overwhelming majority faced capture and subsequent punishment.

Measuring the numbers of Germans who tried to flee proves problematic. One source has identified over 500.[4] 'Ninety-eight men were tried by military courts for attempting to escape from Knockaloe during the war. Not one succeeded in getting away from the Isle of Man.'[5] On one occasion a total of twenty-two prisoners fled from a camp in Sutton Bonington in Nottinghamshire.[6] National newspapers carried regular stories about attempted escapes and the recapture of those who fled. On 27 August 1917 *The Times* reported '16 Fugitives Still Free'. The *Manchester Guardian* of the same day claimed 'Twenty Prisoners Now At Large . . . These include six petty officers, amongst whom are two Zeppelin survivors, who escaped from Stobs Camp' together with four officers who left Colsterdale on the same day. 'Prisoners have also escaped recently from Aldershot and Douglas, and the two men, Richard Eber and Albert Govensky, who got away from Handforth Camp on August 12, have not yet been captured.'

A few sources suggest the reason for escape. One War Office employee claimed that 'prisoners do not escape with any hope of leaving the country. They know it is practically impossible. *They escape rather out of a sense of adventure* – perhaps to relieve something of the monotony of camp life.'[7] Gunther Plüschow, who fled Donington Hall, wrote that:

> In time captivity became unbearable. Nothing relieved the gloom – neither letters, parcels forwarded from home . . . the company of my friends, not even hockey, to which I devoted myself . . . We were greatly depressed owing to our being deprived of war news from German sources . . . Day and night I planned, brooded, deliberated how I could escape from this miserable imprisonment.[8]

Meanwhile, Albrecht Hermann Brugger, captured in October 1918 and interned in Lofthouse Park, became frustrated with waiting for his release during the course of 1919. He anticipated his liberation 'from one week to the next', and 'one disappointment followed another'. The mood in the camp became increasingly depressed, and he eventually 'had enough'.[9] Another internee, who fled from Stobs, felt 'longing for the homeland and the yearning for freedom led me to develop an escape plan'.[10] Paul Rentz, who believed, that as an American citizen he should not even face internment, attempted to escape from Knockaloe in January 1916. During his trial, he declared:

> I only want to repeat once more that I am absolutely fed up with this release business of mine. It has taken the British or American Authorities, or whoever is responsible for it, ten months to give me an answer. I have heard about my case, but the only answer I get is that my case is still going on. Very likely it will take them another year to decide whether they will grant my release or not. Therefore I took the matter into my own hands and tried to regain my stolen freedom.[11]

More than anything else it was the frustration caused by internment that led to escape attempts. While most prisoners did not try to flee and either endured the conditions which led to barbed wire disease or made the best of them by participating in social activities, some individuals decided, like Rentz, to take the law into their own hands.

Because of the difficulties involved in getting out of guarded camps, most internees appear to have planned their escape. Plüschow wrote:

> For hours I walked up and down in front of different parts of the entanglements, whilst I unostentatiously examined every wire and every stake. For hours together I lay in the grass in the vicinity of some of those spots that seemed favourable, feigning sleep. But all the time I was closely guarding every object and noting the ways and habits of the different sentries.[12]

Wilhelm Kröpke described the plans which he drew up to escape from both Queensferry, which ultimately failed, and Alexandra Palace, from where he claimed to have reached Germany.[13] Similarly, Brugger had an elaborate plan which involved his colleagues deceiving the military in Lofthouse Park by moving around during the head count so that they appeared to take his and his companion's places. They escaped through a hole and ended up in a wood, and, according to this 1937 account, the camp authorities did not discover their disappearance for two days.[14] Prisoners also planned for their life beyond the barbed wire, including Wilhelm Jensen and Johann Rastenholz, who fled Frongoch with 'haversacks full of tins of salmon, biscuits and a good supply of other food enough for a few days'.[15]

While most escape attempts involved planning, others appear to have been opportunist. For example, 'four sailors and one air serviceman escaped while with a working party at Pirbright'.[16] In fact, little evidence exists to point to any other examples of internees fleeing from working parties, even though this would appear to have been easier than escaping from established camps. Prisoners working beyond the barbed wire may have felt that they had sufficient freedom in contrast to those confined behind it. One of the most unusual escape attempts, reported by much of the national press, involved a prisoner who, while undergoing transfer from one internment camp to another, jumped from a moving train as it slowed down and approached Walton-on-Thames, and disappeared into nearby Ashley Wood.[17] Meanwhile, Georg von Strang, 'who claims to be a German nobleman and an author, but whose appearance would suggest that he was a tramp', made three attempts to escape from Douglas, all of which seem to have been opportunist, if not desperate. After the first, on 10 July 1916, he received a prison sentence of 112 days. On this occasion he 'succeeded in getting out of the camp at night and made his way to the jetty'. He then jumped into the water with the intention of swimming towards a nearby ship, the *Yarrow*, but did not reach it before it sailed away. A policeman arrested him once he got out of the water. However, after serving his sentence in Walton jail for this 'escapade' he returned to Douglas on 13 October and 'early next morning (at 12–45) came out of his barracks, without any clothes on' and 'started to climb over the barbed wire fence' but was arrested. Before his arrest, 'he went to a barrel of lime and covered his head and body with lime'. Von Strang claimed that he 'was trying to appear as if he were insane, in the hope that he would be repatriated'.[18]

Those prisoners who managed to return to Germany constructed exciting adventure narratives, above all Plüschow, who described climbing over the barbed wire fence at Donington Hall with his companion, Oskar Trefftz, a naval officer 'who knew England remarkably well'. They then used the 'Polar star' to navigate and eventually reached Derby. There then followed a train journey to Leicester, followed by another to London. Plüschow waited for Trefftz on the steps of St Paul's Cathedral, but Trefftz was actually captured at Millwall docks. By this time, their escape had made national news. After spending several days in London, Plüschow eventually got on a boat in Tilbury that was heading for Flushing.[19] Kröpke's story involved even more twists and turns: he claimed that he fled Alexandra Palace and eventually succeeded in boarding a ship sailing from the Scottish coast to Copenhagen.[20] Schmidt-Klafleth, who also escaped from Alexandra Palace, described a more believable story upon his return to Germany in September 1915, which involved him hiding in London and eventually sailing out of the London docks after a week on the run.[21]

Many of those who were recaptured had adventures with similar levels of excitement, especially those who remained on the run for the longest periods of time. For instance, Heinz Justus, who jumped out of a train window near Doncaster, eventually got to London, where he claimed to have watched a play entitled *The Hidden Hand* about German spies in England, caught influenza and then made his way to Cardiff, where the severity of his illness meant that he could not carry on with his plans and consequently found himself taken to Lofthouse Park.[22] Four prisoners who escaped from Frongoch 'walked over forty miles either across the moors or along the roadside, and had a map and a compass to assist them in their avowed efforts to reach Liverpool', but a policeman found them 'lying down in the bracken' near the borders of Flintshire and Denbighshire.[23] Lieutenants von Sandersleben and von Andler, who escaped from a camp in Llansannan, slept in fields for several nights but gave themselves up.[24] Another internee lived 'on berries and nuts in the woods' before capture.[25] Some escapees actually succeeded in going out to sea before facing capture, including one group who sailed 170 miles before a trawler spotted them and they 'were brought to the Tyne'.[26] Meanwhile, 'Ferdinand Kehran, the runaway hunchback who escaped from Islington Internment Camp, more than six weeks ago, was arrested in a liner on the vessel's arrival at Liverpool . . . from New York.' The 'Hun Hunchback', actually the British-born son of German parents,[27] faced internment under regulation 14B of the Defence of the Realm Regulations as an individual of 'enemy origin or association',[28] but probably also because of his 'fire-eating' socialism.[29] Kehran actually reached New York, working as a stoker on the ship which carried him, but was arrested at his destination. The purser recognized him two days into the original journey because of the physical descriptions which had appeared in the press following his escape from the camp in Islington with two other 14B cases.[30] The six weeks of liberty enjoyed by Kehran appears to have been one of the longest periods outside a camp experienced by those individuals who escaped, as most were recaptured in a matter of days. Other lengthy periods of liberty included the seven weeks experienced by Kurt von Gruebner, who fled Catterick on 10 August 1918 with 'plenty of money'.[31] Meanwhile, two German sailors who escaped from Larkhill on Salisbury Plain reached 'a south-east coast port'.

> It was a dark and rough night, but they were seen and caught by an alert look-out patrol. Under a boat on the beach a mile away were found bags of biscuits, bread, fruit, a large bottle of water, a razor, and a shaving brush, which they had hidden.[32]

Temporary liberty ended in a variety of ways, as newspaper stories revealed throughout the war. For example, three prisoners who had fled Alexandra Palace in July 1915 managed to travel eight miles north to Coles Grove in Hertfordshire, where a gardener discovered them hiding in a shed. Two months later, two prisoners who had escaped from Dorchester faced arrest on a train bound for Waterloo after a search.[33] Also in the summer of 1915, 'the troops were on duty watching all the roads' following the escape of three German officers from Dyffryn Aled. A police officer discovered the first of them, Lieutenant Commander Tholens, in a pub in Llandudno. When challenged, Tholens simply surrendered. His companions were arrested forty-five minutes later.[34] In January 1916 four Germans who had fled Knockaloe made it as far as nearby Peel harbour, where they tried to hide in a boat and initially evaded a search party, but when they tried to move from one boat to another, passers-by spotted them and they were arrested.[35] Meanwhile, Lieutenant Paul Scheumann gave himself away when he signed into Bellomo's Hotel in central London after escaping from a camp in Chippenham. Scheumann had aroused suspicion when he signed his name in the hotel register as 'Thomas Mann, High-street 145, Bristol'. The owner stated that 'The 145 being placed at the end of the name of the street' gave him away, 'as all Germans write the number thus'.[36]

While most escapes ended peacefully with the prisoners offering little resistance, some Germans had weapons with them, which meant that their freedom ended with violence, or the threat of it. For example, Heinrich Voegler, who fled from Knockaloe, 'drew a knife and threatened to kill' the police officer who attempted to arrest him. The latter then called for the help of a nearby farmer and labourers. 'Several of the men were armed with guns, but being loth to shoot Voegler, who still maintained a defiant attitude, they contented themselves with surrounding him pending the arrival of the military, who had been sent for. Two soldiers eventually came to the scene, and Voegler then immediately submitted.'[37] In April 1918 a 'dramatic encounter with three escaped prisoners took place' in Burghfield near Reading:

> Police Constable Jordan met three suspicious looking men and said 'Goodnight' to them. As he received no reply, he seized one, and a

> struggle ensued. Both fell to the ground. The other two Germans then came to their comrade's rescue, over powered the constable, and the three Germans made their escape into a thick wood.
>
> During the struggle one of the Germans drew a dagger.

A search party found the three escapees the following day.[38]

After capture, military prisoners faced trial by a military court, which normally resulted in terms of imprisonment of between three and six months with or without hard labour, although Army Council instructions from 1917 suggest that the sentences could be as short as fourteen days' 'military confinement' for military captives, to be served 'in places of detention under military control' for 'a simple escape or attempt to escape'. If officers committed the same offence a second time, they could face up to 112 days' military confinement. The punishment would increase for repeat offences. Civilians would face imprisonment.[39] A few examples illustrate the consequences of attempted escape and capture. Hermann Tholens and his two colleagues who escaped from Dyffryn Aled in August 1915 found themselves before a military court in Chester Castle shortly after capture. Each pleaded guilty to the charge of escape. Tholens complained about being handcuffed following arrest. They each faced a sentence of eight-four days' imprisonment, which they would serve in Chelmsford. These sentences, without hard labour,[40] remained relatively mild compared with some faced by other captured escapees, perhaps because of the men's officer status. Another prisoner who 'was found guilty of attempting to escape from his place of internment' faced nine months with hard labour.[41] Wilhelm Kröpke claimed that he received a sentence of twelve months' hard labour for fleeing internment in Queensferry.[42]

Some officers complained about their treatment after recapture by writing to the United States or Swiss Embassy or by speaking with the inspectors when they visited them. For example, Freiherr Grote wrote to the United States ambassador about the sentence of nine months which he faced for digging a tunnel while in Holyport.[43] Meanwhile, Julius Reinhard Koch and Heinrich Brinkmann, captured after trying to flee from internment in Jersey, listed a whole series of complaints including handcuffing after arrest and the size of their cells while they awaited trial, as well as the fact that they had no access to church services at Easter. Sentenced to eighty-four days with hard labour, they also pointed to numerous faults in the military prison in which they were confined.[44] Meanwhile, two prisoners who escaped from Stobs faced a sentence of nine months with hard labour, which they had to serve in the military prison in Woking, where they found conditions intolerable.[45] One United States Embassy official who visited a prisoner held at Dyffryn Aled, on the other hand, painted quite a positive picture of his environment. 'He is allowed two hours exercise in the open air. I visited the officer in his room, and found him at study. It is a large front room, quite 17 feet square, if not more, occupying a corner of the second floor house, with windows looking east and commanding a pleasant outlook.'[46]

As the above narrative reveals, escape attempts, with few exceptions, resulted in failure. The prisoners who attempted to flee totalled hundreds. The scale may find partial explanation in the number of prisoners actually held. However, the main motivation for attempted escapes ultimately consisted of the frustration which prisoners felt about long periods of confinement. Fleeing the barbed wire, no matter how hopeless the chances of ultimate freedom, represented one way to relieve the boredom and depression caused by confinement.

Release

Some special groups of prisoners, agreed by the British and German governments and also stipulated by wider international agreements including the Hague Convention, found themselves released and returning home as the war progressed. Several problems prevented a general exchange of prisoners between Britain and Germany during the course of conflict, among them different numbers of captives held by the two sides and the issue of Germans interned in the British Empire. The British side did not start returning prisoners *en masse* until the end of the war, by which time, against the background of the intense Germanophobia which gripped the country, the return essentially became an exercise in deportation.

Those prisoners who felt that they should return to Germany contacted whoever they thought should hear their case. For example, in May 1916 E. Kühl wrote from Knockaloe directly to the 'Secretary of State for Foreign Affairs'. He claimed that when he had arrived in Hull at the outbreak of war as 'Chief Officer' of the merchant ship SS *Ursus*, he had been arrested despite the fact

Figure 8.1 Knockaloe artist's impression of the joy of release.

that, at '56½ years', he 'was then wide over military age' and 'I am now in my 59th year'.[47] Similarly, seven doctors contacted the Swiss Embassy in February 1917, complaining that 'for months they have been detained in England in contravention of the terms of the Geneva Convention'.[48]

The desire for repatriation played a significant role in the mentality of prisoners, especially those facing lengthy confinement on the Isle of Man. The ongoing negotiations between the British and German governments caused much discontent among internees, because they were repeatedly raising and then dashing hopes. In September 1916 the head captain of Camp II in Knockaloe sent a letter to the Prime Minister which began by commenting on the various proposals discussed by the two regimes: 'one day we hear that a satisfactory conclusion is close at hand, or has already been arrived at, only to be informed again soon after that the negociations [sic] have fallen through'. He continued:

> We, the more than 20,000 interned civilian prisoners at Knockaloe practically all of us interned for more than a year, most of us for much longer and many of us for more than two years, have gone through a very trying time, but no part of it has been so trying as the last few months, hope continually alternating with fear, high spirits and gloomy despondency.[49]

The following year A. L. Vischer wrote to Louis Waller of the Home Office that the 'most depressing factor' for Knockaloe internees 'is the total stoppage of repatriation, not only for prisoners of war chosen for it, but also for other inmates in the camp'.[50] Vischer would continue to stress this point throughout the war.[51]

As these two extracts suggest, schemes for exchange and repatriation had developed during the course of the war, but tended to focus upon particular groups of internees. The British government resisted a general exchange of civilians largely because there were far more Germans living in Britain than Britons in Germany. At the same time, disagreements surfaced about the fact that Britain also held German internees in its imperial possessions, which further complicated the arithmetic.[52] As early as October 1914 the British and German governments had reached agreement for 'the mutual repatriation of all clergy, medical practitioners, women, children, and males under 17 and over 55', although few of these would ever have experienced internment, except for those who reached the age of fifty-five after the conclusion of the agreement. The Germans had actually requested forty-five as the maximum age, but the British rejected this because they believed that Germans over forty-five still fought in the army as 'volunteers'.[53] By March 1915 a total of 262 men aged under seventeen, 250 over fifty-five and 283 between those ages had returned to Germany.[54] During 1915 there followed agreements for the repatriation of invalid civilians and military captives, according to a strict list of injuries. Also during 1915 the two governments agreed on the repatriation of ships' boys under seventeen, while in early 1916 seamen over fifty-five and those reaching that age could also return home.[55] Throughout the war negotiations occurred through the mediation of the United States and then the Swiss Embassies in London and Berlin.

During the course of 1916 the British and German governments tried to negotiate on a more general exchange of civilian prisoners, especially those over the age of forty-five, but could not come to an agreement, partly, it appeared, because each side wished to control the agenda and course of events.[56] One scheme upon which the two sides reached agreement during 1916 was the transfer to Switzerland of wounded and sick prisoners of war who were 'not sufficiently incapacitated to justify repatriation'.[57] During this year the German government also accepted that repatriation of combatants would take place if it bore the costs and that it could occur only if shipping became available.[58] One journey occurred in December 1916 and involved the hospital ship *St Denis*, which carried '100 disabled military men' to the Hook of Holland.[59]

In January 1917 a significant breakthrough occurred when the two sides finally agreed to the repatriation of all civilians aged over forty-five, including those living in overseas possessions. This excluded twenty prisoners which either side could retain for military reasons. However, only 350 Germans returned home because the German government proclaimed a war zone around British waters, although it agreed to guarantee the passage of the ships carrying prisoners on specific conditions, which the British rejected.[60] Repatriation therefore stopped. But in June 1917 a conference on repatriation and the treatment of prisoners took place in The Hague, chaired by a Dutch diplomat, Jonkheer van Vredenbruch, and attended by several British politicians and civil servants led by Lord Newton, head of the newly created Prisoners of War Department, while General Friedrich fronted the German delegation. On 2 July the two sides reached an agreement, which resumed repatriation under the auspices of the Dutch government, who would provide the necessary steamships, which would become hospital transports. Those suffering from barbed wire disease could go to Switzerland or another neutral state, as could officers who had been interned for more than eighteen months. The agreement provided for the internment in the Netherlands of invalid civilians and combatants from both sides, including these groups, who would total up to 16,000 people.

Repatriation recommenced in October 1917,[61] and proceeded apace in the months which followed. Between 1 November 1917 and 14 February 1918 a total of 1,633 civilians were transferred to the Netherlands including 1,229 over forty-five years of age, 161 invalids, and four clergy and doctors. A total of 1,560 had sailed from Boston.[62] The fourth transport, which arrived in Rotterdam on 4 February, took 806 prisoners including 269 civilians, 291 seriously injured combatants, five doctors and ten first-aiders. On 17 February a further 743 civilians sailed to Rotterdam for repatriation to Germany. One of these had attempted to commit suicide, while another ended up in hospital in Rotterdam because of ill health. The rest proceeded to Germany.[63] The 'numbers of prisoners-of-war to be embarked upon the twelfth sailings of transport from the country under the Hague Agreement', which departed at the end of April 1918, totalled 228 prisoners, made up of a mixture of civilians and military personnel for either repatriation or internment in the Netherlands.[64] Similarly, a sailing of late August 1918, the twentieth under the Hague Agreement, carried 255 prisoners.[65]

But stories began to surface in the German press about the mistreatment of internees who left Britain at this time.[66] The prisoners complained about a range of issues. One group of civilians who arrived in the Netherlands, remembering those left behind, complained about the food, the footwear, the housing, the washing facilities, the crockery and the medical treatment in Knockaloe.[67] Other prisoners returning home made various complaints about their luggage. For example, one former internee claimed, 'While we were gathered in the refreshment room at Boston the British officer in command entered accompanied by ten members of the military police and selected ten of us whose luggage was to be inspected.' He claimed that they 'were marched off like criminals' and that they had various items confiscated. Several of them had photographs of close relatives destroyed.[68] C. R. Manretz, meanwhile, wrote to the Secretary of State for Foreign Affairs in London after arriving in Rotterdam, complaining about the fact that about half of his luggage of 100 lb had disappeared during his journey from Wakefield, as had that of many of those who travelled with him.[69]

Several prisoners also pointed to the disappearance of books from their luggage.[70] Similarly, Richard Noschke, who left Alexandra Palace and then travelled via Spalding and Boston, claimed that the cases of those departing at Boston harbour were handled very badly and smashed 'against each other in such a blind fury as was never experienced before'.[71] Another major issue began to surface during the course of 1918 as civilian prisoners began to complain about the fact that they were departing without their wives and children. This would become highly significant during 1919 and beyond.[72]

As repatriation continued apace during the course of 1918, the British government increasingly became convinced about a general exchange of internees. Consequently, on 8 June a conference opened at The Hague to consider the question of prisoners of war and reached an agreement on 14 July, although it was never ratified. The agreement provided for the repatriation of all those in neutral territory in the Netherlands and Switzerland at this time and also had clauses focusing upon the treatment of prisoners.[73]

Despite the signing of the armistice, repatriation proceeded only gradually and the final prisoners did not return home until the beginning of 1920. Knockaloe still held 15,974 of the total of 24,000 civilian internees (20,500 to them German) who remained in Britain at the signing of the armistice. The former figure declined only gradually during the course of 1919, actually increasing to 15,983 at the beginning of January 1919 but falling by 4,000 during that month. By 1 March the total had declined to 8,472 and by 1 April to 1,493, although the camp did not finally empty until 1 October.[74] Those who departed from Knockaloe in 1919 included George Kenner, who wrote that he left 'burdened with small luggage and 2 rations of tinned meat with bread' and went together with 600 others 'cheerfully down the valley to Peel'. He had to wait another three days because the awaiting boat could take only 300 people, but he eventually 'travelled on a small freight steam-boat on a rather stormy sea to Liverpool'. He and his companions reached their destination after '4 or 5 hours' and then 'travelled across England to another transfer camp'. They then went to Harwich and sailed on to Rotterdam.[75]

In January 1919 a total of 122,121 German prisoners of war still found themselves in Britain.[76] This figure declined equally gradually. In May the total still stood at 90,989.[77] Nevertheless, repatriation did progress during the early part of 1919, as the figures for Knockaloe indicate. Thus five ships carrying a total of 1,934 civilians left Harwich for Rotterdam between 14 and 28 March 1919.[78] Repatriation of soldiers also took place during the course of 1919 but speeded up after the signing of the Versailles Treaty at the end of June 1919. Thus between 24 September and 20 November 4,162 officers and 73,118 'other ranks' returned home.[79] However, even after this date some Germans, especially soldiers, still remained behind barbed wire. A German Red Cross report of 11 December 1919 claimed that 3,621 men still found themselves in Britain, at Donington Hall, Dalston Hospital, Oswestry, Ripon and Wakefield.[80] This figure included the Scapa Flow prisoners, who did not leave until 29 January 1920; this appears to have been the final sailing of a ship carrying German captives, with the exception of three officers and nine other ranks, 'specially retained', who finally went home on 9 April.[81] But in 1921 the imperial finance ministry produced a list of eighty-five prisoners who had not yet returned from English captivity, which included not only Germans held in Britain but also those in France and in British colonies. The list detailed places of capture and the places in which they were last held, together with statements from people who had last seen them. It did not come to conclusions about the current locations of the individuals examined.[82]

Some camps appear to have become clearing stations for repatriation, including one in Spalding. Those who passed through here included Frederick Lewis Dunbar-Kalckreuth in early 1918.[83] Alexandra Palace appears to have played a similar role, as parties of interned civilians went directly from here to Harwich on their way to Rotterdam, although these could also have included the long-term internees living here. Pattishall became a 'repatriation camp' in that those employed in working camps connected to it passed through it on their way home. Prisoners left here for Harwich from 24 September 1919. They could take 'one suit (his uniform or a suit from Government stores) a change of clothing and a good pair of boots' together with 'his private property' of up to 30 lb. 'A two days' ration is provided and issued to the prisoners of war as they embark.'[84]

Some of the prisoners who returned home during 1919 resented the amount of time they had to spend in camps after the armistice awaiting their final return,[85] as one letter to the Prime Minister and the King written by the 'German Senior Officer' from the camp in Redmires indicates. Reflecting the earlier assertions of Vischer, he claimed that the lack of information about 'a definite period of our repatriation' had caused 'dreadful nervous tension' among 'so many thousands of unfortunate prisoners still interned in this country'. These prisoners resented it 'as a bitter wrong that no arrangements have yet been made for our repatriation'.[86]

Unfortunately for those held at Redmires and elsewhere, the issue of repatriating prisoners of war lay towards the bottom of the list of priorities of the victorious Allies. Upon the signing of the armistice, the Germans had to carry out the immediate repatriation of Allied prisoners 'without reciprocity'. The Allies, in contrast, had no such obligation and the armistice annulled all previous agreements concerning prisoners.[87] Despite this, repatriation from Britain did continue during the course of 1919 and intensified in the autumn as a result of clauses 214 to 221 of the Versailles Treaty.[88] However, because of delays in ratification, the executive Supreme Council in Paris decided upon immediate and complete repatriation at its meeting on 28 August, in order 'to diminish as rapidly as possible the sufferings' of prisoners.[89] Both *The Times* and the *Daily Express* welcomed this decision but continued the discourse of the war years by regarding it as an act of clemency and contrasting it with the treatment of the British prisoners in Germany, even though most had returned much earlier.[90]

Despite the claims made by these two newspapers, repatriation took place in the vindictive atmosphere which gripped Britain and the other victorious Allies in 1918 and 1919. While the punishment for military prisoners consisted of holding on to them for as long as possible, punishment for civilians meant deporting them as quickly as possible, despite the fact that they might have lived in Britain for decades and have had English wives and families. In the intense Germanophobia which continued to grip Britain in the immediate aftermath of the Armistice, the Coalition adopted deportation as one of its key policies in the 'Coupon' election campaign, which lasted from 14 November to 14 December 1918.[91] Despite this, the Aliens Advisory Committee came into existence again under Justice John Sankey in order to consider those Germans with British families who did not wish to return home, who could apply to have their cases considered. The committee gave a number of examples of the types of individual who had a case for remaining in Britain. They included a 'German, aged fifty-two, twenty-nine years' residence, the widower of an English wife, with six children, under nineteen and nothing known against him. The children would have gone into the workhouse at once on the father's internment, and only one was old enough to earn anything apart from the oldest girl, who kept the house.' The Committee had to confront highly complicated issues, including that of whether to simply deport the husbands and fathers or also to send to Germany wives and families who had never seen the country. Individual families experienced varying fates, none of which proved particularly appealing in the immediate aftermath of the Great War. The committee considered 4,300 applications for exemption from deportation and granted an overwhelming majority of 3,890, which consisted of people with friendly family ties or long residence. Nevertheless, 84 per cent of those alien enemies interned at the Armistice had been repatriated by October 1919. Deportation, building upon internment, rioting and confiscation of property, helped to decimate the pre-war German community in Britain, whose numbers fell from 57,500 in 1914 to 22,254 in 1919. The number of males actually declined from 37,500 to 8,476, indicating the thoroughness of the deportation process. Close to two-thirds of the women were British-born wives who automatically gained German nationality upon marriage, pointing to the number of broken families caused by the deportation process.[92]

Return

The destruction of families became one of the grim realities caused by the end of internment. Those who had bitterly resented their confinement, together with those who had poeticized the pain it caused and the separation from their wives and children, would find that liberation simply threw up new problems. As the statistics above suggest, the vast majority of civilians had to return home to a country which they had not, in some cases, seen for decades, often without their families. They joined the tens of thousands of soldiers making their way home whose only experience of Britain had consisted of a spell in an internment camp with, perhaps, some time spent in the countryside as farm workers. Although soldiers did not experience the pain of separation from families, they returned to a defeated and depressed Germany, which had to deal with millions of demobilized soldiers and the political and economic consequences of defeat. Several organizations came into existence with the aim of re-integrating them into peacetime society.

Even before they returned home, they had to face the journey. Just as those who had sailed across the North Sea in 1918 complained about their experiences, so did those deported and repatriated in 1919, as a whole series of documents indicate. Attention focused upon both the journey and treatment on arrival in Rotterdam. One note from the German Foreign Office to the Swiss legation complained that 'the steamers . . . are systematically over crowded beyond the limits of their capacity', which meant that 'a number of persons are under the necessity of remaining on deck during the cold nights'. Furthermore, 'Water both for drinking and for washing is withheld and the food is bad and insufficient.' The note went on to focus upon the 'unheard of suffering' on one particular voyage, which had 'resulted in the death of five of the passengers'. This document referred to the *Manitou*,[93] and the claims about poor conditions find support in other evidence. A letter of 5 February 1919 signed by Ruoff, who described himself as 'Sec. Committee of Reception' in Rotterdam, stated that some of the 1,200 badly wounded soldiers and 3,500 civilians who had arrived in January, especially from Hull, had received treatment 'unworthy of human beings' during the journey. He described one of the boats 'which regularly arrive here with civilians' as 'nothing but a cattle steamer' and 'too small for the number of persons it is intended to transport'. Returning Germans also complained about the behaviour of British guards, especially the pilfering of their possessions. Ruoff gave several examples. 'One of the civilians, a certain Albert Keef of 6, Friedrichstrasse, Hamburg, an employee of the Hamburg–America Line, was relieved of the following: his shipping papers and identity card, his certificates of character, and his sick-funds card.' Many civilians also claimed that they had money confiscated.[94] A German 'Note Verbale' of 5 April listed complaints made by civilians, which included the fact that 'they were forced to part with their books and writing which had helped them to bear the suffering of the long internment or were the fruit of their scientific work during all those years'. Furthermore, 'charges are also proffered by all the repatriated civilians with hardly any exception' that 'the very limited luggage they were allowed to take along, is interfered with during the passage to, and at the arrival at Rotterdam to an extent, that would leave them but scanty remnants of their personal effects to arrive with at their homes'. The note also mentioned spoliation of luggage. 'Any remonstrances, it is claimed, are met with by insults and rebuffs, if not brutal assaults committed before the eyes of the onlookers watching the revolting scenes from Dutch soil and to the horror and disgust of all concerned, not least the British-born wives of returning internees.'[95] In fact, the worst story involved the treatment of female relatives of returning internees. Ruoff claimed that three women 'told me and others that they had to undergo corporal examination in England, and were obliged to strip totally naked and stand on a stone floor in the bitter cold'.[96]

As had happened throughout the war, the British government denied allegations of mistreatment of internees on their journey to the Netherlands. Although investigations had taken place into the German claims,[97] it seems tempting to view this episode in Anglo-German relations simply as a continuation of the 'mightier than thou' attitude which had determined the two sides' attitudes to each other's treatment of prisoners throughout the course of the war. On the other hand, we might view the allegations made by returning internees as a continuation of a culture of complaining which many of the middle-class internees and officers had developed during their long and boring confinement in Britain. This, however, seems a rather simplistic interpretation, particularly in view of the number and regularity of complaints which emerged during the repatriation process in 1918 and 1919. The mistreatment ties in with the anti-German violence which had exploded in Britain during the first year of the war, fuelled by a Hun-hating press.

Some of the accounts written by those making the journey across the North Sea do not focus upon mistreatment. This particularly applies to those liberated in the earlier years of the war, although even then some negative accounts emerged. For example, Anton Ditschkowski claimed that on his journey home through Gravesend 'all my things were taken including a stamp collection'.[98] Georg Wagener felt an initial joy and relief at liberation. Writing from a German nationalist perspective, he recalled: 'Thus on Sunday 18 June [1916], we left an inhospitable and hostile England. Our hearts were simply filled with a feeling of deep gratitude on the journey to Holland.' They landed in Vlissingen and then travelled to Goch:

> As we travelled over the Dutch border, we felt like children, who, after a long time, returned to the Fatherland from lunacy, from

> exile and away from a hard fate. With a deep hail which came from the bottom of our hearts towards our Kaiser and Volk we greeted our Fatherland and roared into the German evening: 'Deutschland, Deutschland über alles'.[99]

While only an extreme German nationalist could have produced such words, others shared Wagener's sense of liberation. Hans Erich Benedix remembered saluting a British lieutenant with a whisky and soda on the boat to the Netherlands and being greeted with the words: 'Gentlemen you are free!' Benedix commented: 'These words rang like the music of the Gods.' Like Wagener, he sailed into Vlissingen and then travelled to Goch, although patriotic euphoria did not overcome him.[100]

A German consul met those prisoners who arrived in Vlissingen or Rotterdam in the earlier stages of the war, partly to facilitate their passage to Goch. These meetings remained fairly low-key events.[101] By 1918 and 1919, reception committees began to greet returning prisoners as part of the attempt to re-integrate them into Germany society. By the end of the war the Dutch also warmly greeted the returning Germans, as several accounts recall. One anonymous story even mentioned 'friendly sisters from the Red Cross' on board the ship which carried the author across the North Sea. In fact, several accounts focus upon these Red Cross women, whose youth, beauty and femininity struck prisoners who for years had had virtually no experience of women. The same account mentioned: 'German and Dutch women showered us with flowers and gave us cigarettes, cigars and chocolate as welcome gifts.'[102] George Kenner used almost the same phrase: 'Ladies, all dressed in white, decorated us with flowers and distributed cigars', while the 'Dutch military formed in parade and bid us welcome'.[103] The account of Karl von Scheidt and Fritz Meyer, whose book contains a short section entitled 'Reception in Amsterdam', provided similar details: 'Immediately after our ship moored at the jetty, beautiful women from the Red Cross came aboard and asked us what we wanted and distributed chocolate, cigars and cigarettes. Later there appeared the wife of the German ambassador, His Excellency Rosen, from The Hague and personally presented a bunch of flowers to each individual.'[104] Paul Cohen-Portheim had a different experience when arriving in Rotterdam.

> There was no joyous reception awaiting us; there was, in fact, no one to receive us at all . . . Neither the Dutch nor the German authorities had been warned in time of our coming, it appeared, and as most of them had to come from The Hague, several hours passed before they arrived. It was then discovered that they were not expecting exchange-prisoners at all, but a batch of women and children.[105]

Under the terms of the agreements signed between Britain and Germany, some released prisoners spent time in the Netherlands. These included von Scheidt and Meyer, who found themselves interned in a camp between Hattem and Wapenveld. They painted a positive picture of this location and pointed out that 'Parents, siblings, wives and other relatives had already visited their loved ones here.'[106] Meanwhile, Frederick Lewis Dunbar-Kalckreuth found himself sitting at the same table as an English officer in Rotterdam when he arrived in May 1918. He then visited 'many comrades' in a German camp in Wolfhezen. In the following month he moved to Amsterdam, where he lived in a house with a Herr Beyerheim. He would actually remain in Amsterdam until the end of November, during which time he visited old acquaintances from the Isle of Man, now held in Hattem.[107] Cohen-Portheim found that when he arrived in the Netherlands in February 1918 the camp in which he should have spent time was not yet ready, which meant that he had to find private accommodation. Like Dunbar-Kalckreuth he remained in the Netherlands until November 1918. In May he moved to a hotel in Noordwijk, which he described as 'an ideal place', and he then travelled throughout the Netherlands.[108]

Internees' ultimate arrival in Germany, whether they travelled straight through the Netherlands or remained there during 1918, proved a happy occasion for many of them. One anonymous account recalled the joy of being 'a free man again', which was intensified when, upon returning home, his 'dear wife' opened the door to him and his children surrounded him.[109] Similarly, J. Machner remembered his first night in Wilhelmshaven and then his return to his parents' house, where he saw his mother after many years of separation.[110] For many prisoners homecoming led to tears of joy. One Protestant pastor pointed out: 'Strong men cry like children upon their return.'[111]

The German state made efforts to welcome and relieve the returning prisoners, especially military captives, as did charities.

The Kriegsministerium für Heimkehrende Kriegsgefangene and the Reichzentralstelle für Kriegs- und Ziviligefangene, which came into existence in December 1918 to co-ordinate all government agencies concerned with prisoners,[112] published a short pamphlet in 1919 in order to demonstrate to the returning prisoners 'that the homeland will endeavour to have a full understanding of their situation' and show them 'the right way'. It listed over thirty tasks which local authorities should carry out. All prisoners would initially spend time in a transit camp where they would undergo a process of reorientation, which included getting hold of currency and obtaining advice.[113] These camps also deloused the returning internees and provided each of them with a new set of clothes. Former prisoners further obtained help with tracing their relatives. Eventually their demobilization and release back to civilian life would take place.[114] By September 1919 a total of twenty-five transit camps existed, holding 67,320 returning prisoners from Europe and beyond.[115] In May 1919 a new organization came into existence, the Kriegsgefangenenheimkehr, with branches which helped with the re-integration of German prisoners throughout the country. This attempted to bring together a whole series of official and charitable bodies concerned with prisoners.[116] Its tasks included providing care and advice for returned military prisoners and giving each of them a sum of money. It also had special tasks with regard to former civilian internees which included help with losses and advice on German nationality for those who had lost it.[117] In Württemberg a central reception committee for the return of prisoners of war issued a series of guidelines for the whole process of prisoner return. This mentioned the establishment of committees throughout Württemberg which ran transit camps, convalescent homes and military hospitals. The guidelines recommended the opening of local offices to continue supporting returned prisoners. The help they would receive included assistance with finding employment. The guidelines also recommended the method of reception, which was to include music and coffee or lemonade.[118]

Official bodies worked together with several charities, which also placed much effort into helping prisoners re-integrate into German society.[119] The German Red Cross devoted particular attention to the return of civilians from Britain and its colonies.[120] The Protestant Church carried out much work, building upon its previous efforts in assisting prisoners while abroad. From 1918 it worked in the internment camps established for returning Germans in the Netherlands.[121] In Germany it focused upon the spiritual welfare of the returned internees and also helped in greeting the returnees, including with 'the German homeland song'. The church recognized the significance of re-integrating the former internees into their families because some of them were 'broken' and 'much changed'.[122] It also suggested several pieces of music for greeting returned prisoners, including extracts from Mendelssohn's *Elijah*,[123] which would represent part of a 'church festival'.[124] The church further arranged collections to help returning prisoners.[125] Finally, it also handed out leaflets to returnees to welcome them home and make them feel good about themselves. One of these, entitled 'Once More in the Homeland', told its readers that it would never forget their 'courage', 'suffering' and 'patience' and that they would 'help rebuild a new fatherland from the ruins'. This patriotic note continued in the final sentence, which declared: 'A hearty welcome as colleagues and comrades in arms in the old beloved homeland.'[126]

Despite the range of official bodies which greeted and made efforts to help returning prisoners, few personal accounts recalled their efforts. Instead, they tended to recall, in a positive sense, first seeing women or families. Others focused upon the negative, including the economic and political turmoil in which Germany found itself in 1918 and 1919. Cohen-Portheim, when he arrived in Bremen at the end of 1918, was shocked at the hotel accommodation available, the substitute foods which had become normal by this time as a result of rationing, the British blockade and resultant shortages and the value of the Mark. A walk through the streets 'was enough to make me see that collapse and catastrophe had been inevitable'. He continued: 'The shop-windows showed empty packages, the shoe-shops wooden clogs, the streets were full of men in worn and mended or tattered uniforms, both men and women, still more the children, were thin and worn looking.'[127] Richard Noschke, meanwhile, who eventually made his way to his brother's house, had to confront inflation, shortages, strikes and riots. He concluded that 'the outlook for the future is dark'.[128]

All those who returned to Germany at the end of the Great War would have to confront economic and political upheaval. In addition, some would have to deal with the break-up of their families as a result of the British government's imposition of mass deportation.

This separation had actually begun earlier in the war, as the case of W. Roderwald, who wrote to the Swiss Embassy from Knockaloe, pointed out. During his internment his wife and two daughters 'are in Germany anxiously awaiting for my return', and his son faced conscription into the British army.[129] Family break-up became normal for German internees at the end of the war. For example, the pastry cook Karl Gräßle had moved in 1889 to Manchester, where had he married Sofie Wunzdorf from Hanover, with whom he had six children, now aged between three and twenty-one. He returned to Germany in 1918 and found himself living in Friedrichshafen with his brother but without his wife and children. He complained:

> My wife with her 6 children is still living in Manchester. My 2 eldest daughters are currently employed in an office there, which allows my wife to make ends meet. While I was still in the internment camp, I always had contact with my family. Since then I have received no news from them.[130]

We can surmise that both Roderwald and Gräßle were reunited with their families. This, however, did not happen in the case of Max Gottshalt, who had moved to Britain at the start of the twentieth century and married his wife Thekla, with whom he had five children. He found himself interned in Knockaloe for much of the war, during which time he regularly kept in touch with his wife and children. Nevertheless, after he arrived in the Netherlands in February 1918, his communications became increasingly infrequent. By October 1920 he appears to have lived with his sister, 'who will not assist me any more, work is scarce, millions are out of work, food and everything else is terribly expensive even to write a letter costs about 1 Mark, so you will understand why I do not answer all your letters . . . Do not send me anything in the way of food or money. Keep it for yourself and the children, but also do not send me your complaining letters.' During the course of 1921 he claimed he could not return to London because of his debts and because he would have to leave after three months under new nationality regulations. Max sent his final letter in March 1922. The letters reveal that the reason for separation lay in economic woes, although neither Max nor Thekla ultimately appeared willing to move to the residence of their spouse.[131] The typicality of this story seems difficult to measure, but if we view it against the wider tragedy of the consequences of the First World War for the family unit as a result of conscription in both Britain and Germany,[132] it does not seem unusual. Perhaps Max had found another woman, or perhaps he just could not face the idea of re-integrating into British society and into his family after years of separation. Other Germans who remained in Britain included Heinrich Henkel, released from Knockaloe to a camp in Frith Hill and then to the German Hospital in east London. Although he was reunited with his family, he probably fell victim to another post-war phenomenon in the form of flu, as he died of pneumonia in October 1919. His children spent time in the German Orphanage during the 1920s when their mother also experienced illness.[133]

Not all internment stories ended so tragically. In 1920 the Quaker James Baily travelled to Germany, where he met some former Manx internees. This meeting occurred partly through an organization called the Bund der Auslandsdeutschen, which had developed English branches in various parts of the country including Hanover. Baily addressed a meeting here consisting of 350 former internees, their wives and their friends in February 1920. Although ostensibly on a humanitarian mission, Baily went out of his way to make contact with former Manx prisoners but also bumped into some unexpectedly. Those in the latter category totalled nineteen people, including three waiters working at a hotel in Stuttgart; the head waiter of the Hotel Rampal in Heilbronn; and five waiters at the Wiener Cafe in Constance. Baily also met Herr Rossler, previously held in Douglas and 'now assisting his father' in running a hotel in Baden-Baden, 'where the whole of their staff were ex Knockaloe Po.W.s'. This points to the fact that some returnees managed to resume the careers which they had pursued before the war. Unmarried men appear to have had an easier path on their return than those with wives and children. The head waiter at the Hotel Rampal 'asked advice on getting his fiancée over from England', while another person whom Baily bumped into in Freiburg remained separated from his family in England. Other Germans did manage to bring their wives and children with them. These included 'an English born woman + her German husband late of Halifax who are managing in apartments + longing to get a house of their own'. But 'they have a little daughter living with Grandmother in England'. Baily commented: 'One of the most repeated impressions forced upon me during my three months tour of Germany was the sad plight of the English born wives and children of repatriated Germans living in Germany. Strangers in a strange land', they had little knowledge of the language and also had to face the same privations as the rest of the German population.[134]

The end of internment

Despite the desperate years which some Germans on the Isle of Man in particular spent yearning for the outside world, once they experienced freedom, they found that it did not promise what they had envisaged during their years of depression and contemplation. Much of the yearning had focused upon family reunification, and while some managed to achieve this, others would never see their families again, in some cases through choice. Those who persisted with the desire to reconstruct their family unit usually succeeded as long as they accepted the difficulties involved, in the form of travelling to Germany and bringing wives to a strange land undergoing political and economic upheaval in which they felt like strangers and, essentially, enemies.

Civilian internees who returned with English wives, particularly those who had served in the military, probably did not go through the re-integration process reserved for prisoners, although some provision existed for them. The German government and charities tried to make the returnees feel like heroes, as revealed in the payments they received and the attention devoted to playing the correct pieces of music to greet them.

The internees' feelings upon moving back to Germany varied. Those of a nationalist disposition felt good about setting foot upon German soil, something indicated most clearly by the recollections of Georg Wagener, who arrived even before the development of the sophisticated re-integration efforts at the end of the war. More critical eyes, such as Cohen-Portheim's, focused, in contrast, upon the political and economic problems when he entered Bremen. 'It almost made one's heart stand still to realize the immense tragedy of a great people.'[135]

How the returning prisoners felt upon first setting foot upon German soil was determined, above all, by their level of patriotism and their family status, but all would return to the upheaval described by Cohen-Portheim. As indicated by some of the individuals encountered by Baily in 1920, some Germans managed to continue with the careers which they had begun before the war. Many were waiters, who usually had moved to England before 1914 in order to learn English so that their employment prospects in continental hotels could improve. Rather ironically, the experience of years in Knockaloe, where they could attend English-language classes, may have facilitated this process.[136] Nevertheless, we can conclude this chapter by returning to the story of Max and Thekla Gottshalt. While the surviving correspondence of this couple may not ultimately tell us why this man abandoned his wife and five children, his letters point to the pressure of the economic catastrophe which had befallen Germany, which made him feel that he could not support his family. The cessation of internment may have meant a happy ending for many civilian and military internees, but for others one form of misery followed another.

Notes

1 MNH/MS08562, Thekla to Max Gottshalt, 18 September 1918.

2 Richard Bessel, *Germany after the First World War* (Oxford, 1993); Adam R. Seipp, *The Ordeal of Peace: Demobilization and the Urban Experience in Britain and Germany, 1917–1921* (Farnham, 2009), pp. 165–97, 233–59.

3 Panikos Panayi, 'German Business Interests in Britain during the First World War', *Business History*, vol. 32 (1990), 244–58.

4 See the list in Graham Mark, *Prisoners of War in British Hands during WW1: A Study of their History, the Camps and their Mails* (Exeter, 2007), pp. 236–47.

5 Leslie Baily, *Craftsman and Quaker: The Story of James T. Baily, 1876–1957* (London, 1959), p. 102.

6 NA/HO45/10883/345466, Chief Constable of Nottinghamshire to Home Office, 1 October 1917.

7 *Daily Mirror*, 3 September 1917.

8 Gunther Plüschow, *My Escape from Donington Hall* (London, 1922), pp. 184–6.

9 Albrecht Hermann Brugger, *Meine Flucht aus dem Kriegsgefangenen-Lager Lofthouse-Park* (Berlin, 1937), p. 14.

10 BA/R67/253, DRK, Interner Bericht 102, 4 March 1918.

11 *Isle of Man Examiner*, 12 February 1916.

12 Hugh Durnford et al., *Tunnelling to Freedom and Other Escape Narratives from World War One* (1932; Mineola, NY, 2004), p. 261.

13 Wilhelm Kröpke, *Meine Flucht aus englischer Kriegsgefangenschaft*

1916: Von Afrika über England nach Deutschland zur Flandern-Front (Flensburg, 1937).

14 Brugger, *Meine Flucht*, pp. 19–25.
15 *Daily Mirror*, 9 July 1918.
16 Ibid., 27 September 1916.
17 Ibid., 12 September 1917; *Manchester Guardian*, 12 September 1917.
18 *Isle of Man Weekly Times*, 28 October 1916.
19 Durnford et al., *Tunnelling*, pp. 262–78.
20 Kröpke, *Meine Flucht*, pp. 46–79.
21 BA/MA/RM3/5378, Kapitän Johannes Schmidt-Klafleth, Meine Flucht aus England.
22 Durnford, et. al., *Tunnelling*, pp. 200–15.
23 *Manchester Guardian*, 17 April 1916.
24 *Scotsman*, 12 April 1915; *The Times*, 12 April 1915.
25 *Daily Mirror*, 28 August 1917.
26 *Scotsman*, 5 September 1915.
27 *Daily Express*, 3 January 1917.
28 *The Times*, 21 November 1916.
29 *Daily Express*, 3 January 1917.
30 Ibid., 23 November 1916, 3, 4, 5 January 1917; *The Times*, 21, 23 November 1916.
31 *Daily Express*, 9 October 1918.
32 Ibid., 6 May 1918.
33 Ibid., 26 July, 18 September 1915; *The Times*, 26 July, 18 September 1915.
34 *Manchester Guardian*, 18 August 1915.
35 *Peel City Guardian and Chronicle*, 22 January 1916; *Isle of Man Weekly Times*, 22 January 1916.
36 *Daily Mirror*, 18 October 1917.
37 *Morning Post*, 2 September 1915.
38 *Daily Express*, 29 April 1918.
39 NA/FO383/285, Army Council Instruction No. 1209 of 2 August 1917, Prisoners of War – Instructions to Military Courts for the Trial of Prisoners of War.
40 BA/R901/83158, Zusammenstellung der Nachrichten über die in England erfolgte Verurteilung zu 84 Tagen Gefängnis des Oberleutenants im Regiment des Gardes du Corps Hans Werner von Hellendorff nach Englischen und deutschen Zeitungen, sowie seinen eigenen Briefen; *Daily Telegraph*, 28 August 1915; *Scotsman*, 28 August, 3 September 1915; *Manchester Guardian*, 28 August 1915.
41 BA/R901/85161, Foreign Office to US Embassy, 11 November 1916.
42 Kröpke, *Meine Flucht*, p. 32.

43 NA/FO383/163, Freiherr von Grote to the US Ambassador, 14 June 1916.
44 NA/FO383/164, Julius Reinhard Koch and Heinrich Brinkmann to US Embassy, 30 September 1916.
45 BA/R67/253, DRK, Interner Bericht 102, 4 March 1918.
46 BA/R67/1811, US Embassy Report on Dyffryn Aled, 12 October 1916.
47 NA/FO383/149, E. Kühl to Secretary of State for Foreign Affairs, 15 May 1916.
48 NA/FO383/283, Letter to German Division of Swiss Legation, 13 February 1917.
49 NA/FO383/203, Head Captain of Camp II, Knockaloe, to Prime Minister, 22 September 1916.
50 NA/FO383/276, A. L. Vischer to Mr Waller, 26 May 1917.
51 See, for example, NA/FO383/432, Swiss Embassy Report on Knockaloe and Douglas, 11 September 1918.
52 J. C. Bird, *Control of Enemy Alien Civilians in Great Britain, 1914–1918* (London, 1986), p. 169; NA/HO45/11025/410118, Report of the Directorate of Prisoners of War, September 1920.
53 NA/HO45/11025/410118, Report of the Directorate of Prisoners of War, September 1920.
54 *Hansard* (Commons), fifth series, vol. 70, col. 1758, 15 March 1915.
55 NA/HO45/11025/410118, Report of the Directorate of Prisoners of War, September 1920; FO383/58, Prisoners of War, Conditions of Exchange of the Severely Wounded between Britain and Germany, 27 October 1915.
56 Panikos Panayi, *The Enemy in Our Midst: Germans in Britain during the First World War* (Oxford, 1991), pp. 85–6. See also the relevant correspondence in NA/FO383/172.
57 *Correspondence with the United States Ambassador Respecting the Transfer to Switzerland of British and German Wounded and Sick Combatant Prisoners of War* (London, 1916).
58 NA/HO45/11025/410118, Report of the Directorate of Prisoners of War, September 1920.
59 NA/FO383/149, Letter from W. R. Clark, 11 December 1916.
60 Panayi, *Enemy*, p. 86; NA/FO383/278, Exchange with Germany of Civilian Prisoners over 45 Years of Age.
61 Panayi, *Enemy*, pp. 87–8; *An Agreement between the British and German Governments Concerning Combatant and Civilian Prisoners of War* (London, 1917).
62 NA/FO383/382, Minute, 18 May 1918.
63 BA/R67/1283, DRK, Interner Bericht 102, 4 March 1918.

64 NA/FO383/382, War Office to Prisoners of War Department, 30 April 1918.
65 NA/FO383/383, War Office to Prisoners of War Department, 29 August 1918.
66 See also Chapter 7 above.
67 NA/FO383/432, Note Verbale, 16 April 1918.
68 NA/FO383/410, Note Verbale, 11 April 1918.
69 NA/FO383/410, C. R. Manretz to Secretary of State for Foreign Affairs, 15 April 1918.
70 See correspondence in NA/FO383/438.
71 IWM, The First World War Diaries of Richard Noschke, pp. 44–5.
72 See the correspondence in NA/FO383/411.
73 Panayi, *Enemy*, p. 89; *An Agreement between the British and German Governments concerning Combatant Prisoners of War and Civilians* (London, 1918).
74 NA/HO45/10833/327753, Home Office Memorandum, 18 November 1918; MNH/MS09310, Isle of Man Constabulary Archive, Box 5, Daily Return of Prisoners Interned.
75 MNH/MS11425, George Kenner, Sketches of a German Interned Civilian Prisoner in England (1914–1919).
76 NA/WO394/20, Statistical Information Regarding the Armies at Home and Abroad, 1914–1920.
77 NA/FO608/268, Telegram from Lord Curzon to Lord Balfour, 15 May 1919.
78 NA/FO383/501, Code Telegram to Sir W. Townley, 21 March 1919.
79 NA/WO394/20, Statistical Information Regarding the Armies at Home and Abroad, 1914–1920.
80 LBWHS/M400/2/150, DRK, Rundschreiben 1113, 11 December 1919.
81 NA/WO394/20, Statistical Information Regarding the Armies at Home and Abroad, 1914–1920; *Daily Express*, 3 February 1920.
82 BA/R67/1348, Reichsfinanzministerium, Liste der Kriegsgefangenen, die noch nicht aus England Zurückgekehrt sind, 23 August 1921.
83 Frederick Lewis Dunbar-Kalckreuth, *Die Männerinsel* (Leipzig, 1940), pp. 330–5. See also BA/MA/MSG200/2277, Schilderungen eines Lederfachmannes.
84 BA/R901/83132, Swiss Embassy Report on Pattishall, 17 October 1919.
85 Richard B. Speed III, *Prisoners, Diplomats, and the Great War: A Study in the Diplomacy of Captivity* (London, 1990), pp. 177–8.
86 NA/FO383/502, German Senior Officer, Redmires, to David Lloyd George and His Majesty the King, 5 August 1919.
87 Speed, *Prisoners*, pp. 174–5.

88 NA/FO383/502, War Office to Commandants, Prisoners of War Camps, 31 July 1919.
89 *Daily Express*, 30 August 1919.
90 Ibid.; *The Times*, 30 August 1919.
91 Panayi, *Enemy*, p. 221.
92 Ibid., pp. 96–7; *Daily Mirror*, 18 December 1918; *Manchester Guardian*, 18 December 1918, 1 November 1919; *Report of Committee Appointed to Consider Applications for Exemption from Compulsory Repatriation By Interned Enemy Aliens* (London, 1919).
93 NA/FO383/500, Note Verbale, 24 February 1919; NA/FO383/502, Note Verbale, 30 May 1919.
94 NA/FO383/501, Letter from Ruoff, Sec. Reception Committee, Rotterdam, 5 February 1919.
95 NA/FO383/501, Note Verbale, 5 April 1919.
96 NA/FO383/501, Letter from Ruoff, Sec. Reception Committee, Rotterdam, 5 February 1919.
97 See NA/FO383/501, Chief of the British Armistice Commission to President of German Armistice Commission, 4 May 1919; NA/FO383/505, Memorandum Regarding German Allegations as to Treatment of Repatriated Civilians in 'Manitou'.
98 BA/MA/RM3/5391, Statement by Anton Ditschkowski, 24 October 1916.
99 Georg Wilhelm Wagener, *Meine Gefangenschaft in Südafrika und England vom 15. Sept. 1914 bis 18. Juni 1916* (Brunswick, 1917), pp. 98–9.
100 Hans Erich Benedix, *In England interniert* (Gotha, 1916), pp. 104, 109.
101 Ibid., p. 109; Otto Schimming, *13 Monate hinter dem Stacheldraht: Alexandra Palace, Knockaloe, Isle of Man, Stratford* (Stuttgart, 1919), p. 31; J. Maue, *In Feindes Land: Achtzehn Monate in englischer Kriegsgefangenschaft in Indien und England* (Stuttgart, 1918), p. 81.
102 BA/MA/MSG200/2277, 'Schilderungen eines Lederfachmannes'.
103 MNH/MS11425, George Kenner, 'Sketches of a German Interned Civilian Prisoner in England (1914–1919)'.
104 Karl von Scheidt and Fritz Meyer, *Vier Jahre Leben und Leiden der Auslandsdeutschen in den Gefangenenlagern Englands* (Hagen, 1919), p. 135.
105 Paul Cohen-Portheim, *Time Stood Still: My Internment in England* (London, 1931), p. 205.
106 Scheidt and Meyer, *Vier Jahre*, pp. 135–6.
107 Dunbar-Kalckreuth, *Die Männerinsel*, pp. 339–59.
108 Cohen-Portheim, *Time Stood Still*, pp. 207–30.

109 BA/MA/MSG200/2277, 'Schilderungen eines Lederfachmannes.
110 J. Machner, *Gefangen in England: Erlebnisse and Beobachtungen* (Hildesheim, 1920), pp. 388–90.
111 G. Schrenk, 'Wie helfen wir als Seelssorger zur rechten Begrüßung und Fürsorge für die heimkehrenden Kriegsgefangenen?', in Oskar Goehling, ed., *Frei und daheim! Eine Handreichung für Heimkehrfeiern in Kirche und Gemeinde* (Berlin, 1919), p. 33.
112 *Nachrichtenblatt der Reichzentralstelle für Kriegs- und Ziviligefangene*, January 1919.
113 Kriegsministerium für Heimkehrende Kriegsgefangene (Unterkunfts-Departement) und der Reichzentrale für Kriegs- und Ziviliegefangene, *Merkblatt für heimkehrende Gefangene* (Berlin, 1919).
114 LBWHS/M1/8/231, Kriegsministerium, Grundsätze für die Rückführung Deutscher Kriegsgefangener (Heeresangehöriger), 15 April 1919.
115 *Nachrichtenblatt der Reichzentralstelle für Krieg- und Ziviligefangene*, September 1919.
116 Ibid., May 1919.
117 Professor Hickmann, 'Kriegsgefangenenheimkehr', in Goehling, ed., *Frei und daheim!*, pp. 37–43.
118 LBWHS/M1/8/231, Württembergischer Zentral-Empfangs-Ausschuß für die Kiegsgefangenen-Heimkehr, 'Richtlinien für den Empfang der zurückkehrenden Kriegsgefangenen'.
119 For details of the range of such organizations see, for example: EZA1/788, Hilfsausschuß für Gefangenenseelsorge; and *Nachrichtenblatt der Reichzentralstelle für Kriegs- und Ziviligefangene*, May 1919.
120 EZA1/788, 'Merkblatt für die aus Großbritannien und den britischen Kolonien zurückkehrenden deutschen Zivilpersonen'.
121 EZA1/788, Hilfs-Aussuß für Gefangenen-Seelsorge an den Deutschen Evangelischen Kirchenausschuß, 27 August 1918.
122 Schenk, 'Wie helfen wir', in Goehling, ed., *Frei und daheim!*, pp. 29–36.
123 'Musikalien', in Goehling, ed., *Frei und daheim!*, pp. 44–5.
124 EZA1/788, Verordnung, die Heimkehrer der deutschen Kriegs- und Ziviligefangenen betreffend vom 30. Juni 1919.
125 EZA1/789, Oberkirchenrat Schwerin to Deutschen Evangelischen Kirchenausschuß, 17 June 1920.
126 EZA1/789, 'Wieder in der Heimat!'
127 Cohen-Portheim, *Time Stood Still*, pp. 233–4.
128 IWM, The First World War Diaries of Richard Noschke.
129 NA/FO383/298, W. Roderwald to Swiss Minister, 22 May 1917.
130 LBWHS/M77/1/930, Militärpolizeistelle Friedrichshafen to Stellv. Generalkommando III.A.K, Stuttgart, 11 May 1918.

131 MNH/MS08562, Letters from Max to Thekla Gottshalt, 1915–22.
132 See, for example, Ute Daniel, *The War from Within: German Working-Class Women in the First World War* (Oxford, 1997), pp. 127–230; Richard Wall, 'English and German Families and the First World War', in Richard Wall and Jay Winter, eds, *The Upheaval of War: Family, Work and Welfare in Europe, 1914–1918* (Cambridge, 1988), pp. 43–106.
133 Roy Bernard, *My German Family in England* (Maidenhead, 1993), pp. 26–7.
134 Baily, *Craftsman and Quaker*, pp. 111–12; MNH/MS10417, J. T. Baily, 'Germany 1920, FEC&FWVRS', pp. 1–2, 164, 195.
135 Cohen-Portheim, *Time Stood Still*, p. 234.
136 Panikos Panayi, 'Sausages, Waiters and Bakers: German Migrants and Culinary Transfer to Britain, c1850–1914', in Stefan Manz, Margrit Schulte Beerbühl and John R. Davis, eds, *Migration and Transfer from Germany to Britain, 1660–1914* (Munich, 2007), p. 155.

9

The meaning of internment in Britain during the First World War

As Arthur Marwick asserted nearly five decades ago, the First World War represented a central turning point in the history of modern Britain because of both its short-term and its long-term effects, which were perpetuated further by the Second World War.[1] For any historian working on twentieth-century Europe, especially the first half of it, these two conflicts overshadow all else and led Eric Hobsbawm to describe the 'decades from the outbreak of the First World War to the aftermath of the Second' as 'an Age of Catastrophe'.[2] Although much of Europe suffered during these years, especially the central and eastern part of the continent, two of the key participants were Britain and Germany, which underwent some of the most profound transformations as a result of the wars.[3]

Our concern in this conclusion consists of an attempt to understand the meaning of internment in First World War Britain by placing it into a series of specific themes revolving around this conflict, but also by looking backwards to the nineteenth century and forwards to the Second World War. We can reach a deeper understanding of our story by placing it into three contexts. First is its importance to the lives of those affected. Second is its significance as state policy. And, third, we need to place the control of German prisoners in Britain within the broader European picture of persecution during the First World War in particular, and to try to understand its meaning within the age of catastrophe recognized by Hobsbawm, but also examine the First World War as a turning point in the history of mass incarceration.

During the Great War internment had a significant meaning as part of the propaganda war between Britain and Germany, so that public opinion in both countries focused upon the plight of their own prisoners abroad while claiming that they treated the enemy well at home. The influence of the press in both Germany and Britain meant that the issue remained important in both countries. At the same time, charities in Germany also ensured that the plight of Germans abroad remained a live issue. The memoirs of those who faced life behind barbed wire in Britain and elsewhere became a significant literary genre during and immediately after the Great War in Germany, experiencing something of a mini-revival with the approach and outbreak of the Second World War.

However, we should not forget that for decades the internment of Germans in First World War Britain had no meaning, because it had disappeared from the public and academic memory in both Britain and Germany. It seems reasonable to reiterate astonishment at the fact that this study represents the first attempt by a historian to tell the story of the hundreds of thousands of Germans imprisoned in Britain during the Great War. Drowned out by the Germanophobia of the interwar years, the experience of Great War internment was further erased by the memory of the even more brutal, global and destructive Second World War. New memories virtually crushed the experiences of the earlier conflict, certainly when it came to imprisonment in Britain. This scenario operated especially in Germany, where the final prisoners did not return from the Soviet Union until 1955, a full decade after the defeat of the Nazis.[4]

Internment as a personal experience

First World War internment had the most meaning for those who experienced it. Using a variety of both official and unofficial sources, this book has tried to use individual stories to view internment through the eyes of those involved, whether they were civilians or soldiers. For both of these groups internment had several meanings, some of which applied to both and others of which applied to the two groups separately.

Marwick devised a variety of dimensions of war, one of which consisted of the 'destructive and disruptive'.[5] For virtually every German who found himself behind barbed wire in Britain, the experience clearly disrupted his pre-war life. For those who served in the German army, internment in Britain represented one phase in their lives as soldiers, which may have started in the late summer or autumn of 1914 and ended in 1919. Imprisonment in Britain usually formed a small aspect of First World War experiences, as few German soldiers would have spent more than two years on British soil and most probably remained for less than one. For civilians, whether living in Britain or not, internment represented the central event of their wartime experiences. To return to its disruptive aspects, these come through in many of the accounts which have survived. It applies, for instance, to those individuals who, perhaps naively, thought that they could sail across the Atlantic from the United States to Germany in the late summer of 1914 and expect to get home. Taken off their boat by the Royal Navy, escorted to a British port and gawped at or worse by the local population, they could not have been prepared for the years they might subsequently face behind barbed wire. Members of the German navy as well as German fishermen faced similar experiences later in the war, although they may at least have known of the possibility of internment. Meanwhile, those working or living in the British colonies could face epic journeys to Britain. Some of the most moving and negative accounts came from those who spent their summers in Britain, including Frederick Lewis Dunbar-Kalckreuth, who had come to the country to improve his English, and, above all, Paul Cohen-Portheim. The enraged account written by the latter drips with indignation as a result of the injustice he felt at being confined for years behind barbed wire simply because he happened to spend a few days in the summer of 1914 painting in Britain. Cohen-Portheim's may represent one type of bourgeois experience, which did not apply to those lower down on the social scale, who had always had less control over their lives, although the prevalence of barbed wire disease might suggest otherwise.

Internment had different meanings for civilians and soldiers. For many male enemy aliens living in Britain in the summer of 1914 it represented their central wartime experience because of the amount of time they spent behind barbed wire. They tended to view incarceration more negatively than soldiers for several reasons. Firstly, precisely because for many it represented the central negative aspect of their lives during the war, although some of those who had experienced the rioting of May 1915 preferred to spend time behind barbed wire rather than face the wrath of the xenopbobic British working classes, and therefore surrendered when Asquith called for wholesale internment. Spending years behind barbed wire away from families and with little to do often proved a bitter experience for individuals contemplating their fate. The development of prison camp societies helped to alleviate their depression, although we can see these all-male societies simply as substitutes for the world with women and children outside. Soldiers tended not to view their lives within camps so negatively, although examples of barbed wire disease existed among the military. Nevertheless, as A. L. Vischer recognized, for many soldiers, living in a prisoner-of-war camp represented a relief from the constant threat of death which they had experienced on French battlefields. At the same time, most military personnel, with the exception of officers, could work, often in the British countryside, which meant that they did not spend years of their adult lives essentially playing, whether at sport or in the theatre, for example. Despite the boredom, depression and resentment which a prolonged spell behind barbed wire may have caused for those civilians who encountered it, most soldiers probably preferred this to life in a French trench or a camp on the continent. Perhaps years on the Isle of Man may have represented one of the *easiest* of German male experiences during the Great War, although we should see it as just one of many evils.

The end of the war also had different meanings for soldiers and civilians. Although both groups may have waited in camps for repatriation for up to a year during 1919 as part of the punishment for the defeated Germans at Versailles, the conclusion of the conflict affected the two groups in different ways. The soldiers who had spent relatively little time behind barbed wire in Britain could look forward to some type of stability in the sense that they would return home to former lives. On the other hand, they may have spent as much time as the civilians had away from their families and homes, as the experience of imprisonment formed just one aspect of an overall military life which had included fighting on the western front. Return home meant going back to a completely changed Germany that was undergoing revolution and economic catastrophe. At the same time as attempting to re-integrate into this economic and political upheaval, they had to try to live again with their families, who had undergone completely different wartime experiences.

The various bodies which came into existence to help re-integrate returning internees tried to make the task easier for both soldiers and civilians. But the difficulties facing the latter seem to have been even more overwhelming, even though many of those waiters who had migrated to England before 1914 to improve their job prospects managed to secure employment. However, civilians not only arrived in Germany to face the same upheaval as everybody else, but returned to unfamiliar surroundings which some had not seen for decades. They had no German homes to which to return and therefore often had to live with brothers and sisters, despite the fact that they both had their own families now. Even worse, some of them separated from these families either temporarily or permanently. The years of contemplating freedom behind the barbed wire in the absence of any employment would have raised hopes in many civilians, but these were now crushed by the realities of liberation.

First World War internment in Britain, whether for civilian males or soldiers, formed one aspect of an early twentieth-century German or British experience which, for the entire population of these two countries, became dominated by war. The internees, particularly those civilians who lived in England, found themselves trapped between two cultures. While they bitterly resented their fate, we can see their situation as one possible scenario for males born in late nineteenth-century Europe.

Incarceration as state policy

The implementation of internment in First World War Britain meant a new departure in terms of both soldiers and civilians. Never had the country imprisoned so many people at the same time. The explanation for this partly lies in the fact that Britain had never previously fought a total war. On the last occasion on which Britain had become embroiled in a conflict resembling the scale of the Great War, the French Revolutionary and Napoleonic Wars, it had imprisoned enemy soldiers and tightened its aliens policy but had not introduced mass internment.[6]

However, here, as in much else, the First World War resulted in new departures. Beginning with the incarceration of soldiers, the scale of the conflict and the size of the armies involved meant that the issue of prisoners of war surfaced in a new manner. Although mistreatment became part of the everyday lives of captives throughout Europe,[7] the growing humanitarianism of the nineteenth century meant that those who were incarcerated within Britain itself received relatively good treatment. The reason for transferring soldiers *en masse* to Britain partly lay in the need for labour to keep the wartime economy going and to help with the harvest. The millions of soldiers fighting during the First World War, as well as the consequent number of captives which Britain found itself holding, meant that it had to create numerous camps throughout the world. The combination of total war, which led to mass mobilization and participation in military conflict, and the acceptance of the humanitarian treatment of captives in Britain meant that those who found themselves on British soil faced a relatively comfortable experience. Britain essentially had no choice but to open large numbers of prisoner-of-war camps because of the hundreds of thousands of Germans it captured as the war progressed. Nevertheless, on British soil at least, it played by humanitarian rules.

The internment of aliens, on the other hand, involves a greater degree of choice from a bureaucratic point of view. Britain may not have been the only country to implement internment of civilians during the First World War, but it became the centre of a global system of incarceration. On the one hand this resulted in the transportation of people to the Isle of Man from throughout the world. However, as part of a global empire, decisions taken in London influenced policy throughout Britain's possessions, whether India, New Zealand, Australia or Canada.

When the war broke out Britain had no definite policy with regard to the internment of either soldiers or civilians. Military victories and the capture of soldiers determined the plight of the former. For the first nine months of the war British policy muddled through without coming to any decisions as to how to deal with enemy aliens of military age within its shores. The Aliens Restriction Act, passed on the day after the outbreak of war, indicated the planning which the Home Office in particular had carried out with regard to overall control of enemy aliens. Internment, however, suddenly became an option during the course of August 1914, and over the next nine months the numbers of Germans who found themselves behind barbed wire rose and fell. The panic caused by events on the battlefield and its consequent influence on press and parliamentary opinion helped to force the Home Secretary, Reginald McKenna, to intensify internment, but Asquith's government remained undecided as to the right course.

The turning point consisted of the sinking of the *Lusitania* in May 1915 and the consequent mass rioting against German shops, fuelled by a Germanophobic press. Asquith's announcement in the House of Commons introducing wholesale internment arose partially from the desire to protect Germans from rioters. This explanation receives further support from the fact that many internees simply surrendered themselves to the police at this time.

We might view these events as exceptional in modern British history. Attacks against a foreign population on the scale of those upon the Germans have not occurred since 1915 and had not happened since the (even worse) Gordon Riots of 1760.[8] Yet internment replicated patterns of state behaviour towards ethnic outsiders that were characteristic of twentieth-century Britain. The template was the Aliens Act of 1905 when an anti-alien campaign resulted in the passage of the cornerstone of all subsequent attempts to exclude ethnic groups with the 'wrong' credentials,[9] most notably a series of Acts from the 1950s until the 1970s to limit black and Asian immigrants.[10] From our perspective the closest parallel is the decision to introduce internment in June 1940. Although preparations had existed for mass incarceration before this time, the government implemented wholesale internment in a state of panic as the Wehrmacht conquered continental Western Europe. On this occasion, almost uniquely in modern British aliens policy, the state quickly reversed its decision, realizing that many of those interned (as refugees from the Nazis) had the same enemy.[11] This contrasted with the events of the First World War, when the link between Germans and the Fatherland remained firmly established and survived until the end of the war, as was most clearly manifested in the mass deportations which occurred.

Internment in Britain during the First World War therefore fits into the history of British governmental responses to migrant populations. All migrant groups have faced some sort of hostility, and since the Aliens Act of 1905, governments have found official solutions to the question of dealing with perceived outsiders, usually by introducing legislation to control further entry of the migrant group which is the main focus for hostility at the time. The use of internment against Germans during the First World War may appear distinct in two main ways. In the first place, the resident Germans had become well integrated and largely invisible by 1914, despite the rise of 'spy fever', but suddenly became instantly recognizable, despite their apparent physical similarities to the ethnic majority. Yet the First World War Germans resembled, for example, the Italians, who had faced relatively little animosity in the inter-war years but would experience incarceration along with German Jews, whose entry had caused official and unofficial hostility during the 1930s following Mussolini's declaration of war on Britain on 10 June 1940.[12] More recently, Muslims became visible following the Rushdie affair and the development of wars against Islamic states from the 1990s. The government also introduced measures to control those regarded as dangerous, albeit not on a mass scale.[13] Perhaps the truly unique aspect of mass incarceration during the First World War lies in the extremity of this administrative solution. Xenophobia may have characterized modern British history, but the totality of the exclusion, in both official and unofficial terms, remained unique, encompassing mass internment, mass deportation, mass rioting and wholesale confiscation of property. Britain essentially carried out ethnic cleansing during the First World War, and the incarceration of German males for years represented a transitionary stage.

The importance of the First World War

We therefore need to turn to the importance of the First World War as a turning point in the persecution of minorities. Most scholars working on the plight of ethnic outsiders in Europe in the first half of the twentieth century accept the importance of war as the background for the most extreme acts which occurred, especially in central and Eastern Europe, where, for instance, Mark Levene and Timothy Snyder have also stressed the importance of vulnerable regions in borderlands. Levene pays particular attention to the years 1912–48, which encompassed not simply the era of the two world wars but also the collapse of the Ottoman Empire and the rise and fall of Nazism and its consequences. Snyder focuses upon the Second World War.[14] In addition, we need to remember the army of scholars who have stressed the importance of the Second World War in the Nazi Holocaust, although Donald Bloxham has recently viewed the Holocaust as one of many genocides;[15] this approach is partly inspired by the work of Levene, who regards genocide and ethnic cleansing as part of the nation-building process.[16] But Levene does not remain alone in regarding genocide as almost normal in modernity.[17]

Levene's essay on the 'rimlands' significantly begins in 1912, the era of the Balkan Wars when ethnic cleansing began to gain legitimacy, although it had become increasingly common as the Ottoman Empire collapsed during the nineteenth century.[18] Nevertheless, it was in the era of the First World War that ethnic cleansing and ultimately genocide became legitimate policy. While this happened in several parts of Europe, the Ottoman Empire became the crucible for legitimization, as two episodes in particular illustrate: the Armenian genocide, which resulted in the murder or displacement of perhaps 1.5 million people, and the 'population exchange' which took place between Greece and Turkey in the early 1920s, which again resulted in the displacement of millions of people.[19] Alan Kramer has looked at minority persecution in the Balkans more generally in his study of mass killing during the First World War.[20]

What happened to the German community in Britain during the First World War seems a long way from the events in Turkey and Greece, both geographically and in terms of the plight of the individuals involved. British public opinion felt outraged at both the Armenian genocide and the 'population exchange' between Greece and Turkey.[21] At the same time Britain treated those it interned, whether soldiers or civilians, in a basically humane manner, despite the fact that soldiers experienced some mistreatment upon capture and release. Yet internment of civilians formed part of a process of marginalizing and eliminating the German community in Britain, which came to fruition by 1920. Unlike the situation at the end of the Second World War, when 15,000 German prisoners, admittedly out of a much larger number (peaking at of 402,000 in September 1946), remained in Britain,[22] allowing Germans to stay at the end of the First World War never appears to have become an issue, as official figures indicate that all, except for a handful who seem to have disappeared from the radar, had undergone repatriation by 1920. At the same time, we must not forget the reality of civilian internment. It meant that men faced separation from their families, whether in England, in the case of those settled in the country, or in Germany, for those who happened to find themselves in Britain in the summer of 1914 or who faced transportation to the Isle of Man. Furthermore, we also need to remember that internment formed part of a British policy involving both state and public opinion which included violence and which destroyed virtually every German-owned shop in Britain.

We can understand internment in Britain during the First World

War as a jigsaw piece in a policy of ethnic cleansing which eliminated the German community and which mirrored bloodier jigsaw puzzles on the continent. The concentration camp really came into its own during the First World War. While those states who captured soldiers might incarcerate hundreds of thousands of such individuals, the internment camp also played a role in punishing civilians, whether in Europe or beyond. France and Germany also utilized this form of marginalization of enemy aliens.[23] Yet Britain perfected the system on a global scale because decisions taken in London had implications for German communities all over the world as an imperial internment system evolved.

Ethnic cleansing also became part of state policy during these years. Although it took off during the nineteenth century, the final collapse of the Ottoman Empire in the era of the the First World War intensified such actions, which were legitimized in the Lausanne Treaty of 1923.[24] Ultimately, the actions of the British state did not result in hundreds of thousands of deaths, as happened in the Ottoman Empire. Yet both states practised ethnic cleansing. In contrast to the brutal and chaotic actions of Turkey, Britain carried out its punishment of its marginalized population relatively humanely. The end result, however, ultimately remained the same: the elimination of the perceived enemy.

Internment in Britain during the First World War therefore reflects events elsewhere on the continent as a result of this savage conflict, which killed millions of combatants and civilians. It tells us about the nature of the British state at this time as well as about the nature of armed conflict and it consequences for both soldiers and civilians. While British bureaucracy may ultimately have refrained from extreme violence, it played a significant role in legitimizing civilian and military incarceration on a global scale.

The First World War also acted as a key turning point in the history of mass incarceration within Britain and beyond. While Europe may not have previously experienced total war on the scale of that of 1914–18, it would do so again just two decades later. Whether we examine the European or British situation, the precedents laid down during the Great War served the policy of the makers of the Second World War well. The concentration camp may have reached its peak in the early 1940s but it built upon the prototypes of 1914–19.

In the British case we can see this in civilian internment. As Peter and Leni Gillman demonstrated, some continuity existed in this policy between the two world wars, with the Home Office and War Office playing key roles, although inter-war conferences which also involved the Committee of Imperial Defence had decided not to implement wholesale incarceration, but to pursue deportation and selective internment in view of the variety of Germans who found themselves in Britain, ranging from Nazis to Jewish refugees. However, in an act which almost repeated the events of May 1915, following the success of the German army in Western Europe and the declaration of war on Britain by Mussolini, the British government again opted for mass incarceration. Nevertheless, in this case it did go back to its pre-war policy and, learning the lessons of the First World War, did not pursue mass internment for any length of time, although the situation of the internees was helped by their anti-Nazism and their refugee status.[25]

Mass incarceration reached its peak in central Europe under the Nazis. A clear continuity exists, as scholars such as Ulrich Herbert have demonstrated, in the way in which the precedent of using prisoner-of-war labour during the First World War reached its ultimate manifestation in the Second World War, driven on by a much more overtly racist ideology and also engaging far more victims than during the Great War, so that the Nazi economy became highly dependent upon both its prisoners of war and foreign labourers.[26]

Those Germans and Italian combatants who found themselves held in Great Britain would not experience the type of savage treatment meted out especially to Jews and Soviet prisoners of war,[27] as Dieter Steinert and Inge Weber-Newth and Lucio Sponza have demonstrated. In the British case it seems that the continuities are equally clear, and once again, we might argue that the British government learnt its lesson from the First World War, especially in its greater utilization of prisoner labour.[28]

In the British case mass internment comes to a close with the Second World War. Although the country may have become involved in many wars since 1945 it has never again experienced the scale of military participation of the decades between 1914 and 1949. Nevertheless, it has again fallen into the type of panic which led to the mass incarceration of the First World War. 'Security' has become a catchword for the way in which the British state deals with its citizens.[29] For the purpose of maintaining both 'national' and 'personal' security, internment of the type which occurred during the Great War continues. By the 1970s IRA suspects became victims of such a policy under the Prevention of Terrorism Act, while those regarded as having links to Islamic-based terrorism now find themselves detained.[30] The evolution of multicultural Britain and the fact that few Britons have participated in recent wars ensure that numbers remain small. But we can still see the origins of this process in the First World War.

The Great War represents a key turning point in the history of mass incarceration, both within Great Britain and in Europe as a whole. While Britain may not have carried out the types of intolerance upon its soil which occurred in continental Europe, it did persecute its German population. At the same time, the number of prisoners held by the British Empire points to the fact that it pursued global incarceration in the age of total war. As this book has tried to demonstrate, internment represented a key experience for males in early twentieth-century Europe. Britain played a key role development of mass incarceration.

Notes

1 Although it is rather dated and unfashionable we should not ignore the importance of the pioneering work of Arthur Marwick, whose most important volumes include *The Deluge: British Society and the First World War* (London, 1965) and *War and Social Change in the Twentieth Century* (1965; reprint London, 1986).

2 Eric Hobsbawm, *Age of Extremes: A Short History of the Twentieth Century* (London, 1994), pp. 6–7.

3 Good introductions to Britain in the First World War include Trevor Wilson, *The Myriad Faces of War: Britain and the Great War 1914–1918* (Cambridge, 1986). For Germany see Roger Chickering, *Imperial Germany and the Great War, 1914–1918*, 2nd edn (Cambridge, 2007). For some of the latest research on the Second World see Jeremy Black, ed., *The Second World War*, 7 vols (Aldershot, 2007).

4 See, for instance, Andreas Hilger, *Deutsche Kriegsgefangene in der Sowjetunion, 1941–1956: Kriegsgefangenenpolitik, Lageralltag und Erinnerung* (Essen, 2000).

5 Marwick, *War and Social Change*, pp. 11–12.

6 Elizabeth Sparrow, 'The Alien Office, 1792–1806', *Historical Journal*, vol. 33 (1990), 361–84; Francis Abell, *Prisoners of War in Britain,*

1756 to 1815: A Record of their Lives, their Romance and their Sufferings (Oxford, 1914).

7 Heather Jones, *Violence against Prisoners of War in the First World War: Britain, France and Germany, 1914–1920* (Cambridge, 2011).

8 Panikos Panayi, 'Anti-Immigrant Riots in Nineteenth and Twentieth Century Britain', in Panikos Panayi, ed., *Racial Violence in Britain in the Nineteenth and Twentieth Centuries* (London, 1996), pp. 1–25.

9 Bernard Gainer, *The Alien Invasion: The Origins of the Aliens Act of 1905* (London, 1972).

10 John Solomos, *Race and Racism in Britain* (Basingstoke, 1993), pp. 52–77.

11 See contributions to David Cesarani and Tony Kushner, eds, *The Internment of Aliens in Twentieth Century Britain* (London, 1993) and Richard Dove, ed., *'Totally un-English'? Britain's Internment of 'Enemy Aliens' in Two World Wars* (Amsterdam, 2005).

12 Lucio Sponza, 'The Anti-Italian Riots, June 1940', in Panayi, ed., *Racial Violence*, pp. 131–49; Louise London, *Whitehall and the Jews, 1933–1948: British Immigration Policy and the Holocaust* (Cambridge, 2000).

13 Tariq Modood, *Multicultural Politics: Racism, Ethnicity and Muslims in Britain* (Edinburgh, 2000).

14 Mark Levene, 'The Tragedy of the Rimlands: Nation-State Formation and the Destruction of Imperial Peoples, 1912–1948', in Panikos Panayi and Pippa Virdee, eds, *Refugees and the End of Empire: Imperial Collapse and Forced Migration during the Twentieth Century* (Basingstoke, 2011), pp. 51–78; Timothy Snyder, *Bloodlands: Europe between Hitler and Stalin* (New York, 2010).

15 Donald Bloxham, *The Final Solution: A Genocide* (Oxford, 2009).

16 Levene, 'Tragedy'.

17 Other general histories of genocide include, for example, Cathie Carmichael, *Genocide before the Holocaust* (London, 2009) and Ben Kiernan, *Blood and Soil: A World History of Genocide* (London, 2009). As the titles of these two books suggest, however, while they may focus upon the twentieth century, they recognize, like Levene, the long-term history of genocide.

18 Justin McCarthy, *Death and Exile: The Ethnic Cleansing of Ottoman Muslims, 1821–1922* (Princeton, 1995).

19 Introductory histories to these two episodes include: Vahakn Dadrian, *The History of the Armenian Genocide* (Oxford, 1995); and Renée Hirschon, ed., *Crossing the Aegean: An Appraisal of the 1923 Compulsory Population Exchange between Greece and Turkey* (Oxford, 2003).

20 Alan R. Kramer, *Dynamic of Destruction: Culture and Mass Killing in the First World War* (Oxford, 2007).

21 Akaby Nassibian, *Britain and the Armenian Question, 1915–1923* (London, 1984), pp. 33–66; Matthew Frank, *Expelling the Germans: British Opinion and Post-1945 Population Transfer in Context* (Oxford, 2007), pp. 20–5.

22 Inge Weber-Newth and Johannes-Dieter Steinert, *German Migrants in Post-War Britain: An Enemy Embrace* (London, 2006), pp. 23–31.

23 Matthew Stibbe, *British Civilian Internees in Germany: The Ruhleben Camp, 1914–18* (Manchester, 2008); Jean-Claude Farcy, *Les camps de concentration français de la Première Guerre Mondiale (1914–1920)* (Paris, 1995).

24 Frank, *Expelling*, p. 20.

25 Peter and Leni Gillman, *'Collar the Lot': How Britain Interned and Expelled its Wartime Refugees* (London, 1980).

26 Ulrich Herbert, *A History of Foreign Labour in Germany, 1880–1980: Seasonal Workers/Forced Laborers/Guest Workers* (Ann Arbor, MI, 1990), pp. 87–192.

27 See, for example, Gerhard Hirschfeld, ed., *The Policies of Genocide: Jews and Soviet Prisoners of War in Nazi Germany* (London, 1986).

28 Weber-Newth and Steinert, *German Migrants*, pp. 23–31, 51–70; Lucio Sponza, *Divided Loyalties: Italians in Britain during the Second World War* (Frankfurt, 2000), pp. 123–317.

29 See contributions to B. J. Gould and Liora Lazarus, eds, *Security and Human Rights* (Oxford, 2007), for an international perspective.

30 Catherine Scorer and Patricia Hewitt, *The Prevention of Terrorism Act: The Case for Repeal* (London, 1981); Arun Kundani, *The End of Tolerance: Racism in the 21st Century* (London, 2007), pp. 165–79.

Bibliography

Primary sources

Archival material

Bedford and Luton Archives and Record Centre, Bedford

WW1/AC, War Agricultural Executive Committee

British Library, London, Printed Books Section

Rudolf Rocker, 'Alexandra Palace Internment Camp in the First World War'

British Red Cross Archive, London

Verzeichnis der Kriegsgefangenenlager und Lazerette in Frankreich, Großbritannien, Italien, Russland und Japan, Abgeschlossen am 1. Mai

Bundesarchiv, Berlin-Lichterfelde

R67, Archiv des Ausschusses für deutsche Kriegsgefangene des Frankfurt Vereins vom Roten Kreuz/Archiv für Kriegsgefangenenforschung, Frankfurt am Main

R901, Auswärtiges Amt

Bundesarchiv, Militärarchiv, Freiburg

MSG3, Sammlung von Verbandsdruckgut

MSG200, Elsa-Brändström-Gedächtnisarchiv: Kriegsgefangenenwesen 1867 bis Gegenwart

RH18, Chef der Heeresarchive

RM3, Reichsmarineamt

Evangelisches Zentralarchiv, Berlin

1/788, Hilfsausschuss für Gefangenenseelsorge, 1914–21

1/789, Hilfsausschuss für Gefangenenseelsorge, 1914–21

45/37, Hilfsausschuss für Gefangenenseelsorge, 1914–21

51, Ökumenisches Archiv

Hull History Centre

LDBHR, Hohenrein Papers

Imperial War Museum, London
German Prisoners of War in Great Britain, 1914–18
The First World War Diaries of Richard Noschke
Vorschriften für Kriegsgefangene
82/35/1, Transcript of E. Wolff, 'My Adventures in the Great War 1914/18'

Landesarchiv, Baden-Württemberg, Haupstaatsarchiv Stuttgart
M1/8, Kriegsministerium, Medizinal-Abteilung
M77/1, Stellvertretendes Generalkommando XIII. AK / Generalkommando
M400/2, Heeresarchiv Stuttgart: Kriegsgefangenen-Archivstelle

London Metropolitan Archives
Acc/2805, Office of the Chief Rabbi

Manx National Heritage, Douglas
B115/43q, Camp IV, Knockaloe, I.O.M., Final Report and Statistical Record on the Internal Administration of the Prisoners of War Camp No. IV, 1915–1919
B115/70f, Government Circular No. 581
B115/xf, Internment Scrapbooks
MS06465, Douglas Camp Journal
MS08562, Letters from Max to Thekla Gottshalt, 1915–22
MS09310, Isle of Man Constabulary Archive
MS0937, Catering Records of Knockaloe Detention Camp
MS09379, Douglas Alien Detention Camp, School Papers Belonging to Bruno Kahn, 1914–18
MS09845, Government Office Papers
MS09954, Letters from Archibald Knox to Winifred Tuckfield and Mrs E. T. Holding
MS10417, Papers of James T. Baily
MS11034, Transcripted Correspondence of Edwin Mieg
MS11062, List of Camp Staff at Knockaloe and Douglas Alien Detention Camp
MS11425, George Kenner, 'Sketches of a German Interned Civilian Prisoner in England (1914–1919)'
MS12028, Diary of Karl Berthold Robert Schonwalder

National Archives, London
ADM1, ADM137, Admiralty Papers
AIR1, Ministry of Air Papers
CAB42, Cabinet Papers
FO383, FO608, Foreign Office Papers
HO45, Home Office Papers
MEPO2, Metropolitan Police Papers

NATS1, Ministry of National Service
WO32, WO162, WO394, War Office Papers

Staatsbibliothek zu Berlin
Kriegsgefangenenlager Lofthouse Park

Wellcome Library, London
RAM/488, three letters written by German prisoners of war to their families about their treatment and the torpedoing of the hospital ships taking them to England

Printed works

Official publications

An Agreement between the British and German Governments Concerning Combatant and Civilian Prisoners of War (London, 1917).

An Agreement between the British and German Governments Concerning Combatant Prisoners of War and Civilians (London, 1918).

Bericht des Reichskommisars zur Erörterung von Gewaltätigkeiten gegen deutsche Zivilpersonen in Feindesland über seine Tätigkeit bis zum. 1. Januar 1916 (Berlin, 1916).

Correspondence with the United States Ambassador Respecting the Transfer to Switzerland of British and German Wounded and Sick Combatant Prisoners of War (London, 1916).

Defence of the Realm Regulations Consolidated and Revised, January 31st 1917 (London, 1917).

Deutsche Kriegsgefangene im Feindesland: Amtliches Material, vol. 1, *England* (Berlin, 1919).

Disturbance at the Aliens Detention Camp at Douglas on Thursday November 19th, 1914: Inquiry by the Coroner of Inquests on Friday, November 20th, and Friday, November 27th, 1914 (Douglas, 1914).

Hague Convention, 1907: Hague Convention (IV) respecting the Customs of War on Land and its Annex: Regulations Concerning the Laws and Customs of War on Land, 18 October 1907, ANNEX TO THE CONVENTION: Regulations Respecting the Laws and Customs on Land # Section I: On Belligerents # Chapter II: Prisoners of War, www.icrc.org/ihl.nsf/full/195 (accessed 27 March 2012).

Hansard, Commons, Lords, fifth series, 1914–19.

Kriegsministerium für Heimkehrende Kriegsgefangene (Unterkunfts-Departement) und der Reichzentrale für Kriegs- und Ziviliegefangene, *Merkblatt für heimkehrende Gefangene* (Berlin, 1919).

Report of Committee Appointed to Consider Applications for Exemption from Compulsory Repatriation by Interned Enemy Aliens (London, 1919).

Reports of Visits of Inspection Made by Officials of the United States Embassy to Various Internment Camps in the United Kingdom (London, 1916).

Stenographische Berichte über die Verhandlungen des deutschen Reichstages, 1914–20.

War Office, *Statistics of the Military Effort of the British Empire during the Great War, 1914–1920* (London, 1922).

Newspapers

British

Atherstone Express
Cannock Chase Courier
Chiswick Times
Daily Express
Daily Mirror
Daily Sketch
Daily Telegraph
Dorchester Mail
Globe
Hornsey Journal
Isle of Man Examiner
Isle of Man Weekly Times
Londoner General-Anzeiger
Luton and Bedfordshire Advertiser
Manchester Guardian
Mona's Herald
Morning Post
Observer
Peel City Guardian and Chronicle
Scotsman
The Times
Wakefield Express
Weekly Dispatch

German

Berliner Tageblatt
Die Eiche
Frankfurter Zeitung
Hamburger Fremdenbatt
Hamburger Nachrichten
Kieler neueste Nachrichten
Kölnische Volkszeitung
Kölnische Zeitung

Mitteilungen der Bundesleitung der Reichsvereinigung ehemaligen Kriegsgefangen

Mitteilungen des Reichsbund zum Schutze der deutschen Kriegs- und Ziviligefangenen

Nachrichtenblatt der Reichszentralstelle für Kriegs- und Zivilgefangene

National Zeitung

Norddeutsche allgemeine Zeitung

Tägliche Rundschau

Vossische Zeitung

Internment camp

Deutsche Blätter (Dorchester)

Deutsche Zeitung (Brocton)

Die Hunnen (Knockaloe)

Lager-Bote (Wakefield)

Lager-Echo (Knockaloe)

Die Lager-Laterne (Douglas)

Lager-Zeitung (Knockaloe)

Quousque Tandem (Knockaloe)

Das Schleierlicht (Douglas)

Stobsiade (Stobs)

Unter Uns (Douglas)

Welt am Montag (Knockaloe)

Werden (Knockaloe)

Contemporary books, articles, memoirs and novels

Abteilung des Zweigvereins Gießen vom Roten Kreuz, *Zweiter Bericht des Bezirks-Ausschusses Giessen für Vermißte und Kriegsgefangene Deutsche* (Gießen, 1918).

Arbeitsbericht der Evangelische Blättervereinigung für Soldaten and Kriegsgefangene Deutsche, Bad Nassau (Lahn) über das Tätigkeitsjahr 1917/1918 (Bad Nassau, 1918).

Bauer, Franz, *1915–1918: Mein Erinnerungsbuch zum dreijährigen Bestehen des Camp Theaters Compound 2, Camp 1, am. 20. März 1918, zu gleich ein Überblick über die Tätigkeit aller anderen Bühnen des Lager 1* (Knockaloe, 1918).

Benedix, Hans Erich, *In England interniert* (Gotha, 1916).

Bezirk-Ausschuss Gießen für Vermißte und Kriegsgefangene Deutsche, Abteilung d. Zweigvereins Gießen von Roten Kreuz, *Erster Bericht* (Gießen, 1917).

Bogenstätter, L. and Zimmermann, H., *Die Welt hinter Stacheldraht: Eine Chronik des englischen Kriegsgefangenlagers Handforth bei Manchester* (Munich, 1921).

Brepohl, F. W., ed., *Briefe unserer Gefangenen* (Bad Nassau, 1916).
'British Treatment of Enemy Prisoners: Journalists Visit Manx Camps', *Manx Quarterly*, vol. 17 (October 1916), 73–4.
Brugger, Albrecht Hermann, *Meine Flucht aus dem Kriegsgefangenen-Lager Lofthouse-Park* (Berlin, 1937).
Caine, Hall, *The Woman of Knockaloe: A Parable* (London, 1923).
Cohen-Portheim, Paul, *Time Stood Still: My Internment in England* (London, 1931).
Dunbar-Kalckreuth, Frederick Lewis, *Die Männerinsel* (Leipzig, 1940).
Durnford, Hugh et al., *Tunnelling to Freedom and Other Escape Narratives from World War One* (1932; Mineola, NY, 2004).
Eckhardt, Albin and Maul, Kurt, *Was wir in englischer Kriegsgefangenschaft erlebten und erlitten* (Frankfurt, 1922).
Eckmann, Heinrich, *Gefangene in England* (Leipzig, 1936).
German Prisoners in Great Britain (London, n.d.).
Goehling, Oskar, ed., *Frei und daheim! Eine Handreichung für Heimkehrfeiern in Kirche und Gemeinde* (Berlin, 1919).
Gumprecht, Heinz, *Die magischen Wälder* (Gütersloh, 1933).
Handels-Schule, Camp I, Compound IV, *Bericht über das Winterhalbjahr 1916/1917 und Lehrplan für das Sommerhalbjahr 1917* (Knockaloe, 1917).
Hartmann, R., *Bilder aus dem Gefangenenlager Knockaloe in England* (Bad Nassau, 1918).
Hecklinger, Philipp, *Tagebuchblätter über Krieg und Kriegsgefangenschaft in Kamerun und England* (Stuttgart, 1916).
Hilfe für Kriegsgefangene Deutsche, Landesausschuss für Anhalt, *Arbeitsbericht 1914 bis 31. März 1917* (Dessau, 1917).
Hine, Sophie McDougall, *Bishop Bury: Late Bishop of North and Central Europe* (London, 1933).
Hopkins, Tighe, *Prisoners of War* (London, 1914).
'Karl Emil Markel', *Der Auslandsdeutsche*, vol. 15 (November–December 1932), 317–19.
Ketchum, John Davidson, *Ruhleben: A Prison Camp Society* (Toronto, 1965).
Knauft, Karl, *Die schwarze Stadt: Knockaloe vom Morgengrauen bis Mitternacht* (Knockaloe, 1918).
Köhler, J., ed., *Karte von Grossbritannien, Italien u. den überseeischen Ländern, in denen Kriegs- und Zivilgefangene befinden* (Hamburg, 1917).
Kröpke, Wilhelm, *Meine Flucht aus englischer Kriegsgefangenschaft 1916: Von Afrika über England nach Deutschland zur Flandern-Front* (Flensburg, 1937).
Landesausschuss für Anhalt, *Hilfe für kriegsgefangene Deutsche: Arbeitsbericht 1914 bis 31. März 1917* (Dessau, 1917).

Lawrence, D. H., *Kangaroo* (1923; reprint Harmondsworth, 1985).
—— *Selected Letters* (Harmondsworth, 1978).
MacDonagh, Michael, *In London during the Great War* (London, 1935).
Machner, J., *Gefangen in England: Erlebnisse and Beobachtungen* (Hildesheim, 1920).
Machray, Robert, 'Great Britain's Humane Treatment of German Prisoners of War', in H. W. Wilson and J. A. Hammerton, eds, *The Great War*, vol. 12 (London, 1919), pp. 401–14.
Manchester Guardian History of the War, vol. 4, *1915–16* (Manchester, 1916).
Maue, J., *In Feindes Land: Achtzehn Monate in englischer Kriegsgefangenschaft in Indien und England* (Stuttgart, 1918).
Meyn, Ludwig and Mörlins, Wolfgang J., eds, *Knockaloe Aliens Detention Camp, 1914–1917: Drei Jahre Schul-Arbeit* (Knockaloe, 1917).
Norden, Heinrich, *In englischer Gefangenschaft* (Kassel, 1915).
Plüschow, Gunther, *My Escape from Donington Hall* (London, 1922).
Pörzgen, Hermann, *Theater ohne Frau: Das Bühnenleben der kriegsgefangenen Deutschen, 1914–1920* (Königsberg, 1920).
Pult, D. W., *Siebzehn Monate in englischer Kriegsgefangenschaft* (Siegen, 1917).
Rocker, Rudolf, *The London Years* (1956; Nottingham, 2005).
Roxburgh, Ronald F., *The Prisoners of War Information Bureau* (London, 1915).
Sachse, Fritz and Cossmann, Paul Nikolaus, *Kriegsgefangen in Skipton: Leben und Geschichte deutscher Kriegsgefangenen in einem englischen Lager* (Munich, 1920).
Scheidt, Karl von and Meyer, Fritz, *Vier Jahre Leben und Leiden der Auslandsdeutschen in den Gefangenenlagern Englands* (Hagen, 1919).
Scheller, Walter, *Als die Seele starb: 1914–1918: Das Kriegserlebnis eines Unkriegerischen* (Berlin, 1931).
Schimming, Otto, *13 Monate hinter dem Stacheldraht: Alexandra Palace, Knockaloe, Isle of Man, Stratford* (Stuttgart, 1919).
Schmidt-Reder, Bruno, *In England kriegsgefangen! Meine Erlebninsse in dem Gefangenenlager Dorchester* (Berlin, 1915).
Siegmund-Schultze, F., 'Die Gefangenenseelsorge in England', *Die Eiche*, vol. 6 (1918), 315–49.
Simonis, Henry S., *Zum alten jüdischen Zivilrecht* (Berlin, 1922).
Spindler, Carl, *The Phantom Ship* (London, 1931).
Stoffa, Pál, *Round the World to Freedom* (London, 1933).
Textil-Fach-Schule, Zivilgefangenen Lager Knockaloe, Insel Man, England, Lager I, Compound 4, *Jahres-Bericht, 1917–1918* (Knockaloe, 1918).
The Times History of the War, vol. 6 (London, 1916).

Thomas, Anna Braithwaite, *St Stephen's House: Friends Emergency Work in England, 1914 to 1920* (London, 1920).
Turnverein Knockaloe Compound 6, Gefangenenlager Knockaloe Insel Man, Camp I, *Turnbericht über das Jahr 1916* (Knockaloe, 1916).
Vereinigung Wissenschaftlicher Veleger, *Deutsche Kriegsgefangene in Feindesland* (Leipzig, 1919).
Verzeichnis der Knockaloe-Bücherei (Hamburg, 1918).
Vielhauer, Adolf, *Das englische Konzentrationslager bei Peel (Insel Man)* (Bad Nassau, 1917).
Vischer, A. L, *Barbed Wire Disease: A Psychological Study of the Prisoner of War* (London, 1919).
Vöhringer, Gotthilf, *Meine Erlebnisse während des Krieges in Kamerun und in englischer Kriegsgefangenschaft* (Hamburg, 1915).
Wagener, Georg Wilhelm, *Meine Gefangenschaft in Südafrika und England vom 15. Sept. 1914 bis 18. Juni 1916* (Brunswick, 1917).
Wohlenberg, Christoph, *Kriegsgefangenen in England! Dramatische Beschreibung des 22. Juni 1919* (Bordessholm, 1919).
Zweigverein Worms E.V. d. Hessischen Landesvereins vom 'Roten Kreuz'. Bezirksausschuß f. Vermißte u. Kriegsgefangene Deutsche, *Drei Jahre Vermissten-Ermittlung und Gefangenenfürsorge* (Worms, 1917).

Films

Lee, Roland V., director, *Barbed Wire* (1927).
Powell, Michael and Pressburger, Emeric, directors, *The Life and Death of Colonel Blimp* (1943).

Secondary sources

Published works

Abell, Francis, *Prisoners of War in Britain, 1756 to 1815: A Record of their Lives, their Romance and their Sufferings* (Oxford, 1914).
Adams, R. J. Q., *The Conscription Controversy in Great Britain, 1900–18* (Basingstoke, 1987).
Allen, Vivian, 'Caine, Sir (Thomas Henry) Hall (1853–1931)', *Oxford Dictionary of National Biography*, online edn, www.oxforddnb.com/view/article/32237 (accessed 5 October 2010).
Aly, Götz and Heim, Susanne, *Architects of Annihilation: Auschwitz and the Logic of Destruction* (London, 2003).
Anglo-German Family History Society, *An Insight into Civilian Internment in Britain during WWI* (Maidenhead, 1998).
Applegate, Celia and Potter, Pamela, 'Germans as the "People of Music": Genealogy of an Identity", in Celia Applegate and Pamela Potter, eds, *Music and German National Identity* (London, 2002), pp. 1–35.
—— eds, *Music and German National Identity* (London, 2002).

Audoin-Rouzeau, Stéphane and Becker, Annette, *14–18: Understanding the Great War* (New York, 2002).

Baily, Leslie, *Craftsman and Quaker: The Story of James T. Baily, 1876–1957* (London, 1959).

Barker, A. J., *Behind Barbed Wire* (London, 1974).

Bauman, Zygmunt, *Modernity and the Holocaust* (Cambridge, 1989).

Beckett, Ian F. W. and Simpson, Keith, eds, *A Nation at Arms: A Social Study of the British Army in the First World War* (Manchester, 1985).

Bernard, Roy, *My German Family in England* (Maidenhead, 1993).

Bessel, Richard, *Germany after the First World War* (Oxford, 1993).

Bird, J. C., *Control of Enemy Alien Civilians in Great Britain, 1914–1918* (London, 1986).

Black, Jeremy, ed., *The Second World War*, 7 vols (Aldershot, 2007).

Blackbourn, David and Evans, Richard J., eds, *The German Bourgeoisie: Essays on the Social History of the German Middle Classes from the Late Eighteenth to the Early Twentieth Century* (London, 1991).

Blaschke, Olaf and Kuhlermann, Frank-Michael, eds, *Religion im Kaiserreich: Milieus – Mentalitäten – Krisen* (Gütersloh, 1996).

Bloxham, Donald, *The Final Solution: A Genocide* (Oxford, 2009).

—— *The Great Game of Genocide: Imperialism, Nationalism and the Destruction of the Ottoman Armenians* (Oxford, 2005).

Boghardt, Thomas, *Spies of the Kaiser: German Covert Operations in Great Britain during the First World War* (Basingstoke, 2004).

Bourne, John, *Britain and the Great War, 1914–18* (London, 1989).

Braber, Ben, 'Within Our Gates: A New Perspective on Germans in Glasgow during the First World War', *Journal of Scottish Historical Studies*, vol. 29 (2009), 87–105.

Bretagne 14–18, vol. 3 (2002).

Brinson, Charmian, '"Loyal to the Reich": National Socialists and Others in the Rushen Women's Internment Camp', in Richard Dove, ed., *'Totally un-English'? Britain's Internment of 'Enemy Aliens' in Two World Wars* (Amsterdam, 2005), pp. 101–19.

Brown, Malcolm, *Spitfire Summer: When Britain Stood Alone* (London, 2000).

Bryder, Linda, 'The First World War: Healthy or Hungry', *History Workshop*, vol. 24 (1987), 141–57.

Burgdorf, Heinrich et al., eds, *Zwangsarbeiterinnen und Kriegsgefangene in Blomberg (1939–1945)* (Bielefeld, 1996).

Burnett, John, *Plenty and Want: A Social History of Food in England from 1815 to the Present* (London, 1989).

Burrell, Kathy, *Moving Lives: Narratives of Nation and Migration among Europeans in Post-War Britain* (Aldershot, 2006).

Calder, Angus, *The Myth of the Blitz* (London, 1991).

Carmichael, Cathie, *Genocide before the Holocaust* (London, 2009).

Cesarani, David, 'The Anti-Jewish Career of Sir William Joynson-Hicks, Cabinet Minister', *Journal of Contemporary History*, vol. 24 (1989), 461–82.

Cesarani, David and Kushner, Tony, eds, *The Internment of Aliens in Twentieth Century Britain* (London, 1993).

Chapman, James, 'The Life and Death of Colonel Blimp (1943) Reconsidered', *Historical Journal of Film, Radio and Television*, vol. 15 (1995), 19–36.

Chappell, Connery, *Island of Barbed Wire: Internment on the Isle of Man in World War Two* (London, 1984).

Chickering, Roger, *Imperial Germany and the Great War, 1914–1918*, 2nd edn (Cambridge, 2007).

Cole, G. D. H. and Postgate, Raymond, *The Common People* (London, 1938).

Connelly, Mark, *Christmas: A Social History* (London, 1999).

Creswell, Yvonne, 'Behind the Wire: The Material Culture of Civilian Internment on the Isle of Man in the First World War', in Richard Dove, ed.,*'Totally un-English'? Britain's Internment of 'Enemy Aliens' in Two World Wars* (Amsterdam, 2005), pp. 45–61.

—— ed., *Living with the Wire: Civilian Internment in the Isle of Man during the Two World Wars* (Douglas, 1984).

Dadrian, Vahakn, *The History of the Armenian Genocide* (Oxford, 1995).

Daniel, Ute, *The War from Within: German Working-Class Women in the First World War* (Oxford, 1997).

Davis, Gerald H., 'Prisoners of War in Twentieth Century Economies', *Journal of Contemporary History*, vol. 12 (1977), 623–34.

DeGroot, Gerard J., *Blighty: British Society in the Era of the First World War* (London, 1996).

Dove, Richard, ed.,*'Totally un-English'? Britain's Internment of 'Enemy Aliens' in Two World Wars* (Amsterdam, 2005).

Draper, Laurence and Pamela, *The Raasay Iron Mine: Where Enemies Became Friends* (1990; fifth printing Dingwall, 2007).

Draskau, Jennifer Kewley, 'Prisoners in Petticoats: Drag Performance and its Effects in Great War Internment Camps on the Isle of Man', *Proceedings of the Isle of Man Natural History and Antiquarian Society*, vol. 12 (April 2007–March 2009), 187–204.

—— 'Relocating the Heimat: Great War Internment Literature from the Isle of Man', *German Studies Review*, vol. 32 (2009), 83–106.

—— 'Written between the Lines on Devil's Island: The "Stobsiade"

Anthology 1917: Great War Internment Literature from the Isle of Man', in Richard Pine and Eve Patten, eds, *Literatures of War* (Newcastle-upon-Tyne, 2008), pp. 104–17.

Drower, Jill, *Good Clean Fun: The Story of Britain's First Holiday Camp* (London, 1982).

Ellis, John, *Eye-Deep in Hell: The Western Front, 1914–1918* (London, 2002).

Evans, Richard J., *In Hitler's Shadow: West German Historians and the Attempt to Escape from the Nazi Past* (London, 1989).

Farcy, Jean-Claude, *Les camps de concentration français de la Première Guerre Mondiale (1914–1920)* (Paris, 1995).

Feltman, Brian K., 'Tolerance as a Crime? The British Treatment of German Prisoners of War on the Western Front, 1914–1918', *War in History*, vol. 17 (2010), 435–58.

Ferguson, Niall, *The Pity of War* (London, 1998).

—— 'Prisoner Taking and Prisoner Killing in the Age of Total War: Towards a Political Economy of Military Defeat', *War in History*, vol. 11 (2004), 148–92.

Field, Charles, *Internment Mail on the Isle of Man* (Sutton Coldfield, 1989).

Fischer, Gerhard, *Enemy Aliens: Internment and the Homefront Experience in Australia, 1914–1920* (St Lucia, 1989).

Fischer, Gerhard, 'Fighting the War at Home: The Campaign against Enemy Aliens in Australia during the First World War', in Panikos Panayi, ed., *Minorities in Wartime: National and Racial Groupings in Europe, North America and Australia during the Two World Wars* (Oxford, 1993), pp. 263–86.

Foucault, Michel, *Discipline and Punish: The Birth of the Prison* (London, 1977).

Francis, Paul, *Isle of Man Twentieth Century Military Archaeology*, part 1, *Island Defence* (Douglas, 1986).

Frank, Matthew, *Expelling the Germans: British Opinion and Post-1945 Population Transfer in Context* (Oxford, 2007).

Freitag, Gabriele, *Zwangsarbeiter im Lipper Land: Der Einsatz von Arbeitskräften in der Landwirtschaft Lippes, 1939–1945* (Bochum, 1996).

Friedrich, Jörg, *The Fire: The Bombing of Germany, 1940–1945* (New York, 2006).

Fulbrook, Mary, *German National Identity after the Holocaust* (Cambridge, 1999).

Fussell, Paul, *The Great War and Modern Memory* (Oxford, 1975).

Fyson, Robert, 'The Douglas Camp Shootings of 1914', *Proceedings of the Isle of Man Natural History and Antiquarian Society*, vol. 11 (April 1997–March 1999), 115–26.

Gainer, Bernard, *The Alien Invasion: The Origins of the Aliens Act of 1905* (London, 1972).

Gillman, Peter and Leni, *'Collar the Lot': How Britain Interned and Expelled its Wartime Refugees* (London, 1980).

Goeschel, Christian, *Suicide in Nazi Germany* (Oxford, 2009).

Gordon, Hampden, *The War Office* (London, 1935).

Gould, B. J. and Lazarus, Liora, eds, *Security and Human Rights* (Oxford, 2007).

Grayling, A. C., *Among the Dead Cities: Was the Allied Bombing of Civilians in WWII a Necessity or a Crime?* (London, 2006).

Gregory, Adrian, *The Last Great War: British Society and the First World War* (Cambridge, 2009).

Gullace, Nicoletta F., 'Friends, Aliens and Enemies: Fictive Communities and the Lusitania Riots of 1915', *Journal of Social History*, vol. 39 (2005), 345–67.

Hammond, J. L. and L. B., *The Skilled Labourer, 1760–1832* (London, 1919).

Hansen, Jutta Raab, 'Die Bedeutung der Musik für 26.000 internierte Zivilisten während des Ersten Weltkrieges auf der Isle of Man', in Richard Dove, ed.,*'Totally un-English'? Britain's Internment of 'Enemy Aliens' in Two World Wars* (Amsterdam, 2005), pp. 63–81.

Harris, Janet, *Alexandra Palace: A Hidden History* (Stroud, 2005).

Haste, Cate, *Keep the Home Fires Burning* (London, 1977).

Havers, R. P. W., *Reassessing the Japanese Prisoner of War Experience* (London, 2003).

Held, Renate, *Kriegsgefangenschaft in Großbritannien: Deutsche Soldaten des Zweiten Weltkrieges in britischem Gewarhsam* (Munich, 2008).

Herbert, Ulrich, *A History of Foreign Labour in Germany, 1880–1980: Seasonal Workers/Forced Laborers/Guest Workers* (Ann Arbor, MI, 1990).

—— *Hitler's Foreign Workers: Enforced Labour in Germany under the Third Reich* (Cambridge, 1997).

Heusel, F. E., *Handforth through the Ages* (Chester, 1982).

Hilger, Andreas, *Deutsche Kriegsgefangene in der Sowjetunion, 1941–1956: Kriegsgefangenenpolitik, Lageralltag und Erinnerung* (Essen, 2000).

Hinz, Uta, *Gefangen im Grossen Krieg: Kriegsgefangenschaft in Deutschland, 1914–1921* (Essen, 2006).

Hirschfeld, Gerhard, ed., *Exile in Great Britain: Refugees from Hitler's Germany* (Leamington Spa, 1984).

—— *The Policies of Genocide: Jews and Soviet Prisoners of War in Nazi Germany* (London, 1986).

Hirschon, Renée, ed., *Crossing the Aegean: An Appraisal of the 1923*

Compulsory Population Exchange between Greece and Turkey (Oxford, 2003).

Hobsbawm, Eric, *Age of Extremes: A Short History of the Twentieth Century* (London, 1994).

Holmes, Colin, 'The Myth of Fairness: Racial Violence in Britain, 1911–19', *History Today*, vol. 35 (October 1985), 41–5.

Homze, Edward L., *Foreign Labour in Nazi Germany* (Princeton, NJ, 1967).

Horn, Pamela, *Rural Life in England in the First World War* (Dublin, 1984).

Horne, John and Kramer, Alan, *German Atrocities, 1914: A History of Denial* (London, 2001).

Horne, Julie M., 'The German Connection: The Stobs Camp Newspaper, 1916–1919', *Transactions of the Hawick Archaeological Society* (1988), 26–32.

Hutchinson, John F., *Champions of Charity: War and the Rise of the Red Cross* (Oxford, 1996).

Ibs, Henning, *Hermann J. Held (1890–1963): Ein Kieler Gelehrtenleben in den Fängen der Zeitläufe* (Frankfurt, 2000).

Issmer, Volker, *Niederländer in verdammten Land: Zeugnisse der Zwangsarbeit von Niederländern im Raum Osnabrück während des Zweiten Weltkrieges* (Osnabrück, 1998).

Johnson, Franklyn Arthur, *Defence by Committee: The British Committee of Imperial Defence, 1885–1959* (London, 1960).

Jones, Heather, 'International or Transnational? Humanitarian Action during the First World War', *European Review of History*, vol. 16 (2009), 697–713.

—— *Violence against Prisoners of War in the First World War: Britain, France and Germany, 1914–1920* (Cambridge, 2011).

Kaminsky, Annette, ed., *Heimkehr, 1948* (Munich, 1998).

Kelly, Pat, *Hedge of Thorns: Knockaloe Camp, 1915–19* (Douglas, 1993).

Kennedy, A. L., *The Life and Death of Colonel Blimp* (London, 1997).

Kennedy, Paul, *The Rise and Fall of British Naval Mastery* (London, 1976).

Kennedy, Thomas C., *British Quakerism, 1860–1920: The Transformation of a Religious Community* (Oxford, 2001).

Kiernan, Ben, *Blood and Soil: A World History of Genocide* (London, 2009).

King, Alex, *Memorials of the Great War in Britain: The Symbolism and Politics of Remembrance* (Oxford, 1998).

Koch, Erich, *Deemed Suspect: A Wartime Blunder* (Toronto, 1980).

Kochan, Miriam, *Britain's Internees in the Second World War* (London, 1983).

Korr, Charles and Close, Marvin, *More than Just a Game: Football v Apartheid* (London, 2008).

Kramer, Alan R., *Dynamic of Destruction: Culture and Mass Killing in the First World War* (Oxford, 2007).

—— 'Prisoners in the First World War', in Sibylle Scheipers, ed., *Prisoners in War* (Oxford, 2000), pp. 75–90.

Krammer, Arnold, *Prisoners of War: A Reference Handbook* (London, 2008).

Kundani, Arun, *The End of Tolerance: Racism in the 21st Century* (London, 2007).

Kushner, Tony and Lunn, Kenneth, 'Introduction', in Tony Kushner and Kenneth Lunn, eds, *The Politics of Marginality: Race, the Radical Right and Minorities in Twentieth Century Britain* (London, 1990).

Lafitte, François, *The Internment of Aliens* (1940; London, 1988).

Leese, Peter, *Shell Shock: Traumatic Neuroses and the British Soldier in the First World War* (Basingstoke, 2002).

Lehmann, Albrecht, *Gefangenschaft und Heimkehr: Deutsche Kriegsgefangene in der Sowjetunion* (Munich, 1986).

Levene, Mark, 'The Tragedy of the Rimlands: Nation-State Formation and the Destruction of Imperial Peoples, 1912–1948', in Panikos Panayi and Pippa Virdee, eds, *Refugees and the End of Empire: Imperial Collapse and Forced Migration during the Twentieth Century* (Basingstoke, 2011), pp. 51–78.

London, Louise, *Whitehall and the Jews, 1933–1948: British Immigration Policy and the Holocaust* (Cambridge, 2000).

Lüdtke, Alf, *Eigen-Sinn: Fabrikalltag, Arbeitererfahrungen und Politik vom Kaiserreich bis in den Faschismus* (Hamburg, 1993).

—— ed., *The History of Everyday Life: Reconstructing Historical Experiences and Ways of Life* (Princeton, NJ, 1995).

MacArthur, Brian, *Surviving the Sword: Prisoners of the Japanese 1942–45* (London, 2005).

McCarthy, Justin, *Death and Exile: The Ethnic Cleansing of Ottoman Muslims, 1821–1922* (Princeton, 1995).

Macdonald, Kevin, *Emeric Pressburger: The Life and Death of a Screenwriter* (London, 1994).

Mackenzie, S. P., *The Colditz Myth: British and Commonwealth Prisoners of War in Nazi Germany* (Oxford, 2004).

Manz, Stefan, 'Civilian Internment in Scotland during the First World War', in Richard Dove, ed.,*'Totally un-English'? Britain's Internment of 'Enemy Aliens' in Two World Wars* (Amsterdam, 2005), pp. 83–97.

—— *Migranten und Internierte: Deutsche in Glasgow, 1864–1918* (Stuttgart, 2003).

—— 'New Evidence on Stobs Internment Camp', *Transactions of the Hawick Archaeological Society* (2002), 59–69.

Marder, Arthur J., *From Dreadnought to Scapa Flow: The Royal Navy in the Fisher Era, 1904–1919*, 5 vol (Oxford, 1961–70).

Mark, Graham, *Prisoners of War in British Hands during WW1: A Study of their History, the Camps and their Mails* (Exeter, 2007).

Marwick, Arthur, *The Deluge: British Society and the First World War* (London, 1965).

—— *War and Social Change in the Twentieth Century* (1965; reprint London, 1986).

Mason, Tony and Riedi, Eliza, *Sport and the Military: The British Armed Forces, 1880–1960* (Cambridge, 2010).

Messinger, Gary S., *British Propaganda and the State in the First World War* (Manchester, 1992).

Mielke, Heinz-Peter, *Kriegsgefangenen Arbeiten aus zwei Jahrhunderten* (Viersen, 1987).

Modood, Tariq, *Multicultural Politics: Racism, Ethnicity and Muslims in Britain* (Edinburgh, 2000).

Moeller, Robert G., *War Stories: The Search for a Usable Past in the Federal Republic of Germany* (London, 2001).

Montgomery, J. K., *The Maintenance of the Agricultural Labour Supply in England and Wales during the War* (Rome, 1922).

Moss, Richard and Illingworth, Iris, *Pattishall: A Parish Patchwork* (Astcote, 2000).

Mosse, George L., *Fallen Soldiers: Reshaping the Memory of the World Wars* (Oxford, 1990).

Mosse, W. E., et al., eds, *Second Chance: Two Centuries of German-Speaking Jews in the United Kingdom* (Tübingen, 1991).

Murphy, Robert, *British Cinema and the Second World War* (London, 2000).

Murray, Judith, 'Stobs Camp, 1903–1959', *Transactions of the Hawick Archaeological Society* (1988), 12–25.

Naisk, T. E., 'The German Prisoners of War Camp at Jersey during the Great War, 1914–1918', *Bulletin of the Société Jersiaise*, vol. 15 (1955), 269–80.

Nassibian, Akaby, *Britain and the Armenian Question, 1915–1923* (London, 1984).

Newton, Gerald,'Germans in Sheffield, 1817–1918', *German Life and Letters*, vol. 46 (1993), 82–101.

——'Wie lange noch? Germans at Knockaloe, 1914–18', in Gerald Newton, ed., *Mutual Exchanges: Sheffield Münster Colloquium II* (Frankfurt, 1999), pp. 103–16.

Niven, Bill and Paver, Chloe, eds, *Memorialization in Germany since 1945* (Basingstoke, 2010).

Oeter, Stefan, 'Die Enwicklung des Kriegsgefangenenrechtes: Die Sichtweise eines Völkerrechtes', in Rüdiger Overmans, ed., *In der Hand des Feindes: Kriegesgefangenschaft von der Antike bis zum Zweiten Weltkrieg* (Cologne, 1999), pp. 41–59.

Oltmer, Jochen, 'Einführung: Funktionen und Erfahrungen von Kriegsgefangenschaft in Europa des Ersten Weltkrieges', in Jochen Oltmer, ed., *Kriegsgefangene im Europa des Ersten Weltkrieges* (Paderborn, 2005), pp. 11–23.

—— 'Unentherbliche Arbeitskräfte: Kriegsgefangene in Deutschland 1914–1918', in Jochen Oltmer, ed., *Kriegsgefangene im Europa des Ersten Weltkrieges* (Paderborn, 2005), pp. 67–96.

—— ed., *Kriegsgefangene im Europa des Ersten Weltkrieges* (Paderborn, 2005).

Overmans, Rüdiger, '"In der Hand des Feindes": Geschichtsschreibung zur Kriegsgefangenschaft von der Antike bis sum Zweiten Weltkrieg', in Rüdiger Overmans, ed., *In der Hand des Feindes: Krigesgefangenschaft von der Antike bis zum zweiten Weltkrieg* (Cologne, 1999), pp. 1–39.

—— ed., *In der Hand des Feindes: Krigesgefangenschaft von der Antike bis zum zweiten Weltkrieg* (Cologne, 1999).

Panayi, Panikos, 'Anti-Immigrant Riots in Nineteenth and Twentieth Century Britain', in Panikos Panayi, ed., *Racial Violence in Britain in the Nineteenth and Twentieth Centuries* (London, 1996), pp. 1–25.

—— *The Enemy in Our Midst: Germans in Britain during the First World War* (Oxford, 1991).

—— 'German Business Interests in Britain during the First World War', *Business History*, vol. 32 (1990), 244–58.

—— *German Immigrants in Britain during the Nineteenth Century, 1815–1914* (Oxford, 1995).

—— 'The German Poor and Working Classes in Victorian and Edwardian London', in Geoffrey Alderman and Colin Holmes, eds, *Outsiders and Outcasts* (London, 1993), pp. 53–79.

—— '"The Hidden Hand": British Myths about German Control of Britain During the First World War', *Immigrants and Minorities*, vol. 7 (1988), 253–72.

—— 'A Marginalized Subject? The Historiography of Enemy Alien Internment in Britain', in Richard Dove, ed.,*'Totally un-English'? Britain's Internment of 'Enemy Aliens' in Two World Wars* (Amsterdam, 2005), pp. 17–26.

—— 'Sausages, Waiters and Bakers: German Migrants and Culinary Transfer to Britain, c1850–1914', in Stefan Manz, Margrit Schulte

Beerbühl and John R. Davis, eds, *Migration and Transfer from Germany to Britain, 1660–1914* (Munich, 2007), pp. 147–59.

—— ed., *Violence in Britain in the Nineteenth and Twentieth Centuries* (London, 1996).

—— and Virdee, Pippa, eds, *Refugees and the End of Empire: Imperial Collapse and Forced Migration during the Twentieth Century* (Basingstoke, 2011).

Pelt, Robert Jan von and Dwork, Deborah, *Auschwitz: 1270 to the Present* (London, 1996).

Perry, Joe, *Christmas in Germany: A Cultural History* (Chapel Hill, NC, 2010).

Pfahlmann, Hans, *Fremdarbeiter und Kriegsgefangene in der deutschen Kriegswirtschaft, 1939–1945* (Darmstadt 1968).

Phillips, Howard and Killingray, David, 'Introduction', in Howard Phillips and David Killingray, eds, *The Spanish Influenza Pandemic of 1918–19: New Perspectives* (London, 2003), pp. 1–25.

—— —— eds, *The Spanish Influenza Pandemic of 1918–19: New Perspectives* (London, 2003).

Pöppinghege, Rainer, *Im Lager unbesiegt: Deutsche, englische und französische Kriegsgefangenen-Zeitungen im Ersten Weltkrieg* (Essen, 2006).

—— '"Kriegsteilnehmer zweiter Klasse": Die Reichsvereinigung ehemalige Kriegsgefangener 1919–1933', *Militärgeschichtliche Zeitschrift*, vol. 64 (2005), 391–423.

Proctor, Tammy, *Civilians in a World at War, 1914–1918* (London, 2010).

—— *Female Intelligence: Women and Espionage in the First World War* (London, 2003).

Rachamimov, Alon, 'The Disruptive Comforts of Drag: (Trans)Gender Performances among Prisoners of War in Russia, 1914–1920', *American Historical Review*, vol. 111 (2006), 362–82.

—— *POWs and the Great War: Captivity on the Eastern Front* (Oxford, 2002).

Ramsden, John, *Don't Mention the War: The British and the Germans since 1890* (London, 2006).

Riesenberger, Dieter, *Für Humanität in Krieg und Frieden: Der Internationale Rote Kreuz, 1863–1977* (Göttingen, 1992).

Robinson, Daniel N., *An Intellectual History of Psychology*, 3rd edn (London, 1995).

Rock, David and Wolff, Stefan, eds, *Going Home to Germany? The Integration of Ethnic Germans from Central and Eastern Europe in the Federal Republic* (Oxford, 2002).

Roper, Michael, *The Secret Battle: Emotional Survival and the Great War* (Manchester, 2009).

Rowley, Geoffrey, *The Book of Skipton* (Buckingham, 1983).

Ruge, Friedrich, *Scapa Flow 1919: The End of the German Fleet* (London, 1973).

Sargeaunt, B. E., *The Isle of Man and the Great War* (Douglas, 1922).

Saunders, Michael and Taylor, Philip M., *British Propaganda during the First World War, 1914–18* (London, 1982).

Scheidl, Franz, *Die Kriegsgefangenschaft von den ältesten Zeiten bis zur Gegenwart: Eine völkerrechtliche Monographie* (Berlin, 1943).

Scheipers, Sibylle, 'Introduction: Prisoners in War', in Sibylle Scheipers, ed., *Prisoners in War* (Oxford, 2000), pp. 1–20.

——, ed. *Prisoners in War* (Oxford, 2000).

Schröder, Joachim, *Die U-Boote des Kaisers: Die Geschichte des deutschen U-Boot-Krieges gegen Großbritannien im Ersten Weltkrieg* (Bonn, 2003).

Schwartz, Maxine, *We Built Up Our Lives: Education and Community among Jewish Refugees Interned by Britain in World War II* (London, 2001).

Scorer, Catherine and Hewitt, Patricia, *The Prevention of Terrorism Act: The Case for Repeal* (London, 1981).

Scott, Peter, 'Captive Labour: The German Companies of the BEF, 1916–1920', *Army Quarterly Defence Journal*, vol. 110 (1980), 319–38.

Seeber, Eva, *Zwangsarbeiter in der faschistischen Kriegswirtschaft* (Berlin, 1964).

Seipp, Adam R., *The Ordeal of Peace: Demobilization and the Urban Experience in Britain and Germany, 1917–1921* (Farnham, 2009).

Skirne, Peter, 'Hall Caine's *The Woman of Knockaloe*: An Anglo-German War Novel from the Isle of Man', in Susanne Stark, ed., *The Novel in Anglo-German Context: Cultural Cross-Currents and Affinities* (Amsterdam, 2000), pp. 263–76.

Smith, Leslie, *The German Prisoner of War Camp at Leigh, 1914–1919* (Manchester, 1986).

Snyder, Timothy, *Bloodlands: Europe between Hitler and Stalin* (New York, 2010).

Soldern, Adelheid von, 'Im Hause zu Hause: Wöhnen im Spannungsfeld von Gelegenheiten und Aneigungen', in Jürgen Reulecke, ed., *Geschichte des Wohnens*, vol. 3, *1800–1918: Das bürgerliche Zeitalter* (Stuttgart, 1997), pp. 145–332.

Solomos, John, *Race and Racism in Britain* (Basingstoke, 1993).

Southerton, Peter, *Reading Gaol* (Stroud, 2003).

Sparrow, Elizabeth, 'The Alien Office, 1792–1806', *Historical Journal*, vol. 33 (1990), 361–84.

Speed, Richard B. III, *Prisoners, Diplomats, and the Great War: A Study in the Diplomacy of Captivity* (London, 1990).

Spoerer, Mark, *Zwangsarbeit unter dem Hankenkreuz: Ausländische Zivilarbeiter, Kriegsgefangene und Häftlinge im Deutschen Reich und im besetzten Europa* (Stuttgart, 2000).

Sponza, Lucio, 'The Anti-Italian Riots, June 1940', in Panikos Panayi, ed., *Racial Violence in Britain in the Nineteenth and Twentieth Centuries* (London, 1996), pp. 131–49.

—— *Divided Loyalties: Italians in Britain during the Second World War* (Frankfurt, 2000).

Steinbach, Daniel Rouven, 'Defending the *Heimat*: The Germans in South-West Africa and East Africa during the First World War', in Heather Jones, Jennifer O'Brien and Christoph Schmidt-Supprian, eds, *Untold War: New Perspectives in First World War Studies* (Leiden, 2008), pp. 179–208.

Stent, Ronald, *A Bespattered Page? The Internment of His Majesty's 'Most Loyal Enemy Aliens'* (London, 1980).

Stephenson, Jill, *Hitler's Home Front: Württemberg under the Nazis* (London, 2006).

Stevenson, John, *British Society, 1914–45* (London, 1984).

Stibbe, Matthew, *British Civilian Internees in Germany: The Ruhleben Camp, 1914–18* (Manchester, 2008).

—— 'Elisabeth Rotten and the "Auskunfts- und Hilfstelle für Deutsche im Ausland und Ausländer in Deutschland"', in Alison S. Fall and Ingrid Sharp, eds, *The Women's Movement in Wartime: International Perspectives* (Basingstoke, 2007), pp. 194–210.

—— *German Anglophobia and the Great War, 1914–1918* (Cambridge, 2001).

—— 'The Internment of Civilians by Belligerent States during the First World War and the Response of the International Committee of the Red Cross', *Journal of Contemporary History*, vol. 41 (2006), 5–19.

—— 'Introduction: Captivity, Forced Labour and Forced Migration during the First World War', *Immigrants and Minorities*, vol. 26 (2008), 1–18.

—— 'A Question of Retaliation? The Internment of British Civilians in Germany in November 1914', *Immigrants and Minorities*, vol. 23 (2005), 1–29.

—— ed., *Captivity, Forced Labour and Forced Migration in Europe during the First World War* (London, 2009).

Strachan, Hew, *The First World War*, vol. 1, *To Arms* (Oxford, 2001).

Sullivan, Matthew Barry, *Thresholds of Peace: Four Hundred Thousand German Prisoners and the People of Britain, 1944–1948* (London, 1979).

Sweetman, John, *Bomber Crew: Taking on the Reich* (London, 2005).

Taylor, A. J. P., *English History 1914–45* (1965; reprint Harmondsworth, 1985).

Teuteberg, Hans-Jürgen, 'Food Provisioning on the German Home Front, 1914–1918', in Ina Zweiniger-Bargielowska, Rachel Duffett and Alain Drouard, eds, *Food and War in Twentieth Century Europe* (Farnham, 2011), pp. 59–72.

Towle, Philip, *Japanese Prisoners of War* (London, 2003).

van der Vat, Dan, *The Grand Scuttle: The Sinking of the German Fleet at Scapa Flow in 1919* (London, 1982).

Wagner, Jens-Christian, *Ellrich 1944/45: Konzentrationslager und Zwangsarbeit in einer deutschen Kleinstadt* (Göttingen, 2009).

Wall, Richard, 'English and German Families and the First World War', in Richard Wall and Jay Winter, eds, *The Upheaval of War: Family, Work and Welfare in Europe, 1914–1918* (Cambridge, 1988), pp. 43–106.

Walling, John, *The Internment and Treatment of German Nationals during the 1st World War* (Grimsby, 2005).

Watson, Alexander, *Enduring the Great War: Combat, Morale and Collapse in the German and British Armies, 1914–1918* (Cambridge, 2008).

Weber-Newth, Inge and Steinert, Johannes-Dieter *German Migrants in Post-War Britain: An Enemy Embrace* (London, 2006).

Welch, David A., 'Cinema and Society in Imperial Germany, 1905–1918', *German History*, vol. 8 (1990), 28–45.

West, Margery, *Island at War: The Remarkable Role Played by the Small Manx Nation in the Great War 1914–1918* (Laxey, 1986).

Wilson, Trevor, *The Myriad Faces of War: Britain and the Great War, 1914–1918* (Cambridge, 1986).

Winter, Jay, *Sites of Memory, Sites of Mourning: The Great War in European Cultural History* (Cambridge, 1995).

Winterbottom, Derek, 'Economic History', in John Belchem, ed., *The New History of the Isle of Man*, vol. 5, *The Modern Period, 1830–1999* (Liverpool, 2000), pp. 207–79.

Wittlinger, Ruth, 'Perceptions of Germany and the Germans in Post-War Britain', *Journal of Multilingual and Multicultural Development*, vol. 25 (2004), 453–65.

Wood, Peter, 'The Zivilinternierungslager at Lofthouse Park', in Kate Taylor, ed., *Aspects of Wakefield 3: Discovering Local History* (Barnsley, 2001), pp. 97–107.

Wurzer, Georg, *Die Kriegsgefangenen der Mittelmächte in Russland im Ersten Weltkrieg* (Göttingen, 2005).

Theses

Dewey, P. E., 'Farm Labour in Wartime: The Relationship between Agricultural Labour Supply and Food Production in Great Britain during 1914–1918, with International Comparisons' (Ph.D. thesis, University of Reading, 1978).

Francis, Andrew, '"To Be Truly British We Must be Anti-German": Patriotism, Citizenship and Anti-Alienism in New Zealand during the Great War' (Ph.D. thesis, Victoria University of Wellington, 2009).

Websites

Anglo-German Family History Society, www.agfhs.org.uk (accessed 15 September 2010).

Volksbund Deutsche Kriegsgräberfürsorge, Cannock Chase www.volksbund.de.kgs/stadt.asp?druckvorschau-true+stadt-1068&st-1 (accessed 15 September 2010).

Index

Lightning Source UK Ltd.
Milton Keynes UK
UKOW05f1101250414

230577UK00003B/31/P